In recent years policymakers and scientists have become increasingly interested in the economics of science, and in particular in the relationship between accounting and science. This book, originally published as a special issue of the journal *Science in Context*, explores the intersections between the sociology and history of science and the sociology of accounting. Embodying a truly interdisciplinary spirit the book draws attention to the constitutive role that practices of economic calculation in general, and of accounting in particular, play for the conduct of science and for the forms of economic life within which science is embedded. The contributors explore a number of issues, including the role of accounting as a distinctive form of administrative objectivity; conceptual exchanges between science and business administration; actuarial practices and their claims to scientificity; conceptions of the factory as a form of laboratory; accounting for research and development expenditure; the emerging role of patents in the physical sciences; and models of scientific accountability. One recurrent theme throughout the book is the manner in which forms of accounting practice construct possibilities for thought and action.

Cambridge Studies in Management 26

Accounting and science

Cambridge Studies in Management
Formerly Management and Industrial Relations series

Editors
WILLIAM BROWN, *University of Cambridge*
JOHN CHILD, *University of Cambridge*
ANTHONY HOPWOOD, *University of Oxford*
and PAUL WILLMAN, *London Business School*

Cambridge Studies in Management focuses on the human and organizational aspects of management. It covers the areas of organization theory and behaviour, strategy and business policy, the organizational and social aspects of accounting, personnel, and human resource management, industrial relations and industrial sociology.

The series aims for high standards of scholarship and seeks to publish the best among original theoretical and empirical research; innovative contributions to advancing understanding in the area; and books which synthesize and/or review the best of current research, and aim to make the work published in specialist journals more widely accessible.

The books are intended for an international audience among specialists in university and business schools, undergraduate, graduate and MBA students, and also for a wider readership among business practitioners and trade unionists.

For a list of titles in this series, see end of book.

Accounting and science
Natural inquiry and commercial reason

Edited by

Michael Power

London School of Economics and Political Science

Published by the Press Syndicate of the University of Cambridge
The Pitt Building, Trumpington Street, Cambridge CB2 1RP
40 West 20th Street, New York, NY 10011-4211, USA
10 Stamford Road, Oakleigh, Melbourne 3166, Australia

Originally published by Cambridge University Press in 1994 as a
special issue of the journal *Science in Context*.

First published as *Accounting and science: natural inquiry and
commercial reason*, with a new foreword, by Cambridge University
Press in 1996.

Printed in Great Britain at the University Press, Cambridge

A catalogue record for this book is available from the British Library

Library of Congress cataloguing in publication data

Accounting and science: natural inquiry and commercial reason /
    edited by Michael Power.
        p.   cm. – (Cambridge studies in management: 26)
    Includes index.
    ISBN 0 521 55325 3 (hc). – ISBN 0 521 55699 6 (pbk.)
    1. Accounting. 2. Management science. 3. Commercial statistics.
I. Power, Michael. II. Series.
HF5657.A2565   1996
657–dc20   95–38403   CIP

ISBN 0 521 55325 3 hardback
ISBN 0 521 55699 6 paperback

KS

Contents

Illustrations and tables

Contributors

MADELEINE AKRICH
Centre de Sociologie de L'Innovation

TIMOTHY ALBORN
Department of History, Harvard University

STEVE FULLER
Department of Sociology and Social Policy, University of Durham

MYLES JACKSON
Department of History and Sociology of Science, University of Pennsylvania

BRUNO LATOUR
Centre de Sociologie de L'Innovation

JOHN LAW
Department of Sociology and Social Anthropology, University of Keele

PETER MILLER
Department of Accounting and Finance, London School of Economics and Political Science

PHILIP MIROWSKI
Department of Economics, University of Notre Dame

TED O'LEARY
Department of Accounting, University of Cork

THEODORE PORTER
Department of History, University of California, Los Angeles

MICHAEL POWER
Department of Accounting and Finance, London School of Economics and Political Science

KEITH ROBSON
Manchester School of Management

BRAD SHERMAN
Faculty of Law, University of Brisbane

Foreword: The flat-earthers of social theory

Bruno Latour

Flat-earthers have a bad reputation; they are supposed to be just a bunch of cranks who really deny that the earth is spherical. And yet there is a stream of sociology which is made of flat-earthers, all the same. For these people, society is essentially, ontologically flat. They share, if you wish, a geographical intuition (that's the only charitable interpretation I can have of their world view). When they travel by train along the countryside, they are amazed at the distance that separates each farm, each road, each village, this tyranny of distance which is so costly to overcome that you need to walk over to go from one point to the next, or to drive a car, or to fetch a phone, or to send an invoice in order to reach someone else. It is as if there were no third dimension for them, no society, no big animal, as if those places, those people, those interactions were not under any other sky but *the sky*.

I have told you they are flat-earthers and deny the obvious! Even when their commuter trains slowly reach the big cities, the geographical intuition still gets hold of their mind. In Capitol Hills, Elysées Palaces, Wall Street skyscrapers, they see nothing but flatness, as if there were no three dimensions even there, but only flat slices of interactions piled onto one another. In what we call institutions, they see only buildings, doors, desks, forms, pens, in-trays, out-trays, organigrams, charts, and never, never an institution, as everyone else does. It is as if they were blind. Everyone else, when thinking of society, feels the weight of a pyramid or of a sphere made up of other spheres. Size increases with height and weight so that one feels overpowered by the span of a structure so much larger, so much wider, so much older than the puny interactions taking place in it. For everyone else, society is vertical. But not for the flat-earthers who live in the realm of sociology like those 2-D creatures described in *Flatland*.[1] Bugs, that's what they are, bugging sociologists who had so much trouble, over a century, to make political scientists, philosophers and psychologists accept the essential transcendence of society and

---

[1] Edwin A. Abbott, *Flatland: a romance of many dimensions* (originally published in London, 1884) with illustrations by the author (New York: Dover Publications, 1992).

its *sui generis* origin. And here they are, those cranks, denying the existence of a society, of a social context, undoing the work of their predecessors, unknitting what had been knitted stitch after stitch, statistic after statistic, form after form, file after file, in-tray after out-tray, cash-register after cash-register. They are much worse than those interactionists who had for years insisted on the importance of local, face-to-face interactions among people repairing on the spot the fragile fabric of social linkages. These at least respected the social context; they simply filled in the details with dialogs, utterances and lively exchanges; they were just fine-tuning the small discrepancies of social order, without ever claiming that society was as flat as those pragmatic interactions themselves. Never did they claim that these face-to-face adjustments could form, by mere addition, the overarching structure of society itself. Interactionism was just a branch of sociology, excellent for street corners, shop talks, jazz orchestras, and pop and mom stores, but beyond, beneath and above, the real society stood. It was made of another stuff – more sturdy, more real, more elevated – and other sociologists, equally more sturdy, more important and more elevated, were fortunately in charge of studying it.

But look at those flat-earthers! They do not have the modesty of interactionists. They claim to account for big things as well as for small talks, for agencies as well as for structures. Yes, it is the market they want to explain, and the state and nation and Classes and Society itself while they are at it. They have no shame, no restraint! You talk to them about a company managerial structure – terms that everyone understands easily (I mean the 3-D people) – and those 2-D analysts will ask you about the office space in which one manager sits, then the bookkeeping procedure she uses, then the chart on which she has labelled the names of her collaborators, then the chain of command which allows her to call meetings, then the pie chart which she has received from marketing and that describes consumer response to her latest campaign. Do these statistics measure the demand for the product? Does the organization chart reveal the corporate structure? Not a bit, and that is what is so terrible with them. Those instruments do not measure anything, they make the things they measure! They are "performative" – that's their buzz word. Consumers? Made up by statistical networks of questionnaires and pollsters. Capital? Made up by double-entry bookkeepings and piles of forms and paper slips. The bottom line is not a metaphor, it is really, literally, sillily, the bottom line. You ask about the strength of market forces? They will describe to you the British statistical bureaux or the INSEE office in the outskirts of Paris. It is as if economies were a mere consequence of the science of economics! Incredible, they confuse the scientific disciplines and what these disciplines the study of. They behave like the proverbial Chinese moron and when asked to look at the moon they focus with glee on her finger tips! I told you they are blind to what everyone else sees clearly. And they do not stop at that. You ask them, "But what about Britain, and France and Germany? Don't they exist for good even if their economies don't? Are they not real agencies expressed by customs, cultures and mores?" They don't waver, those cranks. They will tell you that another network, another scientific discipline, is "performing" nation boundaries and that without the work of geographers and historians and land surveyors and civil engineers and border patrols, no one could even think about the borders of Britain, France or Germany, and could not inspect them with their eyes. Agency becomes a consequence of narration.

And if you wish to go further and shift from social to natural sciences and start talking about the geology of Britain, the hydrography of France, or the meteorology of Germany, they will answer by showing you geologists drawing maps of Britain; you will learn everything about instrument networks along French rivers; and instead of the weather above Munich, they will list the satellites and weather stations and computers that "make up" the meteorological charts and draw the polar fronts on your evening newspaper. To performative disciplines they will add more performative disciplines, like tortoises on the top of other tortoises, all the way down (except there is no down). Every normally verticalized person is able to go from form to content, from pie chart to what is charted, from statistics to the market forces, from bookkeeping to profit, from words to the reference of the words, from story-telling to agency, but no, not them; they are like so many blind termites, unable to see beyond the forms, the numbers, the charts, the stories, the inscriptions (another of their buzz words) that collectively, they argue, create all those representations by a certain kind of speedy circulation.

If you object that everyone else sees what they fail to see, it does not bother them in the least, and they will retort, "Who is everyone else? How many of them are there? How strongly have they been connected? How long did it take to knit their consensus? How costly is it to maintain it from one year to the next?" And they will busy themselves trying to answer those absurd questions! They take everything literally, like kids really, unable to grasp the figurative meaning of all these words the grown-ups use. When we talk loosely about what the market wants, Germany wishes, classes insist on, or how much goods are worth, they will launch into another inquiry, as blind and obsessive and mad as the previous one to find a realistic meaning to these expressions. This time they will explore the "metrology" and "standardization" of those instruments (those are some of their other big words). If economies exist, it is because, they argue, economics has spread, as have accounting and management and insurance and all those despicable cameral sciences. And by this they do not even mean what everyone else means by "spreading," as if every decent manager had finally come to realize the usefulness and efficiency of those convenient instruments. No, they deny the very independent existence of "usefulness," and "efficiency," and "rationality," and "convenience" and keep asking which real, local, practical instruments are measuring those values, and on which reading device (by which they literally mean the hand of a clock or the head of the computer printer). When you mention what "everyone has in mind," they don't think of ideas, but only of meters, textbooks, teacher–pupil relations, curricula, reviews, and yes also, cash-registers, ticket-counters, software packages, paper slips, until they have obtained a standardized interaction which accounts for the dissemination of a body of practice. Ah! practice, they worship practice. According to them, the very notion of profit does not escape the networks of accounting more than the volt could escape the metrological chain of electricity, or social structure the networks of the sociological discipline.

These rascals not only claim to remake social structure from top to bottom (except of course there is no up and down in their limited horizon), but they also include sociologists, that is us, the dismal profession, inside their "reflexive" inquiry (as they like to say with what is to me a very misplaced undertone of pride). Fancy that! 2-Ds teaching dimensions to 3-Ds; the blind teaching colors. Yes, they confess that "society" comes from sociology, in the same way as the calculation of bottom lines comes from accounting, or chromosomes from the feeding of drosophiles in the network of turn-of-the century geneticists. Since society is flat and interactions are all there is, every time a synoptic vision exists, a bird's-eye view, a gaze from Mars, a synthesis of any sort, it means that a local panopticon has been built. And for their blind eyes, sociologists are those panopticon builders who, through questionnaires, newspaper clippings, theories, quotations, American Sociological Association meetings, advisory boards, textbooks and social workers, end up locally building a scenario of what society is, of what it is made up, and how it is going to change. Sociology is as fiercely localized and as dependent on instruments as meteorology or chemistry.

It is quite discouraging, I must say, to have to fight that sort of reasoning in 1996. There is no way to make them realize that sociology describes society, and does not perform it. We are not limited to our networks and to their extension through metrology. We are not – how should I say? – mere chemists, or biologists. We sociologists see through our instruments and reach toward social structure, social evolution, market forces as they really are. We are not simply adding our instruments and concepts and interpretations to those of the actors who should remain for ever in their place as so many informants. But there is no way to discuss with flat-earthers; everyone knows that. When we make large gestures with both hands to describe the society in which everything is included, the big picture that ignoramuses should always be reminded of, they believe we are drawing in the air something like a pumpkin! Really childish, I tell you. I can't decide what is worse: their disbelief in the methods of science or their doubt over the existence of society. It is as if for them the two were related like Siamese sisters. They behave like that bizarre breed of physicists who are unable to decide if they are dealing with a wave or a particle. For them all the data are simultaneously descriptions of an outside world and inscriptions circulating as fast as possible inside networks of heavily equipped professionals. Simultaneously. They can't make up their minds.

Oh yes, I almost forgot, there is worse: they cannot say a word about our most important issue, the debate between actor and social structure, the freedom of individual agents versus the necessary determination of social forces! That debate leaves their minds absolutely blank. Poor things, we should not be too cruel with them; they lack a dimension. They are no more able to visualize the problem than a flatlander could a cylinder, or a circle for that matter. For them there is simply no social structure, but, strangely enough, that does not leave them just with individuals either. No, I told you they were a bit dense, they simply ignore the dichotomy, and thus all the work we had to do over the decades in overcoming it. In their flat-society sociology, they have none of these niceties to embellish their interiors. It is as if there were only triangles, apexes, so that any individual interaction leads to many others but without ever jumping through the mediation of the social order. Networks they call them; and when there is a gathering of these nets, a synthesis, it is still another very local and particular interaction. In their world, nothing is bigger or smaller than anything else, but simply more tightly or more loosely connected. Threads and lines everywhere, no surfaces, no volumes, that is the deprived and barren landscape of their flat earth.

You would think that they would at least confess that something is missing from their picture, that they would have a sort of remorse, a nostalgia for the vertical dimension they have lost. Not at all. They are perfectly satisfied. Even what puzzles us most, the transportation in one local situation of the weight and necessity of social power, is, they claim, no problem at all. We have not invented the language we speak, the nation in which we are born, the customs we obey, the duties we fulfill, the institutions in which we fulfill a role; every local interaction, every act of individual freedom, every internal representation is partially determined by these obvious forces coming from elsewhere, and this is the intuition that really made our discipline, created our own profession. That they don't deny. They accept all of it and share the same intuition as if they really wanted to remain members of our club and to call themselves sociologists in spite of their obvious deficiency. But their actors are not individuals equipped with an inside and an outside, with degrees of freedom and with minds over which a society would consist of a different matter altogether. No, they are traversed by actions of which they are not the origin but simply the mediators. So are they cultural dopes, puppets manipulated by social forces, mere expressions of what goes through them? No, since these forces and these *sui generis* entities simply do not exist for them. They have to invent a completely implausible theory of action, with no actor; only actions and actants! The result is pitiful. It is not even a structure with positions to be occupied by replaceable entities.

They have events everywhere. Historical events at all points. Radical historicism. And to transport forces from one event to the next, what do they rely on? Objects, those very objects we had so much trouble in chasing away to avoid the dictatorship of science and technology, to carve our own professional space. They are thick with objects in charge of transporting at a distance the action of other times and places. And do not believe that they are able to distinguish at least the material part of these objects from their symbolic or social dimensions. Alas not. The word "symbolic" means nothing more to them than the debate of the actor versus the structure. Objects have no symbolic dimension but they are not material either. They believe that objects are social partners like you and me. You see that the mathematical recreation of *Flatland* is nothing compared to the bizarre world of flat sociologists. That's how they hope to fill in the specifications of social order, to foot the bill of power and force and hierarchy and domination and exploitation. Local interactions, plus objects and instruments, plus number of connections, plus accounting procedures! That's all there is in their *Meccano*! Were it not so sad it would be laughable. They dissipate our most cherished treasures, our rich explanatory causes, and replace them with an endless list of consequences! And they are happy with it. Although they are as flat as a square, they feel so superior to us that they call us pre-relativist, non-reflexive, neo-positivist sociologists! They want to make sociology, they argue, thoroughly empirical, but this obsessive blindness makes them positivist to an incredible degree. No, no we should not let them have their way. We have abandoned too many vertical dimensions, already, lost too many transcendences. This flat sociology is too impoverished to serve as a substitute for sociology. Let us level the flat-earthers.

I told you that writers of forewords are old-fashioned; you should never have asked me to write a foreword.

Bruno Latour

1 Introduction: from the science of accounts to the financial accountability of science

Michael Power

The Pacioli effect

Luca Pacioli, mathematician and teacher, is often mistakenly credited with the invention of double-entry bookkeeping (Swetz 1987, 24). Nevertheless, in 1994, the quincentenary of his *Summa de Arithmetica*, accountants from Edinburgh to Venice have been determined to celebrate the "founding father" of "scientific" accounting. But how can accounting aspire to be scientific, and what is its peculiar logic? For Max Weber, double-entry bookkeeping was much more than a mere business technique; it was paradigmatic of a pervasive formal-legal rationality that was increasingly calculative in nature. Werner Sombart pushed Weber's insights even further and argued that double-entry bookkeeping, famously eulogized (without irony) by Goethe as one of the "finest inventions of the human mind," was a necessary condition of capitalism by virtue of the fact that it enabled abstract economic calculation. Capital as a category did not exist outside the double-entry world view.

The flaws in Sombart's claims are perhaps too obvious to rehearse. As Yamey (1949, 1964) has suggested, double-entry bookkeeping was used less than Sombart imagines – without detriment to the march of capitalism. And the independent development of the Chinese double-entry method, similar to that of the Italian (Jun Lin 1992), undermines necessitarian claims. But whatever the truth of Sombart's thesis (Edwards 1989, 61–62), it represents a distinctive tradition of thinking about accounting: "Weber was seeking to differentiate between *calculation* in terms of money, and money's actual use. Thus he opened up the space for a consideration of the distinctiveness of economic calculation" (Miller and Napier 1993, 635). Weber's (1978) few brief passages on accounting have had "far reaching consequences for the writing of accounting history" – notably that of Sombart: "From such a starting point, an entire historiography has been built around questions of the causal links

1

between 'scientific bookkeeping' and 'the rise of capitalism'" (Miller and Napier 1993, 636).[1]

It is not my purpose to engage these questions of historical scholarship directly but to use them as the pretext for this collection. Even if it is trivial to state that accounting emerged from the same Enlightenment project as science, history – especially bad history and its heroes – can be a contemporary resource. In the figure of Pacioli, accounting has a certain potential for placing itself close to the origins of modern rationality itself. However, it would be too simple to claim a legitimizing role for the Pacioli myth. In the United Kingdom at least, public images of the accountant have moved far beyond that of double-entry bookkeeping. Accountants now work in many different roles: as consultants, auditors, tax advisers and insolvency practitioners. Accordingly, the rise of professional accounting is to a large extent a dissociation from the mechanics of double-entry bookkeeping. The claimed expertise of the financial adviser now has little to do with humble routines that can readily be delegated to clerks. Indeed, the success of accounting in professionalization terms has much to do with the subordination of routine expertise (Abbott 1988,125). As Hopwood (1992) has put it, accountants are now more significant than accounting.

Accordingly, the 1994 celebrations of Pacioli are ambivalent. A quincentenary dear to the hearts of a small body of accounting historians must be set in the context of a professional practice that is increasingly confident of its economic and social position. Practicing accountants no longer need to trace their conceptual origins to that most legitimate of cultural projects – science. Indeed, despite public failures and criticisms, accountants increasingly promulgate a commercial rationality that looks set to eclipse the cultural authority of science. Whatever remains to be said by scholars about the Pacioli of 1494, in 1994 his reexposure comes at a time when accounting is increasingly implicated in the reorganization of research practice around such ideals as "cost effectiveness," "value for money," and "efficiency."

As mathematicians, architects, and others celebrate those parts of the *Summa* relevant to the history of their discipline, university departments of mathematics and architecture are increasingly subject to the agencies of accounting. Accounting as an academic field is relatively young, but as a practice it is coming to shape organizations in new ways, subjecting them to a more detailed and explicit economic logic than hitherto. This

---

[1] There is a distinct and extensive tradition of concern with economic calculation and capitalist accounting within Marxist economics. See Bettelheim (1976) and Thompson (1986, chap. 3). In addition, there is a neoromantic tradition of reaction against all forms of economic calculation (Power 1992a).

intensification of economic calculation is perhaps most evident in the changing management of public science. Where once the image of science shaped the legitimacy of other practices, the cultural authority of science is now beginning to unwind. It was scientism as the hegemonic self-understanding of science that so preoccupied the sociologists of the Frankfurt school, and concerns about the authority of scientists and technological experts persist in a variety of areas. But a form of financialism looks set to displace scientism, an irony that provides the underlying theme of this introduction.

The emphasis in this collection on economic *calculation* rather than on economics is deliberate. I shall suggest below that the hopes for a consistent economics of science fall well short of providing an account of the calculative practices within which economic reason is instantiated and through which its impact on scientific practice can be gauged. An "economics of science," which claims a new orientation for studying science in context, will prove to be a paradoxically disembodied and contextless program in the absence of a consideration of calculative practices. The relationship between economics and accounting is varied and complex (Hopwood 1992). Accounting does not necessarily stand in a subordinate relation to economics (though economists may like to think this). On the contrary, economics draws from accounting in crucial ways (Klamer and McCloskey 1992; Hoskin and Macve 1993). And there can be little doubt that abstract economic models assume away the very contexts of economic calculation that are relevant to science studies.

In this introductory essay, I attempt to provide a schematic guide to an emergent field of inquiry: science and accounting. This guide sketches a prototype for a research agenda which unites the collection of essays which follow and must be articulated with two points firmly in mind: a nonessentialist view of what counts as accounting and a constructivist symmetry in the treatment of science and accounting.

The first point requires us to look beyond Sombart and double-entry bookkeeping to all those "accountings" that are implicated in economic activities: costing, budgeting, cost-benefit analysis, risk assessment, censuses, samples, and so on. We must constantly ask what counts as accounting. The second point requires that the varied "constructivist" sensibilities about science must be extended to the forms of economic calculation that provide its context. Though it will not be possible in this essay to explore the many different senses of "social construction," this point is crucial. One might consistently be a realist about both accounting and science. One might even be constructivist about accounting while remaining a scientific realist of some kind. But it seems inconsistent to be constructivist about science while remaining a realist about accounting, although existing attempts to construct an economics of science tend to do precisely this.

In the next section I consider that strand of thinking concerned with the "scientific" status of accounting. This looks initially like a fairly standard story about scientism, about science as a cultural model for other practices, and is articulated by a small number of theorists concerned to make accounting practice and accounting research more "scientific." However, this standard story can be retrieved as an episode in what Daston (1992,1994) and Porter (1992,1994) have called "the history of objectivity." In section 3 I consider some developments in the history and sociology of science that open up science to its economic context; and in section 4 I am critical of the extent to which these developments lean toward an economics of science that abstracts from concrete processes of calculation. In section 5 I consider the recent social turn in accounting research, which is partly an internal reaction against the prominence of economics-based methodology and which can be aligned with broader historical and sociological reflections on the rise of quantification. I argue that analyses of science in economic context would benefit from newly contextualized understandings of accounting itself. Indeed, while the social turn in accounting has drawn on social studies in science, the reverse has not occurred. One of the conspicuous contributions of the new accounting research has been the recognition of the symbolic and ritualistic properties of accounting practices and their growing cultural hegemony in making activities visible in economic terms. In the light of this research, I go on to consider the role of accounting for science. In short, the replacement of the cultural hegemony of the scientist with that of the accountant can be traced in the shift from preoccupations with the scientificity of accounts to the financial accountability of science.

Accounting as calculating science

Appeals to the scientificity of practices, and the reception of the image of science in different fields, tell us much about the nature of these fields, their preoccupations and their search for institutionalized legitimacy. For many years financial accounting discourse had been concerned with the nature of economic measurement, in particular income recognition and asset valuation. As academic accounting established itself, it was perhaps inevitable that these questions should acquire an epistemological flavor and that images of science should intrude (e.g., Mautz and Sharaf 1961).

Miranti (1986, 1988) explores the idea of "scientific accountancy" in the early years of the American accounting profession and in the writings of Haskins, one of its founding members. Haskins appealed to the epistemological affinity between accountancy and the apparently indigenous traditions of statistical thinking in Emerson's writings. Accountancy was linked to ideals of social progress and order, a view that contrasted with the "British" emphasis on the limitations of statistics in the face of professional judgment and the "approximate" nature of accounting:[2] These early reflections represent attempts to lift accounting and audit practices beyond the status of craft knowledge and to connect them with relatively established forms of scientific thinking. But these ways of talking about accounting were at best symbolic. According to later theorists, such as Chambers (1991) and Sterling (1979), accounting practice suffered and continues to suffer from the pervasive subjectivity of its calculative operations. In their view, accounting practice could become more scientific only by concerning itself with the objective economic *measurement* of independent phenomena.

Stamp (1981) rejected these appeals to science, preferring instead to explore jurisprudential models for understanding accounting. From Chambers' and Sterling's points of view, Stamp is a kind of relativist. But from Stamp's point of view, Chambers and Sterling misunderstand the fundamental nature of both accounting and science. Where Sterling desires "tests rather than tastes," Stamp argues that the accounting project is fundamentally judgmental and that the myth of objective measurement hides the forms of social agreement that support calculative practice.[3] It would be a mistake to see this accounting debate purely in philosophical terms, although such terms provide its currency. As I have argued elsewhere (Power 1986), the Sterling–Stamp debate is difficult to understand if we seek to identify it too closely with philosophical debates about realism and relativism, notwithstanding the use of key philosophical terms. Stamp is not simply a "methodological anarchist," and Sterling is not a "naive realist." Rather, both are deeply preoccupied with the nature of stability and consensus in accounting practice. Arguing that they have got their physics wrong (cf. Stamp 1993), though strictly correct, is to miss the broader significance of these preoccupations. Sterling's and Stamp's exchanges must be understood in relation to a

[2] Such differences may explain why the United States, as contrasted with the United Kingdom, was fertile ground for the development of statistical sampling in auditing. Indeed, scientific accounting finds its counterpart in the hopes for auditing to ground its inferential claims in the authority of statistical sampling (Vance 1950; Power 1992b; Carpenter and Dirsmith 1993). Even though sampling remained controversial within mainstream statistics, it could acquire practical certainty as it moved into other fields and lent those fields their own peculiar scientific authority. As Collins (1985, 145) reminds us, claims become more certain the further they travel from their origins.

[3] Sterling's appeal to science to support the elimination of judgment looks strange. Contra Popper, Sterling regards science as a basis for *eliminating* controversy rather than for institutionalizing "conjecture and refutation."

growing self-consciousness about the purpose of financial accounts (American Accounting Association 1966) and the project to develop a conceptual framework for financial reporting, a project that has consumed a great deal of time and money in North America in recent years. As Lyas (1984, 109) puts it, "Accounting seems to be in a Cartesian frame of mind and to be engaged on a fundamental inquiry into its own foundations."

In other words, a debate between a small group of theorists reflects and articulates wider regulatory concerns about the state of accounting. What is accounting for? What is its basic structure? How can consensus for accounting policy be secured? While academics could recast these preoccupations in epistemological terms, regulators were confronted by the inevitable compromises of practice and the need to carry the support of a critical mass of practitioners. Consequently, the conceptual framework project has been heavily constrained by the need to appear rational while retaining the bulk of existing practice as it is. This quest for foundations in the form of a conceptual framework is philosophically rather unfashionable and manifestly unscientific, at least in Popperian terms. But the conceptual framework in accounting is more an administrative than a philosophical enterprise. Indeed, it can be regarded as an attempt to prevent the overt politicization of the process of setting accounting standards by appeal to an agreed set of axioms. Yet this has only exacerbated the politics of the process, especially as the conceptual framework leaves most substantive accounting issues untouched. Thus any suggestion of philosophical realism by ideals of "representational faithfulness" within this framework must be regarded with caution. Such ideals are simply one value among others and must be traded against other practical concerns.[4]

These debates about the status of accounting practice and the nature and purpose of economic measurement constitute a distinctive tradition of theorizing about accounting, one with discernible connections with the interests and aspirations of practicing accountants even when informed by philosophical reference points. But another more pervasive development has taken place that has served to marginalize Sterling, Stamp, and other theorists concerned to reconstruct the mission of financial accounting. This is what can be described as an "empirical turn" in the social sciences, of which the rise of so-called "positive" research in accounting and related disciplines is an example. Though the history of this empirical turn is undoubtedly complex, within accounting research it has become evident that questions of scientificity have shifted away from

---

[4] See the essays in Mumford and Peasnell 1993 for a further exploration of this claim.

concerns about first-order accounting practice. The emergence of quantitative programs for the *explanation* of practice has displaced the question of scientificity from practice to research. Scientificity is no longer a question of legitimacy for accounting *practitioners* but for a growing body of *researchers*. One important condition of possibility for this transformation has been the advances in information technology that have made available data on capital market prices. These data bases have enabled researchers to conduct empirical studies of the impact of accounting information, and, particularly in North America, accounting research has professionalized and normalized around social scientific canons of experimental method (Whitley 1986).

Across the social sciences, meta-debates about methods have borrowed heavily from those in the philosophy of the natural sciences. The recent history of accounting research is instructive: the emergence of "positive accounting theory" (Watts and Zimmerman 1986) as a research handbook is supported by views, albeit crude ones, of what it is to be properly scientific. According to this view, accounting theorists must no longer concern themselves with "better" accounting, a normative issue of little empirical interest. Their role is to explain practice as they find it. Methodological discussion in these contexts is the public relations arm of a new empirical research style. As a consequence, theorists such as Mattesich (1989) who have attempted to reconnect this science of accounting research to the ends of practice have generally found themselves isolated. More generally, concerns have begun to emerge about the "gap" between academic research and accounting practice.

To the casual observer, these developments provide evidence of the reach of scientism. But their interest may end there. Neither first-order concerns about scientific accounting, whatever that could mean, nor second-order preoccupations with research methodology need to be taken too seriously. Indeed, it could be argued that these debates are hopelessly muddled and that the invocation of the likes of Popper, Lakatos, and Feyerabend can be explained away as so much intellectual fashion and at worst as philosophically incompetent: methodology debates within accounting research have given accounting academics an excuse to play with philosophy to demonstrate their intellectual credentials. But if this were all there was to the various accounting fascinations with the image of science our story could end here. Interestingly, it would be a story with an underlying scientism of its own, insofar as it reinforces traditional intellectual territories: incompetent accountants can never contribute to the philosophy of science.

However, another interpretation suggests itself, one that locates the reception of the scientific image in the accounting field as an episode in the "neglected" (Daston 1992) history of objectivity. Scientism and the exported images of science are important components of this history, and an understanding of objectivity debates in context must remain indifferent to such qualms about the philosophical expertise of those who appeal to philosophy. Even epistemologically "flawed" reasoning reflects the preoccupations of a field of knowledge and may have some bearing on programs for social and administrative control enacted in the name of science. It is with this in mind that Porter (1992, 636) revalues the "scientific" debates in accounting during the 1960s as "unsung classics in science studies" and suggests a starting point for developing a broader appreciation of the scientificity of accounting.

Concerns about objectivity in accounting contexts must be seen in terms of preoccupations with the stability and replicability of professional judgment processes. Replication is a regulative ideal, both for knowledge production and for administration and, as Collins (1985, chap. 6) has shown, for the determination of the boundaries of expert communities. Hence the concept of objectivity is implicated in professional sensibilities and in the negotiated balance between expert discretion and impersonal rules. Seen in such terms, philosophical debates reflect competing views on rule making and authority. Within financial auditing there are recurrent debates about the role of structure in the audit process. In such contexts, the claimed objectivity of formal structure has little to do with realism in any traditional sense and much to do with defendability in a court of law if things go wrong. As Van Maanen and Pentland (1994) show, auditing records have a rhetorical function, and formal methods of "writing up" practice provide a public face for the consumption of lawyers. Accordingly, the objectivity of procedure (Megill 1994) is closely related to its adversarial potential. More generally, "objectivity" in this sense of a publicly visible code of practice may be constituted for complex regulatory and professional purposes. From this point of view, standardization projects, such as the conceptual framework for financial reporting, have less to do with accurate representation and more to do with preserving institutional structures of self-regulation. Conceptual framework projects simply dress up questions of procedural fairness as cognitive issues.

Once we understand that certain preoccupations with the scientificity of practices have little to do with representing reality but reflect complex episodes of institutional change, then the "science of economic calculation" emerges in a different light. An intellectual *volte-face* is required, from questions about the scientificity of economic calculation to questions about the implication of calculative practices for the self-understanding of science. Such a shift necessitates a recognition of the deep affinities between quantitative practices, such as statistics and accounting, and administrative and managerial concerns. As one accountant put it (Rorem 1927), "Accounting and statistics are similar in their use, for both are tools of control"; and Miranti (1989) argues that the new regulatory order of the Interstate Commerce Commission, which emerged at the end of the nineteenth and beginning of the twentieth centuries, depended for its efficacy on the construction of accounting and statistical uniformities to enable comparative analyses to be made. In this respect accounting sharpens the "mind's eye" of administrative reform or, in the words of Porter (1992, 641), the "ambit of accounting . . . is first of all adminis-trative and not cognitive." Defining objectivity as the statistical variance of measurement practices (Ijiri and Jaedicke 1966) may be privately sup-ported by realist intuitions about the ultimate elimination of this variance and a convergence upon *the* measure. But such a definition implies that the greater agreement among accounting measurers, the greater the objectivity of the measure. Accounting objectivity is an administrative rather than an ontological product.

The emergence of state financial apparatus in eighteenth-century Germany, and the varied needs for a "science" of state finances, the *Kameralwissenschaften*, illustrate the interpenetration of statistical, finan-cial and administrative practices. Cameralism, concerned centrally with forestry and mining practices, aspired to unify the fields of science, tech-nology, and finance as elements of *polizei* science (Forrester 1990, 291). For example, Lowood (1990, 321) describes the resource management initiatives for forestry, which require the forest to be described in quan-titative terms before subjecting it to economic reason. In this context, dif-ficulties in establishing the mass of wood and the use of estimation techniques for irregular bodies led to the standardization of the *Normalbaum*. The physical forest balance sheet, with its conceptual roots in forestry science, was then linked to the financial balance sheet of the cameralist by the concept of "yield." Regulation of the forest in this way required a new configuration of administrative expertise to keep the forest's books in terms of both wood and gold. As Lowood (ibid., 337) puts it, "the recurrent themes of equilibrium and the balance sheet har-monized with those of administrative convenience and scientific resource management." The forest became objective and normalized for manage-ment purposes.

The scientific aspirations of economic forms of calculation, and their implications for rethinking the history of objectivity, must also be set in the context of an intensification of the use of numbers in modern polit-ical argument. As Rose (1991) argues, political choices are involved in decisions about what to measure, and numbers have the capacity to constitute new realities and new possibilities for surveillance. In this way numerical ideas of the world are constitutively social within it. Like Porter, Rose draws attention to images of procedural "fairness" constituted by the faith in numerical representation. Similarly Barry (1993) argues that a sociology of measurement and calculation provides a link between the history of science, the sociology of knowledge, and social theory more generally. According to Barry, "a range of technologies historically associated with the engineering of spatial relations" (ibid., 463) have constructed new objectivities around forms of calculation that are solutions to both the problem of long-distant control and the construction of new hyperspaces of number. Measurement and other forms of scientific representation are deployed "in the regulation of social and economic relations" over large distances.

This theme is echoed in Porter's contribution to the present volume, which focuses on the role of impersonality in projects of quantification. He notes a strong preference for standardization, via agencies of "quantitative impersonality," in contrast to ideals of accuracy and precision. It is a relative preference traceable to regulatory initiatives in North America between the 1920s and 1950s. Realist intuitions played little role in these regulatory developments. For example, in the search for costs and benefits, Porter claims that numbers "emerged . . . with only a modest degree of thingness" and that therefore numerical abstraction from qualities is an imperative of control rather than accurate representation. "To create new concepts is to create new things," and these new things embody possibilities for regulatory action. Furthermore, "Numbers react back on the processes they are designed to measure, and are themselves important actors in the economic process." Thus, according to Porter, crime and death rates and other public statistics can describe reality because they define it. In defining it they create newly "rational" forms of behavior, new incentive structures and motives. Indeed, "the numbers can just as well be self-undermining as self-vindicating: precisely because they have become powerful, it is attractive to circumvent them."

The spread of quantification also corresponds to a reconfiguration of expert knowledge and stimulates projects of professionalization. Alborn's contribution to this volume emphasizes the administrative nexus between science and forms of calculation, and its implications for forms of collective mobility. Centers of calculation as networks of allies in Latour's sense emerge. For example, Victorian actuaries formed an alliance with scientific values in the early part of the nineteenth century only to abandon it later when they were more occupationally established. The history of actuaries' professional mobilization demonstrates that appeals to scientific authority could be made very selectively, and a certain ambiguity in the whole notion of "scientificity" enabled the benefits of symbolic capital to be acquired while retaining sufficient credibility for commercial purposes.

Alborn focuses less on the contribution of actuaries to an emerging body of scientific thought, which could later dispense with them, than on the reasons that actuaries sought this alliance in the first place. The management of commercial boundary disputes within insurance depended on fluid ideals of objectivity, publicity, and universality. Alborn shows how these ideals became as much sources of tension as of legitimacy because actuaries needed to manage an alliance with science, with its newly impersonal and universalistic mission, while preserving the idiosyncratic and private nature of their expertise. This complex project of alignment with and distantiation from what Daston calls the "moral economy of science" provides a very specific case of the intersection between science and the economically driven calculations of actuaries. Alborn demonstrates the contingency of this interaction in the fundamental fragility of attempts to formulate a knowledge base that is sufficiently public to attach itself to scientific values but not so public as to be replicable by all and sundry, thereby opening up undesirable competition (Abbott 1988, 102–4).

To summarize: questions of the scientificity of calculative practices such as accounting reinforce the scientistic image of science. In so doing they tend to understate the local "objectivity" problems that stimulate the appeal to science in the first place and that require ambiguity in the very idea of "scientificity" for such appeals to succeed. Affinities of communicative style between science and economic administration point less to the colonization of the latter by the former, the hegemony of a technical interest in Habermas' sense, and more to shared preoccupations with transparency, control, replication, and fairness. Indeed, these affinities both make possible and reinforce conceptual exchanges between the scientific and economic domains. Accordingly we need to shift our focus from the unidirectionality of science *as* context to the multidirectional image of science *in* context.

Science and technology in economic context

The exchange of metaphors between scientific and economic fields has been well documented. Whether in the case of physics (Mirowski 1989) or biology (Morgan 1995), such transfers involve complex forms of reception and adaptation, especially as fields begin to constitute themselves as discrete domains. As Jackson's contribution to this volume demonstrates, Goethe's science was simultaneously a managerial moral. In this respect natural research and administrative management come together in contingent biography. Goethe's concept of "budget" links his natural and administrative investigations, and its ambiguity permits a ready transfer between problems of financial calculation and the natural equilibrium of a closed system. Nature is organized in such a way that its own "economy" is isomorphic with its economic management.

According to Jackson, Goethe was familiar with double-entry bookkeeping in mining and water management contexts, and his administrative duties drew upon and reconstituted his natural knowledge. Goethe's relation to the *Kameralwissenschaften* was complex and selective, and he sided with physiocrats on many economic issues. The notion of an "organic law of compensation," an organism's inherent ability to balance itself, provided the natural ideal against which "artificial" economic budgets could be judged. Nature was the perfect economy, and budgets were the tool to illustrate its closed and self-balancing flow of resources. Another instance of conceptual "exchange" is provided by Wise (1988), who argues for the societal and mediating function of machines as a set of ideas that makes the interaction between truth and utility possible. From this point of view the steam engine is an intellectual mediator that instantiates a specific concept of labor value. In turn this symbolizes industrial progress and, through ambiguous concepts of "work" and "energy," enables a transfer between the idea of optimizing economy and the concept of force. Science is thereby conceptually embedded in material productive process such that physical and economic measurement are intertwined.

In Wise's sense of shifting concepts, budgets and steam engines are "two-way windows" that link specialist and nonspecialist. Through these windows members of society can "view" the activities of natural philosophers in one direction, and natural philosophers can view society in the other. This metaphor of a two-way window and the conceptual network it expresses is another version of the idea that science, technology, and society are a "seamless web" (see Bijker et al. 1987). Accounts of the structure of this web and the nature of the "context" within which science and technology are to be understood are varied. The reading that is relevant to the present volume concerns the economic and commercial shaping of scientific and technological "discourse" via technologies of calculation and accounting, in particular costing.

The problem of calculating cost lies at the heart of large scale technological developments such as railways, electricity, and telecommunications. For example, the interdependencies between forms of accounting and scientific activity are visible in Thomas Hughes' (1979) study of Edison as an inventor-entrepreneur. Hughes describes the close relation between detailed economic calculation/accounting and the development of the electric light bulb. From the point of view of the modern accountant Edison's estimates of capital depreciation look remarkably low, and this has a crucial bearing on judgments about the viability and profitability of his research. Reading these estimates with the benefit of hindsight one might suspect that they must have involved a good deal of "creativity," in the sense of Edison's determination to represent the project as potentially profitable.

This suggests a point that will be developed at greater length below: rather than functioning as a neutral and disinterested piece of objective economic calculation, Edison's accounting is a peculiar kind of rhetoric. Evidence from more recent studies (such as Brunnson 1989) suggests an important role for accounting in rationalizing and justifying decisions that have already been taken, rather than enabling those decisions in the first place. Of course, in the context of Edison these are merely suggestions and speculation: Edison may well have believed that the depreciation rates corresponded to the probable life of the technology. But it would be wrong to assume that Edison's economic calculations were somehow "objective" just because in retrospect we can say that electric light was viable. It could be said that Edison's calculations, and those of his advisers, did not so much *reflect* the underlying viability of electric light as play a critical role in *constituting* that viability by persuading bankers and other backers.

The focus of science and technology studies has tended to be material technology, artifacts and instruments, rather than bureaucratic control systems. However, as McGaw (1985, 704) has argued, the line between technology and business technique is often a difficult one to draw. She recognizes the role of accounting techniques in "making visible and manipulating important aspects of the business environment" of technology and applies this to a study of cost accounting in the paper industry. McGaw rejects the "modern" view that early technological innovators failed to adopt the capital accounting methods that their technologies required. Rather, modern depreciation techniques could not have helped their decision making given the rapid nature of technological change.

McGaw also draws attention to the emergence of costing techniques by engineers; "Rather than judging industrial performance by comparing present costs to records of previous costs, standard costing measures worker efficiency or raw material waste against an ideal, but obtainable, performance carefully established under test conditions. Thus, standard costing is more an engineering concept than an accounting one" (ibid., 719). Hausman and Neufeld's (1989) study of strategies for pricing electricity develops this suggestion and compares the approaches of engineers and economists to the issue of cost. They argue that the engineer tended to be preoccupied with the "correct" way to analyze fixed cost, presupposing there was a determinate answer, and they conclude that the primary difference between the two experts was the greater sensitivity of the economist to the effect of pricing on consumer behavior (ibid., 102).

Cost accounting in technological context suggests the diversity of strategic orientations and expert cognitive styles to which it may be linked. Furthermore, in positioning science and technology "in context," forms of economic calculation such as costing must be regarded, in part at least, as agonistic, as persuasive resources rather than as technologies of neutral representation. Problems of costing in large-scale settings continue to provide difficulties today because cost is not simply a technical matter but is also a technology of social production that requires elaborate negotiation. Noble (1977), quoting from Leon P. Alford's account of Charles Babbage, makes a similar point: "In order to succeed in a manufacture, it is necessary not merely to possess good machinery . . . The domestic economy of the factory should be carefully regulated." Babbage's ideas about calculating machines, about the accuracy of measurement and about rational factory management, were closely interdependent (Schaffer 1994). His intuitions were systematic: the world system was a macroscopic version of a factory whose rational organization corresponded precisely to the rational organization of computation. Hence it was natural for Babbage to suggest that "scientists follow the example of manufacturers."

Although Babbage's ideas were shortlived in Britain, a similar version of them (without the metaphysics) flourished briefly some fifty years later in America.[5] In Taylor's *The Principles of Scientific Management* (1911), forms of economic calculation came to be implicated in the engineering of the workplace itself. Engineers, whose primary competence lay with material technologies, became pioneers of rational economic procedures in the form of cost accounting and statistical control (Noble 1977, 261). At the turn of the century in America a distinctive engineering-management nexus was formed that involved "a shift of focus on the part of engineers from the engineering of things to the engineering of people" (ibid., 263–64).

The conceptual consensus sustaining this program was short-lived. Its mechanical views of human nature and its practical difficulties soon

---

[5] Space does not permit a development of the reasons why ideas of rational factory management failed to take hold in Britain in contrast with North America. But differences in administrative styles and philosophies would play an explanatory role.

became evident (standard costing emerged as a coherent practice only after World War II). Furthermore, the optimism that foresaw the American engineer as an applied microeconomist began to fade. This episode in the "expanding notion of engineering practice" (ibid., 311–12) illustrates the contingency of the relations between science, technology, and economic calculation. Miller and O'Leary (1989) locate the source of this contingency in a fragile coalition of new managerial concerns about the functional space of the organization. These concerns linked hierarchical management structures to progressivist ideals of efficiency and justified, albeit temporarily, a concentration and transformation of industrial authority. Scientific management offered a "conception of the efficient enterprise as a functional space administered according to a neutral regime of facts and techniques." An optimism in the reforming potential of science and technology enabled a reconstructed managerialism to become the solution to diverse progressivist concerns, such as the belief that efficiency would eradicate conflicts between labor and employer.

Though Taylorism lost its cultural authority in the wake of the depression in the United States and the rise of more "cooperative" thinking, scientific management and the "search for costs" provide an important context in which science, technology, and economic calculation interact. But how far does this interaction go as we move further into the institutional territory of science, into spaces of experimentation and theorization itself? Recent developments in the history and sociology of science express new ways of thinking of the "mesh" of theory, experiment, and practice that take us beyond *conceptual* exchange between emerging fields of science and business to those of the *material* interaction between science and administrative practices. This suggests a reading of context that deprioritizes the role of theory, adopts a constructivist view of experimental phenomena, and eschews any crude science or technology reductionism. "Opinions vary on just how narrowly or how broadly to construe the relevant contexts" (Lenoir 1988, 7), and one option is a political economy of practices in which scientific knowledge is credentialized by the same interests that organize society. From this point of view questions of science and economic calculation can be posed in broad terms. However, more restricted construals of context suggest another possibility. For example, Pickering (1992, 1994) alludes to a symbiosis of practice and concepts, the constant adjustment of phenomena of interest to consumers in which financial resources will be significant. And this suggests a potential for a microeconomics of science.

Beyond the economics of science

According to Lenoir (1988), Latour and Woolgar (1982) translate the
hitherto theory-dominated approach to science into their own microsoci-
ological terms. In their view the fortune of factual claims depends on
cycles of credibility in which there is a process of conversion between
money (financial capital), prestige (reputational capital), and data (epistemic capital). Within this cycle for the production of accredited scientific facts, Latour and Woolgar play heavily with the economic language
of investment and circulation. This echoes Bourdieu's (1975) earlier work
comparing scientists directly with modern businessmen as having strategies to maximize their symbolic capital by accumulating symbolic profit.

The criticisms of this program are probably well known.[6] It has been
argued that it fails to give an adequate account of why scientists are interested in reading each other's work. Furthermore, such ways of describing
science may only reflect the dominant role of economic metaphors in
society itself. The way such metaphors become modes of self-description
is not peculiar to science, does not imply that everyone is a rational cal-
culator, and does not enable the construction of an economics of science.
As Knorr-Cetina (1982, 108) has put it: "Part of the difficulty arises from
the fact that the notion of symbolic capital is a conceptual composite
whose components are neither clearly defined nor assigned unequivocal
consequences."

Another kind of objection to anthropological explorations of an
economy of science is that they seem to be more concerned with
debunking a certain view of scientific truth than with the mechanics of
economy. When Latour and Woolgar (1982, 42) say that "the link
between the scientific production of facts and modern capitalist economics is probably much deeper than mere relation," it is difficult to disagree. But the only way in which such a link could be clearly
demonstrated, and therefore for the anthropology of science to move
beyond the analogy of exchange, is by giving attention to the theory and
practice of economic calculation. For example, Latour and Woolgar
(ibid.) state that "the question of the calculation of resources, of maxi-
mization, and the presence of the individual are so constantly moving
that we cannot take them as our points of departure." So far so good.
But how exactly does the calculation of economic or reputational consequences take place, and against the background of which sets of information is this rational? Bourdieu talks of the production of knowledge in

---

[6] It should be noted that anthropological readings of economic transactions in terms of
symbolic exchange have been used before to characterize scientific activity – e.g.,
Hagstrom 1965 – and Peirce's 1967 [1879] paper, "Note on the Theory of the Economy
of Research," predates Popperian notions of knowledge production from competition.

an economy of symbolic goods. But this is an economy in the abstract, without context and without calculation. Or at least, forms of economic calculation are assumed to work unproblematically as a "conversion of resources." Such conversion processes presuppose an accounting that is not made explicit.

A problem begins to emerge. Critiques of science, and of dominant theory-based understandings of science, have turned to economics for conceptual leverage.[7] But in doing so a certain economic orthodoxy – of disembodied and costless calculation – has been left untouched. Hands (1994) sees the problem in terms of a somewhat uncritical appropriation of neoclassical economics. Certainly, Latour and Woolgar are not wholeheartedly "applying" economics to science, since this would constitute an economic reductionism inconsistent with their program. Nevertheless their work reflects the attraction of economic metaphors that have inspired more explicitly neoclassical programs for an economics of science. According to Hands, reflexivity is necessary to avoid the tension between social constructivist views of scientific knowledge and practice and the individualist and anti-constructivist leanings of neoclassical economic models. Furthermore, economics tends to presuppose calculative practices that stand outside theory. Even an economics of information presupposes rational forms of metacalculation around different information strategies.

Knorr-Cetina's (1982) critique of quasi-economic models of science concerns their underlying individualism, which indirectly reproduces heroic images of scientists – only this time in the guise of entrepreneurs. In her view, the focus on the scientific community as the unit of analysis retains the very internalism of the older models of inquiry from which these economic models of science are trying to escape. Indeed, science in economic context is much more a question of the commodification of scientific labor than its celebration in symbolic exchange. The shift in orientation that this provokes makes the walls of the laboratory porous: "We may have to exchange the picture of the scientist-capitalist in a community of specialists for one which recognises the basic dependencies of scientific work that lead us beyond these communities" (Knorr-Cetina 1982, 114).

Knorr-Cetina's conception of "transepistemic" arenas of inquiry suggests that the technical and cognitive selections of the laboratory are not limited to the scientific community but also involve funding agencies, industry salesmen, and perhaps even accountants. Knorr-Cetina substi-

---

[7] In the same way, some historians of science and technology have turned to contexts of industrialization and capital formation and others have turned to more general social histories for rethinking context.

tutes the dynamics of transepistemic resource relationships for the speciality group focus, and chains of problem translations for cycles of credibility: "It is exactly through these elaborations that financing agencies and scientists negotiate what the problem is, and how it is to be translated into actual research selections" (ibid., 123). What is at stake here is less an economics of science than a feel for the reciprocal influence of business and scientific practices. Accounting is at the heart of those influences.

A variation on this theme is provided by Fuller (1992, 414), who invokes the motif of a "scientific management of science." Like Knorr-Cetina he is drawn to the notion of science as work, in contrast to traditional science studies, which are still caught up in the "expert" language of science, unable to "integrate talk about science within the categories normally used to talk about the rest of society" (ibid., 415). In his view science is a complex cluster of behaviors in which labor and communication are organized. Where Fuller's social epistemology differs from other expanded notions of the context of laboratory practice is in its normative program to extract the accountability conditions for knowledge production in order to inform science policy (ibid., 419). Fuller is concerned with the extent to which scientific workers (experts) themselves are to be subject to external critical scrutiny. And Taylorism, for all its weaknesses, reflects this commitment to making expertise transparent.

This is a theme that Fuller develops further in this volume. Philosophies of science, he argues, embody implicit social accountability conditions for scientific practitioners, conditions that will in turn implicate policies for "accounting for science." He illustrates this general claim in the context of the differences between Mach and Planck. Their respective positions on the "ends of science" embody contrasting views about the social reproduction of scientific knowledge. Fuller contrasts Mach's democratic instincts with Planck's defense of the integrity of the scientific community. Whereas Mach saw science in terms of its labor saving potential, Planck tended to see science as valuable and "value adding" in its own right. For Mach it was scientists who needed education about their role; for Planck it was the public who needed to recognize the value of science. According to Fuller, these differences represent a decisive turning point in the history of the accountability of science. Mach's allegiances with the "folk" science values of the *Naturphilosophen* lost out to Planck's world view and its implicit support for Big Science. From Fuller's critical point of view an economics of science is to be welcomed to the extent that it disturbs the closed world of scientific expertise and poses afresh the question of the public accountability of public science.

How far Latour and Woolgar, Knorr-Cetina, and Fuller really differ is clearly an important issue for science studies specialists. But each raises the material stakes of an economics of scientific knowledge and so provides logical spaces within which understandings of economic calculation in context might be brought to bear on science in context. The conjunction of laboratory practices and accounting statements thus becomes a sensible rather than a silly problem, and new sensitivities within the history and sociology of science can be linked not to neoclassical economics but to a body of work on accounting in context.

Economic calculation in context

The economic shaping of technology is an important theme within the field of technology studies. In part this theme takes its lead from Marx's recognition that economic laws, and the forms of calculation through which they are realized, are not universal but specific to forms of society: "Even if in all societies people have to try to reckon the costs and benefits of particular design decisions and technical choices, the form taken by that reckoning is importantly variable . . . Economic calculation presupposes a structure of costs that is used as the basis for that calculation. But cost is not an isolated, arbitrary number of pounds or dollars. It can be affected by, and itself affect, the entire way a society is organised" (Mackenzie and Wajcman 1985, 15, 17). These "social constructivist" insights are mainly preoccupied with the relation between labor costs and technological development and have not been systematically developed in science and technology studies. Indeed, despite the work of Lave (1986) on arithmetic and Hacking (1990) and Desrosières (1994) on statistics, a form of naive realism about economic numbers persists.[8] So what does a constructivist reading of "accounting in context" imply? Without doubt there is enormous variety, evident in such journals as *Accounting, Organizations and Society, Critical Perspectives on Accounting,* and others, but a number of common themes are visible.

First, the understanding of accounting in context breaks with the narrowly technical and highly ethnocentric understandings of accounting that inhabit the twilight world between theory and practice. Second, it eschews the quantitative research orientation of positive accounting studies, even though such studies have a certain debunking mission of

---

[8] Here another irony of intellectual exchange is evident. Although I have implied that the work of Latour and others lacks a full-blooded theory of economic calculation, theorists of accounting in context have drawn partial inspiration from science studies. Science studies researchers may rediscover their own work in the accounting context. Porter (1992) more or less implies this.

their own. Third, it attempts to break out of the orbit of double-entry bookkeeping and the tradition of sociological and historical inquiry initiated by Weber. For example, Miller and Napier (1993) emphasize the heterogeneity and temporary stability of all forms of accountings. In this view, accounting has no essence: the same technical practice can be allied with a multiplicity of aims and objectives, at corporate and state levels, and at different places and times may or may not be considered as "accounting." Accordingly, the function and mission of accounting can never be simply presupposed, and official images of accounting, widespread in textbooks, as an abstract and timeless calculus must be recognized by the analyst as highly particular expressions of calculative rationality with a complex and contingent history. Political economy theorists of accounting (Cooper and Sherer 1984; Tinker 1985) might not go so far with the theme of contingency, preferring to see in the production of accounting statements a reflection of the same social interests as those that tend to be more generally dominant. Nevertheless, there is sufficient common ground to talk loosely of a "critical accounting school." Much of this common ground derives from an application of the insights of social and institutional theories to accounting.

It has become well established that organizations rarely make decisions in a classical, rational manner (Powell and DiMaggio 1991; Meyer and Scott 1992). The contingencies of information production, use, and (significantly) nonuse are central to this understanding. At one extreme accounting functions as a symbolic resource to provide *ex post* legitimacy to "decisions" that have already been made by other means, to ascribe responsibility to organizational agents (Brunsson 1989).[9] Though the role of accounting in decision making is ambiguous, it has acquired a certain ideological dominance as a symbol of economic rationality (Montagna 1990). Accounting is a rhetorical resource for economic agents, particularly in adversarial settings (McBarnet et al. 1993). Accounting is therefore a hermeneutic enterprise, a form of economic interpretation that makes possible a certain style of communication. Carruthers and Espeland (1991) emphasize the role of accounts as a way of framing decisions as "rational" and thereby making them legitimate. Indeed, these insights from contemporary institutional theory can be read back into the classical history of accounting itself. Accordingly, techniques such as double-entry bookkeeping can be regarded as the presentation of convincing arguments. Statements of profit and net worth express not simply economic conditions but the "moral legitimacy" of a prudent, disciplined, and ultimately rational mind.

---

[9] Such views will be familiar to sociologists of large-scale technological projects. See Mackenzie and Wajcman (1985, 18) and Gansler (1982).

In light of these analyses, the constructed nature of accounting implies varying degrees of nonrealism about economic reality. This probably has greater intuitive leverage than nonrealist views of natural reality.[10] It is particularly plausible in those cases where there is no independent "fact of the matter" that would determine "correct" accounting and where the outcome is largely a matter of negotiation in which appeals to "reality" have a rhetorical character. In other words, even a close technical reading of accounting yields to nonrealist conclusions, and many practitioners of "creative" accounting would probably agree. As Dodd (1994, 113) puts the point in the context of monetary exchange, "To transmit and receive information . . . is not simply to project an independent body of facts through space and time, but to bring those facts into being as facts."

Another important constructivist theme is the idea that accounting has real consequences by virtue of creating categories of significance. The role of systems of classification in constituting styles of thought and patterns of action is hardly a new idea, particularly for anthropologists (Douglas 1987). But as accounting practices assume an increasingly central role in the reproduction of social life the point is of more than academic interest. Accounting representations tend to reinforce their solidity as economic action is conducted using them. Accounting exercises that are inherently subjective such as valuation, can acquire an institutionalized objectivity by virtue of being widely presupposed to be valid. As Porter implies, numbers are objective because they are stable, not the other way around.[11]

A few examples will reinforce this point.[12] Hines (1988) probably pushes the constructivist reading of accounting as far as it can go. Her analysis is driven by a concern that the environmental effects of corporate activity are often invisible within traditional accounting systems. From this point of view, the issue is not so much the need to attach appropriate economic costs to external effects as the need to reflect upon the image of the organization and its boundaries, which is symbolized and reinforced by traditional accounting. Similarly, Hopwood (1987) draws attention to the manner in which accounting is often mobilized by an abstract image of its potential, a dynamic in which a domain of economic facts can be created in new arenas. These newly visible realities then become subject to regulatory control at a temporal and spatial distance from their point of origin via the language of cost. New relations

[10] To be fair to mainstream economics, the importance assigned to expectations is consistent with an antirealist view of economic reality.

[11] This is particularly apparent in the case of net present value (NPV) calculations (Miller 1991) and brand accounting (Power 1992c).

[12] For a good overview of the relevant literature, see Morgan and Willmott 1993 and Hopwood and Miller 1994.

of dependency emerge within a continuous economic dialogue between the possible and the actual. From this point of view accounting becomes a way of actualizing economics, and economic ideas in turn provide the rationale for new accountings. Miller and O'Leary's (1987) analysis of the history of standard costing pushes this story in a different direction. In rendering reality in such a way that it can be known, individuals are enmeshed in projects of national efficiency and programs for rational administration. This constructivist reading of accounting also extends to the construction of subjects of accounting (Miller 1994). Power is exercised through a certain kind of freedom, in which zones of discretion are created and within which decision making is possible.

The contrast in tone between these studies, some of which are loosely related to the work of Foucault, and Porter's reading of quantification provides a contrast between different constructivist readings of economic calculation. Whereas Porter (and Fuller to some extent) links quantification to traditions of democratization and empowerment via the impersonality and transparency of expertise, Miller and O'Leary emphasize the "governing" potential of accounting, as does Hopwood. This difference in tone has a bearing on the directions that analyses of science and economic calculation may take.

Accounting for science

Other than as a corrective to a crude economics of science, what further insight is gained by importing constructivist readings of economic calculation into science and technology studies? The answer reflects another twist in the fortunes of science and commercial reason. The theoretical and methodological shifts that dislodged theory-dominant conceptions of science are not only intellectual transformations in the history and sociology of science and technology. The reconfiguration of the status of instrumentation, experiment, and laboratory organization in such a way as to emphasise context, contingency and environment has added a contemporary pertinence to the "new management" of science.

To say "new" here is not to suggest that science was never managed or that a golden age of free inquiry has fallen prey to the language of income, expenditure, and profit. Science has never been free from diverse forms of accountability to peers, patrons, and publics. But in both the United Kingdom and North America, Big Science is being subject to increasing scrutiny, as widespread demands for accountability in public services take effect. Furthermore, these demands are being shaped increasingly by the language of accountancy. Initiatives to improve the "Public Understanding of Science" (PUS) reflect this new mood of public accountability, a demand for rethinking the relations between science and its "stakeholders."[13]

In North America these demands for accountability have been spiced by preoccupations with scientific fraud and the need to restore trust in the public mission of science. Practices of data audit have emerged, journals addressing the accountability of scientific research have been launched, and studies of scientific fraud are beginning to appear (La Follette 1992). Scientific audit is a "newly emerging area of inquiry" (Cassidy and Shamoo 1989), and Francis (1989, 11) notes the growing opinion that peer review is an exaggerated quality-control mechanism. New demands have been made for more formal and independent forms of audit. In this context the links between replication, quality control, and regulation take a particular form.[14] The traditional narrative of science reproduces the belief that fraud and error are exposed by the process of replication. However, this view fails to acknowledge the importance of institutionally established incentives to replicate. Not only is pure replication pointless (Collins 1985), but because of this it has no institutional value – it produces no capital, symbolic or otherwise, for the replicator.

Mirowski's contribution to this volume provides an example of this point. He develops an analogy between the pursuit of precision measurement of physical constants and forms of economic arbitrage. He claims that the concept of arbitrage represents a non-neoclassical rationality that provides greater insights into the stability of scientific practice than existing studies in the economics of science. According to Mirowski, a virtual economy exists "to police the otherwise unexplained diversity of opinion" (p. 566) and to punish inconsistency. The value of constants is constructed out of this process of intellectual arbitrage. Indeed, the arbitrage model has the advantage of nonrealism, since only relative values matter for the stability of the network of prices or constants. In such a view, measurement error corresponds to abnormal profit, and arbitrage opportunities exist for both traders and meta-analysts, subject to transactions costs, to discover and eliminate inconsistency.

Mirowski sketches a history of quantitative error that locates it within accountability structures for science and in which the distinction between random and systematic measurement error is constituted to maintain

[13] However it should be noted that, unlike demands for financial accountability, the PUS initiative reinforces the image of elite experts and ignorant publics, an image contested by analysts of popular science.

[14] It has been said that "where priority is a matter not just of scientific credit but of patent rights – whether for a test for the AIDS virus or for a putative cold fusion process – or when a clinical trial can clear the way to market for a billion-dollar drug, then threats to scientific work loom larger. Unless work in areas like this is fully published, and tested by the appropriate expert community, then the quality of science may be at risk" ("Fraud and Suspicion in Science" 1992).

temporary stabilities in the network of constants. A key figure in Mirowski's story is Raymond Birge, whose talent for reevaluation of the experimental reports of others created the "job of the meta-analyst," who would "supervise actively the attribution of error throughout the interconnected network of constants . . . doggedly imposing consistency" (p. 235). According to Mirowski, error analysis has become a "thriving industry" that is internalized by many Big Science laboratories producing their own "error budgets." "It is no accident that the bureaucratization of error audits spreads in tandem with the bureaucratization of scientific inquiry" (p. 238). Such developments parallel political worries about accountability and fraud in science, worries that favor a layer of supervision and audit. However, unlike market arbitrage, where the arbitrageur has an obvious incentive to exploit inconsistency for profit (thereby eliminating the inconsistency as a by-product), no one is personally motivated to accumulate results of error arbitrage. In other words, being an error auditor is likely to be as low-status as being a financial auditor. But error auditing will no doubt acquire its own aura of expertise in due course.

In making science auditable, Francis (1989, 15) argues that there are dangers of monitoring the individual scientist rather than the incentive structure of science itself. Furthermore, it is in the nature of audit and accounting practices, whether financial or nonfinancial, to create their own layers of bureaucratic reality and to generate new incentives for creative avoidance of monitoring systems (Power 1994). For example, Cozzens (1986, 9) raises the question of how the agenda of research may be affected: "What are the effects on science of the changing rationales advanced to justify government support of scientific research?" She notes that "historical description has not yet been synthesised into a general notion of the relationship between science and its sources of support in the contemporary period" (ibid., 10).

The complexity of this relation between funding and knowledge growth requires close attention to specific forms of economic calculation. But despite new sensitivities to the brokering role of program managers and, in contrast to traditional social and historical studies, the suggestion that the new unit of analysis is the funding program rather than an idealized scientific community, the "funding of science" literature tends to regard the financial context of science rather unproblematically. For example, Dixon-Long's (1971) analysis embodies rather orthodox views of the role of budgeting, and Remington (1988) tends to presuppose a realist view of costs. In contrast, the language of "costs," "budgets," and "profitability" must be understood as part of the "social production of credibility" and as central to the construction of the scientist-manager.

In other public policy areas, such as health care in the United Kingdom, it is increasingly evident that medical discourse is profoundly transformed by new commitments to economic calculation. New categories of cost have been created, general practitioners have been transformed into budget holders, and demands for efficiency fit uneasily with older languages of care. Whether parallel transformations in scientific research are occurring remains to be seen, but a recent government paper (*Realising our Potential* 1993) indicates the determination of the state to subject science to very similar changes. The individual scientist is no longer a passive actor in this process but, following Miller and O'Leary (1987), may be actively constructed as a self-managing economic agent. There is already some evidence for this in the plethora of management courses for scientists being offered by some U.K. universities. That laboratory scientists should attend courses on project costing and financial management would have been unthinkable until recently. It is through these newly intensive processes of socialization that economic calculation will come to have a constitutive effect on laboratory practice.

The contribution to this volume by Law and Akrich documents the emergence of a managerial discourse of "customers," to replace users, at a large public sector laboratory. The changes involve the creation and management of "good customers" to find out what can reasonably be expected of the research facility. The needs of these customers is also paralleled by a new attention to cost in laboratory work and the formation of a project-relevant accounting system. However, cost control is much more than a technical initiative, especially given the general technical problem of central cost allocation. Law and Akrich suggest that while a market orientation was introduced for only a small proportion of the work of the laboratory, it may have had far-reaching effects on the climate of management. Notably, they suggest that appropriation of an economically driven mode of strategic thinking by a bureaucratic and scientific context is neither simply a question of colonization by economic reason nor of decoupling, but a complex symbiosis of elements permitting the management of discretion around a problematic accounting system. Decisions about cost and allocations of cost reflect local organizational concerns rather than a natural economic reality.

Law and Akrich are skeptical of a "total marketization" of science, as if markets and science embodied monolithic logics. They stress the contingency of the impact of calculable orderings and the multivalent nature of "calculable spaces" in Miller's (1994) sense. There is no consistent discourse across different contexts (the laboratory, the accountant's office, the requisitions store), and the same individuals adjust their roles accordingly. Accounting also carries with it the sources of its own delinquency by constituting local spaces of discretion; its capacity to "act at a distance" must therefore be weighed against the new proximities that accounts generate. For Law and Akrich, "accounting is merely another addition to the more or less ramshackle technologies of modern governmentality."

Sherman's contribution to this volume also concerns the changing conceptions of the management of U.K. public science and the distinctive role that patents are playing within broader concerns for accountability, efficiency, and value for money. The commercial potential of patentable products has given rise to technology and intellectual property "audits," and has given a further stimulus to financial accountability initiatives. Sherman argues that law presupposes certain distinctions between pure and applied research, distinctions that, for all their crudity, nevertheless have effects. Researchers are being required to operate explicitly as commercial agents, and a new culture of economic calculation is emerging around the patentable product. These changes also impact on the way results are described, such that the form of information disclosure is changing: secrecy and fraud have heightened sensitivities about the timing of information release. Sherman argues that patents are not neutral in their effects but shift the visibility of scientific activity toward what are perceived as applied products, such as biotechnology. Consequently, to the extent that patents have become performance indicators for scientists, a certain style of governance of science has been established. Patent law allows research "to be presented as a bounded, stable object" and to be translated into a unit of valuation that enables diverse projects to be compared and ranked for funding purposes. As researchers reconstruct their own professional identities around this process, both indirectly and directly in the form of training in legal and accounting disciplines, the patenting process becomes self-fulfilling.

Sherman shows that forms of economic calculation, and associated legal instruments such as patents, mediate and represent external interests, such as those of the state, within scientific research activity. Robson's essay also demonstrates the importance of making science visible in economic terms. During the 1980s one of the ways in which the British government attempted to influence levels of private sector research and development was to require the disclosure of corporate expenditure in the published financial statements. Such a belief in the role of financial accounting was naive, to say the least, particularly the hope that British companies might be "shamed" into increasing their investment in R&D to the benefit of the national economy as a whole. Accounting was enrolled to function as a pseudo-anonymous, apolitical medium, through which the state could act on corporate laboratories "at a distance." In this way, local forms of accounting became linked to broader macroeconomic accountings of performance. Accordingly, accounting for R&D is not simply a technical issue but is implicated in broader government programs for stimulating industrial research and for improving economic performance. Under these conditions, the precise details of how R&D expenditure is calculated are less important than the program for influencing the private sector without contradicting liberal philosophies of control.

Quite apart from external attempts to influence them, corporate laboratories have always wrestled with problems of internal financial accountability. According to Dennis (1987, 481), "The founding of corporate laboratories . . . marked the beginnings of a new set of relations between American scientists and their patrons." This development involved complex realignments of expertise in which the academic's role as consultant stimulated debates about laboratories as "universities in exile." An increasingly blurred relation between science and technology emerged, and corporate goals came to have an important influence on the certification of knowledge via publication practices. Thus the development of large corporate laboratories provides for a new political economy of science in which the poles of science and commerce are locked in an ongoing debate and from which the concept of "industrial research" begins to take shape. According to Dennis (1987, 508), in the 1920s "new markets for physical scientists, especially in corporate laboratories, created both new career paths and new vocabularies" as a system of scientific knowledge was constructed. These developments make it possible to ask: "To what extent, if any, did the successful production of the fruits of corporate research hinge upon the transformation of the manufacturing plant into a laboratory?" (Dennis 1987, 511).

It is precisely this question that Miller and O'Leary address in their contribution to the present collection. In place of traditional preoccupations with the subsumption of the laboratory within certain productive and economic imperatives, they describe a spatial reordering of work relations in which the factory can be understood in much the same way as a laboratory can. Once the concept of science and laboratory practice admits material and organizational elements and adopts a more localized view of experimentation, in which instrumentation and testing are intercalated (Galison 1988), then the boundaries between laboratory and factory are blurred. Both can be regarded as organizations with complex assemblages of elements for the production of knowledge.

In their study of management changes at Caterpillar Inc., a manufacturer of heavy-duty industrial vehicles, Miller and O'Leary emphasize the interrelation between instrumentation and visualization in the redesign of the factory as a system of knowledge. Furthermore, they observe how such internal programs for redesign are informed by broader conceptions of the mission of manufacturing industry and ideals of the customer and the product. In this way a new political economy of the factory can inform laboratory studies, and the motif of a new "economic citizenship" for factory workers provides insights into the financial reconstruction of the culture of public science that parallel those of Sherman as well as Law and Akrich.

It has already been said that the contributions of Miller and O'Leary, Robson, and Sherman reflect constructivist sensibilities about economic calculation that differ from those of Porter and, to some extent, Fuller. On the one hand accounting can be viewed as a selective technology that shapes actors' opportunities for decision making and, by making their actions visible to regulatory centers of control, influences processes of identity formation. On the other hand accounting can be viewed in terms of liberal values as an instrument for rendering transparent hitherto obscure relations of dependency and for enabling public scrutiny of private expertise. This opposition reflects different nuances of liberal thinking, which cluster around the problems of control and accountability respectively. The liberal *control* problem is how to manage indirectly "at a distance" by creating zones of autonomy (Rose and Miller 1992). The *accountability* problem is how to equalize knowledge opportunities and make social institutions more transparent, a problem that can also be framed in more radical terms. The quantifying spirit embodies this essential tension: between an objectivity that shapes and one that enables social action. This tension gives rise to different constructivist emphases on the effects of accounting in science: accounting as governance technology and accounting as democratization of expertise. But perhaps these differences are ultimately matters only of degree: both emphases undermine the image of science as expertise *sui generis* and suggest its "interactive stabilization" with forms of economic calculation.

Conclusion

This essay is part introduction and part genre creation, an attempt to weave together the history and sociology of science and the history and sociology of accounting. I have tried to untangle some of the themes that may be at stake in the relationship between science and economic calculation. The task is part speculation, part critical re-reading of existing social and historical studies of science, and part explication of the new constructivism in accounting research. I have attempted to sustain a broad reading that could have implications for a newly sensitized research agenda. Along the way I have drawn on the diverse sensitivities to context in science studies and have made some critical remarks about the "economics of science" and the ironies of a radical program that uses very traditional resources. However, despite the efforts of accounting researchers to dislodge realist intuitions about costs and profits, the economics of science programs will start to look more plausible as science in practice becomes more explicitly perceived and managed in economic terms. Ideas can "become true" if the world changes.

The schematic story that locates the various essays in this volume is certainly not historical. But I have tried to suggest a line of development from the "history of objectivity," in which disciplines such as accounting have sought to solve problems of objectivity in particular ways and have evoked the image of science to do so, to contexts of knowledge production in which forms of economic calculation and experiment are intertwined. Here economic calculation may play a variety of roles, ranging from the influencing of research agendas to the construction of the accountant-scientist. It is this awkward line of development that reflects the title of this introduction: the transition from the science of accounts to the financial accountability of science. This is an intellectual and social transition in which the authority of science, or at least myths of that authority, confronts the newly confident authority of economic calculation. Greater sensitivity to accounting in scientific context could provide a new direction to science policy studies that have been preoccupied with the vulnerability and indeterminacy of scientific authority in quasi-legal contexts (see, for example, Cambrosio et al. 1990).[15] More generally, as Jasanoff (1987) has shown, the boundaries between science and other disciplines are highly contested in policy contexts where legitimation may depend on rational justification in a mixture of scientific, economic, and legal terms. Jasanoff's study typifies an emphasis on legal process, but her claims about competing forms of authority, the contested nature of the boundary-defining language, and the strategic significance of new conceptual categories could apply equally to forms of economic calculation. Contemporary slogans of "value for money," "best available technology not entailing excessive cost," and the like are precisely problematic boundary categories in her sense. Furthermore, economic theories of science are also constitutive of the boundaries of scientific practice, making it receptive and porous to the influence of accounting and other commercial practices. From the contemporary point of view the Frankfurt school seems to have overestimated the hegemony of science and

---

[15] First-order policy theorists have been prompted to argue, in the case of forensic science, for the need to remove it from an adversarial environment and make it available to prosecution and defense alike. See "Scientists Call for Re-Trial on Evidence" 1992.

technology. Even later Weberian "corrections" to critical theory by Habermas understate the knowledge-constitutive role of forms of economic calculation and the institutional momentum they have acquired in 1994. Whether Pacioli would be proud of this or not, we can only guess.

ACKNOWLEDGEMENT

I am grateful to D. Wade Hands, Peter Miller, Christopher Napier, Brad Sherman, and Andrew Warwick for comments on earlier versions of this essay.

REFERENCES

Abbott, Andrew. 1988. *The System of Professions: An Essay on the Division of Expert Labor.* Chicago: Chicago University Press.

American Accounting Association (AAA). 1966. *A Statement of Basic Accounting Theory.* Evanston, Ill.: American Accounting Association.

Barry, Andrew. 1993. "The History of Measurement and the Engineers of Space." *British Journal for the History of Science* 26:459–68.

Bettelheim, C. 1976. *Economic Calculation and Forms of Property.* London: Routledge & Kegan Paul.

Bijker, Wiebe, Thomas Hughes, and Trevor Pinch, eds. 1987. *The Social Construction of Technological Systems.* Cambridge, Mass.: MIT Press.

Bourdieu, Pierre. 1975. "The Specificity of the Scientific Field and the Social Conditions of the Progress of Reason." *Social Science Information* 14(6):19–47.

Brunnson, Nils. 1989. *The Organization of Hypocrisy: Talk, Decisions and Action in Organizations.* Chichester: John Wiley.

Cambrosio, Alberto, Peter Keating, and Michael Mackenzie. 1990. "Scientific Practice in the Courtroom: The Construction of Sociotechnical Identities in a Biotechnology Patent Dispute." *Social Problems* 37(3):275–93.

Carpenter, Brian and Mark Dirsmith. 1993. "Sampling and the Abstraction of Knowledge in the Auditing Profession: An Extended Institutional Theory Perspective." *Accounting, Organizations and Society* 18(1):41–63.

Carruthers, Bruce, and Wendy Espeland. 1991. "Accounting for Rationality: Double-entry Bookkeeping and the Rhetoric of Economic Rationality." *American Journal of Sociology* 97(1):31–69.

Cassidy, Marie, and Adil Shamoo. 1989. "First International Conference on Scientific Data Audit, Policies and Quality Assurance." *Accountability in Research: Policies and Quality Assurance* 1:1–3.

Chambers, Ray. 1991. *Foundations of Accounting.* Geelong, Victoria: Deakin University Press.

Collins, Harry. 1985. *Changing Order: Replication and Induction in Scientific Practice.* London: Sage.

Cooper, David, and Michael Sherer. 1984. "The Value of Corporate Reports: Arguments for a Political Economy of Accounting." *Accounting, Organizations and Society* 9(3/4):207–32.

Cozzens, S. E. 1986. "Funding and Knowledge Growth." *Social Studies of Science* 16:9–21.

Daston, Lorraine. 1992. "Objectivity and the Escape from Perspective." *Social Studies of Science* 22:597–618.

1994. "Baconian Facts, Academic Civility, and the Prehistory of Objectivity." In *Rethinking Objectivity*, edited by Alan Megill, 37–64. London: Duke University Press.

Dennis, Michael. 1987. "Accounting for Research: New Histories of Corporate Laboratories and the Social History of American Science." *Social Studies of Science* 17:479–518.

Desrosières, Alain, 1994. "Official Statistics and Business: History, Classification, Uses." In *Information Acumen*, edited by Lisa Bud-Frierman, 168–86. London & New York: Routledge.

Dixon-Long, T. 1971. "The Government of Science: A Comparative Approach." *Science Studies*, 263–86.

Dodd, Nigel. 1994. *The Sociology of Money: Economics, Reason and Contemporary Society*. Cambridge: Polity Press.

Douglas, Mary. 1987. *How Institutions Think*. London: Routledge & Kegan Paul.

Edwards, John. 1989. *A History of Financial Accounting*. London: Routledge.

Forrester, David. 1990. "Rational Administration, Finance and Control Accounting: the Experience of Cameralism." *Critical Perspectives on Accounting* 1:285–317.

Francis, Jere. 1989. "The Credibility and Legitimation of Science: A Loss of Faith in the Scientific Narrative." *Accountability in Research: Policies and Quality Assurance* 1:5–22.

"Fraud and Suspicion in Science." 1992. *Times Higher Education Supplement*, 4 September.

Fuller, Steve. 1992. "Social Epistemology and the Research Agenda of Science Studies." In *Science as Practice and Culture*, edited by Andrew Pickering, 390–428. Chicago: Chicago University Press.

Galison, Peter. 1988. "History, Philosophy and the Central Metaphor." *Science in Context* 2(1):197–212.

Gansler, Jacques. 1982. *The Defense Industry*. Cambridge, Mass.: MIT Press.

Hacking, Ian. 1990. *The Taming of Chance*. Cambridge: Cambridge University Press.

Hagstrom, Warren. 1965. *The Scientific Community*. New York: Basic.

Hands, Wade. 1994. "The Sociology of Scientific Knowledge and Economics: Some Thoughts on the Possibilities." In *New Directions in Economic Methodology*, edited by Roger Backhouse, 75–106. London: Routledge.

Hausman, William, and John Neufeld. 1989. "Engineers and Economists: Historical Perspectives on the Pricing of Electricity." *Technology and Culture* 83–104.

Hines, Ruth. 1988. "In Communicating Reality We Construct Reality." *Accounting, Organizations and Society* 13(3):251–61.

Hopwood, Anthony. 1987. "The Archaeology of Accounting Systems." *Accounting, Organizations and Society* 12:207–34.

1992. "Accounting Calculation and the Shifting Sphere of the Economic." *European Accounting Review* 1(1):125–43.

Hopwood, Anthony, and Peter Miller, eds. 1994. *Accounting as Social and Institutional Practice.* Cambridge: Cambridge University Press.

Hoskin, Keith, and Richard Macve. 1993. "Accounting as Discipline: The Overlooked Supplement." In *Knowledges: Historical and Critical Studies in Disciplinarity,* edited by E. Messer-Davidow, D. R. Shumway, and D. Sylvan, 25–53. Charlottesville and London: University of Virginia Press.

Hughes, Thomas. 1979. "The Electrification of America: The System Builders." *Technology and Culture* 20:125–39.

Ijiri, Yuji, and Robert Jaedicke. 1966. "Reliability and Objectivity of Accounting Measurements." *Accounting Review* 41:474–83.

Jasanoff, Sheila. 1987. "Contested Boundaries in Policy Relevant Science." *Social Studies of Science* 17:195–230.

Jun Lin. 1992. "Chinese Double-entry Bookkeeping before the Nineteenth Century." *The Accounting Historian's Journal* 19(2):103–22.

Klamer, Arjo, and Donald McCloskey. 1992. "Accounting as the Master Metaphor of Economics." *European Accounting Review* 1(1):145–60.

Knorr-Cetina, Karin. 1982. "Scientific Communities or Transepistemic Arenas of Research? A Critique of Quasi-economic Models of Science." *Social Studies of Science* 12:101–30.

La Follette, Marcel. 1992. *Stealing into Print: Fraud, Plagiarism, and Misconduct in Scientific Publishing.* Berkeley: University of California Press.

Latour, Bruno, and Steve Woolgar. 1982. "Cycles of Credit." In *Science in Context,* edited by Barry Barnes and David Edge, 35–43. Milton Keynes: Open University Press.

Lave, Jean. 1986. "The Values of Quantification." In *Power, Action, Belief: A New Sociology of Knowledge,* edited by John Law, 88–111. London: Routledge.

Lenoir, Timothy. 1988. "Practice, Reason, Context: The Dialogue between Theory and Experiment." *Science in Context* 2(1):3–22.

Lowood, Henry. 1990. "The Calculating Forester: Quantification, Cameral Science, and the Emergence of Scientific Forestry Management in Germany." In *The Quantifying Spirit in the Eighteenth Century*, edited by Tore Frängsmyr, J. L. Heilbron, and Robin Rider, 315–42. Berkeley: University of California Press.

Lyas, Colin. 1984. "Philosophers and Accountants." *Philosophy* 59(227):99–110.

McBarnet, Doreen, Syd Weston, and Christopher Whelan. 1993. "Adversary Accounting: Strategic Uses of Financial Information by Capital and Labour." *Accounting, Organizations and Society* 18(1):81–100.

McGaw, Judith. 1985. "Accounting for Innovation: Technological Change and Business Practice in the Berkshire County Paper Industry." *Technology and Culture* 26:703–25.

Mackenzie, Donald, and Judy Wajcman. 1985. "Introductory Essay." In *The Social Shaping of Technology*, edited by Donald Mackenzie and Judy Wajcman, 2–25. Milton Keynes: Open University Press.

Mattesich, Richard. 1989. "The Scientific Approach to Accounting." In *Modern Accounting Research: History, Survey and Guide*, edited by Richard Mattesich, 1–19. Canadian Certified General Accountants' Research Foundation, Research Monograph No. 7. 2nd ed.

Mautz, Robert, and Hussein Sharaf. 1961. *The Philosophy of Auditing.* Sarasota, Flo.: American Accounting Association.

Megill, Alan. 1994. "Introduction: Four Senses of Objectivity." In *Rethinking Objectivity*, edited by Alan Megill, 1–20. London: Duke University Press.

Meyer, John, and Richard Scott, eds. 1992. *Organizational Environments: Ritual and Rationality.* London: Sage.

Miller, Peter. 1991. "Accounting Innovation beyond the Enterprise: Problematizing Investment Decisions and Programming Economic Growth in the UK in the 1960s." *Accounting, Organizations and Society* 16(8):733–62.

    1994. "Accounting and Objectivity: The Invention of Calculable Selves and Calculable Spaces." In *Rethinking Objectivity*, edited by Alan Megill, 239–64. London: Duke University Press.

Miller, Peter, and Christopher Napier. 1993. "Genealogies of Calculation." *Accounting, Organizations and Society* 18:631–48.

Miller, Peter, and Ted O'Leary. 1987. "Accounting and the Construction of the Governable Person." *Accounting, Organizations and Society* 12:235–65.

    1989. "Hierarchies and American Ideals 1900–1940." *Academy of Management Review* 14(2):250–65.

Miranti, Paul. 1986. "Associationalism, Statistics and Professional Regulation: Public Accountants and the Reform of Financial Markets, 1896–1940." *Business History Review* 60:438–68.

    1988. "Professionalism and Nativism: The Competition in Securing Public Accountancy Legislation in New York during the 1890s." *Social Science Quarterly* 69(2):361–80.

    1989. "The Mind's Eye of Reform: The ICC's Bureau of Statistics and Accounts and a Vision of Regulation, 1887–1940." *Business History Review* 63:469–509.

Mirowski, Philip. 1989. *More Heat Than Light: Economics as Social Physics, Physics as Nature's Economics.* Cambridge: Cambridge University Press.

Montagna, Paul. 1990. "Accounting Rationality and Financial Legitimation." In *Structures of Capital: The Social Organization of the Economy*, edited by Sharon Zukin and Paul DiMaggio, 227–60. Cambridge: Cambridge University Press.

Morgan, Glenn, and Hugh Willmott. 1993. "The 'New' Accounting Research: On Making Accounting More Visible." *Accounting, Auditing and Accountability Journal* 6(4):3–36.

Morgan, Mary S. 1995. "Evolutionary Metaphors in Explanations of American Industrial Competition." In *Biology as Society, Society as Biology: Metaphors*, edited by S. Maasen, E. Mendelsohn and P. Weingart. 311–337. Dordrecht: Kluwer.

Mumford, Michael, and Kenneth Peasnell, eds. 1993. *Philosophical Perspectives on Accounting: Essays in Honour of Edward Stamp.* London: Routledge.

Noble, David. 1977. *America by Design: Science, Technology and the Rise of Corporate Capitalism.* Oxford: Oxford University Press.

Peirce, Charles S. [1879] 1967. "Note on the Theory of Research." *Operations Research* 15:642–48.

Pickering, Andrew. 1992. "From Science as Knowledge to Science as Practice." In *Science as Practice and Culture*, edited by Andrew Pickering, 1–26.

Chicago: Chicago University Press.

1994, "Objectivity and the Mangle of Practice." In *Rethinking Objectivity,* edited by Alan Megill, 109–27. London: Duke University Press.

Porter, Theodore. 1992. "Quantification and the Accounting Ideal in Science." *Social Studies of Science* 22:633–52.

1994. "Objectivity as Standardization: The Rhetoric of Impersonality in Measurement, Statistics and Cost-Benefit Analysis." In *Rethinking Objectivity,* edited by Alan Megill, 197–238. London: Duke University Press.

Powell, Walter, and Paul DiMaggio. 1991. *The New Institutionalism in Organizational Analysis.* Chicago: University of Chicago Press.

Power, Michael. 1986. "Taking Stock: Philosophy and Accountancy." *Philosophy* 61:387–94.

1992a. "After Calculation? Reflections on *Critique of Economic Reason* by André Gorz." *Accounting, Organizations and Society* 17(5):477–99.

1992b. "From Common Sense to Expertise: Reflections on the Pre-history of Audit Sampling." *Accounting, Organizations and Society* 17:37–62.

1992c. "The Politics of Brand Accounting in the United Kingdom." *European Accounting Review* 1(1):39–68.

1994. "The Audit Society." In Hopwood and Miller 1994, 299–316.

Realising our Potential: A Strategy for Science, Engineering and Technology. 1993. White Paper. Cm 2250. London: HMSO.

Remington, J. 1988. "Beyond Big Science in America: The Binding of Inquiry." *Social Studies of Science* 18:45–72.

Rorem, C.R., 1927. "Similarities of Accounting and Statistical Method." *Accounting Review* 3:10–18.

Rose, Nikolas. 1991. "Governing by Numbers: Figuring out Democracy." *Accounting, Organizations and Society* 16:673–97.

Rose, Nikolas, and Peter Miller. 1992. "Political Power beyond the State: Problematics of Government." *British Journal of Sociology* 43(2):173–205.

"Scientists Call for Re-Trial on Evidence." 1992. *Times Higher Education Supplement,* 10 January.

Schaffer, Simon. 1994. "Babbage's Intelligence: Calculating Engines and the Factory System." *Critical Inquiry,* 21: 203–227.

Stamp, Edward. 1981. "Why Can Accounting Not Become a Science Like Physics?" *Abacus* 17(1):13–27.

Stamp, Philip. 1993. "In Search of Reality." In *Philosophical Perspectives on Accounting: Essays in Honour of Edward Stamp,* edited by Michael Mumford and Kenneth Peasnell, 255–314. London, Routledge.

Sterling, Robert. 1979. *Toward a Science of Accounting.* Houston: Scholars Book Co.

Swetz, Frank. 1987. *Capitalism and Arithmetic: The New Math of the Fifteenth Century.* La Salle, Ill.: Open Court.

Taylor, Frederick. 1911. *The Principles of Scientific Management.* New York: Norton.

Thompson, Grahame, ed. 1986. *Economic Calculation and Policy Formulation.* London: Routledge & Kegan Paul.

Tinker, Tony. 1985. *Paper Prophets: A Social Critique of Accounting.* New York: Holt, Rinehart and Winston.

Van Maanen, John, and Brian Pentland. 1994. "Cops and Auditors: The Rhetoric of Records." In *The Legalistic Organization,* edited by S. Sitkin and R. Bies, 53–90. London: Sage.

Vance, L. L. 1950. *Scientific Method for Auditing.* Berkeley: University of California Press.

Watts, Ross, and Jerold Zimmerman. 1986. *Positive Accounting Theory.* Engelwood Cliffs, N.J.: Prentice-Hall.

Weber, Max. 1978. *Economy and Society: An Outline of an Interpretive Sociology.* Edited by Guenther Roth and Claus Wittich. Berkeley: University of California Press.

Whitley, Richard. 1986. "The Transformation of Business Finance into Financial Economics: The Roles of Academic Expansion and Changes in US Capital Markets." *Accounting, Organizations and Society* 11(2):171–92.

Wise, M. Norton. 1988. "Mediating Machines." *Science in Context* 2(1):77–113.

Yamey, Basil. 1949. "Scientific Bookkeeping and the Rise of Capitalism." *Economic History Review* II 1(2,3):99–113.

    1964. "Accounting and the Rise of Capitalism, Further Notes on a Theme by Sombart." *Journal of Accounting Research* 2(2):117–36.

2   Making things quantitative

Theodore M. Porter

Quantification is normally taken to be a problem for scientists, a problem of knowledge. But like most problems of knowledge, this one is social and political as well. The political dimension long predates science, reaching back to the beginnings of accounting and surveying in the ancient world. In modern times, too, quantification has been as closely tied to administration as to science. Indeed, its use in science derives not only from a faith that the laws of nature are written in mathematical language but also from the rigors of scientific communication, the administration of knowledge, and the need for trust. Among the most important roles of statistics in science, for example, is to render an accounting of belief (Porter 1992b). Scientists, social scientists, and engineers depend especially on such tools to justify their activities to governments and to the public at large.

One important meaning of the scientific ideal is an aspiration to escape the bounds of locality and of culture. Not all uses of numbers reflect that aim, and some long preceded it. Economic exchange could not possibly depend on fancy quantitative tools or concepts. Yet the scientists' quest for rigor and precision is not for that reason inconsequential. Numbers defined by fixed rules and communicated in writing are different in important ways from those that emerge in exchanges based on face-to-face bargaining. A shift toward impersonality implies a move toward a more public form of knowledge. It promotes the fixing of conventions, the creation of stable entities that can be deployed across great distances. Standardized quantitative rules have been almost as fertile as standard experiments and mass-produced instruments in the making of new things.

These are sometimes given old names, such as "intelligence," "costs and benefits," or "work." But the sense of such terms cannot remain fixed. If quantifiers are unable to impose narrower and more consistent meanings on older terms, their measures will seem inadequate. Rarely, if ever, are preexisting qualities simply made more precise by being quantified. At issue, rather, is the creation of new entities, made impersonal and (in this sense) objective when widely scattered people are induced to count, measure, and calculate in the same way.

36

Neither scientific nor accounting activity is inherently distinguished by this kind of objectivity. Both have been decisively urged in its direction by the need to satisfy an audience of researchers, clients, and regulators whose lack of personal trust reflects their physical or cultural distance. Scientists and accountants are not, in every respect, natural allies. Natural knowledge is rarely conceived in terms of objects that can be equated with money, the universal substance of accounting. Yet a problematic like that of accounting is apparent, for example, in the energy accounts of physicists and ecologists, or in chemists' equations of mass (Mirowski 1989,127–32; Wise 1989, 90; Worster 1985, chap. 14; Porter 1981). Here, while I give some attention to the explicitly financial, I am concerned with accounts in a broader sense that includes quantities such as mass, population, and probability. I ask how quantified qualities are brought into existence, through a combination of scientific and administrative activity.

Quantifying quantities: the problem of standardization

Before inquiring into the making of new quantitative entities, it will be useful to consider a simpler case. Sometimes the entities, and indeed their quantitative nature, are not in doubt. This is likely to be true more often in routine bureaucratic matters than in issues at the forefront of creative research. Still, it is anything but easy to create and maintain bureaucratic routines, including routines of measurement. Consider the monumental task faced by the (American) National Bureau of Standards, and by comparable agencies in other countries. Their job is to provide officials at every level of government with specifications and tolerances for all kinds of measures. Nowadays, much of their attention is necessarily devoted to regulatory matters. An especially important one is the control of air, water, and ground pollution through an accounting of discharges. But in order to regulate potentially harmful substances, there must be prescribed ways to measure them. J. S. Hunter (1980) writes: "We have reached the stage where there is a federally mandated method for measuring almost every physical, chemical, or biological phenomenon." Such measurements, it has been (officially) estimated, absorb 6 percent of the gross national product of the United States. Even so, most are plagued by inconsistencies. To get farms, laboratories, factories, and retailers to report, in the same form and following the same measurement protocol, the quantities of the myriad substances they discharge has proved overwhelmingly difficult.

Measurement for public purposes is rarely so simple as applying a meter stick. Hunter speaks grandly but appropriately of "measurement systems." In the case of waste discharges, he proposes, an adequate measurement system must include criteria for sampling, measurement, calibration, custody, data analysis and reporting, training of personnel, and control of interlaboratory bias. Adequate measurement means disciplining people as well as instruments and processes, particularly when, as in most measures of discharge concentrations, there is advantage to be gained from deception. Failure to enforce the prescribed procedures will create opportunities to cheat and may lead to a fatal loss of credibility. Even if everybody is honest, systematic differences among laboratories will mean that some manufacturers are treated more harshly than others. Hence rules and specifications must be put into effect at millions of diverse locations, by calibrating millions of instruments and millions of people to the same standard.

Standardization and proper surveillance are in some ways more important to a public measurement system than is close approximation to true values as defined by elite research laboratories. Only when uniform methods have been put in place is it possible to talk of adequate quantification. Then can one plausibly combine and manipulate data, to account for discharges, to regulate people. The bureaucratic context is important. Accommodating variation in measurement practices requires a good deal more trust than is normally available, especially in an adversarial regulatory culture like that of the United States (Jasanoff 1990). If an eccentric manufacturer were to invest extra resources to perform a state-of-the-art analysis, this would be viewed by the regulators as a vexing source of interlaboratory bias, and very likely an effort to get more favorable measures by evading the usual protocol, not as a welcome improvement in accuracy. There is a strong incentive to prefer readily standardizable measures to highly accurate ones, where these ideals are in conflict.

Similar considerations apply in the human sciences. In census debates, for example, nobody ever argues that populations are inherently non-quantitative, or that demographic numbers are mere fictions. But any actual count depends on the specification and political acceptance of a whole array of conventions. First there are definitional problems: deciding on the standing of tourists, legal and illegal aliens, and, when this category of people existed, slaves. Then it must be determined what efforts will be made to locate and tally people who reside at new addresses, or who can never be found at home, or who live in the streets (Alonso and Starr 1987; Anderson 1989). The credibility of sampling procedures as a substitute for or correction to results of the complete count has been vigorously debated in many countries. While it is generally accepted among professionals that skillfully designed samples can be more accurate than exhaustive surveys, they are not used for many purposes because they lack sufficient credibility (Desrosières 1993). The American census bureau has not been permitted to adjust its raw figures using an estimate of the undercount. In this and other cases, greater accuracy is deemed to come at too high a cost if it requires discretionary adjustments to the results of an intuitively plausible and relatively mechanical procedure.

Mechanizing judgment: the cult of impersonality

This preference for rules over unconstrained judgment is common both within science and in the larger political arena (Porter 1992a). The free exercise of judgment invites suspicion of arbitrariness or bias. Such considerations have inspired efforts to identify rules of right reasoning, even to quantify judgment. The theory of probability itself arose as a way of measuring rational belief in conditions of uncertainty. Games of chance were studied not mainly because of their inherent interest or importance, but because they provided readily quantifiable analogues to practical decisions made by jurors, merchants, and voters (Daston 1988). The very concept of "probability" is an outstanding example of a quality whose meaning changed radically when it was quantified (Hacking 1975). It referred originally to the credibility of a witness or authority, or of a statement to which such a person had attested. By analogy it could be applied to impersonal testimonies, the evidence of nature. The mathematization of probability, avidly pursued by mathematicians and philosophers during the eighteenth century, was to permit the evaluation of such testimonies and sources of evidence according to fixed quantitative rules. By the nineteenth century the priority had been reversed; probability became a branch of mathematics with some possibility of application to practical decisions. And indeed there was by then much skepticism about the applications, which seemed increasingly to derive from the excesses of Enlightenment rationalism. Probability was caught up in arguments surrounding the French Revolution.

These debates about the applicability of calculation to elections and judicial decisions had an unmistakable political dimension. But the classical theory of probabilities seemed also to fail on its own terms. Most damaging was the charge that there is something fundamentally arbitrary about the choice of the parameters to be inserted into the calculations, especially when it is desired to turn an observed frequency into a Bayesian measure of belief. In this case, nineteenth-century critics found no reason to assume that two people applying this calculus to a problem should come up with the same answer. Probability, as applied to the affairs of ordinary life, seemed no longer to have unambiguous meanings, either quantitative or qualitative. Where it seemed merely subjective, that was sufficient to discredit it.

The ideal of mechanized judgment did not quite disappear, though. If by 1820 or 1840 probability seemed too loose to guide the judgments of everyday life, it could still apply where quantitative measurements were abundant and the task was simply to infer a parameter by manipulating these numbers. This occurred first of all in astronomy, at the beginning of the nineteenth century. Its success there provided an incentive to redefine other fields, such as psychology, as measurement disciplines (Stigler 1986). Statistical manipulation, after all, was a most promising means for attaining objectivity, for generating consensus by renouncing arbitrariness and reducing scientific judgment to a kind of accounting. In the twentieth century it became customary in studies of agriculture, medicine, social science, and industrial quality control to quantify degrees of certainty using R. A. Fisher's inferential statistics. In many fields a probability value, most commonly .05, became synonymous with adequate evidence for a scientific conclusion (Gigerenzer et al. 1989; Danziger 1990).

These inference rules have given valuable service to the task of quantification by acting as a constraint on subjectivity. Karl Pearson ([1892] 1957), whose philosophical writings were highly influential among early twentieth-century social scientists, applauded science for its "sequences and laws admitting no play-room for individual fancy" and argued that the "scientific man has above all things to strive at self-elimination in his judgments." Little wonder that he devoted most of his career to the creation of mathematical statistics, as a tool of eugenics but also as a general method of scientific inquiry. Statistics, as Pearson and others defined it, has contributed invaluably to that control over people whose critical role in precise measurement was noted by Hunter. Especially among scientists in relatively insecure fields, the appreciation for precise and impersonal results runs so strong that a preoccupation with statistical significance seems often to have left no room for considerations of substantive significance (McCloskey 1985).

Along with statistics, the great agency of quantitative impersonality in recent times has been accounting itself, along with some of its close relatives. This affects natural scientists mainly in regard to activities they consider of subordinate interest, such as the administration of grants. It is often more central to engineering, medical, and social science work, especially insofar as these have come to bear on public policy. A glorified form of accounting, cost-benefit analysis, has been widely advocated as the rational basis for public regulatory and investment decisions of all kinds. We associate this now with economics, but it was created and made effective by engineers, an extension of their increasingly quantitative methods for designing public projects.

The key agency in all this was the civil division of the United States Army Corps of Engineers. Its members used numbers to bring rationality to public decisions concerning navigation and flood control. This is no case of simple opposition between scientific rationality and political expediency. Rigorous quantification was a concession to politics, or rather a strategy for forestalling it. The language of economics had been used routinely by public engineers, at least in the European tradition, since the eighteenth century. The drive for rules by which projects were to be evaluated arose much later, and always in response to explicitly political challenges. Rigorous cost-benefit analysis was part of an effort to weaken opposition and mitigate rivalries by diminishing the opportunity for self-interested distortion (Porter 1995b, chap. 7).

This story is not only an American one, but most contemporary forms of cost-benefit analysis may be traced to initiatives within the United States bureaucracy from the 1920s to the 1950s. From the beginning, the Corps of Engineers used the language of economic rationality as a basis for approving some proposed navigation or flood-control projects and rejecting others. A key event in this history was the Flood Control Act of 1936, which required that any flood control project receiving federal money should show benefits in excess of costs. Still, the legislation did not dictate how costs and benefits were to be measured. The Corps preferred to endorse projects where they encountered no serious opposition, and in such cases there was little chance that their economic analyses would be scrutinized by outsiders. Since the projects had to be approved by a Board of Engineers in Washington, made up of high-ranking Corps officers, there was at least some pressure for consistency from within the Corps itself (U.S. War Department 1943). But army engineers resisted congressional attempts to reduce their economic analyses to inflexible rules (U.S. Congress 1957).

The push to formalize these methods, and hence to turn "costs" and especially "benefits" into measurable entities, came not from some logic intrinsic to science and engineering but from political conflict. This appeared primarily in two forms. One was opposition to Corps projects by powerful interest groups, mainly railroads and electric utilities, whose managers and shareholders preferred not to face government-supported competition in inland transportation and electric power generation. The other was bureaucratic conflict within the federal government. Several agencies, especially the Soil Conservation Service of the Department of Agriculture and the Bureau of Reclamation of the Department of the

Interior, were also involved in flood control. They operated under different statutes, and their claims on projects could be enhanced or damaged according to the allocation of benefits. Like the Corps, they were disposed to maximize estimated benefits for services, such as flood control and navigation, for which no local contribution was normally required, since this helped them generate local political support. Sometimes this competition could degenerate into an unseemly bidding war (U.S. Congress 1952). The only solution was to impose some control on cost-benefit analysis. Various strategies of reducing discord, including governmental reorganization, interagency cooperation, and oversight by the Bureau of the Budget, were tried during the late 1940s and early 1950s. These attempts at standardization opened up a space into which economists entered during the 1950s.

Perhaps the most heroic effort to turn "benefits" into a quantitative entity that would have the same meaning throughout the United States government (if not the world) was undertaken in the late 1940s, in the wake of a series of prolonged and embarrassing disputes between the Bureau of Reclamation and the Corps of Engineers, the worst of which involved a proposed dam on the Kings River in California. The fight was not simply a consequence of bureaucratic imperialism. The problem was that agency disagreement had quickly spread outward into the political domain, from which it could no more be reclaimed than the water itself. Local interests in California polarized over the enforcement of acreage restrictions on recipients of federally subsidized water. In Washington this dispute became a node in a continuing power struggle between the executive and legislative branches of government (Maass 1951). The leaders of the affected agencies hoped to avoid such situations in the future by harmonizing the laws under which the agencies operated, and in particular by establishing uniform quantitative criteria to determine once and for all the amount and allocation of benefits. For this purpose, in April of 1946 a Subcommittee on Costs and Benefits was created within the Federal Inter-Agency River Basin Committee, and charged with working out uniform economic methods.

It is clear from the record of their meetings that the agencies radically underestimated the difficulty of this task. Costs and benefits, according to a familiar rhetoric, are real quantities, used routinely in private business to make investment decisions. But when examined closely, they proved startlingly elusive. It took the subcommittee about two years even to record in mainly qualitative form the cost-benefit practices in effect at the principal agencies. Meanwhile a few economists from the Bureau of Agricultural Economics had been asked to formulate an "objective analysis" of the problem, meaning one that ignored all statutes and existing practices, and answered only to the logic of economics and of numbers. Their report had initially been expected within a matter of weeks or months. It was finally distributed in mimeographed form after about three years, following several frenetic weeks of negotiation and compromise.

By this time it was painfully apparent that representatives of the agencies could find no other basis for consensus. The appearance of the objective analysis in July of 1949 was followed by a flurry of subcommittee meetings, "centered around the practicality and applicability of the theoretically sound procedures to agency programs" (U.S. National Archives 1946–53). Finally, in May of 1950, the subcommittee issued its report, *Proposed Practices for Economic Analysis of River Basin Projects* (U.S. FIARBC 1950). The report was of considerable significance in the history of cost-benefit analysis and came to be known affectionately among practitioners as the "Green Book." It failed, however, to win the assent of all the constituent agencies. "Costs" and "benefits," on this account, emerged from these discussions with only a modest degree of "thingness." They remained too amorphous, too open, to be capable of settling controversies. The engineers and economists were willing to supplement the results of economic rationality with somewhat arbitrary conventions, in the interests of administrative coordination. But in this case, too many powerful and divergent interests were at stake for mere conventions to hold up.

Instruments and instrumentalism: quantitative positivism

Where science is better shielded from controversies in the political order, it has sometimes proved possible to reach a working consensus by ignoring fundamental disagreements, at least provisionally. The alliance of quantification and positivism is illustrated in an exemplary way by eighteenth-century experimental physics. "Experimental physics" was an ambitious term to describe the physical study of heat, light, electricity, and possibly chemistry. At the beginning of the century, these had been more closely allied to natural historical fields such as botany than to mechanics or astronomy. Scientists of the late eighteenth century were committed to raising the level of these studies through experimentation and, above all, measurement. To this end, great effort was made to improve such instruments as thermometers and electrometers. Measurement activities were very little impeded by the utter lack of consensus about what sorts of things heat and electricity were. Experimental physics rested to a large degree on the hope that one could begin with instrumental measurements without presupposing too clear an idea of the things measured. Successful measurement meant balanced accounts, the sign of a conserved substance.

In the early eighteenth century, heat was almost exclusively a phenomenon of everyday experience. "Temperature" was a medical concept, which described the condition of the atmosphere in much the same way as temperament related to the constitution of a person (Feldman 1990). This is typical of the rich variety of connotations once associated with entities that seem now to be unproblematically quantitative. Such polyvalent concepts could never be subject to unidimensional measurement, still less reduced to mathematical law. To quantify was necessarily to ignore a rich array of meanings and connotations. This recalls Nietzsche's observations on history: the form of life epitomized by quantification depends on the art of forgetting. To quantify qualities is to abstract away much of their conventional meaning. Critics not only of social science but also of mathematical physics have complained of this. The Hegelian natural philosopher Georg Friedrich Pohl, for example, argued against Georg Simon Ohm's mathematical treatise on the flow of electricity that it was like a report on travels through a new and interesting country by a correspondent who wrote down nothing but the times of arrival and departure of the trains (Jungnickel and McCormmach 1986, 1:86; Gillespie 1960, passim).

To abstract from a rich complex of meanings is to lift up and preserve what can most easily be controlled and communicated to other specialists in other places. And promiscuous measuring, guided by a keen interest in whatever can be made unequivocal, has often led to the identification of stable concepts. The mercury thermometer was regarded as a promising way to measure heat, or temperature, long before either of these was well understood physically, because it at least seemed to rise monotonically as things became hotter. Whether a fixed expansion of mercury represented the same increase of heat at different levels or for different substances was at first anybody's guess. But precision could get researchers a long way, even without a proper theory. When equal weights of hot and cold water, mixed together, could be made to give water of mean degree, then the lines on the thermometer could be defined as homogeneous units. Physicists and chemists armed with thermometers, scales, and calorimeters could now measure the "heat capacity" of various substances and the "latent heat" that somehow disappeared as ice was melted or water boiled. These purely descriptive results in the experimental physics of heat, and similar ones for electricity, were modestly offered as data on which researchers of diverse theoretical persuasions could agree (Roberts 1991; Heilbron 1979).

Few natural philosophers gave up the ambition to understand the objects and events underlying their measures. But there were credible philosophical reasons not to be too much embarrassed by these lapses of realism. As Joseph Fourier wrote a bit later, the chief virtue of mathematics "is clearness; it has no marks to express confused notions" (quoted in Smith and Wise 1989, 149). In the late eighteenth century, Etienne Bonnot de Condillac had argued that clarity and simplicity of language were much to be preferred over any aspiration to seize the essence of things. Nominalism was best for science. Condillac did not take this to imply that everything flows into everything else, so that we must forever live in a sea of confusion. Rather, the denial of fixed types freed humans to impose on passive nature whatever order would best serve their purposes (Rider 1990; also Foucault 1973). Sensible classification was for him synonymous with clear thinking. Quantification, too, was valuable mainly as a way of ordering perceptions. Science is a well-made language. The model language is algebra. Gillespie (1980, 65) observes that Condillac's logic of science was thoroughly quantitative, in a way rather akin to accounting.

The displacement of concepts by quantities is perhaps best illustrated by the new language of chemistry, proposed in A. L. Lavoisier's 1789 textbook as the crucial element of the revolution he hoped to effect in that science. The proper basis for any scientific language, he explained, had been defined in Condillac's *Logic*. On this basis Lavoisier began to describe the operations of chemistry using equations, the language of algebra. Each of the simple substances that go into a reaction, the left side of the equation, must also show up in the finished product, the right side. Testimony that nothing has been lost is provided by the equal sign, representing equality of weight on a balance. There were no deep truths implied by this language. It was, to be sure, capable of expressing fundamental truth claims – that, for instance, oxygen is the cause of combustion and of acidity. Its real virtue, though, was that it could describe chemical operations without assuming knowledge of the causes of chemical properties. It easily survived the refutation of Lavoisier's beliefs about acidity that gave oxygen its name.

Lavoisier's was very much an operational nomenclature, a guide to the manipulation of substances in the laboratory. This is what Condillac expected of a well-formed language. The inspiration for this one came not only from philosophy but also, and perhaps more fundamentally, from mineralogy and mining. Chemistry was through and through a practical science. The decision to base chemical names on the simple substances that a mineral contained was first made by practical mineralogists in Sweden and Germany as part of an effort to classify and name minerals in a way that would be most useful to miners. Chemical knowledge, in short, was to be a tool of rational administration. Mining chemists had little practical interest in the customary purpose of chemical explanation, to find the causes of the properties of substances. They wanted to know what metals could profitably be extracted from ores. Lavoisier, who successfully adapted this mineralogical program to chemistry, was not so devoted a follower of Condillac that he had abandoned all hope of explanation. He had definite ideas about what chemical elements were truly simple, and of how the properties of substances were transformed in chemical reactions. But he thought it more important for a language of chemistry to be practical – descriptive and quantitative – than for it to be explanatory (Porter 1981; Lundgren 1990). This quantitative style epitomizes what many critics on the left and the right have found most objectionable in science. As the Frankfurt philosophers argued, positivist science permits men to "replace the concept with the formula, and causation by rule and probability" (Horkheimer and Adorno 1969, 11).

Making things with numbers: quantitative realism

These remarks on the natural sciences emphasize the destructive effects of the quantitative impulse. Friendly and hostile observers alike have often been more impressed by the disappearance of meanings than the smuggling in of new ones. On this account a working philosophy of "descriptionism" or "positivism" has often been allied to systematic efforts at quantification, in the social and natural sciences alike (Porter 1994). But it would be quite wrong to suppose that scientists are compelled to choose between concepts, or qualities, and quantities. Quantification has an important constructive role. With numbers one can often make new things, or at least transform old ones.

Ian Hacking (1983) and Bruno Latour (1988) have shown to what extent experimental science works by remaking nature and not merely by describing it. In its most extreme form, this argument implies that the power of science in the world ought to be understood not as following from the validity of scientific knowledge but as the effect of a much vaster intervention, the transformation of nature into what Simon Schaffer has called an "extramural laboratory." The argument that the entities of experiment are new and artifactual is at least usefully provocative for understanding the natural sciences. It is perhaps most powerful and convincing, though, in regard to the social and behavioral sciences. Social objects change depending on how people understand them. Accordingly, to create successful new concepts is to create new things. Statistics, preeminent among the quantitative tools for investigating society, is powerless unless it can make new entities. Its methods, wrote Francis Galton, deal comprehensively with entire species, and with entire groups of influences, just as if they were single entities, and express the relations between them in an equally compendious manner. They commence by marshalling the values in order of magnitude from the smallest up to the largest, thereby converting a mob into an orderly array, which like a regiment thenceforth becomes a tactical unit. (Galton 1901, 7)

Even the most elementary operation of statistics, counting, is senseless unless the objects counted can be mobilized and defended as homogeneous.

The rhetoric of our own time abounds in constructed entities that have taken on a vigorous life of their own. We find them in almost every domain. A multitude of figures surrounds commercialized athletic activities, preeminently cricket and baseball. The pioneering statisticians of baseball were moralists, looking to create measures that would draw attention away from self-aggrandizing heroics and reflect the essential virtues of a team sport. By now the statistics very nearly define athletic prowess. A variety of economic measures provides the backbone to most modern business news. Unexpectedly high inflation numbers will cause a surge in interest rates. Favorable figures on trade or the purchase of consumer durables will drive up the stock market, or rather (to be precise) the stock indexes. Changes in gross domestic product will be used by international lending agencies to decide how effectively a "developing" country is absorbing foreign capital, or whether an industrialized economy is pulling out of recession. And a recession is often a shadowy entity, defined by the movement of an aggregate of numbers. It would be going too far to say there is no such thing as an economy at all, but neither can one plausibly talk about an economy developing according to its own laws, which the numbers merely represent. Numbers react back on the processes they are designed to measure, and are themselves important actors in the economic process (Gigerenzer et al. 1989, chap. 7).

The concept of "society" is in part a statistical construct. When quantitative records of crimes and suicides first became widely available in the 1820s, the numbers were generally found to be shocking. It was not so much their magnitude as their steadiness that inspired wonder. Crime, wrote Adolphe Quetelet in 1835, is "a budget that is paid with frightening regularity . . . a tribute that man acquits with greater regularity than that he owes to nature or the state treasury" (quoted in Porter 1986, 54). Why, he wondered, should something so lawless as murder, so disorderly and irrational as suicide, occur in almost uniform numbers from year to year? What form of fatality could drive people to do away with themselves according to so strict a budget?

A new entity made it all seem natural. Crimes are not the misdeeds of isolated individuals. Rather, they are properties of the "social body." These regularities, he argued, show that society bears responsibility for crime. The individual criminal on the scaffold is merely an expiatory victim. Quetelet regarded "statistical laws" as the most powerful evidence available for the reality of society. Emile Durkheim, though critical of Quetelet, invoked these broad regularities to similar ends.

The creative power of statistics is not limited to such global entities as society. Many social concepts that now seem indispensable, such as rates of crime or unemployment, were made real by statistical accounts. The accounts themselves, in turn, required effective administrative intervention to be stabilized. This is true even of death rates, at least from the standpoint of insurance companies. The first generation of professional actuaries, working in early-Victorian England, considered the careful selection of lives at least as important as the construction of sound life tables for calculating safe premiums. Indeed, they considered reliance on mortality rates for the whole population to be an unsatisfactory makeshift for a new company, which after some years would replace these general tables by better ones reflecting its own experience. That experience, in turn, would depend on its success at selecting lives of excellent quality to insure.

Rates of illness were still more problematical. An expert actuary, John Finlaison, testifying for a select committee of the House of Commons in 1825, openly doubted that sickness could ever be reduced to law. The select committee found this unacceptable, since many friendly societies provided insurance to their members against the consequences of illness. If sickness varied unpredictably, they were all threatened with bankruptcy. It strong-armed Finlaison into conceding the possibility of laws of sickness. In 1849 another witness explained how a system of careful surveillance and elimination of perverse incentives permitted his organization to stabilize rates and hence to offer such insurance securely. Policing the boundaries of sickness has become all the more important in recent times. Otherwise the public treasury will be drained by epidemics of impermissible maladies, and following the logic of the new Ricardianism, all surplus value will pass ineluctably into the hands of physicians (Hacking 1990; Porter 1995a).

Statistical categories are scarcely easier to maintain than accounting definitions. The numbers they define are threatened by misunderstanding as well as self-interest. Alain Desrosières and Laurent Thévenot (1988) discuss the problems of coding, and report that in up to 20 percent of cases a repeat interview will assign an employee to a different occupational category from what was reported initially. Even this much consistency can be attained only with a trained and relatively cohesive work force. In many cases it is not enough. Aggregate numbers are routinely used, preeminently in the United States, as a basis for apportioning political power and for allocating public revenues. Add to this the obligatory political rhetoric of rapidly growing economic numbers, and it is easy to conceive why statistics are so often disputed.

On occasion these debates go deeper and the categories themselves are challenged. Racial and ethnic categorization inspires great passion and is always highly contentious in the United States. Activists and bureaucrats created the category "Hispanics" out of Americans of Mexican, Cuban, Puerto Rican, Iberian, and Central and South American descent, though this was by no means universally supported among these various groups (Peterson 1987). Still, the disputes should be regarded not simply as evidence of the vulnerability of statistics. They also supply noisy testimony to their power. Statistics participate actively in the formation of individual and collective identities. Consider the *cadre*, which can be roughly translated as professional manager (Desrosières 1989, 1990). In 1930 the term scarcely existed. It was imprinted on the public consciousness above all by its adoption as a statistical category in postwar French economic planning. By now it can be used unproblematically in newspapers or conversations to designate a class of people, existing *an sich* and perhaps even *für sich*. French students can aspire to attend an Ecole des Cadres in Paris, to be formed into this variety of humanity by learning, among other things, to manipulate numbers, speak business English, and play golf. Thévenot (1990) makes stories like these central to this formation of social classes, which, he argues, are inseparable from the instruments of social statistics that contribute to their articulation. Public statistics are able to describe social reality partly because they help to define it (Porter 1993).

Extramural accounting: a world made safe for numbers

It would be quite false to suppose that numbers are useless for description. But in the human and natural sciences alike, successful description always depends on some variety of control – at least of observers, if not of interventions. This need not always be highly centralized. Nor is it necessarily self-affirming. I certainly would not imply that the world accepts passively the forms impressed on it by some quantitative *force majeure*. In economic and social affairs, quantitative predictions and management by numbers often create inducements for business people, medical patients, taxpayers, and criminals (among others) to alter their behavior in a way that undermines the numbers. That is, though the world described by social as well as natural scientists is partly a world of their own construction, they cannot make it however they choose. The numbers can just as well be self-undermining as self-vindicating; precisely because they have become powerful, it is attractive to circumvent them. The "bottom line" is never determined unambiguously by the activities it summarizes. Where there is incentive to deceive, the job of keeping the numbers honest will depend on ever more detailed regulations, and on spies and auditors who are in a position to examine things in relatively full detail. This means opening up black boxes, thus compromising those key virtues of detachment and economy that made the numbers valuable in the first place.

Officials often find ways to adjust numbers in a desired direction. When the United States Forest Service was enjoined by Congress to cut no more timber than is renewed by annual growth, its scientists quickly learned creative accounting. By calculating the anticipated effects of new pesticides, fertilizers, and stronger tree varieties, they projected an increase in forest growth rates – thereby permitting the immediate harvest of more big trees (Hays 1987, 48; Caufield 1990, 68). Cooking the books, though, may not be the worst form of quantitative deception. Responsible officials sometimes change their behavior in order to outwit the quantifiers. Corporate managers put off maintenance for the sake of better short-term numbers (Hopwood 1973). Schoolteachers adjust the curriculum to improve performance on standardized tests.

With these examples, though, we have crossed over from the domain where quantitative rules are found wanting when confronted by a recalcitrant world into one that displays their remarkable if perverse ability to remake that world. Alexander Zinoviev's novel *Homo Sovieticus* (1985) defines the paradigm case:

Any hopes that one can make scientific discoveries in the sphere of predicting the future are without foundations. First of all, in the Soviet Union predictions about the future are the prerogative of the highest party authorities, and so scientific small fry are simply not allowed to make any discoveries in this area. Secondly, the Party authorities don't predict the future, they plan it. It is in principle impossible to predict the future, but it can be planned. After all, in some measure history is the attempt to correspond to a plan. Here it's like the five-year plans: they are always fulfilled as a guide to action, but never as predictions.

Moreover, quantitative successes feed on one another. Theodor Adorno (1969) noted this in some remarks on the relation of quantification to capitalism in the culture industry. As an American refugee scholar, by one of the odder quirks of fate in intellectual history, he had become associated with a study of radio headed by another émigré, the archquantifier Paul Lazarsfeld. Adorno reminisced: "When I was confronted with the demand to 'measure culture,' I reflected that culture might be pre-

cisely that condition that excludes a mentality capable of measuring it."
But this mattered little for the study of mass entertainment. "It is a
justification of quantitative methods that the products of the culture
industry, second-hand popular culture, are themselves planned from a
virtually statistical point of view. Quantitative analysis measures them by
their own standard." It goes without saying that he did not think that
standard a very high one.

It has been urged that accounts have less to do with representing facts
than with guiding behavior in large organizations. There is more than a
hint here of a false dichotomy. Numbers that have no credibility as truth
claims will be less effective also at projecting power and coordinating
activity. But the imperative mood tends to define the indicative.
Adequate description counts for little if the numbers are not also reasonably standardized. Only in this way can calculation establish norms
and guidelines by which actors can be judged and can judge themselves.

Ambitious social scientists generally think of physics when they con-
template the possibilities of quantification. But numbers and quantitative
manipulations are at least as important for the management of public life
as they are for any of the sciences. Forms of quantification such as
accounting can teach us as much about the sources and consequences of
social science quantification as can an elevated view from the vantage
point of natural science triumphant. Indeed, I would go further and argue
that the practical quantitative imperative has contributed in several
important ways to the pervasiveness of numerical reasoning even in
physics. Everywhere it assists the enforcement of a certain discipline and
hence is active on the level of power as well as knowledge (Thompson
1967; Landes 1983, chap. 3; Schaffer 1988; Olesko 1991). Everywhere it
acts as a filter, which, if it clarifies, does so by removing impurities and
isolating what Nancy Cartwright (1989) calls "capacities" from the complex maze of phenomena that we confront in the world outside the laboratory. What is abstracted away might from another standpoint be
regarded as most essential. And what is preserved in the analysis may
also be perpetuated by artifice – by experimental manipulation, industrial
manufacture, or bureaucratic intervention. Administrative power is as
difficult to separate from the methods of social science as is technology
from the sciences of nature.

The social sciences are often regarded, not least by their own practitioners, as weak. In many spheres of life, though, they have been strikingly successful not only in describing the world but in remaking it.
Standardized tests work well for predicting success in school in part at
least because they have helped to form the institutions in which they are
most heavily used. E. G. Boring's famous proposal that intelligence be

defined as what the tests measure was intended as a statement of experimental operationalism; but it is perhaps better understood as testimony to the power of professionals in alliance with administrators to shape people and institutions, and in this way to make concepts mean what they want them to mean (see Hornstein 1988). Such tests have traditionally been less successful at predicting success outside of school. But the network within which these measures are valid extends increasingly beyond the walls of educational institutions. The public culture of business depends on forms of quantitative analysis taught in business schools. Doctors inhabit a world of charts and graphs, and of clinical studies written in the language of significance levels from inferential statistics. There is much evidence that people do not spontaneously analyze their daily problems in anything like the terms of mathematical probability. But in a quantified world they cannot be competent unless they learn to think in formal, quantitative terms.

The reconfiguration of expert knowledge implied by the spread of quantification is exemplified by recent quantitative studies of judgment and decision making. Psychologists now commonly use probabilistic calculations as a standard against which to assess the ability of subjects to make accurate judgments under conditions of uncertainty. This began with some optimism but led ineluctably to the view that human reasoning is defective. An especially controversial conclusion emanating from this research program holds that even the clinical judgment of experts is generally inferior to rigid quantitative rules for predicting behavior. But the quantifiers have constructed the world in which they excel. The judgment of lay subjects is normally assessed by posing for them a Bayesian probability problem, where base rates are expressed numerically and where there is little richness of detail. Clinicians are typically asked to make predictions based not on long interviews with patients but rather using numbers generated by a test such as the Minnesota Multiphasic Personality Inventory. In such cases, not surprisingly, expert judgment can add little beyond what computers can do following mathematical rules. In a world defined by quantification, quantitative methods reign supreme. That world is no longer confined to the laboratory and the computer (Gigerenzer et al. 1989, chap. 5; Kleinmuntz [1984] 1986; Holt 1978).

To quantify a quality is not merely to solve an intellectual problem. It is to create what Latour calls a center of calculation, surrounded by a network of allies. Not so long ago, only a utopian like Condorcet could aspire to create such a world. But now the network is largely in place. It includes computers and software packages. It includes millions of scientists, engineers, government officials, and clerks busily engaged in adding to the world's supply of numbers. And it includes administrators of all kinds who evaluate people according to these numbers. The quantification of qualities is as much an administrative accomplishment as an intellectual one. And no matter what the skeptics may say, many social qualities have already been successfully quantified, in a variety of ways. Those who seek to do it differently, or to spread the net of quantified qualities still wider, need to consider not only epistemological questions but also moral and political ones. There is strength in numbers, and anyone who proposes to wield them more effectively must ask not only about their validity but also about how the world might be changed by adopting new forms of quantification.

ACKNOWLEDGEMENTS

I wish to thank the Earhart Foundation, the John Simon Guggenheim Memorial Foundation, and National Science Foundation (grant DIR 90–21707) for their support of this research. The paper was originally written for a conference on "The Measurement of Achievement" sponsored by the Achievement Project, Oxford, England.

REFERENCES

Adorno, Theodor. 1969. "Scientific Experiences of a European Scholar in America." Translated by Donald Fleming. In *The Intellectual Migration: Europe and America 1930–1960*, edited by Donald Fleming and Bernard Bailyn, 338–70. Cambridge, Mass.: Harvard University Press.

Alonso, William, and Paul Starr, eds. 1987. *The Politics of Numbers*. New York: Russell Sage.

Anderson, Margo. 1989. *The American Census: A Social History*. New Haven, Conn.: Yale University Press.

Cartwright, Nancy. 1989. *Nature's Capacities and Their Measurement*. Oxford: Clarendon Press.

Caufield, Catherine. 1990. "The Pacific Forest." *The New Yorker*, 14 May, 46–84.

Danziger, Kurt. 1990. *Constructing the Subject: Historical Origins of Psychological Research*. Cambridge: Cambridge University Press.

Daston, Lorraine. 1988. *Classical Probability in the Enlightenment*. Princeton, N.J.: Princeton University Press.

Desrosières, Alain. 1989. "Les spécificités de la statistique publique en France: Une mise en perspective historique." *Courrier des Statistiques*, no. 49 (January): 37–54.

  1990. "How to Make Things Which Hold Together: Social Science, Statistics and the State." In *Discourses on Society, Sociology of the Sciences Yearbook*, vol. 15, edited by P. Wagner, B. Wittrock, and R. Whitley, 195–218.

  1993. *La Politique des grands nombres: Histoire de la raison statistique*. Paris: Editions la Découverte.

Desrosières, Alain, and Laurent Thévenot. 1988. *Les catégories socioprofession-nelles.* Paris: Editions la Découverte.

Feldman, T. 1990. "Late Enlightenment Meteorology." In Frängsmyr et al. 1990, 143–77.

Foucault, Michel. 1973. *The Order of Things.* New York: Vintage.

Frängsmyr, Tore, John L. Heilbron, and Robin Rider, eds. 1990. *The Quantifying Spirit in the Eighteenth Century.* Berkeley: University of California Press.

Galton, Francis. 1901. "Biometry." *Biometrika* 1.

Gigerenzer, Gerd, et al. 1989. *The Empire of Chance: How Probability Changed Science and Everyday Life.* Cambridge: Cambridge University Press.

Gillespie, Charles. 1980. *Science and Polity in France at the End of the Old Regime.* Princeton, N.J.: Princeton University Press.

Hacking, Ian. 1975. *The Emergence of Probability.* Cambridge: Cambridge University Press.

——— 1983. *Representing and Intervening.* Cambridge: Cambridge University Press.

——— 1990. *The Taming of Chance.* Cambridge: Cambridge University Press.

Hays, Samuel P. 1987. "The Politics of Environmental Administration." In *The New American State: Bureaucracies and Policies since World War II,* edited by Louis Galambos, 21–53. Baltimore: Johns Hopkins University Press.

Heilbron, John L. 1979. *Electricity in the Seventeenth and Eighteenth Centuries.* Berkeley: University of California Press.

Holt, Robert R. 1978. *Methods in Clinical Psychology,* vol. 2: *Prediction and Research.* New York: Plenum Press.

Hopwood, Anthony. 1973. *An Accounting System and Managerial Behaviour.* Lexington, Mass.: Lexington Books.

Horkheimer, Max, and Theodor W. Adorno. 1969. *Dialektik der Aufklärung: Philosophische Fragmente.* Frankfurt: S. Fisher Verlag.

Hornstein, Gail A. 1988. "Quantifying Psychological Phenomena: Debates, Dilemmas, and Implications." In *The Rise of Experimentation in American Psychology,* edited by Jill G. Morawski. New Haven, Conn.: Yale University Press.

Hunter, J. S. 1980. "The National System of Scientific Measurement." *Science* 210 (21 November):869–74.

Jasanoff, Sheila. 1990. *The Fifth Branch: Science Advisors as Policymakers.* Cambridge, Mass.: Harvard University Press.

Jungnickel, Christa, and Russell McCormmach. 1986. *Intellectual Mastery of Nature: Theoretical Physics from Ohm to Einstein,* 2 vols. Chicago: University of Chicago Press.

Kleinmuntz, Benjamin. [1984] 1986. "The Scientific Study of Clinical Judgment in Psychology and Medicine." In *Judgment and Decision-Making,* edited by Hal R. Arkes and Kenneth R. Hammond, 551–67. Cambridge: Cambridge University Press.

Landes, David. 1983. *Revolution in Time.* Cambridge, Mass.: Harvard University Press.

Latour, Bruno, 1988. *Science in Action.* Cambridge, Mass.: Harvard University Press.

Lundgren, Anders. 1990. "The Changing Role of Numbers in Eighteenth-Century Chemistry." In Frängsmyr 1990, 245–66.

Maass, Arthur. 1951. *Muddy Waters: The Army Engineers and the Nation's Rivers*. Cambridge, Mass.: Harvard University Press.

McCloskey, Donald. 1985. *The Rhetoric of Economics*. Madison: University of Wisconsin Press.

Mirowski, Philip. 1989. *More Heat Than Light: Economics as Social Physics; Physics as Nature's Economics*. Cambridge: Cambridge University Press.

Olesko, Kathryn M. 1991. *Physics as a Calling: Discipline and Practice in the Königsberg Seminar for Physics*. Ithaca, N.Y.: Cornell University Press.

Pearson, Karl. [1892] 1957. *The Grammar of Science*. New York: Meridian.

Peterson, William. 1989. "Politics and the Measurement of Ethnicity." In Alonso and Starr 1989, 187–233.

Porter, Theodore M. 1981. "The Promotion of Mining and the Advancement of Science: The Chemical Revolution of Mineralogy." *Annals of Science* 38:543–70.

1986. *The Rise of Statistical Thinking, 1820–1900*. Princeton, N.J.: Princeton University Press.

1992a. "Objectivity as Standardization: The Rhetoric of Impersonality in Measurement, Statistics, and Cost-Benefit Analysis." *Annals of Scholarship* 9:19–59.

1992b. "Quantification and the Accounting Ideal in Science." *Social Studies of Science* 22:633–51.

1993. "Statistics and the Politics of Objectivity." *Revue de Synthèse* (4)1:87–101.

1994. "Death of the Object: Fin-de-siècle Philosophy of Physics." In *Modernist Impulses in the Human Sciences*, edited by Dorothy Ross. Baltimore: Johns Hopkins University Press.

1995a. "Precision and Trust: Early Victorian Insurance and the Politics of Calculation." In *The Values of Precision*, edited by M. Norton Wise. Princeton, N.J.: Princeton University Press.

1995b. *Trust in Numbers: The Pursuit of Objectivity in Science and Public Life*. Princeton, N.J.: Princeton University Press.

Rider, Robin. 1990. "Measure of Ideas, Rule of Language: Mathematics and Language in the Eighteenth Century." In Frängsmyr 1990, 113–40.

Roberts, Lissa. 1991. "A Word and the World: The Significance of Naming the Calorimeter." *Isis* 92: 198–222.

Schaffer, Simon. 1988. "Astronomers Mark Time: Discipline and the Personal Equation." *Science in Context* 2:115–45.

Smith, Crosbie, and M. Norton Wise. 1989. *Energy and Empire: A Biography of Lord Kelvin*. Cambridge: Cambridge University Press.

Stigler, Stephen. 1986. *The History of Statistics: The Measurement of Uncertainty before 1900*. Cambridge, Mass.: Harvard University Press.

Thévenot, Laurent. 1990. "La politique des statistiques: Les origines des enquêtes de mobilité sociale." *Annales: Economies, Sociétés, Civilisations*, no. 6:1275–1300.

Thompson, E. P. 1967. "Time, Work-Discipline, and Industrial Capitalism." *Past and Present* 38:56–97.

U.S. Congress, House of Representatives. 1952. *Economic Evaluation of Federal Water Resource Development Projects: Report . . . from the Subcommittee to*

Study Civil Works, 82nd Congress, 2nd Session, House Committee Print No. 24.

U.S. Congress, Senate, Committee on Public Works, Subcommittee on Flood Control-Rivers and Harbors. 1957. *Hearings: Evaluation of Recreational Benefits from Reservoirs*, 85th Congress, 1st Session.

U.S. FIARBC (Federal Inter-Agency River Basin Committee), Subcommittee on Costs and Benefits. 1950. *Proposed Practices for Economic Analysis of River Basin Projects*. Washington, D.C.: U.S. Government Printing Office.

U.S. National Archives, Washington, D.C., 1946–53. "Records of the Federal Inter-Agency River Basin Committee Subcommittee on Benefits & Costs." Record Group 315, Entry 6, Boxes 1–5.

U.S. War Department, Corps of Engineers, Los Angeles Engineers District. 1943. *Benefits from Flood Control: Procedure to be Followed in the Los Angeles Engineer District in Appraising Benefits from Flood Control Improvements*. Mimeo, National Archives, Pacific Southwest Region (Laguna Niguel, Calif.), RG77, 800.5.

Wise, M. Norton. 1989–90. "Work and Waste: Political Economy and Natural Philosophy in Nineteenth-Century Britain." *History of Science* 17:263–301, 391–444; 18:221–61.

Worster, Donald. 1985. *Nature's Economy: A History of Ecological Ideas*. Cambridge: Cambridge University Press.

Zinoviev, Alexander. 1985. *Homo Sovieticus*. Translated by Charles Janson. Boston: Atlantic Monthly Press.

3   Natural and artificial budgets: accounting for Goethe's economy of nature

Myles W. Jackson

Introduction

"We live in credit and debt," declared Werner in *Wilhelm Meisters Lehrjahre*, Goethe's classic *Bildungsroman*, published in 1795. Werner was overtly concerned with the economics of his time. He informed the main character, Wilhelm:

At that time, you had no true idea at all of trade, while I could not think of any man whose spirit was, or needed to be, more enlarged than the spirit of a genuine merchant. How fantastic it is to see the order which prevails throughout his business! Via this order he can, at any time, survey the general whole, without needing to perplex himself with the details. What advantages he derives from the system of double-entry bookkeeping [*doppelte Buchhaltung*]! It is among the finest inventions of the human mind; every prudent master of a house [*Haushalter*] should introduce it into his economy. (Goethe, WA I, 21, 51; my translation)[1]

Werner, the "prudent manager," was Goethe's perfect foil to Wilhelm. Wilhelm replied, "You begin with the form, as if it were matter: you businessmen commonly forget, in your additions and balancings, what the proper sum total [*Facit*] of life is" (ibid.). Werner responded, echoing Goethe's own beliefs, by claiming that

order and clarity increase the desire to save and to purchase. Anyone who mismanages [*übel haushält*] soon finds himself in the dark . . . A good manager, however, finds no greater pleasure than to pull together each day the sum of his increasing happiness. . . . Natural and artificial productions of all regions of the earth [have become] articles of necessity for men. How pleasant and how intellectual a task it is to calculate, at any moment, what is most required, and yet is wanting or hard to find, to procure for each easily . . . ; to lay in your stock prudently beforehand, and then to enjoy the profit of every pulse in that mighty circulation . . . You will then see the smallest piece of ware in its connection with the whole mercantile concern . . . everything augments the circulation by which you yourself are supported. (Ibid., 51–52)

Wilhelm Meisters Lehrjahre was written during one of the most prolific and ambitious periods in Goethe's life. This period witnessed Goethe's

---

[1] All references to the *Weimarer-Ausgabe* of Goethe's collected works are abbreviated WA in the text, followed by the volume, section, and page numbers.

active engagement with natural research and administrative management. Although he no longer participated directly in the privy council (*Das geheime Consilium*), he was deeply engrossed in his administrative duties at the Ilmenau mine. He had completed his *Beiträge zur Optik and Die Metamorphose der Pflanzen* earlier in that decade and was now turning his attention to morphology, a term he had coined for the scientific and artistic study of organic forms. It was also the time when he was familiarizing himself with Adam Smith's *Wealth of Nations*.

As I have argued elsewhere (Jackson 1992a, 460; 1992b, 143–44), Goethe's science represented a managerial moral. The natural world of Saxe-Weimar-Eisenach was managed in the same manner as the administration of that region, and Goethe was the *Hofmeister*. Goethe, using Kant's definition of genius in *Kritik der Urteilskraft* as a resource, fashioned himself as the genius who could interpret natural laws and manage their application to civil cases (Goethe, WA I, 29, 146).

This paper discusses two aspects of accounting. The first, typified by the natural budgets found throughout Goethe's morphological writings and by his own practices in the administration of the Ilmenau mine, is the static, "technical mechanism for recording transactions" (Miller 1990, 316). The second, more dynamic, aspect of accounting "attributes financial values and rationales to a wide range of social practices, thereby according them a specific visibility, calculability and operational utility" (ibid., 316–17). As we shall see, Goethe's financial support of and scientific interest in chemical practices necessary for amalgamation did not merely represent an attempt to bolster the regional economy by increasing the amount of metal obtained from the mine, it also served as an example of how chemistry was transformed from a subservient subject tainted by its working-class status and associations with alchemy into an independent university discipline (Golinski 1988, 1–3). Precisely because mining officials such as Goethe attributed financial value to chemical practices relevant to mining and many other industries, chemistry became much more visible and operationally useful. Chemistry also provided a means whereby a more precise quantification of metal ores became possible. The costs incurred by the smelting, mining, and chemical processes were recorded on the debit side of Goethe's balance sheet, while the precious metals obtained by these processes were recorded on the credit side.

Goethe's use of *Wasserwirtschaft*,[2] as developed by the geologist Abraham Gottlob Werner, combined both aspects of accounting. On the one hand, it was an artificial economy attempting to keep track of the

---

[2] *Wasserwirtschaft* is generally translated as hydraulic engineering. Yet such a translation loses the implication of an economy. It is literally translated as water economy.

distribution of water in the mine. *Wasserwirtschaft* itself, as discussed below, embodied the notion of economy. On the other hand, *Wasserwirtschaft* was of immense financial value, as it permitted miners to exhume metals from the earth much more efficiently. Therefore, Goethe's accounting procedures attributed financial value to practices involved in *Wasserwirtschaft*. Such practices included the manufacturing of hydraulic pumps and the digging and reinforcing of the mine's shafts.

Goethe's notion of budgets in his accounting procedure was purposely ambiguous so that he could create linkages between investigating nature and administering Saxe-Weimar-Eisenach. Natural budgets were inviolate balances. They were nature's allotment of force for performing functions crucial to the development of a particular organism. According to Goethe, nature was the perfect economy. In administration, however, accounting budgets were merely assessments of the total amount of money needed to perform functions relevant to the state. They were artificial and therefore were inferior to natural budgets. Goethe needed to systematize the duchy's financial records; so he created budgets. While conducting his morphological research, however, Goethe sought not to create budgets but to reveal nature's inherent ability to budget. The genius researcher of nature, which Goethe considered himself to be, used budgets as a heuristic tool to trace nature's developments. Budgets, whether natural or artificial, were instruments of order. Not only did they actively rectify chaotic accounting procedures, they also passively depicted balanced, organic forces present in nature.

Thus the organizing principles of nature were for Goethe the same as the methods used in investigating it. Goethe's administrative rhetoric – including such words as "budget," "balance," "economy," "law," and "order" – was also applicable to the relationships inside both the organization of the state and natural philosophy. The role of a late eighteenth and early nineteenth-century *Naturforscher* tied these relationships together. A *Naturforscher's* job as court official was necessarily political, and laws that governed human knowledge in eighteenth-century Weimar were, according to Goethe, natural and not artificial.

Goethe's administration of Weimar from 1776 to the 1790s

Before Goethe's appointment to the privy council, Weimar had been an impoverished and underdeveloped community. Manufacturing, which had formed the economic basis of much larger cities such as Frankfurt on Main and Leipzig, had been marginal in Weimar. The duchy had possessed a minute economy based on *Handwerker*, crafts, retail trade, and a farming community.

Goethe entered into Weimar's court culture in November of 1775[3]. On 11 June 1776 he became a member of the *Geheimen Legationsrat*, receiving voting privileges on 25 June of that year. On 5 September 1779 he was appointed privy councillor (*Geheimnen Rat*) and played an active role in the *Geheime Consilium*, the duchy's most powerful administrative body, until departure for Italy in July of 1786 (Goethe, AS I, p. xiii).[4] The privy council was an instrument of the ruling duke based on the principles of enlightened despotism. The council was responsible for advising the duke on, among other things, managerial and fiscal matters (ibid., I:iv). Goethe's primary role within the privy council was balancing the books. He needed to bring financial order to the *Finanzverwaltung*, which his predecessor, von Kalb, had left in utter chaos.

During the 1770s and 1780s, Duke Carl August appointed young, bourgeois lawyers such as Goethe, Schmid, Schnauss, and Voigt to the privy council in order to supplement the aging court officials who had been appointed by Carl August's mother, Anna Amalie (Hubschke 1958, 60–63, 80, 82–86). These officials, such as von Kalb and von Fritsch, were members of the aristocracy. Tensions quickly arose between the two classes of administrators, as Goethe spearheaded a plan of reform for Saxe-Weimar-Eisenach (Goethe WA IV, 5, 73, 236, 311–12).

Goethe often opposed general tax increases proposed by his elder aristocratic colleagues, claiming that taxing the poor was a very inefficient and unfair means of raising capital. As evidenced by his stance against taxation in order to obtain capital for the mine at Ilmenau and by his decisions on the project to reconstruct the Weimar castle after a fire had gutted it in May of 1774, Goethe wished to increase capital within the duchy by investment in industry and manufacturing. Thus he often supported attempts at mechanization (ibid., IV, 12, 50–51; Hoffman 1950, 295–300).[5]

The Ilmenau mine had been a valuable source of income for the region for centuries (Wagenbreth 1983, 19–38). Carl August had decided early in his reign that the mine was worth repairing after the destruction it had incurred during the Seven Years' War. On 18 February 1777, after Bergrat Friedrich Wilhelm Heinrich von Trebra had conducted a comprehensive study of the potential income the mine could generate and the feasibility and cost of its repair, Carl August established a mining commission to

---

[3] For the most detailed account of Goethe's managerial life, see von Bradish 1937 and Pitt 1987

[4] All references to Goethe's *Amtliche Schriften* are abbreviated AS, followed by the volume and page numbers.

[5] These sentiments were also present in Goethe's report "Über das Maschinenwesen. Gutachten über den Vorschlag des Tischlermeisters Röntgen von 24. February 1797," Goethe- and Schiller-Archive, Weimar, Germany.

which Goethe was appointed. The older members of the privy council had claimed that the initial capital needed to repair the Ilmenau mine should be procured by taxing the residents. Goethe, however, strongly opposed the plan. After traveling to Ilmenau with Carl August in 1776, he had become aware of the region's poverty. Another tax would simply destroy any hope for a future economy. Thus his decision, along with that of Hofrat von Eckhardt and Geheimrat C. G. Voigt, proved to be a significant contribution to the development of the Ilmenau mine and to the regional economy. These three members of the mining commission concluded that the duchy should offer mining shares (*Kuxe*) which would encourage investment in Ilmenau. Von Eckhardt's "Nachricht von dem ehemaligen Bergbau bei Ilmenau, und Vorschläge, ihn durch eine neue Gewerkschaft wieder in Aufnahme zu bringen," written under Goethe's close supervision, detailed their plans. Carl August provided a portion of the original investment, as well as paying for the mining commission (ibid., 45). Von Eckhardt's document ensured the mining company of Ilmenau a series of liberties and privileges unlike any other mining agreement of the period. Miners and mining advisers had total control of their own shares and profits, with options to mortgage or sell them as they pleased (Goethe, LA I, I, 65–70; Wagenbreth 1983, 42–43; Voigt 1912, 47–50).[6] After the initial three years the duke, as regal owner and ruler, received one-wentieth of all the procured metal and one-tenth of the total profits.

The scheme enjoyed a resounding success. By late summer 1783, all 1,000 shares were sold at 20 taler each. The secretary of the mining commission, Johann Gottfried Schreiber, claimed that had there been 3,000 shares available, they would all have been bought up (Thüringer Staatsarchiv Weimar B 16232, fol. 10). Investors as far away as Nurenberg and Berlin purchased shares (Wagenbreth 1983, 47; Voigt 1912, 166–67), with noblemen outside of Saxe-Weimar-Eisenach accounting for 566 of the 1,000 shares. In the duchy itself, Goethe, Wieland, and Herder were all shareholders. The Ilmenau mine, as a result of the triumph of Goethe and von Eckhardt's investment scheme, opened on 24 February 1784.

But Goethe's attempt to invigorate Saxe-Weimar-Eisenach's economy was not restricted to the Ilmenau mine. In January of 1779 he was appointed director of the commission of streets and paths (*Wege-baudirektion*) and of the War Committee (Goethe, AS I, xiv). As the former, Goethe increased the number of roads from Weimar to larger cities in the region, including Erfurt and Gotha. He also enlarged the network within the duchy by creating routes between Weimar, Jena, and

---

[6] All references to the *Leopoldina-Ausgabe* of Goethe's collected scientific works are abbreviated LA in the text, followed by the section, volume, and page numbers.

Eisenach. Such a network of routes helped to stimulate trade both within the duchy itself and with surrounding states. As director of the War Commission, Goethe increased revenue for the duchy by slashing the number of soldiers in the Weimar militia (Henning 1976, 267–69). All of these administrative enterprises involved balancing the books by double-entry accounting (Goethe, AS I, xvi).

One of Goethe's first responsibilities while in Weimar was the creation of a budget for the chamber (*Kammer-Etat*) (ibid., 5–15) and the Weimar court (*Hof-Etat*) (ibid., 18–19). On 11 June 1782 Goethe replaced von Kalb, one of the older, aristocratic members of the privy council, as director of the chamber (*Kammer*), which dealt with the heart of the financial concerns of the privy council (ibid., xvi).[7] Although Goethe's involvement in the privy council waned considerably after his return from Italy, he continued his work on the *Bergwerkskommission* of the Ilmenau mine.

Like many eighteenth-century investigators of nature, Goethe possessed a predilection for collecting natural artifacts such as minerals and plants. It is therefore appropriate that his administrative duties included the organization and management of cabinets of nature, scientific institutes, and museums. In 1779 he set up a natural history cabinet in Jena. In 1794 he and C. G. Voigt became codirectors of the Botanical Institute Commission in Jena. Nine years later both men were responsible for the creation and maintenance of all the scientific collections of the Jena Museum, which included mineralogical, zoological, astronomical, and physical chemistry cabinets (ibid., xiv–xx). Their responsibilities grew to include the Jena observatory in 1812 and the veterinary medical school in 1816. Hence a large part of Goethe's administrative duties involved managing knowledge of nature.

Goethe and the *Kameralwissenschaften*

The cameral sciences (*Kameralwissenschaften*) were university curricula that late seventeenth- and eighteenth-century cameralists developed to instruct bureaucrats on how to serve regional rulers (Tribe 1984, 266–76; Forrester 1990, 290–92). The cameral sciences were generally divided into three distinct yet related categories: *Oekonomik*, *Polizei* Science, and *Cameralistik*. *Oekonomik* included the theoretical social sciences, economics, and technologies related to agriculture, forestry, and mining. *Polizei* Science dealt with the implementation of the cameralists'

---

[7] Although Goethe was acting director of the *Finanzverwaltung* (financial administration chamber), he never enjoyed the official title of the *Kammer–präsident*, as had von Kalb (see Goethe, AS I, p. xvi).

curricula, particularly in relation to the regional militia, which policed and regulated the people with the aim of achieving the common good of the state. The third component, *Cameralistik*, concerned itself with the control of the state's finances (Forrester 1990, 291).

Goethe typically chose elements and practices of Enlightenment ideology that he could adapt to his own use without totally accepting the epistemological claims of that ideology. The cameral sciences were no exception. He subscribed to the view that *"Cameral-Wissenschaft* concerns itself with the means of raising revenues for the *Landes-Fürst*, their [*sic*] general improvement and utilization in the maintenance of the commonweal (*gemeinen Wesens*) so that every year a surplus remains" (Dithmar 1745, 225; translated in Tribe 1984, 264). Goethe supported instruction in the cameral sciences at the University of Jena (Goethe, AS II, 2, 668). His administration of the Ilmenau mine drew on the scientific, technological, and economic practices associated with *Oekonomik*. Mercantilism and cameralism promoted the view that the wealth of a ruler and his people depended on the amount of cash flow and metals. These economic systems claimed that the export of metals to other regions would activate trade. Goethe's work as director of finances of Saxe-Weimar-Eisenach fitted squarely into the domain of *Cameralistik*. However, from the outset he strongly opposed the *Polizei* role of the state, hence his reduction of the Weimar militia. He did not implement any portion of *Polizei* science.

Cameralism as an economic ideology began to wane in popularity during the 1770s and 1780s. During that period it became evident that cameralism and mercantilism could not be successfully adopted by small German duchies such as Saxe-Weimar-Eisenach (Mahl 1982, 134). Weimar's meager manufacturing ability combined with its limited degree of industrialization rendered such forms of economy useless. Cameralism was slowly being replaced in many German states by a new economic theory, French physiocracy.

Physiocratic doctrine proclaimed that social phenomena, like their counterparts in nature, are subject to laws: just as natural laws control and regulate nature, social laws, established by human reason, guarantee order (Sagave 1976, 109). François Quesnay, the founder of physiocracy, wished to establish an economic theory of an *ordre naturel*. He believed in the existence of self-evident truths (*Evidenz*), which took the form of physical laws in nature and moral laws of human behavior (Hutchinson 1990, 280–81).

The physiocrats divided the population of France into three categories: the productive class, composed of farmers, miners, and fishermen, who reaped the fruits of the earth; the proprietary class, which owned land

and were the sources of capital; and the artisan or "sterile" class, which manufactured and distributed the goods generated by the productive class (Hankins 1985, 178). Believing, like Quesnay, that every citizen had natural rights, the physiocrats sought to guarantee the sanctity of property and a free market (ibid.).

During the 1770s physiocracy took root in the German states through the translation of the works of Mirabeau and de Nemours. Margrave Karl Friedrich's agricultural reforms in Baden, to which Goethe paid close attention, were based on the physiocratic principles of these two men (Jackson 1992a, 464; Sagave 1976, 111). Goethe undoubtedly sided with the physiocrats on many issues during the 1770s and 1780s, and indeed implemented a portion of their policies. The importance of property for the duke's subjects, soil enrichment, the dissipation of large, seigneurial goods, and the necessity to build trade routes were all economic aspects of physiocracy that Goethe supported (Mahl 1982, 187).

In short, from 1776 to the mid-1790s Goethe played an active role in the economic development of the duchy of Saxe-Weimar-Eisenach. By picking and choosing among the elements of differing economic theories, Goethe was attempting to manage the duchy as efficiently as nature managed itself. It was precisely during this period that Goethe began formulating his view that nature was the perfect economy; and morphology was the discipline Goethe created in order to depict this perfect economy.

Goethe's morphology

Goethe's work on morphology in particular and his biology in general was vitalistic in nature. Although he readily admitted that physics and chemistry help elucidate the properties of living organisms, he vehemently opposed any attempt to reduce biological phenomena to physico-chemical principles. In his essay "Bildung und Verwandlung" ("Formation and Transformation"), Goethe argued that "analytical efforts, if continued indefinitely, have their disadvantages. To be sure, the living thing is separated into its elements, but one cannot put these elements together again and give them life" (Goethe, WA II, 6, 8, as translated in Goethe 1952, 23). In his "Vorarbeiten zu einer Physiologie der Pflanzen" ("Preliminary Notes for a Physiology of Plants"), written in the mid-1790s, Goethe declared:

From the physicist in the strict sense of the term, the science of organic life has been able to take only the general relationship of forces, their position and disposition in the given geographical location. The application of mechanical principles to organic creatures has only made us more aware of their perfection; one might almost say that the more perfect living creatures become, the less can mechanical principles be applied to them. (Goethe, WA II, 6, 295, as translated in Goethe 1952, 89)

Goethe was attacking the mechanical philosophy of French rationalism, which had dominated European thought for over a century and a half. He despised the French depiction of organisms as complex machines. In *Dichtung und Wahrheit*, Goethe recalled his reaction to the mechanistic nature presented throughout Baron d'Holbach's *Système de la Nature*, published in 1770:

We found ourselves deceived in the expectation with which he had opened the book. A system of nature was announced, and therefore we truly hoped to learn something of nature, our idol. . . . But how hollow and empty we felt in this melancholy, atheistic half-night [*atheistische Halbnacht*], in which the earth vanished with all its images, the heaven with all its stars. (Goethe, WA I, 28, 69–70)

It was this mechanical ideology of the French that had driven the young Goethe to Shakespeare, where he had discovered the notion of genius, the creative spirit of man and the creative spirit of nature (ibid., 71–77).

Goethe was, of course, not alone in his condemnation of the French *Weltanschauung*. His *Sturm und Drang* cohorts, and later the early Romantics, echoed Goethe's disdain and indignation. All of them fundamentally opposed the notion of mechanical laws of nature. Nature was to the late eighteenth-century German-speaking investigators of nature and *Naturphilosophen* a dynamic, not a static, entity. Although united in their belief in a living, non-mechanical nature, not all of them agreed on the governing primary principles of nature's system. In short, there were two responses to a nature ruled by mechanical laws: one was to reject the notion of natural law altogether; the other to base nature on organic laws. Goethe, the privy councilor, believed that organic laws were the principles governing nature; they accounted for natural order. His linkage between the state and the organism, discussed below, illustrates the claim that organic laws served as the organizational principle of both his views of nature and his administration of Saxe-Weimar-Eisenach.

Like all his views on nature, Goethe's organicism was based on the law of polarity: nature was a unity of opposing forces and entities. For example, in his *Zur Farbenlehre*, which was published in 1810 and was the culmination of two decades of research on color theory, Goethe classified all colors under two categories, plus and minus, and ascribed corresponding attributes to each.

Considered from a general point of view, color is determined toward one of two sides. It thus presents a contrast, which we call a polarity, and we may designate this by the expression "plus and minus."

plus	*minus*
yellow	blue
action	negation
light	shadow
force	weakness
warmth	coldness
proximity	distance
repulsion	attraction
affinity with acids	affinity with bases (Goethe, WA II, 1, 277)

Polarity, which Goethe claimed to be a natural property, was of fundamental importance to his botanical and morphological studies. For example, in his 1790 treatise, *Die Metamorphose der Pflanzen*, Goethe contrasted the two major forces in plants: expansion and contraction. The cotyledons and corolla of a plant are worked on by an expansive force, while the calyx and coronas are affected by a contractive force.

By repeating here a remark made earlier, that styles and stamens represent the same stage of development, we can further clarify the cause of this alternate expansion and contraction. From the seed to fullest development of stem leaves we noted first an expansion; thereupon we saw the calyx developing through contraction, the petals through expansion, and the sexual organs again through contraction; and soon we shall become aware of the maximum expansion in the first and the maximum contraction in the seed. In these six steps nature ceaselessly carries on her eternal work of reproducing the plants by means of the two sexes. (Goethe, WA II, 6, 62–63, as translated in Goethe 1952, 60–61)

Returning to Goethe's essay "Preliminary Notes for a Physiology of Plants," in a section entitled "Organische Entzweiung" ("Organic Duality") he contrasted the root and leaf of a plant.

Origin of root and leaf. They are united by origin; indeed, they cannot be imagined without the other. They are also by their origin opposed to each other . . . root embryos develop downward and the leaf embryo upward, by saying that they are opposed, in keeping with the general dualism of nature, which here becomes specific. . . . We find that the roots require moisture and darkness to develop; the leaf requires light and acridity. Thus, from the beginning to end these needs are opposed . . . Chief differences between the root and leaf embryo: the former always remains simple. The leaf embryo, on the other hand, develops most directly, and step by step approaches perfection. Light and darkness foster elaboration. Moisture and darkness restore it . . . We reach the climax of organic duality in the division of the two sexes. (Goethe, WA II, 6, 307–8, as translated in Goethe 1952, 95–96)

These passages are noteworthy for two reasons. First, polarity illustrates nature's balancing abilities; equal and opposite forces exist in nature. Nature is, therefore, balanced. Although his notions owed much to the *Naturphilosophie* of Schelling,[8] Goethe's polarity and balance, unlike

---

[8] For a good summary of Goethe's organicism, see Wetzels 1987.

Schelling's, were also applicable to the relationships within administrative accounting. Schelling had no interest whatsoever in serving the state, and his *Naturphilosophie* did not link the organism to the state. Indeed, this is one very important difference between Goethean depictions of nature on the one hand and the natural views of the *Naturphilosophen* and many of the early Romantics on the other. For Goethe, who was very much a part of Weimar's court culture, the linkages between nature and polity were of much more concern than for his cohorts in Jena.

Second, these passages reveal that Goethe believed in the existence of external laws – i.e., laws external to the organism. French mechanistic accounts of nature held the view that mechanical laws govern living organisms, and that those laws are inherent to the organism and are not present in the environment. Goethe countered such a depiction of nature first by claiming that natural laws governing life are organic, not mechanical, and second by asserting that natural laws are not restricted to the organism but are also present in the environment. Goethe's belief in internal, organic laws, such as the *Bildungstrieb*, or formative force, implied that nature is not simply a projection of man's ego, as Schelling would later insist.

The concept of the formative force is not originally Goethe's. In fact, Goethe's vitalist view belonged to the Kant-Blumenbach tradition (see Jardine 1991, 22–28; Lenoir 1989, 17–35). Vitalism denied the role of a rational agent in nature and sought to base the understanding of nature on vital forces. Indeed, one of the major features of vital materialism and morphology was a central commitment to these vital forces, such as Blumenbach's *Bildungstrieb*. Much of Goethe's work on morphology resulted from his anatomical investigations with Blumenbach (Bräuning-Oktavio 1956, 79–86).

In his work of 1781 entitled *Ueber den Bildungstrieb und das Zeugungsgeschäfte* ("On the Formative Force and the Generative Activity"), Blumenbach described the various directions that the *Bildungstrieb* could take in the multifarious life forms, both internally and externally (Jardine 1991, 27–28). Within certain limits, external stimuli can produce variations in the formative force thereby creating slight modifications in the structure of the organism (Lenoir 1989, 22). Goethe lauded Blumenbach for basing development on an anthropomorphic entity, the *nisus formatives*, or *Trieb*, rather than reverting to the notion of *Kraft*, which Goethe condemned as being mechanical and "a dark incomprehensible point" (*ein dunkler unbegreiflicher Punkt*) in the organization of living matter (Goethe, WA II, 7, 72).

As in Blumenbach's account, every organism in Goethe's scheme had an allotted sum of formative force, which remained constant throughout the organism's lifetime. The formative force was allocated to different organs depending on the needs of that organism in response to its environment. In his essay "Erster Entwurf einer allgemeinen Einleitung in die vergleichende Anatomie, ausgehend von der Osteologie" ("First Outline of a General Introduction in Comparative Anatomy, Starting from Osteology") of 1795, Goethe spoke of an organism's inherent ability to budget its *Bildungstrieb*.

> The rubric of [*the Bildungstrieb*'s] budget (*Etat*), in which it divides up the cost, are prescribed to the organism. What it will direct to each part is to some extent up to the organism itself. If it wants to direct more [force] to one part, it is not completely hindered as long as it simultaneously takes away the same amount from another part. Thus nature can never be in debt, nor can it become bankrupt [*bankrutt*]. (Goethe, WA II, 8, 16)

He continued by elaborating on nature's budgets.

> To illustrate this notion of budgetary give and take [*haushältische Gebens und Nehmens*], let us cite a few examples. The snake is a highly organized creature. It has a strongly marked head, with a perfectly developed auxiliary organ – an extensible lower jaw. Its body on the other hand is, as it were, infinite; and this is possible because it needs to waste neither substance nor strength on auxiliary organs. No sooner do such auxiliary organs appear in some form or other – the short arms and legs of the lizard, for example – than the infinite length shrinks into a much shorter body. The long legs of the frog greatly shorten into body, and by the same law [*Gesetz*] the shapeless toad is extended in breadth. (Ibid., 18–19)

Goethe spoke of the "preponderance" (*Übergewicht*) of certain organs with respect to others. For example, "the neck and extremities of a giraffe are encouraged [to develop] at the cost of the giraffe's body, whereas just the opposite occurs in the mole" (ibid., 16). Goethe called this budgeting ability of nature the organic law of compensation, or the correlation of the parts to the whole. This law declares that "no part can gain something without another part losing something, and vice versa" (ibid.). At the end of this section in the essay, Goethe reiterated the importance of external laws that keep the internal organic law of compensation in check: "The *Typus* must comply, to a certain degree, with the general external laws [*allgemeine äussere Gesetzen*]" (ibid., 19). Throughout his morphological writings he continually spoke of the natural principle of balance (*Gleichgewicht*), the preponderance of the parts of an organism, and the principle of giving and taking (ibid., 309, 312). According to Goethe, no internal part of an organism can be superfluous when an external part of that organism is useless (ibid., 309). In his preparatory notes for the aforementioned essay Goethe sketched out the following notion:

1. Law [*Gesetz*]

The *Typus* has a certain amount of forces, which is independent of its size. This mass of forces must be used by nature. Nature cannot exceed the limit, nor can it fall below that limit . . . The sum of the forces of one animal is the same as the sum of the forces of another [of the same *Typus*]. (Ibid., 316)

The best-known example of Goethe's law of compensation is the inverse relationship between the development of horns and front teeth in the upper jaw of certain animals. Goethe argued that because the lion, like all members of the cat family, has both upper incisors and large canine teeth, it cannot possess any horns (ibid., 60). Hence the *Bildungstrieb* of the lion is spent on the development of teeth. The ox, on the other hand, has neither upper incisors nor canine teeth but does have horns. Likewise sheep (ibid., 17–18). The budgeted allotment of *Bildungstrieb* of oxen and sheep is expended on horns (Wells 1978, 20–21).

The law of compensation became for Goethe a "fundamental truth" (*Hauptwahrheit*) of nature. In 1830, while critiquing the debate between Baron Cuvier and Geoffroy de Saint Hilaire, Goethe wrote: "Economical nature [*haushältische Natur*] has prescribed a budget [*einen Etat, ein Budget*] in which . . . the main sum [*Hauptsumme*] remains the same, for if too much has been given on one side, it subtracts it from the other side and balances it out in no uncertain manner" (Goethe, WA II, 7, 205–6; Nisbet 1972, 21).

Goethe's use of the term *Haushalt* throughout the above quotations is noteworthy. The concept of a *Haushalt* was often employed by cameral-ists throughout the eighteenth century in order to equate the state with a large family where the ruler was the *Hausvater* responsible for the happiness of his family, the subjects (von Schroder 1752, par. 11, as translated in Tribe 1988,19). As Tribe has argued, the *Oekonomie* of household management was well established in the literary genre of the cameral sciences during the seventeenth and eighteenth centuries (Tribe 1988, 26). In the eighteenth century the *Kammer* in general, and the *Finanzverwaltung* in particular, became the advisers of the head of the family. The household in this period, then, was tantamount to the economy of the state. As J. H. G. von Justi claimed in his *Curieuser und nachdencklicher Discurs von der Oeconomia und von guten Oeconomis*, "For what is a good Chamber-President or Cameralist if not an experienced, good and prudent *Oeconomus* or householder" (von Justi 1754, 14, as translated in Tribe 1988, 35). "The art of householding" was defined by G. H. Zincke in his *Allgemeines Oeconomisches Lexicon*, published in 1744, thus:

The art of keeping house, oeconomy, oeconomic science, is a practical science, wherein the wisdom, prudence and art of nearly all learned sciences are applicable to the end of rightful concern for provisioning and economy [*Nahrung- oder Wirtschafts Geschäffte*]. (Zincke 1744, col. 1099, as translated in Tribe 1988, 51).

In short, morphology provided investigators of nature with an investigative methodology that could depict nature's perfect economy. By recording the allotment of *Bildungstrieb* to the differing organelles, natural researchers could provide a *Bauplan*. This *Bauplan* enabled Goethe to illustrate nature's diversity while simultaneously allowing him to proclaim its unity. All organisms possessed *Bildungstriebe* in varying amounts, but the variance of the organisms was due to the distribution of *Bildungstrieb* as directed by the external laws, the climate. Budgets were the methodological tool used to illustrate nature's complex relationship and inherent order. They also permitted investigators of nature to trace a natural, morphological network by depicting the different ways in which the *Bildungstrieb* manifested itself. Similarly, administrators utilized an accounting budget to link various administrative enterprises that formed a financial network. Goethe hoped that his artificial budgets would approximate the accuracy of the natural budgets.

Goethe and mining

Mining was for centuries a vital source of income for the German duchies in Saxony as well as for the Prussian kingdom. J. H. G. von Justi had argued in the mid-eighteenth century that mines were "the most certain path to wealth" (von Justi 1754, 4). In his *Staatswirtschaft* of 1754, von Justi had claimed that the university curriculum of the cameral sciences needed to be supported by a professor of chemistry "who was conversant with smelting techniques and an instructor of mechanics who was familiar with mining machinery" (von Justi 1754, xxxii, as translated in Tribe 1988, 67). Daniel Gottfried Schreber had proposed an academy of cameral sciences at Bützow in which the president would be assisted by five instructors: a professor of cameral sciences or economics who would teach *Haushaltungswissenschaft*, a professor of mathematics and physics who could teach pure mathematics and its practical applications such as the surveying of fields and mines, a professor of natural history, a professor of mineralogy and chemistry to teach the chemistry applicable to mining, and a professor of manufacturing and commerce (Schreber 1763, 417–36; Tribe 1988, 92–93). Schreber had envisaged the professor of mineralogy and physics as playing a pivotal role within the academy. He would teach *physikalische und ökonomische* chemistry. Physical chemistry was taught in a laboratory, while economic chemistry was the lecture portion of the course discussing topics on the chemical processes related to manufacturing, such as dyestuffs, ceramics, glass making, and metallurgy. The course would also include lectures on topics within the sciences of mining (*Bergbauwissenschaften*) such as the refinement and use of the products of mining in foundries (ibid.).

In 1765 an academy combining mining with the study of the cameral sciences, chemistry, mining law, economy and other related disciplines had been established, the Freiberg Bergakademie. Although it would go beyond the scope of this paper to provide a comprehensive history of the Mining Academy at Freiberg and its renowned leader, Abraham Gottlob Werner, it is necessary to mention briefly the connection between mining and economy.

Werner's Bergakademie had been designed specifically with the interests of the state in mind. He wrote, "Every *Wissenschaft* has its worth; they only differ in the degree of utility and the degree of applicability to everyday life" (Werner 1962, 48). He had underscored the point that *Geognosie* could also be extremely useful for the state economist (*Staatswirtschaftler*), "for those at the helm and for those whose interest it is to obtain the riches which spring out of the inner portion of the earth which procure the greatest riches for the nation" (as quoted in Ospovat 1967, 310). Werner had envisaged his Bergakademie as an institution that would educate and train young bourgeois men to serve their country or duchy "in order to make a nation, through enlightenment: honest, dangerous (*gefährlich*), industrious, comprehensible, well-connected, courageous and obedient" (ibid.). According to Werner, it was up to the state to utilize its natural resources to its economic and political advantage. Before becoming director of the academy, Werner had taught economics at the Leipzig School of Economics.

The importance of the academy to the governments of Prussia and Saxe-Weimar-Eisenach cannot be overestimated.[9] Both governments had sent promising young civil servants to be trained in mining, law, and financial administration. Indeed, the financial reformer and Prussian Minister of State von Heinitz had been one of the founders of the academy. Werner's students included Alexander von Humboldt, Novalis, Heinrik Steffens, F. X. von Baader, and J. C. W. Voigt. On becoming director, Werner had altered the curriculum to offer his students a much more thorough training as civil servants. He had placed a major emphasis on the economic considerations of all mining practices. The chemist

---

[9] For the importance of the Freiberg *Bergakademie* to the German states in general, and to Goethe's operation of the Ilmenau mine in particular, see Wagenbreth 1983, Voigt 1912, Herman 1955, and Ziolkowski 1990, 18–63. It should be noted that despite the crucial role the academy played in the economic development of the German states in the late eighteenth century, Lowood 1991 fails to give an account of it.

Lampadius had taught practical mining chemistry courses that were visited by cameralists and economists throughout Germany (Benseler 1853, 1167–68). Werner had divided the lectures on *Bergbau* into four sections: mineralogical, technical, mathematical, and economic. He had also added instruction in *Wasserwirtschaft* (water management). Finally, he had stressed the importance of mining organization and management (Baumgärtel 1967, 151).

Goethe drew heavily on the resources that the Mining Academy provided him. His involvement in mining technology and geology resulted from his need to advise the duke on policy issues. Goethe's views on nature and administration were being co-produced during the 1770s and 1780s.[10]

I came to Weimar totally ignorant of all studies of nature, and the need to be able to give practical suggestions to the duke in his various undertakings, buildings, layouts, propelled me to study nature. Ilmenau cost me much time, trouble and money, but I learned something from it and have acquired a view of nature that I would not like to exchange for any price. (Goethe 1909–11, III:87–88)

I actually first entered the active, working life as well as the sphere of *Naturwissenschaft*, when the honorable Weimar circle accepted me, where, among other precious advantages, I could happily exchange the street air for the country, forest and garden atmosphere. (Goethe, LA I, 10, 321)

Goethe called upon von Trebra to assist him at Ilmenau after von Trebra had completed his study of the Ilmenau mine for Carl August. Von Trebra had been the Freiberg Mining Academy's first student (Hermann 1955, 62). Thus von Trebra, Goethe, C. W. Voigt, and Duke Carl August formed a mining community that was based on the teachings of the Freiberg Academy. Goethe convinced Carl August to provide financial support for the education of young civil servants – among them J. C. W. Voigt, who studied mining under Werner's tutelage from 1776 until 1778:

Joh[ann] Carl Wilhelm Voigt . . . wishes to dedicate his services to you in one way or another after having sent him to the Freiberg Academy and having travelled in the Saxony area. . . . Perhaps Your Excellency will not be opposed to appointing him as mining secretary of the commission . . . He will provide useful services in this field and perhaps others as well. (Goethe, LA I, 1, 27)

In return, the young Voigt assisted Goethe at Ilmenau.

The Bergakademie provided the impetus for Ilmenau's redevelopment by supplying Goethe with not only the necessary mining machinery but also trained individuals with the required technical skills. Conversely, to be a miner or a mining administrator in the German states during the late

---

[10] Shapin and Shaffer 1989 and Latour 1991 have provided us with a methodology that saves us from asking naively causal questions.

eighteenth century, one needed to pass through Werner's academy and acquire the necessary skills. The critical link between mining and the governing chamber was made explicit by von Trebra. When Goethe wanted to send his son, August, to Freiberg before appointing him *Kammerassessor*, von Trebra remarked, "Where can he sit in a *Kammer* without knowing anything about mining?" (as quoted in Hermann 1955, 73). Other students of Werner's assisted in forging the Ilmenau mine: Johann Friedrich Mende and Karl Gottfried Baldauf were advisers on technical machinery; J. G. Schreiber was responsible for maps and boundary marking and became supervisor of mining works (Goethe, LA I, 1, 109); and Voigt became *Bergrat* (mining adviser) and the technical director of the Ilmenau mine in 1783 (Hermann 1955, 40–41). Werner provided Goethe with the personnel to create a booming mining economy.

There are two examples of Goethe's attempt to balance the mining accounts. First, much of Goethe's interface with mining was in an administrative capacity. Therefore, not surprisingly, a great deal of his scientific writings on geology included detailed budgets for setting up and operating the mine at Ilmenau (Goethe, LA I, 1, 172–75, 182–84, 202–3, 238–41). For Goethe, these budgets were artificial; they were his estimates of credits and debits; unlike his morphological budgets, they were not based on a natural network. Assessment budgets kept a record of the financial transactions over a period of time. Goethe shared the common belief that mining itself represented a micro-economy: as riches (*Reichtümer*) were exhumed from the earth, nature's equilibrium was destroyed. However, the profit from those riches was quickly overtaken by the costs of the mining machinery and the water damage sustained during periodic flooding (Wagenbreth 1983, 73–74). The credit side of Goethe's double-entry accounting was to be bolstered by the investment scheme discussed in the introduction to this essay and by the process of amalgamation.

Amalgamation was the newly invented chemical procedure, developed by Ignaz von Born in 1780 which separated the precious metals from the slate and sand (Lowood 1991, 303–6). Goethe researched the possibility of reducing the cost of – or simply by-passing – the expensive smelting operations. In the amalgamation process the metal was dissolved from the slate and then combined with mercury to form an amalgam from which the metal could be easily separated. In 1786 von Trebra, while in Glashütte near Chemnitz, learned the new procedure of amalgamation and immediately informed Goethe and Voigt accordingly (Wagenbreth 1983, 60). Goethe himself witnessed this technique in the Erz Mountains and in Silesia. On 15 October 1790 he wrote to the *Bergbauamt* at

Ilmenau:

Differing mineralogical and chemical observations made during my last visit to Silesia have made me wonder if one cannot handle the copper slate nearly as well or as comfortably as other ores through pounding and sludge [to free it from particles] and thus save the entire operation of crude stone work (*Rohsteinarbeit*) and bring the entire slate immediately to amalgamation. I am informing you of these thoughts and hope that they will be further tested, and that at least a small experiment will be made. (Goethe, WA IV, 9, 231)

By April of 1793, 2,500 tons of copper slate and sand mixed with ores reaped from the mine were brought to the smelting master, Schraeder. But chemical analysis performed in the smelting laboratory revealed quantities of a mere 0.003 percent of silver and copper. A new smelting oven was built later that same year in the hope of procuring a higher percentage of metal. Such hopes were never realized. Schraeder could not successfully separate a significant proportion of copper and silver from the Ilmenau mine (Wagenbreth 1983, 62–63). Ilmenau became an enormous liability, rather than an impressive credit, for the duchy. Goethe had approved the expenditures for the chemical and geological practices necessary for obtaining the precious metals. He claimed that amalgamation was crucial to the credit side of his double-entry accounting (Thüringer Staatsarchiv Weimar, B 16248, ff. 15–16). In essence, Goethe rendered these scientific practices visible, since he attributed to them the properties of quantification and operational utility. Thus they represented a major portion of his accounting practices at Ilmenau.

On 12 April 1793 Goethe summarized the entire Ilmenau enterprise in the form of a budget.

It is necessary to present a summary of the entire economic situation of the works from the accounts. It is noticeable from the outset that while on the one hand the direction [of the works had cost] more than had originally been planned because the actual working of the strata and the general expense needed to accomplish this was greater than originally expected, on the other hand the cost of executing such work had not been subtracted from the original figure in the conceived plans. One therefore had more expenditures and less income than was previously reckoned. (Goethe, LA I, 1, 223)

Goethe himself asserted that his interests in economics and technology were sparked by his general interest in mining. Reflecting back on the summer of 1770, when he was in Elsa, Lothringen, Saarbrück, and Duttweil, Goethe wrote in *Dichtung und Wahrheit*,

Here I actually steeped myself in the interest of the mountain region, and the desire for economic and technical considerations, with which I have occupied myself for a large portion of my life, were first aroused. We heard of the rich Duttweil mines of pit-coal, of the iron and aluminum works, yes even of a burning mountain. (Goethe, WA I, 27, 330)

Goethe went on to state that one of the critical factors tying together his scientific and mercantilistic interests was mining chemistry, "He [Herr Stauf, an applied chemist] belonged to the old school of chemists, which abtrusively stressed the trivial and unimportant details of the subject . . . rather than researching the usefulness of the subject with respect to economic and mercantilistic considerations" (ibid., 334).

The above are crucial passages because they illustrate how Goethe's chemical and mineralogical observations were made with a specific interest in mind: the application of those particular physical sciences to the governmental activity of mining. These passages also depict Goethe as a frugal administrator of natural knowledge who used pioneering technological advances to perform tasks more efficiently and more cheaply. A part of Goethe's economy of nature had its roots in his administrative duties at Ilmenau. His language of the economy of nature obtained its meaning because it represented his practical orientation of mining research. Much of Goethe's interface with nature from the 1770s to the 1790s was in an economic and industrial capacity. The economy of nature was thus not metaphorical in Goethe's eyes, since nature was the perfect economy. A note of Goethe's from 1793 intimately linked natural research and administration. He was hoping to increase the amount of metal ores obtained from the mine's shafts for the amalgamation process:

Pass [a scheme to impede water leakage in one of the tunnels] through everyone, the oldest miners, mining master, mining lawyer, secretary . . . pit foreman and miners . . . Advice on the scheme. Pass the mining acts according to the newest report of the mining master. Tunnels. Upheaval, lighted ditches. Shaft. Machines. Build on these, billeting, sketches, places, disassembled stretches, stamp and wash mills. Idea, situation, incline, cleft, descent. Scheduled time, execution time, money, experiments, effect, hindrance, what is still required . . . personnel, mechanics. (As quoted in Wagenbreth 1983, 62)

It is clear from the above passage that Goethe was attempting to forge and reinforce connections between the bureaucratic, mining, and artisan enterprises. He faced these problems of linkage in his daily routine as an administrator. The bureaucrats provided the finances and tested the feasibility of the scheme, the miners performed the actual labor, and the mining chemists and smelters analyzed the metal ore content. Because such descriptive notes are commonplace, their importance is often neglected. Goethe was building a network in which the *Bauplan* represented the network's record. Accounting practices afforded an opportunity to create artificially a network that strove to resemble the natural network of formative forces, which Goethe revealed in his morphological works.

Another example of Goethe's artificial economy was his use of *Wasserwirtschaft*. Goethe employed Wernerian *Wasserwirtschaft* to prevent flooding of the mine. Werner provided Goethe with a working technique that did more than assist in augmenting the duchy's economy; the practices inherent to Werner's techniques also reflected the notion of economy. Water management was imperative to the proper functioning of mines, and Ilmenau was no exception. Goethe's assistants at Ilmenau had enrolled in Werner's *Lehre von Wasserhaushalt*.[11] Because water was the energy source powering the mines, it needed to be conserved, redistributed, and managed in an orderly and frugal manner. Water was the currency of mining. Since water power was used to tunnel into the earth, it was the formative force of the mine, the inorganic equivalent of the *Bildungstrieb*. Water management was tantamount to a financial economy and was the artificial counterpart to the natural economy depicted in Goethe's morphological writings.

Goethe spent much time and money to effect a system of water economy in Ilmenau. To keep the increasing levels of water in check, the mining ditches were lengthened and every portion of the ditch that was not waterproof was sealed. Goethe personally inspected the water-proofing on 4 and 8 June and 11 November 1785 (Wagenbreth 1983, 49). It took a constant battle of available forces and technical support to solve the water problem in the Johannes shaft (ibid., 50). Other water problems sprang up, however, throughout the late autumn of 1787 and the winter of 1787–88. Leaks became commonplace. On returning from his Italian journeys, Goethe wrote to Carl August on 1 October 1788, "I am proceeding to Ilmenau where they are quite seriously busying themselves to overcome the water" (Goethe, WA IV, 9, 36). He then detailed the procedures for increasing the number of pumps in order to expedite the restoration of order. By 1790 the situation was severe enough for Goethe to call upon the expertise of the Bergakademie once again. Baldauf returned to Ilmenau in February 1790 and offered technological advice to solve Ilmenau's problems (Wagenbreth 1983, 54). During the late summer and early autumn of 1790, Goethe traveled to Upper Silesia, where he studied other mines and devoted his time to water economy. On 12 September 1790 Goethe wrote to C. G. Voigt: "In Tranowitz I find solace in Ilmenau. They have . . . a far greater quantity of water to hoist" (Goethe, WA IV, 9, 225). The first steam engines to hoist water (*Wasserhebungsdampfmaschine*) were operating in Upper Silesia by 1788. Goethe was introduced to a Newcomen steam engine and a water column engine (*Wassersäulemaschine*) during his visit there.

Both of these machines were subsequently used for pumping water out of the mining shafts in Ilmenau (Wagenbreth 1983, 55).

[11] Terms such as *Wasserwirtschaft* and *Wasserhaushalt* clearly illustrate that eighteenth-century bureaucrats and mining instructors believed "hydraulic engineering" to be itself a form of economy.

In January of 1791, Baldauf was consulted once again. This time a massive engineering effort ensued to conquer the ever-present water. Goethe made the necessary funds available and work commenced in June of that year. But their success was ephemeral. Leaks reoccurred in 1793, and a fatal collapse of the Martinrodaer tunnel on 8 November 1796 resulted in the close of the Ilmenau mine. Goethe's administrative project was a complete failure. He was so frustrated and disappointed that he did not return to Ilmenau for another twenty years. His artificial budgets had failed to match their natural counterpart.

Conclusion

From the time he entered the service of Duke Carl August, Goethe began to co-produce his views regarding nature and administration. Both in nature and in the regime he served, Goethe saw enlightened despotism. His notion of the organic state reflected his natural epistemology. Goethe the *Hofmeister* daily constructed linkages between nature and culture. During the 1790s these linkages resulted in an intricate network. In the first half of that decade Goethe's managerial and scientific skills were at their zenith. He busied himself with his research on color theory and morphology, and the Ilmenau works took up a great deal of his administrative time.

The common organizing principle, serving as the major link between enterprises, was the budget. Natural budgets not only illustrated that nature was the perfect economy, they also provided Goethe with an epistemology that was applicable to his morphological studies. The budgets of the duchy, which were artificial and also based on double-entry bookkeeping, were attempts to keep a record of transactions and to balance Weimar's chaotic financial situation. A micro-artificial economy, *Wasserwirtschaft*, was implemented as a technological system that could augment the duchy's macro-economy.

Research into Weimar's court culture and its administrative policies has revealed how much overlap existed between nature and culture. The vast majority of the secondary literature on Goethe severs the numerous enterprises that he himself so desperately sought to unite. New historiographies in the history of science have emphasized the importance of viewing the scientific enterprise as a cultural one. By recovering the context of Goethe's writings on morphology and mining technology, a vast cultural network can be established in which Goethe's *Naturanschauung* was deeply and inextricably embedded.

ACKNOWLEDGEMENTS

I would like to thank Nicholas Jardine, Simon Schaffer, and the anonymous referees for their comments on and constructive criticisms of
earlier versions of this essay, which formed a portion of my Ph.D.
dissertation at the University of Cambridge.

REFERENCES

Baumgärtel, H. 1967. "Abraham Gottlob Werner als Lehrer und Forscher auf
    dem Gebiet des Bergbaus." In *Abraham Gottlob Werner: Gedenkschrift aus
    Anlass der Wiederkehr seines Todes nach 150 Jahren am 30 Juni 1967*, 149–56.
    Leipzig: VEB Deutscher Verlag für Grundstoffindustrie.
Benseler, Gustav Eduard. 1853. *Geschichte Freibergs und seines Bergbaues.*
    Freiberg: J.G. Engelhardt.
Bräuning-Oktavio, Hermann. 1956. "Vom Zwischenkieferknochen zur Idee des
    Typus: Goethe als Naturforscher in den Jahren 1780–1786." *Nova Acta
    Leopoldina* 18:126.
Dithmar, Justus Christoph. 1745. *Einleitung in die öconomischen Policey- und
    Cameralwissenschaften*, 3rd ed. Halle.
Flach, Willy. 1952. "Goethe und Verwaltungsgeschichte. Goethe im Geheimen
    Consilium 1776–1786." In *Thüringische Archivstudien*, vol. 3. Weimar:
    Hermann Böhlaus Nachfolger.
Forrester, David A. R. 1990. "Rational Administration, Finance and Control
    Accounting: The Experience of Cameralism." *Critical Perspectives on
    Accounting* 1:285–317.
Goethe, J. W. v. 1887–1918. *Goethes Werke. Herausgegeben im Auftrage der
    Grossherzogin Sophie von Sachsen,* Weimar edition (abbreviated WA in the
    text), 143 vols. Weimar: Verlag Hermann Böhlaus.
    1909–11. *Goethes Gespräche.* Edited by F. Iodoard Freiherr von Biedermann,
    5 vols. Leipzig: F. W. v. Biedermann.
    1949ff. *Die Schriften zur Naturwissenschaften*, Leopoldina edition (abbreviated
    LA in the text). Weimar: Verlag Hermann Böhlaus.
    1950–72. *Goethes Amtliche Schriften* (abbreviated AS in the text), 4 vols.
    Weimar: Verlag Hermann Böhlaus.
    1952. *Goethe's Botanical Writings.* Edited by Barbara Mueller. Honolulu:
    University of Hawaii Press.
Golinski, Jan. 1988. "Utility and Audience in Eighteenth-Century Chemistry:
    Case Studies of William Cullen and Joseph Priestley." *British Journal for the
    History of Science* 21:1–31.
Hankins, Thomas L. 1985. *Science and the Enlightenment.* Cambridge:
    Cambridge University Press.
Henning, Hans. 1976. "Die Entwicklung Weimars in der Zeit der Emanzipation
    des Bürgertums und im Jahrhundert Goethes." In *Geschichte der Stadt
    Weimar*, edited by Gitta Günther and Lothar Wallraf, 230–337. Weimar:
    Hermann Böhlaus Nachfolger.
Hermann, Walther. 1955. *Goethe und Trebra: Freundschaft und Austausch zwis-*

chen Weimar und Freiberg. Freiberger Forschungshefte D9. Berlin: Akademie Verlag.

Hoffman, A., ed. 1950. *Werktätiges Leben im Geiste Goethes.* Weimar: Hermann Böhlaus Nachfolger.

Hubschke, W. 1958. "Forschungen zur Geschichte der führenden Gesellschaftsschicht im klassischen Weimar." In *Forschungen zur thüringischen Landesgeschichte: Festschrift für Friedrich Schneider*, 55–114. Weimar: Hermann Böhlaus Nachfolger.

Hutchinson, T. 1990. *Before Adam Smith. The Emergence of Political Economy, 1662–1776.* Oxford: Blackwell.

Jackson, Myles W. 1992a. "The Economy of Goethe's Nature and the Nature of His Economy." *Accounting, Organizations and Society* 17:459–69.

1992b. "The Politics of Goethe's Views on Nature." *Enlightenment, Nature and Nurture in Eighteenth-Century Britain* 2:143–57.

Jardine, Nicholas. 1991. *The Scenes of Inquiry: On the Reality of Questions in the Sciences.* Oxford: Clarendon Press.

Latour, Bruno. 1988. *The Pasteurization of France.* Translated by Alan Sheridan and John Law. Cambridge, Mass.: Harvard University Press.

Lenoir, Timothy. 1989. *The Strategy of Life: Teleology and Mechanics in Nineteenth-Century Germany Biology.* Chicago: University of Chicago Press.

Lowood, Henry E. 1991. *Patriotism, Profit, and the Promotion of Science in the German Enlightenment: The Economic and Scientific Societies, 1760–1815.* New York: Garland.

Mahl, B. 1982. *Goethe's ökonomisches Wissen. Grundlagen zum Verständnis der ökonomischen Passagen im dichterischen Gesamtwerk und in den "Amtlichen Schriften."* Frankfurt am Main: Peter Lang.

Miller, Peter. 1990. "On the Interrelations between Accounting and the State." *Accounting, Organizations and Society* 15:315–38.

Nisbet, H. B. 1972. *Goethe and the Scientific Tradition.* London: Institute of Germanic Studies Publication 14.

Ospovat, Alexander M. 1967. "Abraham Gottlob Werners Gedanken über Wissenschaft und Bildung." *Neue Hütte* 12:308–13.

Pitt, Armin Peter. 1987. *Goethe als Manager: Eine Führungslehre.* Hamburg: Steintor Verlag.

Sagave, P.-P. 1969. "Französische Einflüsse in Goethes Wirtschaftsdenken." In *Festschrift für Klaus Ziegler*, edited by E. von Catholy and W. Hellmann. Tübingen: Max Niemeyer.

1976. "Ideale und Erfahrungen in der politischen Praxis Goethes im ersten Weimarer Jahrzehnt." *Goethe Jahrbuch* 93:105–15.

Schlegel, Friedrich. 1958ff. *Kritische Friedrich-Schlegel-Ausgabe* (abbreviated KA in the text). Edited by E. Behler, J.-J. Anstedt, and H. Eichner. Munich: F. Schöningh.

Schreber, D. G. 1763. "Entwurf von einer zum Nutzen eines Staats zu errichtenden Academie der öconomischen Wissenschaften." *Sammlung verschiedener Schrifter* 10:417–36.

Shapin, Steven and Simon Schaffer. 1989. *Leviathan and the Air-Pump: Hobbes, Boyle, and the Experimental Life.* Princeton, N.J.: Princeton University Press.

Tribe, Keith. 1984. "Cameralism and the Science of Government." *Journal of Modern History* 56:263–84.

———. 1988. *Governing Economy: The Reformation of German Economic Discourse, 1750–1840.* Cambridge: Cambridge University Press.

Tümmler, Hans. 1952. *Aus Goethes Staatspolitischen Wirken.* Essen: W. T. Webels.

———. 1976. *Goethe als Staatsmann.* Göttingen: Musterschmidt Verlag.

Voigt, Julius. 1912. *Goethe und Ilmenau.* Leipzig: Xenien Verlag.

von Bradish, Joseph A. 1937. *Goethes Beamtenlaufbahn.* New York: B. Westermann.

von Justi, J. H. G. 1754. *Aufhöchsten Befehl an Sr. Röm Kaiserl. und zu Ungarn und Böhmen König. Majestät erstattetes allerunterhänigstes Gutachten von dem vernünftigen Zusammenhange und practischen Vortrage aller Oeconomischen und Cameralwissenschaften.* Leipzig.

———. 1758. *Staatswirtschaft oder systematische Abhandlung aller Oeconomischen- und Kameralwissenschaften, die zur Regierung eines Landes erfordert werden.* Part 1, 2nd ed. Leipzig.

von Schröder, W. 1752. *Fürstliche Schatz- und Rentkammer.* Leipzig.

Wagenbreth, Otfried. 1983. *Goethe und der Ilmenauer Bergbau.* Weimar: Nationale Forschungs- und Gedenkstätten der Klassischen Deutschen Literatur.

Wells, George A. 1978. *Goethe and the Development of Science, 1750–1900.* Alphen aan den Rijn: Sijthoff & Noordhoff.

Werner, Abraham Gottlob. 1962. *On the External Characteristics of Minerals.* Translated by A. V. Carozzi. Urbana: University of Illinois Press.

Wetzels, Walter D. 1987. "Art and Science: Organicism and Goethe's Classical Aesthetics." In *Approaches to Organic Form: Permutations in Science and Culture*, edited by Frederick Burwick, 71–85. Boston: D. Reidel.

Zincke, G. H. 1744. *Allgemeines Oeconomisches Lexicon*, 2nd ed. Leipzig.

Ziolkowski, Theodore. 1990. *German Romanticism and Its Institutions.* Princeton, N.J.: Princeton University Press.

4   A calculating profession: Victorian actuaries among the statisticians

Timothy L. Alborn

Introduction

In 1867 a bright young actuary named William Makeham revealed a new law of mortality to the London Institute of Actuaries. In his address he suggested to his fellow members why the formula, which smoothed incoming mortality data into a constantly sloping curve, was so important. "The very worst course that could possibly be adopted," warned Makeham,

is to pin our faith upon the crude results of observation, and hoodwink ourselves into the belief that in so doing we are following the path indicated by experience. Let us have the *facts* by all means, but unless we also possess the power to interpret their meaning – to evolve the hidden laws of which they are the rude exponents – we shall . . . turn them but to a very poor account. (Makeham 1867, 346)

A generation later, after the Institute had officially adopted Makeham's law to calibrate its newly collected "Healthy Males" tables, one of its council members, Thomas Young, revealed a formula that could be used to dispel a different variety of rude exponents from their midst. The occasion for Young's speech was a meeting of the Birmingham Insurance Institute, one of a growing number of provincial clubs established in the 1890s to assist in the social improvement of insurance agents and managers. The aim of his formula was to soften manners, not mortality: the rude exponents were those men whose enthusiasm in peddling their product had exceeded the bounds of politeness. Announced Young:

We pass into these halls from the heated and personal asperities of competitive struggle, and gain the valued knowledge of each other in our personal aspect, with the roughnesses of business conflict – which too often obscure our real selves – softened or removed; and we thus tend to import into our rivalry that courtesy and considerateness which only frank and open personal intimacy can produce. (Young 1891, 143)

When Makeham contrasted "hidden laws" with "the crude results of observation," and when Young later sought to smooth the social "roughnesses" he witnessed in his salesmen, both were exhibiting signs of a profession easing into maturity. By the final third of the nineteenth century, British actuaries had served commercial life insurance as part of a more or less formal professional body for fifty years.[1] Their "collective mobility project," to use M. S. Larson's phrase, had passed through stages of formation and crisis, and was in the process of being reestablished on a more stable basis (Larson 1977, chap. 6). These changes in status and organization had accompanied major transitions both in the insurance market and in the practice of calculation by professional groups whose expertise bordered that of the actuaries. Early in the century, when the number of life offices was small and competition at a minimum, actuaries succeeded in establishing informal social bonds among themselves and with mathematicians who took an amateur interest in insurance matters. In the 1840s, when a burst of commercial competition challenged their claims to professional status, actuaries reformed themselves on a more explicitly "scientific" basis: the Institute, established in 1848 as a society for the generation of expert knowledge, was the physical manifestation of this new spirit. But their new styles of language and organization soon encountered a contrary problem. The meaning of science in the 1850s, in a general normative sense as well as in the more specific sense of new trends in statistics and probability, was changing just as actuaries were pinning their hopes for status and commercial stability on a vaguely defined "'scientific" ideal. Unlike the older informal norms actuaries had imbibed in the 1820s, science was increasingly being restructured to refer to disciplined research programs; and probability, once the province of gentleman mathematicians, was being pushed by civil servants like William Farr in the direction of "collectivist" social reform.[2] If actuaries followed their newly blazed scientific trail too far, they risked sacrificing their prior professional claims and alienating their employers with too much talk of social reform. If they backed away, they risked playing into the hands of the new offices, which claimed that hiring an actuary was a needless expense.

In this context, the programmatic statements of Makeham and Young can be seen as efforts to preserve professional status and commercial relevance in an era when there was no such thing as a simple appeal to outside scientific authority. Their strategy, which generally succeeded,

[1] Throughout this article "actuary" will be understood to mean "commercial actuary" – i.e., a person who calculates contingencies for a commercial insurance company – and not other contemporary job descriptions encompassing civil servants and insurance managers. The modern term "life insurance" will also be used instead of "life assurance," which was a common nineteenth-century synonym.

[2] For general changes in British scientific norms and organization in this period see (e.g.) Berman 1987 and Yeo 1993. On the evolving links between probabilism and collectivism see Eyler 1979.

was to borrow freely from contemporary scientific culture without ever losing sight of the unique demands for their services that had arisen since the 1840s. The increase in life insurance business in Britain following the mid-century boom had added whole new classes of clients to the companies' rolls, and hence had introduced a need to recalculate tables on the basis of the incoming stream of experienced mortality. Especially in the days before mechanical data processing, actuaries could legitimately claim sole responsibility for refining these "crude results" by means of the appropriate mathematical formulae, of which Makeham's law was a prime example. Secure in this role, they could spend less time worrying about the ample contributions being made by other statisticians to social policy or probability theory. Young's warnings against commercial "roughnesses" similarly secured a space for actuaries between the all-out competition of the mid-nineteenth century and the collectivist aims of state-employed statisticians. As in past generations, actuaries like Young made a strong appeal to the value of collegiality that they saw at work in neighboring scientific disciplines. But the new generation of actuaries had the advantage of preaching their ethic to an audience that was far more likely to listen: the aspiring professional community of insurance agents. Unlike the competing offices in the 1840s, which had made do without certified actuaries, life insurance salesmen in the late nineteenth century recognized the advantage of heeding the advice of their more seasoned colleagues. When Young preached to them about "courtesy and considerateness," they kept inviting him back – if only to convince potential customers that a salesman who listened to a courteous actuary was likely to be courteous himself.

Besides taking advantage of these new cognitive and social opportunities that presented themselves in the last third of the century, British actuaries turned the commercial fallout from the mid-century boom into a professional plus. Makeham's law, and the new premium tables that accompanied it, made good business sense to life offices that had weathered the recent commercial storm. Most of the new firms that had been floated in the 1840s, despite their confident proclamations about the untapped market for insurance, failed to generate enough business and had to sell out to older companies within a few years. Actuaries could step into this situation and warn the remaining offices about the dangers of relying on undoctored data. The new offices, they claimed, had failed by charging rates based either on their own isolated experience, which provided too narrow a numerical basis for the prediction of future risks, or on outside data, which might encompass more information but be less relevant to their specific needs. Far better, they argued, to use information that had first been pooled from all the offices, then "regulated" in accord with a general law such as Makeham's. Changing commercial conditions also aided the actuaries' efforts to privilege collegiality over competition. Competition in late nineteenth-century life insurance had moved away from the head-to-head struggle among offices that had marked the 1840s, and instead pitted against one another contending agents who reported to a single head office. This new context narrowed the field of necessary commercial converts to the actuaries' professional program, from the earlier wide range of upstart projects to a much smaller number of conservative boards of directors.

This overview of the professional strategies and intellectual products of British actuaries, which will be developed in greater detail below, poses a challenge to the two main perspectives that have touched on such issues: one deriving from the history of science and the other from the sociology of professions. For the purpose of this article, the most relevant studies by historians of science have been those of John Eyler (1979), Theodore Porter (1986), and Ian Hacking (1990), each of which provides a revealing narrative about early alliances between actuaries and organized science but says much less about actuarial practice once that alliance faded. Eyler, in his biography of the sanitary reformer William Farr, has revealed Farr's debt to the actuary Thomas Rowe Edmonds for an important component of his theories of mortality and morbidity. Porter has emphasized the place of actuarial thinking, especially that of Augustus De Morgan and his friends in commercial insurance, in the transition from classical "subjectivist" to modern "frequentist" theories of probability. And Hacking, in a brief chapter on John Finlaison at the National Debt Office, inserts actuaries into his story about "the new imperialism of statistical law" in the early Victorian period (Hacking 1990, 54). Yet all three accounts, while unearthing important points of contact between science and commercial or bureaucratic practice, say little about actuaries in the later nineteenth century. Actuaries appear as supporting actors who play a crucial role in the transition from one form of scientific thinking to another. Their significance lies in what they contributed to an emerging body of scientific thought, not in the reasons (both cognitive and commercial) they had for placing themselves in a position to make that impact, or for distancing themselves from "scientific" thought after mid-century. Perhaps the most representative statement by a historian of science about actuarial practice, in this light, is Donald Mackenzie's footnote in a book that claims to locate the *science* of statistics in the "social context" of late-Victorian Britain: "By this period," he writes,

the major technical instruments of actuarial work, such as the life table, had been developed. There was, of course, much theoretical and empirical work to be done to improve them, but this had become a fairly specialised line of work. Actuarial work was thus rather insulated from developments in statistical theory generally during this period. (Mackenzie 1981, 250)

Another important perspective on actuaries, from the sociology of professions tradition, has recently appeared in its most suggestive form in Andrew Abbott's *The System of Professions* (1988), which depicts the "division of expert labor" as a series of ever-changing boundary disputes and consequent patterns of differentiation among neighboring professional groups. Although Abbott does not include actuaries or statisticians among his cases, the questions he asks are just as relevant for them. In the process, he offers a healthy warning to historians who focus on a single professional group (in this case science) in isolation. It is precisely this practice, he argues, that relegates to the footnotes the "fairly specialised" or "rather insulated" practice of those professions that exist at the boundaries of science. As he suggests it should, a new focus on "inter-professional competition" accounts for the content of actuarial practice as well as its organizational forms in the late nineteenth century. When actuaries at this time developed sector-specific mortality laws and acted as professional mentors for insurance agents, it was because these tasks were in demand from the offices that paid their salaries and because actuaries possessed a comparative advantage over other professions in their ability to perform them. Likewise, if late-Victorian actuaries did not extensively research public health issues or the latest developments in probability theory it was because other professions at the Home Office and Cambridge had demonstrated comparative advantage in those domains. Especially in light of the actuaries' shaky position at mid-century, their story after that time seems to confirm Abbott's thesis that "control of knowledge and its application means dominating outsiders who attack that control" (Abbott 1988, 2).

What Abbott's approach does not do is explain why actuaries ever chose to align themselves so closely with organized science in the first place, or why that choice led to so many problems in the 1840s. Although he may be correct that "control without competition is trivial" (ibid.), it is equally true at other stages in a profession's development that control without alliance formation is impossible. And it is the latter condition for professional survival, which a focus on competition fails to address, that best describes the initial success and eventual problems stemming from the actuaries' informal partnership with science in the early nineteenth century.[3] Early commercial actuaries relied on men of science like De Morgan and Charles Babbage to make their mark in the insurance

---

[3] Nelson and Trubek 1992, 19–21, similarly criticize Abbott's overemphasis on marginal competition, which they claim leads him to overlook the role of professional ideology.

community; just as, to a lesser extent, people like De Morgan and Babbage relied on actuaries as part of their effort to extend science to the middle classes. An alliance between the two groups, if not inevitable, was certainly convenient. It was also strong enough to lead men of science to overlook occasional departures by the actuaries from their newly honed scientific values, and to keep actuaries attached to the ideals of science even when "interprofessional competition" came to call for different forms of organization and expertise. The success or failure of actuaries to achieve professional differentiation, in other words, depended on their ability to know when to borrow from the available "scientific" models of neighboring statisticians in order to enhance their competence and status, and when to forfeit claims to current forms of scientific knowledge in order to stake out territory that was uniquely their own. Hence in order to write a history of their efforts to "professionalize," it is necessary to understand the central tenets of "science" as practiced by contemporary statisticians and to determine the relative worth of these tenets to the actuaries at different points in time. The discussion that follows is loosely organized around three such tenets, or values: objectivity, publicity, and universality.

The value of objectivity, at least in its modern form, conflicted with the actuaries' important professional claim to possess uniquely marketable skills. As Lorraine Daston has argued, the appearance of "aperspectival" objectivity as a scientific value in the early nineteenth century, with its emphasis on precise measurements and replicable experiments, correspondingly weakened the role of judgment and skill. Still, Daston admits that this value was "honored only in the breach": an admission that gains in significance when applied to the actuaries, who never fully internalized nineteenth-century scientific values (Daston 1992, 610–14). Especially in the 1820s, when "objectivity" had as much to do with making a rhetorical point as with enforcing uniform social practice, actuaries could claim to be objective while still selling a set of thoroughly subjective skills to their commercial employers. Mathematicians like Babbage and De Morgan acted as "modern scientists" when they argued that regular distributions of events, which were equally visible to all who cared to look, nudged the merely "probable" into the category of the certain (Porter 1986, 73–76). Life insurance, a business enterprise based on the certainty of statistical law, illustrated the practical utility of this new objectivity. But the reformist hope that a multiplication of facts would counter an overreliance on elite scientific judgement did not translate into a call for the multiplication of insurance companies. John Herschel, who claimed there was "no result which places in a stronger light the advantages which are to be derived from a mere knowledge of the *usual order of nature* . . .

than the institution of life assurances," worried in the same paragraph that "a too great multiplication and consequent competition" among life offices would seriously detract from their utility (Herschel 1830, 57–58). These contrary impulses on the part of early nineteenth-century men of science – to open science to all observers but restrict commerce to prudent capitalists – allowed actuaries to retain skill and judgment as defining traits without appearing to be "unscientific." A generation later, when the "breach" widened within which objectivity was honored as a scientific virtue, actuaries needed to recalculate the costs of allying themselves with science. As Porter has shown, "scientific" statistical thought after 1840 moved in the direction of relying solely on discoverable regularities in a distribution curve, to the point where irregularities were assumed to exist in the events themselves and not in the observer's uncertain mental state (Porter 1986, 78–83). Actuaries, for whom it remained important to distinguish their own capacity for judgment from that of their competitors, ultimately refused to follow this path.

Publicity and universality entered into actuaries' professional calculations in a similar fashion. When these values first appeared in the scientific community they were ambiguous enough to allow actuaries to depart from them in practice without impairing their social links with men of science. Early Victorians made science public when they wrote textbooks for the Society for the Diffusion of Useful Knowledge and held British Association meetings at a different provincial city every year, and they proclaimed their aspiration to universal knowledge in grand systems like William Whewell's *Philosophy of the Inductive Sciences*. But when the British Association published its *Transactions* it exerted editorial control that kept certain forms of science at the margins, and its public meetings always threatened to attract the "wrong" element. The lofty goal of universal knowledge similarly foundered in the early nineteenth century along class and national lines (Morrell and Thackray 1981; Orange 1975; Desmond 1989; Alborn 1989). These ideological tensions, however, persisted among British scientists throughout the nineteenth century without seriously threatening their institutional stability, since most of them could usually agree to depart quietly from their ideals when the alternative involved welcoming "disruptive" mesmerists or social reformers into their fold.

For actuaries, these fortunate social circumstances applied only in the period roughly stretching between 1820 and 1845. At that time, as at other times in the century, their location in the private sector made periodical departures from publicity and universality an occupational necessity: fully public mortality statistics would have diminished an individual office's competitive edge, while national or universal mortality laws were associated with anticompetitive social legislation. But only in the 1820s and 1830s did market conditions allow actuaries to uphold values and practices that stood in contradiction, and only then were their scientific friends willing to look the other way when they did so. Although early Victorian men of science did chafe at extreme forms of privatised knowledge, they commonly supported the actuaries' underlying appeal to private enterprise. De Morgan, for instance, defended their practice of restricting research to local mortality distributions on the grounds that a national insurance scheme would "fail in its operation, by the mere difficulty of arranging its enormous details, the frauds to which it would give rise, and the temptation to idleness it would hold out to the young" (De Morgan 1838, 238).[4] This concurrence between actuarial and scientific attitudes, however, did not survive the company mania of the 1840s, when new offices drummed up business by calling for "universal" coverage and complained that the older actuaries' private ways were monopolistic. Nor did it survive changes in scientific organization, in which an increasingly secure community of scientists felt less compelled to complicate their appeals to publicity and universality by simultaneously proclaiming the contrary values of mammon. Once again actuaries needed to make a choice, and this time they split the difference – opting for public knowledge, in the form of the Institute and its quarterly journal, while resolutely limiting that knowledge to the sort that was only pertinent to commercial life insurance.

Generating consensus in British life insurance (1820–45)

Actuaries and men of science in the 1820s and 1830s needed each other. Actuaries offered scientists a valuable rhetorical weapon in their attempt to reinvigorate a community that many perceived to be lagging behind discoveries on the Continent. Insurance figured prominently in the "useful knowledge" campaign waged by scientific reformers in the 1820s, and a decade later De Morgan was still hoping that the theory of life annuities would "attract many from its commercial utility" and thence provide "the gate through which some will find their way to . . . other branches of science" (De Morgan 1838, xiii–xiv). The special attraction of actuarial work lay in its combination of empirical rigor with commercial profit. Only by paying close attention to empirically derived laws of probability would actuaries be able to provide the sort of advice that

---

[4] For an example of the critical side of the scientists' view of private knowledge, see Herschel's complaint in the *Preliminary Discourse* about self-interested "practical men" who had closely guarded their discoveries as "mysteries known only to adepts," with "their own languages and their own conventions" (Herschel 1830, 70–71).

rendered property secure against unexpected contingencies. And over time, their success in achieving that useful goal would reflect greater glory back onto less obviously practical scientific pursuits. In its very vagueness, this formula allowed scientists to overlook important inconsistencies between their ideals and the commercial practice of the actuaries. And when Babbage or De Morgan did pay closer attention to actuarial practice, they discovered methodological loopholes that allowed them to persist in presenting commercial life insurance as a case in which science, as they defined it, paid off in the real world.

This inclusion of insurance in the category of scientific knowledge added luster to actuarial work at the most general level; and scientists further supported actuaries at the more personal level of positive book reviews and letters of recommendation. But it was in the realm of epistemology, in which reformers found room in the newly "objective" scientific discourse for the values of their commercial allies, that scientific legitimation took on its most precise form. De Morgan contributed the most to this project when he developed a sophisticated distinction between the objective law of averages and subjective probability. In this he followed the example of the Cambridge-trained mathematicians J. W. Lubbock and J. E. Drinkwater, who had distinguished between "certainty" and "certitude": "the one to express the ratio of the favourable to all the cases possible, the other denoting the opinion consequent on the perception of that ratio."[5] This distinction allowed actuaries to rely on "objective" data without relinquishing their claims to exercise special judgment. Under such an arrangement actuaries would collect mortality and financial statistics that provided the necessary empirical grist to check their calculations, while at the same time seeking proper training in mathematics and social etiquette to learn how to form an unbiased opinion. Only then could they be trusted to make reasonably reliable (but still subjective) management decisions.

The marriage of convenience between scientific reformers and actuaries was possible only under certain commercial circumstances. Like Goldilocks and her porridge, actuaries could excel in their scientific program only as long as competition among life offices was neither too cold nor too hot. Minimal competition meant that an office could charge whatever it wanted for policies, with the consequence that any knowledge of probability theory its actuary might possess was rendered irrelevant. This had been the situation at the Equitable, which formed in 1762 as the first

---

[5] De Morgan changed the relevant terms to "facility" and "probability," retaining Laplace's subjective definition of the latter concept, but kept the basic demarcation. See Lubbock and Drinkwater 1830, 2, and Porter 1986, 75–76. Lubbock, a London financier, doubled as director of the Royal Exchange insurance office.

commercial office to offer whole-life policies. As Lorraine Daston has observed, it "flourished in spite of [the] mathematical probability and mortality statistics" provided by its actuary William Morgan, and many other offices that formed around 1800 with similarly high rates made do without any actuary at all (Daston 1988,183; Pearson 1990). As actuaries would discover by the mid-nineteenth century, too much competition also could be a threat to professional status. A crowded market tempted offices to charge less than the actuary recommended as safe, in order to undersell their competitors, and encouraged customers to take advantage of the resulting lower rates without pausing to consider what future consequences might befall them. Commercial conditions were "just right" in the intervening years of 1820–45, when there were enough firms to generate a demand for competitive premiums, and hence for actuaries to calculate margins of error, but not so many that competition burst the informal social bonds connecting different chief executives with one another. The shameless hawking of insurance that Dickens and Thackeray would spoof in the following generation had yet to make much impact; policies at this time were more likely to be sold behind closed doors between trusted friends. Life insurance in the quarter-century before 1845 was a comfortable cartel, in which large offices like the Alliance, the Amicable and the Sun divided up middle-class clients at their leisure (Trebilcock 1985, 570–76).

It was owing to the stable commercial conditions of the 1820s that actuaries who consciously adhered to De Morgan's prescriptions were able to secure the social status that was so important for a nascent profession. Directors at the larger offices hired as actuaries well-cultivated mathematicians whose scientific honors added to the firms' upscale reputation. When the Alliance advertised for an actuary in 1824 its directors picked Benjamin Gompertz, a retired stockbroker and Royal Society member who arrived with a glowing letter from John Herschel; in 1833 the Amicable chose the astronomer Thomas Galloway over De Morgan, a close friend; and the Guardian in 1820 took William Morgan's advice and hired Griffith Davies, a quarryman-savant whose precocious scholarship had caught Morgan's fancy (Walford 1871–80, 1:53; De Morgan 1882, 60–61; Barlow 1855, 339–42). These actuaries established a kind of Royal Society colony in their new commercial surroundings. They held regular private meetings at Davies' house during the early 1830s, at which gin was sipped and vital statistics discussed (Burridge 1895, 3). They also took care that those with whom they mixed outside the life insurance community shared their social and intellectual pedigree. Suitable friends might be Galloway's fellow star charters at the Astronomical Society or the gentleman-naturalists who dug for fossils in Devonshire; unsuitable, at least after the mid-thirties, were the suspect characters who discussed railways and gasworks at the London Statistical Society. Some of these Statistical Society members were renegade actuaries, who worked for smaller firms or government agencies and harbored unorthodox views about insurance. Jenkin Jones of the National Mercantile office, for instance, was a former poor law commissioner who thought the spread of insurance would be the perfect way to keep people off the dole; Thomas Rowe Edmonds of the Legal and General was an Owenite socialist who thought the best way to equalize risks was to equalize wealth as well (Jones 1847; Beer 1920, 1:230–36). Actuaries with these views were more likely to spend their evenings writing letters to *The Lancet*, as Edmonds frequently did, than privately discussing statistics with Gompertz and Galloway. This arrangement suited the more elite actuaries just fine, since it posed little threat to their professional standing as long as commercial circumstances kept the highest market share in their corner.

Once actuaries had secured the requisite social credentials for exercising proper judgment, it remained for them to add further weight to their opinions by acquiring the right sort of data. With that in mind, they set about exploiting the natural resources of their new colony, industriously processing the mounds of statistics that had been piling up in the life offices' account books. Galloway computed a new rate table for the Amicable based on its own mortality experience; Davies divined new rates for the Guardian in 1823 based on data from the Equitable provided to him by Morgan; and the Sun's actuary Joshua Milne turned eight years' worth of parish mortality records into the so-called "Carlisle tables," which would be a staple among a majority of life offices for two generations (Alborn 1991,121–30). Such forays into the realm of raw figures provided elite actuaries with a competitive edge over offices that had not hired them. Milne stressed that empirically accurate tables allowed the actuary "to obtain those kind of advantages in such inquiries, that astronomy and natural history owe to the science of optics" (Milne 1815, xlix). And tables like Milne's, which displayed much lower mortality than those employed by Morgan and other eighteenth-century actuaries, offered the additional advantage of producing cheaper rates that still fell within the bounds of financial security.

The actuaries' alliance with people like De Morgan and Herschel, besides legitimating their status as a skilled elite, allowed them to depart occasionally from the values of publicity and universality without forfeiting their "scientific" stamp. They could do so because the scientific values from which they departed coexisted with a fear, common among middle-class agitators in the age of reform, that any call for changing science would end up producing more harm than good. Actuaries had the advantage, in this context, of being hand-picked members of a new class of scientific investigators, a "labor aristocracy" of sorts, that would protect the margins of science against incursions by people whose values were even less "scientific" then their own. Even though actuaries did not fully live up to their friends' prescriptions, they came close; and closeness counted in more ways than one among an alliance such as this. They may not have valued complete publicity, but they did exchange information openly within their exclusive social circle; and perhaps more to the point, they freely passed on their information to men of science if called upon to do so (Alborn 1991, 51–54). As for universal knowledge, the actuaries pooled their findings into sufficiently large piles to demonstrate that collective knowledge was more useful than the isolated discoveries of individuals. They did not need to extend that practice to its extreme form of national statistics to validate the basic contrast between collective and individual discovery, and it was this basic contrast that was most important for the scientists' methodological reforms. Yet although departing from "scientific values" did not jeopardize the alliance between actuaries and men of science in the short term, it did make actuaries more vulnerable to criticism from socially marginal statisticians like Jones and Edmonds, who could compensate for their weak social position by pointing out inconsistencies between what the elite actuaries said and what they did.

Public communication of knowledge became one of these sites of contested professional values in 1820, when Benjamin Gompertz urged in a Royal Society paper that "the actuaries of the different societies may, by their mathematical skill, collect for the common good of all, from multiplied resources, that which they cannot gain from a less general observation" (Gompertz 1820, 21 The actuaries' location in an informal cartel rendered their notion of "the common good" different from that usually adopted by their scientific friends. When a group of them took up Gompertz' suggestion to combine statistical forces, ultimately producing the so-called "Seventeen Offices' Experience" in 1843, publicity was not high on their list of priorities. The initial spur for the project, in fact, had been a proposal by Edmonds to the London Statistical Society for collecting and *publishing* the statistics of insured lives. Within two weeks of discovering his Plan, Davies' circle of actuaries had delivered an opinion that "it would be desirable that the Offices should from their own records contribute the requisite data to a common weal to afford the means of determining the Law of Mortality which prevails among assured Lives, without reference to the Statistical Society" (Guardian . . . 1821–73, 5:289). They took care to keep the resulting data in manuscript form and restricted its availability to member offices. But their plans for keeping the results private fell through when Jenkin Jones, whose office had not been party to the collection, gained illicit access to the data in 1843. He published nineteen premium tables based on the results, urging that it was "of the utmost importance that the public should be made acquainted with the fact that such a committee has been formed, and have availed themselves of the most extensive and special experience that could be obtained" (Recknell 1948, 18–21; Jones 1843, xx). In the ensuing controversy over Jones' piracy, even the limited aims to which the Seventeen Offices had intended to put the tables came to nothing. Neither Jones' published tables nor the privately circulated data ever caught on among life offices, most of which continued to rely on the late eighteenth-century mortality figures embodied in Milne's Carlisle tables.

A second situation in which the actuaries' practices clashed with their avowed scientific values, relating to the universality of their collective knowledge, surfaced in Gompertz' attempt to formulate a mortality law that could be used to create smooth curves out of rough data. His formula relied on the assumption of a "law of human mortality" that displayed life expectancy as geometrically decreasing with age. Even though he compared the geometrical expression of the law to universally acting "natural effects" such as "the exhaustions of the receiver of an air pump by strokes repeated at equal intervals of time," in practice he imposed limits on its universality. Based on the assumption that some deaths were random events and others were the result of "an increased inability to withstand destruction," his formula exponentially related age with the random chance of dying (represented by the function q^x, where x = age and q = constant), then related that function to the initial "power to avoid death"; the latter power was expressed as a constant, a, that needed to be determined empirically (Gompertz 1825, 517–19). He intended his formula to apply only to a group of people with the same allegedly innate ability to withstand death who desired to insure their lives. For this reason he left it open for individual offices to supply the constant, a, that would correspond to their unique experience. Unlike the Seventeen Offices' Experience, Gompertz' law was actually used by some actuaries to calibrate rate tables, but only when, as he had intended, the tables were based on a single office's experience (see, e.g., Galloway 1841).

There was nothing intrinsic to Gompertz' law, however, to prevent an actuary with different views collecting more data and positing a universal value for the constant, a. This is in fact what Edmonds did in 1830 when he published a set of tables along with a new law of mortality that he claimed was "fixed and immutable, for all human life in all ages of the world." His law described three different logarithmic death-rate curves, corresponding to the stages of infancy, manhood, and old age. Despite his claim that the slope of each curve was "fixed by nature," he allowed that the age range over which they operated could be perturbed by variations in food supply, labor conditions, and environment. In many respects, Edmonds' touted "law of mortality" was identical to that announced by Gompertz a decade earlier. His reference to an increasing "force of mortality" duplicated Gompertz, "increased inability to withstand destruction," and their formulas describing the curve were the same. Yet Edmonds dismissed Gompertz' work as an "imperfect" approximation to his own. The perfecting touch, in his eyes, was the premise that the same constant slopes applied to everyone – unlike Gompertz' curves, which were unique for each individual. Edmonds' assertion of universality was related to the sort of evidence he used to confirm his law. Unlike Gompertz' formula, which smoothed the curves of data collected by individual life offices, Edmonds' described mortality statistics were gleaned from national census data. When he used it to smooth this data, it was not simply with a mind to group together similarly low risks but rather to prevent conditions like hunger and overwork from producing disparate risk groups in the first place. The "most favourable state of life," as represented by statistics that corresponded to Edmonds' table, was a society where all individuals performed the "gentle labour" typical of the middle classes (Edmonds 1832, v–x, xvi–xvii). His departure from the actuaries' commercial and intellectual norms guaranteed a cold professional response. De Morgan rebuffed Edmonds in an 1839 installment of the *Penny Cyclopaedia* for having adopted Gompertz' theories "without anything approaching to a sufficient acknowledgement"; and the rest of the actuarial elite followed suit by greeting Edmonds with pointed silence and refusing to use his tables. Unbowed, Edmonds simply sold his tables to a friendlier customer, William Farr at the General Registrar's office, whom he had conveniently met while serving on a Statistical Society committee in the late 1830s (De Morgan 1839, 414; Cullen 1975).[6]

Competition and professional crisis (1845–60)

Jones' illicit publication of the Seventeen Offices' data and Edmonds' alternative law of mortality revealed fissures in the informal consensus that actuaries enjoyed through the 1830s. Although these were easily patched up at the time, they would soon grow. Newly formed offices after 1840 equated any quest for professional status with attempts by older

[6] For more on the transfer of ideas between Edmonds and Farr, see Eyler 1979, chap. 4.

firms to restrict competition, and this challenged actuaries to face the ambiguities that inhered in their loose collection of scientific values. Around the same time, changes in scientific norms and statistical practice were eroding many of the assumptions on which the actuaries' intellectual program had been based and weakening the status of their closest allies within the scientific community. Actuaries responded to these changes by bringing into sharper focus certain of their commitments to "science" as a value system. First, they established their research on a more "objective" basis, when they tried to discover those "natural laws" that marked out the lower limit to which competition could safely drive premium rates. They also pulled back from the more obvious manifestations of exclusive and local knowledge that had previously marked their practice. But in all these areas their new efforts to revamp their practice threatened to undo their primary purpose, which was to calculate insurance premiums in such a way as to keep their companies competitive. More often than not in the 1850s, the actuaries' appeals to "objective" economic laws merely worsened the monopolistic image of the older companies, and their new embrace of public and universal knowledge conveyed political and economic messages that ran counter to their primary location in the thick of the marketplace. Although actuaries ultimately emerged stronger than ever from their mid-century crisis of commercial fortune and professional identity, the process of recovery was neither preordained nor easy.

As market conditions shifted in the 1840s, the collegiality of the insurance community in the preceding debate was rudely interrupted by a torrent of new life offices. Legislators responded to the torrent of over-competition with the Joint Stock Companies Act of 1844, which required all new offices to provide lists of directors and balance sheets to the Registrar's Office. Far from achieving its aim, however, the 1844 Act gave scores of company promoters the appearance of government approval without providing real accountability. Combined with an increasingly low interest rate after 1847 and the burgeoning popularity of self-help rhetoric, the new law led to a flurry of new insurance companies: between 1844 and 1853, 355 new life offices were projected, although only 149 of these were actually founded and only 59 survived the 1850s (Alborn 1991, 226–27; Supple 1970, 138–45). Even the fraction of companies that did survive marked a twofold increase in the number of life offices doing business in London, and their success was largely due to relatively novel features such as lending money to policyholders, accepting unhealthy lives at higher rates, and stepping up the supply of posters, pamphlets, and door-to-door salesmen. But while such features did succeed in popularizing insurance, only a handful of offices were able to translate their rhetorical claim of unlimited demand into a booming business. Most new projects, if they got off the ground at all, possessed a fleeting life span of five to ten years before transferring their trickle of paying customers over to larger firms.[7] Despite their low level of success, however, they managed to inflict damage on older firms that had problems of their own. The same low interest rates that encouraged the formation of new companies made it especially difficult for older companies to invest their substantial stock of premium income at a profitable rate.

If the new commercial pressures were not enough, actuaries at mid-century also needed to be more careful in making scientific friends. Statisticians whose ideas had most closely meshed with those of the actuaries now carried less weight, both among fellow intellectuals and among the politicians who would make the final choice about the actuaries' professional authority. Babbage's early attraction to commerce earned him a lifelong reputation as a money-grubbing opportunist, as evidenced by an 1865 cartoon depicting him holding up a fish for sale at one-and-a-half pence (MacLeod and Collins 1981, 88). De Morgan's stubborn refusal to participate in intellectual politics was similarly starting to cost him friends: regardless of his high-minded motivations for boycotting the Royal Society on account of its creation of "a kind of order of knighthood" or for resigning from the Astronomical Society in 1861 following a corrupt election, such actions got in the way of scientific progress as defined in the later nineteenth century. And his approach to probability theory, which had given equal weight to the number of observations and the observers' capacity for judgment, was losing ground among younger logicians like George Boole and mathematicians like R. L. Ellis (De Morgan 1872, 18–22; Porter 1986, 78–82). Mid-century politicians, meanwhile, had grown to trust the numbers generated by civil servants and members of the London Statistical Society, many of whom took up methodological positions that were closer to Ellis than to De Morgan. When Parliament called for expert testimony on life insurance in 1853, they invited Farr and Edmonds as star witnesses along with John Finlaison from the National Debt Office. Although commercial actuaries were also well represented at the hearings, their older scientific friends were nowhere to be seen.

These changes in the commercial and intellectual landscape in the decade after 1844 created a serious crisis for elite actuaries. Directors of life offices were now as likely to be fly-by-night adventurers as the staid financiers who had dominated the industry in the 1820s. Policyholders,

---

[7] Cornelius Walford took pleasure in producing many examples of this nature in his *Insurance Cyclopaedia*. See, for instance, Walford 1871–80,1:301–2, 375–77, 398, 2:17, 45, 266–67, 286–87, 491, 505).

similarly, had been caught up in the race to find the cheapest office and could not be trusted to adhere to the conservative wisdom of the actuary. Members of the actuarial elite complained repeatedly after 1844 about "the bonuses which the cormorant-public now so eagerly demands" or about how "very intelligent persons, who, after reading the accounts sent forth by a company, form evidently the most erroneous ideas from them" (Porter 1861, 285; Jellicoe 1853, 9.2054). Worst of all, they feared that their own profession was being dragged down by unqualified quacks whose claim to understand the science of probabilities was belied by an inadequate grounding in statistics. When these promoters confidently supported small upstart offices, they threatened to betray "one of the principal advantages of the system," according to one actuary, namely, "the combination of a large number of individuals in one body, with the purpose of equalizing their individual losses" (Brown n.d., 1).

Some actuaries responded to these threats by receding further into the informal collegiality that had marked their earlier practice; others tried to reform the profession by requiring actuaries from the new offices to meet a set of formal entry requirements. The former group, comprising representatives from a dozen of the oldest firms, formed the Actuaries' Club, the members of which discussed questions of interest over private dinners and generally bewailed the volume of business being lost to the new firms (Simmonds 1948,10, 25–26; Burridge 1895). A larger group of actuaries founded the Institute of Actuaries in 1848 as a forum for presenting scientific papers and giving certifying examinations. Worried by the prospect of company promoters passing themselves off as qualified to calculate premiums, the Institute devoted itself to a "collegiate or educational character" in order to provide insurance with "that consistency and purity in its operation, without which it was liable to become a public pest rather than a public blessing" (Anon. 1851, 121).[8] Although the ringleaders of the campaign against the newer companies were all members of the Institute, its officers claimed neutrality in the debate between old and new companies. Instead of openly siding with the old companies, they used the controversy as a way of drawing attention to their demands for official recognition, urging that the best way to maintain security without interrupting free trade would be to endow the Institute with authority to certify new actuaries.

Actuaries at the Institute consciously related their desire for a "collegiate" character to the parallel aims of "science." Institute leaders described themselves as "lovers of science in general" and informed members that "those who love science for its own sake cease to be actuated

---

[8] On the origins of the Institute of Actuaries, see Simmonds 1948, chaps. 1–3.

by merely selfish motives" (Farren 1850, 114; Brown 1854a, 285). Unlike their earlier appeals to science, though, this time around actuaries made a conscious effort to practice what the scientists seemed to be preaching. In particular they assiduously upheld the claims of "objective" knowledge, which assisted their argument that too much competition among life offices was bad for everyone. Here "objectivity" merged with the dire Ricardian warning that natural laws forbade economic growth beyond a certain point: no amount of actuarial *judgment*, accordingly, could prevent these natural limits from kicking in. In this vein Samuel Brown claimed that the actuary's "scientific knowledge" was "devoted only to ascertain the true law of nature by which [insurance] contracts are governed, not with the least hope of being able to vary it when discovered." Or, as he later argued, it was "of the utmost consequence in all branches of our business to know, not from conjecture, but from actual facts, how far we can go, and where our safety ends" (Brown 1854b, 10; 1852a, 209). This sort of argument was even strong enough to lead actuaries to welcome Edmonds into their fold, at least for the brief duration of their dispute with the new offices. Edmonds, who joined elite actuaries in condemning overcompetition, received Brown's praise in 1850 for filling in the laws of mortality with "actual numerical results" and received permission from the editor of the Institute journal to use its pages throughout the 1850s as a platform for his views (Brown 1850, 26).[9]

If a stronger appeal to objectivity helped actuaries shoot down new offices, a stepped-up call for publicity helped the Institute distinguish itself from the Actuaries' Club. The Institute's journal was offered as an expressly public forum for the exchange of information and ideas, to which end its editor in 1850 called on "some of the older of the Proprietary Companies" – implicitly those with which Actuaries' Club members were affiliated – to submit annual statistics for publication so as to confirm the reputation of vital statistics as "one of the most important points of political economy" (Anon. 1850, 88). These actions represented a conscious snub to the more secretive ways that had previously been the norm and that continued to be practiced at the Actuaries' Club. In 1848 the Institute welcomed Jones as a fellow, much to the dismay of many Club members, who had still not gotten over his treachery; and six years later Brown favorably cited Jones' complaint in his 1843 *Tables* that "the method[s] of registering ages" in the Seventeen Offices' Experience were "so different, that some of the returns, after the time and toil expended, were quite useless for the purpose required" (Brown 1854a, 284).

---

[9] While Edmonds sided with the Institute in opposing overcompetition, his remedy of national insurance would have struck the actuaries (had they stopped to think about it) as erring in the opposite extreme.

The most significant shift in the actuaries' constellation of "scientific" ideals after 1845 concerned the universal applicability of their knowledge and, by extension, the universal applicability of life insurance. They felt a strong pull in this direction, owing to the successful efforts by government actuaries like Farr and Finlaison to achieve status by setting up "objective" professional entry barriers. The example of civil service exams, for instance, allowed one member to claim that the "academical triumphs" of rising FIAs "were not fugitive distinctions" (Porter 1854, 118); while naming Finlaison as their inaugural president and inviting Farr to speak at public meetings produced the sort of exposure that a group composed entirely of office managers could not have achieved on their own. Since these government statisticians had an occupational yen to think of data at a national as opposed to a local level, their example in this regard led actuaries to consider departing from their previously narrower focus on mortality statistics. Institute papers in the 1850s branched out into such areas as sanitary statistics, fire and marine insurance, and taxation – all on the basis of a broad definition of actuarial science as "embracing all monetary questions involving a consideration of the separate or combined effects of interest and probability" (Anon. 1851, 263). In addition to accepting Edmonds' papers for publication, actuaries contributed papers of their own on epidemiology and on "the uniform action of the human will" that suggested an interest in vital statistics that went far beyond the confines of the life office (Porter 1860; Brown 1852b).

In all three of these newly honed values, actuaries soon discovered that it was not going to be as easy as in past years to stave off unwanted intruders by appealing to science, however sincere that appeal might be. The problem of inconsistency between ideals and practice, which had always existed beneath the surface of the actuaries' professional ideology, now appeared with newfound urgency. Both the insurgent promoters at the new offices and the actuaries themselves came to realize that it was impossible to uphold all these "scientific" values and still work for a commercial life office. The promoters struck first, challenging the actuaries' commitment to "objective" science and taking advantage of their public, and hence more vulnerable, self-presentation. Instead of directly attacking the actuaries' Ricardian economic arguments, which were too close to the mark to be disputable, their opponents honed in on the actuaries' educational program, which was allegedly based on the same objective foundation. One supporter of new firms ridiculed the "unmeaning technicalities" of the "so-called science of Assurance" as practiced by the Institute, which he called a "self-constituted conclave"; another denied the Institute's ability to keep out unqualified members, claiming that many certified "Fellows" had "not learnt even the ABC of mathematical science" (Strousberg 1853, 42; Carpenter 1860, 264).

That such language left its mark seems clear from the Institute's effort in 1851 to distance itself from "the productions of philosophers, mathematicians, and men of letters," which stood in contrast with the "ordinary professional minds" of FIAs; or from a member's rush to condemn the "showy and pungent" use of calculus that had appeared in an essay on life insurance "for no better reason than to gratify the desire for a little display" (Anon. 1851, 263; Anon. 1853, 260). Simply retreating from an excessive appeal to science, however, left the actuaries vulnerable to the claim that their "professional minds" were in fact so ordinary as to be useless. According to this claim, actuarial calculation was a relatively simple skill that any clerk could perform. As one new office claimed, "no discernment, no examination of individual cases is required; the whole affair is left simply to the operation of the law of average" – implying that hiring actuaries, with their careful selection techniques, was an expensive luxury (Walford 1871–80, 1:377). Ironically, the Institute's concession to the scientific dictum that knowledge be made public only made matters worse, since it rendered it more vulnerable to attack from new offices than the more exclusive Actuaries' Club. Unlike the latter organization, which by keeping to itself stayed out of the papers, the Institute's prominence made it the single most convenient public target for opponents of older firms.

The biggest problem with the actuaries' new professional program, however, appeared whenever they flirted with the universal laws promoted by state statisticians like Farr. Despite real affinities between commercial and government actuaries in terms of merit-based education and the value of public knowledge, occupational differences were bound to obstruct any permanent alliance between the two camps. The morning after he had chatted about numbers with Institute members, Farr returned to his desk at the General Registrar's Office where he sifted through nationwide figures and targeted pestilent slums for special attention. When commercial actuaries went to work the following day, in contrast, they tabulated policy stubs and turned applicants away for having tubercular parents. Although Farr gladly accepted the recognition offered to him by the Institute, he had relatively little interest in the restricted segment of the population to which most Institute officers catered. Instead, his commercial interests were devoted to extending the benefits of insurance to the lower classes, which made him especially prone to endorse new offices with their pious strains of "insurance for the millions" (Eyler 1979, 82–84). Once commercial actuaries realized the professional problems that came with upholding Farr's ideal of universal knowledge, they started to doubt other parts of his program as well. Especially after the debate with the new offices had died down and "objectivity" had lost its usefulness as a response to overcompetition, actuaries remembered how important subjective judgment had always been to their professional aspirations – and they also noticed, for the first time in over a decade, its relative absence in the approach to statistics taken by Edmonds and Farr.

The chief intellectual manifestation of this occupational divide concerned Farr's assumption that collecting universal data on mortality was both possible and useful. Most commercial actuaries, for all their new-found criticism of private knowledge, continued to restrict their data pool to the select lives of insurance companies. From Farr's perspective, such a view guaranteed inaccurate conclusions because they were based on such a small store of facts. He claimed, instead, that it was possible to conform imperfections in data to universal truths by changing the actual data – that is, by changing the social conditions that were responsible for bringing about deviations from the norm. In 1843 he constructed a set of life tables corresponding to a typical "healthy district" with a mortality rate of 17 per 1,000, which he used to locate environmental factors that had produced deviations from the baseline in other districts and which challenged common assumptions about the role of the actuary. The *English Life Tables* were expressly *national* tables, constructed entirely with census data and intended for use in determining public health policy. To calibrate the tables, he employed Edmonds' law of mortality, complete with its "universal" constants. And instead of resorting to the cautious judgment of the actuary to determine which of the data should be included in his tables, he took the data as he found them to the point of suggesting in 1843 that "Mr. Babbage's machine" might be employed so as to dispense with the actuary altogether (Eyler 1979, 20–82; Farr 1860,140).

Actuaries responded to these differences not by challenging Farr outright, since to do so would have meant abandoning the chief source of legitimation for their professional model. Instead they indicated their qualms by chipping away at Farr's intellectual supports: census takers, medical examiners, and second-tier statisticians like Edmonds. An example of this response was H. W. Porter's review of the *English Tables*. Although Porter vouchsafed that Farr could be trusted as to "correctness of computation," he found several reasons to dispute the tables that were less directly related to Farr. To start with, he noted the inapplicability of Farr's data to the actuaries' commercial needs: "The labouring classes, as well as paupers, vagrants, criminals, and dissolute persons, comprise, by far, the larger proportion of the whole population; and it is not upon such lives that assurances and annuities are granted." He also suspected the original census data on which Farr had constructed his tables: "Minuteness of calculation . . . is of no avail," he wrote, "unless the census enumerators succeed in obtaining exact information." Here the problem lay both with those being enumerated, especially women (whom Porter accused of pathologically lying about their age), and with those doing the counting, especially inexperienced medical officers who often assessed the age of death "altogether at hazard" (Porter 1861, 282–88). These claims all indicated a persistent suspicion of objectivity as a professional value fit for actuaries. At least implicitly, Porter was suggesting that Farr himself had gone wrong by trusting in the observations of people whose minds were liable to error.

A more telling sign that actuaries had rejected Farr's appeal to "objectivity," while still doing their best to retain the organizational benefits that came from his support, appeared when they moved from Porter's moderate criticism of the *English Tables* to a no-holds-barred attack on Edmonds' law of mortality, which Farr had used in their construction. Picking on Edmonds, whose only prestigious advocate was Farr, was a safer task for actuaries than picking on Farr himself. In addition, the attack took shape in the course of a dispute over who truly qualified as the discoverer of the "law of mortality," Gompertz or Edmonds, which allowed them to skirt the wider issues concerning scientific values that divided them from Farr as well as Edmonds.[10] Still, they settled the question of priority almost wholly on two issues related to such values: whose method preserved the most room for subjective uncertainty and whose mind was more trustworthy. Gompertz won the first point by being more "philosophical" than Edmonds – by which his supporters meant, in essence, less cocksure about man's knowledge of universal laws. As future Institute president Thomas Bond Sprague argued: "The reason Mr. Gompertz has stated no definite limits of age is obviously because he did not believe them to be fixed in the same nearly invariable manner as Mr. Edmonds does." And to underscore Edmonds' failure to preserve room in his formula for the intervention of subjective judgment, a German actuary who was an honorary member of the Institute added that "the only point we can arrive at in the present state of science is to discover a formula which gives a numerical approximation for the numbers contained in the table of mortality; any discovery of the natural law of mortality cannot be contained in a formula only" (Sprague 1861a, 293; Lazarus 1862, 283).[11]

[10] The priority dispute surfaced at this time (1860) when Farr nominated Edmonds to be a member of the Royal Society on the basis of his law and De Morgan responded by reviving his earlier claim that Edmonds had inadequately expressed his debt to Gompertz.

[11] Edmonds did not help matters by exaggerating his original claim of universality, brag-

In addition to accusing Edmonds of making universal assertions on the basis of scanty data, the actuaries extended their critique to a more personal level, contrasting the calm rationality of Gompertz' mind with Edmonds' intrinsic liability to error. Here, above all, social pedigree and judgment went hand in hand. Gompertz, as a founding father of the actuarial profession and "one of the greatest mathematicians of Europe," stood head and shoulders above Edmonds, an outsider whom one actuary accused of "want of familiarity with the principles of integral calculus." Sprague responded to Edmonds' charge that Gompertz himself had never publicly accused him of plagiarism by questioning his judgment ("Truly a very positive statement to base upon so slender a foundation of fact, or rather belief!"), followed by a large helping of status differentiation: "I happen to have heard from a gentleman, himself a Fellow of the Royal Society, that Mr. Gompertz has . . . in the course of a conversation at the Royal Society . . . expressed in emphatic language his belief that his theory had been adopted without proper acknowledgement." Edmonds had little hope of beating these odds. When he made much of a string of typographical errors in Gompertz' Royal Society papers, Sprague excused these on the grounds that it was "to be presumed that that gentleman, like so many others of scientific eminence, does not write a very legible hand" and instead blamed "a want of proper supervision of the [Royal Society] press" (Woolhouse 1862, 122; Sprague 1861a, 290–91; 1861b, 37, 41). Gompertz, who died of gout during the middle of the dispute, emerged as its posthumous victor. Edmonds went from participating fully in the Institute during the 1850s, to being written off by Sprague in 1861 as "the plagiarist of Mr. Gompertz," to being written out of the actuaries' history books altogether (Sprague 1861b; Deuchar 1882, 60–63; King [1885] 1902, chap. 6).

Discipline and collect: professional reformation (1860–1900)

Although the priority dispute between Gompertz and Edmonds allowed the actuaries to thump their chests for a year or two, it took much longer for them to resolve the deeper institutional and intellectual problems that faced them in the early 1860s. Institute membership in 1862, though steadily on the increase for five years, still stood at only two-thirds the 1854 level.[12] And a government charter, the *sine qua non* of professional

ging at one point that his mortality constant had "existed as long as man has existed, and forms part of the foundations of the universe" (Edmonds 1860, 177).

[12] Membership dropped from 242 in 1854 to 127 in 1857, owing mainly to a secession by the Institute's Scottish members, and stood at 167 in 1862.

legitimation, remained a distant hope as long as the Actuaries' Club continued to be recognized as a rival group of experts. Nor were the actuaries' frustrations limited to the institutional variety. Their support of Gompertz, whose modest methodology created few problems of calculation to be ironed out, left them in an intellectual quandary. If the only challenge for the actuary was to determine empirically his own office's rate of mortality, what use was there in regular papers being exchanged among professional colleagues? Even worse, in terms of their attempt to base their status claims on a solidly "scientific" foundation, Gompertz' law of mortality offered little by way of a research program that could guide the Institute's educational agenda: fewer "objective" tasks for lower-tier actuaries to perform translated into less status for senior actuaries who administered the qualifying exams. The pages of the Institute's journal through the mid-1860s reflected this lack of a guiding paradigm. Instead of new empirical work on mortality, members were mainly treated to warmed-over installments of De Morgan's *Budget of Paradoxes* and abstruse discussions of interpolation, summation, and compound interest that bore very little on the actuaries' commercial concerns.

By the end of the century, owing to a series of fortunate choices about the relative place of such values as objectivity, publicity, and universal knowledge in their professional ideology, the actuaries had solved nearly all their problems. In 1898 Institute membership stood at 860, over five times the 1862 level; the Institute was a chartered body with its own textbook, lecture series, and plans to host an international congress of actuaries; and in William Makeham's law of mortality it finally had a paradigm that suited its occupational needs. Each of these gains stemmed from the actuaries' success at modifying their collective values in such a way as to stake out a realm of expert knowledge that was uniquely their own. Public communication, which had most clearly distinguished Institute members from their rivals at the Actuaries' Club, became firmly entrenched as a primary actuarial virtue; while objectivity and the quest for universal knowledge, which had appeared with new prominence in the Institute's "scientific" self-presentation at mid-century, once again receded into the background. Actuaries did not so much abandon these latter values as reshuffle their order of priority. They continued to appeal to the "objective" security of large numbers, but they also took care to subordinate those facts to Makeham's "hidden laws." And instead of simply rejecting the premise of universal laws of mortality, they defined the discovery of general laws as a project for future actuaries to sort out. For the present, actuaries in the late nineteenth century had plenty to keep them busy and did not want to risk their professional status by taking on anything new.

None of these revisions would have been possible had the insurance market continued to spiral in the topsy-turvy fashion of the 1850s. The centrifugal force of commercial competition and the centripetal pull of superior status exerted by neighboring professions, between which actuaries had been buffeted in the 1850s, had begun to wane by the mid-1870s. Competition dried up as a predictable outcome of the new offices' exaggerated assumptions about the demand for their services. When the bottom fell out of the insurance market in the late 1850s, many of the newer offices had no option but to sell out to more established firms, creating a partial return to the relatively small nurnber of large firms that had typified life insurance in the 1820s. But economics alone cannot account for the ensuing commercial stability. Notwithstanding the high hopes of mid-Victorian moralists, industry leaders in this age of *laissez faire* did not typically learn from past failures, choosing instead to plunge headlong into the next boom after waiting a few years to catch their breath (Kindleberger 1979). In this context, life offices displayed unique levels of restraint, much of which can be traced to an ability on the part of actuaries to sell their organizational reforms to their employers. Actuaries took over the supervision of insurance agents, which had once been done on the basis of personal reputation and which now became a matter of supervised inspection. They convinced offices to require competitive examinations in hiring clerks and to establish time-management systems to ensure top performance. Such experiments in office rationalization produced economic results, and it did so quickly enough to convince insurance companies to heed their actuaries' advice (Alborn 1991, 253–60).

Success at their individual offices boosted the actuaries' status and allowed them to apply their ethos of collegiality to the industry-wide problem of overcompetition. The merger boom of the early 1860s produced an avalanche of Institute papers on valuation, with actuaries arguing about the safest and most equitable terms to offer failed companies for their policies (e.g., Jellicoe 1858, Sprague 1858, Tucker 1862). Members of the Institute, lacking a clear statistical paradigm to keep themselves busy at their monthly meetings, warmed to the concrete task of setting limits on their firms' expenditure. In the process they proved willing to sacrifice certain ethical claims, such as the goal of charging equitable rates, to preserve the greater good of commercial stability. The most popular arrangement for transferring policies they arrived at was for the buying office to pay a large lump sum to the directors of the selling office, then recoup the loss by jacking up premiums on the policies that had been transferred. This made the directors at both offices happy, since profits were guaranteed on both sides. The only losers were the unfortunate policyholders who had made the mistake of answering a bubble company's advertisement, and whose long-term investment in the policy made them powerless to resist paying the new rates. The career of Charles Jellicoe, editor of the Institute's *Journal,* embodied the advantages accruing to an actuary who was good at playing the merger game. Between 1855 and 1862, the Eagle single-handedly received policies from eight companies (Hunter 1865). With such a burst of new accounts came more work for the actuary and still more occupational status for the profession.

Not all firms followed the actuaries' advice; but those who did not paid for their mistake much more quickly and explosively than the offices that had spurned them two decades before, making the actuaries' professional standing among surviving offices all the more secure. In 1869 a distinctly unhappy ending of this sort surfaced when the Albert, which had spent a decade making a living from cheaply purchased transfers, was unable to pay its claims. The fact that no Institute member could be connected to the failure meant that the actuarial elite could wash their hands of the matter with little difficulty.[13] More important, the Institute was well placed for shaping the legislation that followed in the wake of the Albert collapse. The failure had brought a larger-than-usual smattering of calls for a state audit of life offices, as was already the policy in Germany and most American states (Anon. 1869a, Anon. 1871, Macfadyen 1870). At the same time, there was still a large body of commercial opinion in Britain that assumed, in the words of one anonymous actuary, that the insurance industry "would only languish and wither were it subjected to the mephitic influence of red-tape regulations and restrictions" (Anon. 1869c, 7). Instead of these opposing views creating the stalemate that had led to the ineffectual legislation of 1844, however, this time the Institute succeeded in presenting itself as the best way out of the situation. In 1870 Institute members assisted Parliament in drafting legislation that called for regular valuation statements that were complicated enough for few besides actuaries to understand.[14] All these political triumphs added up, and in 1884 the Institute convinced Parliament to grant its long-awaited charter despite resistance from the still-powerful Actuaries' Club (Nicoll 1898, 206–20).

These fortunate social and commercial conditions gave actuaries the space they needed to set up boundaries between their own expertise and

---

[13] The only Institute affiliate who had some trouble demonstrating clean hands was Augustus De Morgan, who had given the Albert a positive audit in 1862: see De Morgan 1882, 279–80.

[14] The actuaries' movement away from direct communication of their expertise to the general public (as opposed to public communication with one another) accompanied a similar effort to distance themselves from contemporary efforts to popularize the actuarial basis of life insurance: see, e.g., the faint praise directed at Cornelius Walford's *Insurance*

that of their former allies in science and the civil service. Just as important, those former allies were also starting to forget why they had ever been so interested in what the actuaries were up to. By the 1870s each of the three main groups of British statisticians – actuaries, civil servants, and mathematicians who directly applied probability theory to physics and biology – were able to tell the difference between a useful division of labor and an ungainly alliance that was past its prime. Government statisticians like Farr, once they had given up supporting bubble companies that promised "universal" coverage, settled down to the more pragmatic task of selling working-class insurance through existing state institutions; and by the turn of the century statisticians like George Udny Yule and Karl Pearson had set their sights firmly on "pure" mathematics and newly specialized fields like biometry (Mackenzie 1981; Porter 1986, pt. 4). In both domains, commercial actuaries took the hint and kept their expertise to themselves as well. Instead of trading their professional stake in middle-class insurance for jobs with the emerging welfare state, they were content to accept the government actuary's departure from their midst as beneficial to both parties. When Farr introduced and superintended the sale of life policies at post office savings banks in 1864, Institute members reacted to it with equanimity as "a business we do not at all covet" (Adler 1864, 12). Actuaries similarly shed few tears when the new standard-bearers of organized science stopped going out of their way to involve themselves in life insurance. As the Institute's journal passed the quarter-century mark, De Morgan's probability puzzles gave way to prize essays by recent FIAs on such issues as surrender values and distribution of surplus. By that point actuaries were expending most of their energy arguing the relative merits of accounting by the "net premium" or "pure premium" method, and deciding other questions that similarly would have been neither comprehensible nor interesting to a trained statistician who did not happen to work in a life office.

With this display of cognitive autonomy came a clarification of the "scientific" values of objectivity, publicity, and universality that had always held such an ambiguous place in the actuaries' collective identity. The best single illustration of this newly arranged value system first appeared in 1862, when the Institute embarked on an industry-wide collection of mortality experience and then later used those data to provide

---

Guide and Handbook (Anon. 1868b) in a book review published in the Institute's journal. While granting that Walford (who was an Institute member but not a practicing actuary) did "not write as an actuary, and is, therefore, not to be judged by the severe rule which would rightly be applied to one having more pretentions," the anonymous reviewer spent most of the article challenging Walford's credentials as an investment adviser and faulting him for leaving out the actuaries' most recent contributions to science.

empirical support for Makeham's "hidden law" of mortality. The new information itself, which was intended as a revised version of the previous generation's Seventeen Offices' Experience, was an indirect tribute to the tumultuous growth experienced by the insurance industry at mid-century and the subsequent stability of the profession. All those new companies had added masses of lives to the rolls; but these lives could be tabulated in something resembling a collective endeavor only once the industry had stabilized sufficiently to allow for interoffice cooperation.

The collection that would result in the "Healthy Males" or "H^M" tables a decade later demonstrated the professional advantages that came from privileging an open and efficient exchange of knowledge. The original inspiration for the new tables, in fact, reversed the story of how the Seventeen Offices project had originated. Instead of privately collecting data in order to quash a plan to publish data on insured lives, progress toward the *published* series of H^M tables was originally instigated when Samuel Brown heard that the Actuaries' Club was involved in a *private* collection of mortality data. In 1857 J. J. Downes, who had been on the Seventeen Offices committee in 1838, spearheaded an attempt by the Actuaries' Club to update that store of facts. With advice from his brother O. G. Downes, who clerked under him at the Economic office, he had developed a card system to calculate that firm's mortality for the years 1823 to 1855, and he hoped to use the Actuaries' Club to extend the benefits of the system to a wider body of facts (Downes 1862, 3–6). In deference to the traditions of the Club, however, which consistently refused to engage in any activity as a body, Downes was forced to offer its members the choice of adopting his card system or retaining the more traditional circular format. In the end the Club's statistics, despite allegedly being in "a state of forwardness" in 1862, went no further. The project sputtered to a halt, with only a brief entry in the minute books in 1865 complaining of no progress (Actuaries' Club 1848–83, 2:76–79, 109, 3:6, 34–35, 54–57, 103).

In 1862 Samuel Brown contacted the Actuaries' Club to see if it would mind sharing the results of its collection. The Club responded by jealously guarding its figures, much as a dog guards a bone that it never intends to eat. Although Brown may not have snared the Club's bone, in the form of its raw data, he did come away with Downes' card system, which he and his colleagues at the Institute turned into a well-oiled mechanism for processing large quantities of data. Within ten years this machinery had produced a wide range of information encompassing 180,000 lives from twenty offices. From this material Institute actuaries constructed their H^M table (encompassing some two-thirds of the tabulated lives) as well as tables for sick men, healthy women, and a combined table for both sexes (Champness 1879, 229–33; Institute of Actuaries 1848–65, 2:251–52, 264–65). In 1869 actuaries christened the tables "a remarkable proof of the utility of the Institute." This claim was soon justified, as foreign offices applied the Institute's methods and numbers to tables of their own and as British life offices gradually revised their premiums to correspond with the H^M experience. In 1868 it was announced that insurance companies in Germany were collecting their own experience on the Institute's model; and two years later an American actuary argued that the Institute's tables were superior to any possible American collection, since no U.S. office had been in existence long enough to produce comparable figures (Anon. 1869b, 162; Anon. 1868a, 336; McCay 1870, 20–33). In 1872, at the bidding of their actuary Samuel Brown, the Guardian became the first British office to issue new premium tables based on the H^M data (Guardian . . . 1821–73, 12:269).

The importance of the new tables went beyond demonstrating the advantages of public cooperation among actuaries. The tables also helped to legitimate William Makeham's new "law of mortality," which was taking shape at the same time as the H^M data were piling up. And that law, in turn, served as a new paradigm that stabilized the connections in the actuaries' professional ideology between skill and "objective" precision and between local and universal knowledge. What Makeham accomplished was to retain the elegance of Gompertz' formula while discovering a more useful place for knowledge of the sort that would soon be embodied in the H^M tables. In place of Gompertz' formula Bq^x, which referred to the individual's exponentially decreasing "power to avoid death," Makeham offered the formula $Bq^x + \psi(x)$, with the extra function referring to "certain partial forces, which we assume to be, in the aggregate, of equal amount at all ages" (Makeham 1867, 335).[15] Whereas Gompertz' law portrayed an unswervingly geometrical increase in mortality with age, Makeham's function added an arithmetic component to the curve that also needed to be determined empirically. Furthermore, the new function was *disease*-specific, not specific to each individual charted in mortality tables. Makeham suggested that Gompertz' formula by itself worked for diseases affecting the organs (implicitly the repositories of "vital power") – such as heart, liver, and lung disorders, where "the force of mortality somewhat more than doubles itself in 10 years" – while his additional function encompassed all other diseases. As such, his law promised to make use of the "cause of death" entries on the 180,000 policyholder cards (ibid., 335–37).

Makeham's law secured an important distinction between the inter-

---

[15] The form of Gompertz' law given here is Makeham's version, in which the constant a referred to earlier in this article is replaced by B.

pretive skill of the Institute's leaders and the careful precision expected
from its subordinate members, a distinction that significantly improved
the actuaries' efforts to differentiate their practices from those of neighboring statisticians. For different reasons, the previous candidates for
"laws of mortality" that had been offered by Edmonds and Gompertz
had failed to establish this distinction. Edmonds' law had failed because
it was based on census data that were not restricted to the insurance community, hence diminishing its commercial relevance as well as its connection to the collecting activities of subordinate Institute members.
Gompertz' law was commercially relevant, but it failed to set in motion
a fruitful dynamic between subordinate collectors and elite interpreters of
their data. Makeham's law, in conjunction with the new tables, delivered
on both counts. When Institute president William Hodge observed in
1872 that the tables had "singularly falsified" earlier assumptions that
"all that remained to be done was to make accurate observations and
apply them to the scientific formulae then established," he cited
Makeham's law as the foremost interpretive aid that would "open up a
wide field for us in improving our calculations" (Anon. 1872, 147).[16]

The intellectual harvest that Hodge predicted would result from
Makeham's law was possible only because of the wide dispersion of facts
that had been supplied by the H^M tables. Although Makeham developed
his law without direct reference to the H^M project, it supplied his findings
with crucial empirical support. Prior to the tables' publication he had
been forced to rely on collections of data like the Seventeen Offices'
Experience and John Finlaison's government annuitant figures to show
that his predicted rates of mortality corresponded to empirical regularities attested to by the "law of large numbers"; he also relied heavily on
Farr's medical breakdown of the census to support his hunch concerning
organ disorders (Makeham 1866, 309–12; 1867, 336–37). [17] Some of these
sources of data, like Farr's, fell prey to Porter's criticism that they were
irrelevant to life insurance, while others were not sufficiently up-to-date
or based on enough lives to warrant the respect of his peers. Many actuaries, fresh from scolding Edmonds for asserting too much from a
limited store of facts, greeted Makeham's theory with similar caution:
"No set of tables should be forthwith graduated in accordance with any

---

[16] It should be noted that *some* form of "mortality law" was an occupational necessity for
actuaries through the late nineteenth century for the simple reason that calculating
machines were not yet in use that could translate data into premium rates without
requiring recourse to a necessarily approximate formula. On reasons for the delayed
appearance of such machines in the British insurance industry (working models were
available by the 1860s), see Campbell-Kelly 1993.

[17] In the 1866 article he also referred to A. G. Finlaison's friendly society statistics from
1853 and sets of privately collected data on the peerage and the clergy.

preconceived hypothesis," warned Samuel Brown (Institute of Actuaries 1866, 10). It was not until 1870, when the Institute's vice president W. S. B. Woolhouse undertook the task of turning the H^M figures into a smoothly graduated table, that Makeham's law was accepted. The sheer bulk of these new data, as well as the trustworthiness of their collectors, allowed Woolhouse to conclude that the "final results" of his graduation, "on being differenced to second differences, are generally found to be remarkable for their orderly progression." From these uniform facts he quickly proceeded to deduce values for Makeham's theoretical constants, from which he assumed "important and reliable aid" would be derived (Woolhouse 1870, 394, 409).

Of equal importance to the presence of the facts themselves was the social meaning those facts embodied. These were not just any mortality statistics. H^M lives had been selected by head actuaries in twenty of the largest British insurance offices (hence the adjective "healthy") and *collected* by a diligent army of up-and-coming members of the actuarial profession. Makeham's dependence on the H^M data suggests that wayward clerks, as well as wayward facts, had to be taught to conform before the fruits of their labor would be accepted as empirically valid. In 1854 Charles Jellicoe had addressed a similar problem of smoothing rough edges in the Eagle's mortality experience and had concluded that "with some little management a remedy can generally be supplied" (Jellicoe 1854, 207). He had hoped to "manage" the numbers directly, by means of dextrous grouping and interpolation; but as Makeham was to discover, this response to roughness was not enough to achieve consensus among his fellow actuaries. Fortunately, though, an additional type of management was available in the 1860s, in the form of twenty teams of closely supervised clerks who annually added thousands of new cards to the Institute's stores. Satisfactory empirical evidence that Makeham's law really did soften inequalities without destroying "any distinctly marked feature" was possible only once the Institute had replicated his epistemological smoothing exercise in the more tangible world of the counting house. With the help of Downes' card system, the Institute secured its tables from being corrupted by errant facts, while offering moral improvement to the collectors so they themselves might one day be entrusted with "managing" numbers as well as merely compiling them. Woolhouse noted both these qualities when he praised the card system for diminishing the "liability to error in making long and tedious transcriptions" and when he reprinted Downes' claim that arranging the cards in piles and transcribing them "would afford pleasant fireside amusement to any domesticated actuary and his family" (Woolhouse 1866, 82n).

With this new distinction between interpretive skill and precise transcription came a similar shift in the relation between universal and local knowledge as a feature of actuarial work. Makeham allowed actuaries to walk a middle path between Edmonds' law, which in its assertion of universal application was relevant only to national (and hence noncommercial) insurance, and Gompertz' law, which had left actuaries with no basis for collective intellectual activity. The difference owed more to Makeham's style of presentation than to anything inherent in his new law. Instead of claiming that all the relevant constants were fixed in stone, or denying that such constants could ever be calculated, he announced that "there are certain partial forces of mortality (how many I do not pretend to say) which increase in intensity with the age in a constant geometrical ration, while there are also certain other partial forces which do not so increase," adding that "medical science is not sufficiently advanced . . . to separate the whole category of diseases into the two classes specified" (Makeham 1867, 335–36). By suggesting the existence of partial forces "out there" that could some day be discovered, he redefined the empirical project of actuaries from the office-specific one of discerning unique constants to the profession-wide one of figuring out these general laws. But significantly, he did "not pretend to say" where to draw the line between static and constantly increasing forces of mortality. His willingness to leave the determination of general constants to future investigators allowed his fellow actuaries to select who those investigators would be and what counted as legitimate empirical support for such generalizations. As the Institute's official textbook later revealed, this disciplinary function of his elusive "law of nature" was potentially quite useful: "Just as the search for the philosopher's stone, which has never been found, led to great and useful discoveries in chemistry, so the quest after the law of human mortality has resulted in formulas which, if not absolutely embodying that law, at least confer very great practical benefits" (King [1885] 1902, 69).

This last component of Makeham's law, which suggested that universal laws would finally be revealed if only clerks kept at their jobs, could be extended to salesmen as well, and actuaries tried to do this in order to quell a new wave of overcompetition that flared up in the 1880s. Instead of clashing head offices, the problem this time was traveling salesmen and branch managers whose eagerness for commissions and promotions led them to engage in ruthless tactics against their rivals. Careful calculations by actuaries in the head offices ensured that the business generated by these agents was sold at safe rates, but the actuaries had less control over how the sales were made. Inspection systems could not completely prevent agents from misrepresenting their office when they knocked on peoples' doors, and actuaries constantly lamented "large and promiscuous commission allowances" that encouraged "a laxity in the morality of some agents" (Crisford 1880, 189). They responded by trying to get agents and managers to subordinate their unwieldy commercial passions to "laws" of social intercourse that would be revealed in the indefinite future. One day salesmen would be sufficiently "improved" to be able to produce the perfect combination of competition and prudence, just as actuaries would one day collect enough facts to know the true laws of mortality. Thomas Young, soon to be elected Institute president and a devotee of "the all-embracing genius of Mr. Herbert Spencer," interpreted the insurance business in 1896 as moving rapidly along the road "from the simple to the complex under the force of advancing civilization." After "ranging the phenomena of Insurance under the sway of the general evolutionary principles which Mr. Spencer has expounded," he diagnosed excessive competition among agents and managers as lamentable human failings that would gradually disappear as the predestined laws of "complex organization" took hold (Young 1896, 248, 251–52, 259).

Actuaries in the 1890s busied themselves with encouraging the formation of institutions that would help speed this closer fit between unruly staff members and the insurance industry as a whole, just as they had successfully used the H^M project to bring unruly numbers and universal laws of mortality closer together. Young praised the foundation of a Life Offices' Association in London, which he depicted as "a combination of Companies attempting to guide and render uniform, without coercion, the practical character" of the industry (ibid., 254). And by the late 1880s, with the active assistance of London actuaries, similarly designed insurance institutes had cropped up across the provinces as meeting grounds for actuaries, managers, and agents to discuss their common interests (see Liveing 1961). When actuaries were invited to speak at these meetings, Makeham's law and the H^M tables were popular items of discussion, being "that noble result of united effort and highest actuarial skill . . . published under the authority of the Institute of Actuaries" (Monilaws 1891, 10). More often, actuaries hoped that the institutes themselves would teach the value of subordinating human error to natural laws. Young called on the social intercourse at the institutes to provide the "restraining and softening spirit and influence . . . which alone can preserve our business rivalry from degenerating into a harsh and deplorable contest" (Young 1891, 143). Or, as the Scottish actuary Archibald Hewat put it in celebrating the "social or friendly element" of the Irish Insurance Institute in 1893: "We cannot come here, smoke our pipes, sip our coffee, and have a friendly chat, and then go off to-morrow to poach among our erstwhile friend's agents" (Hewat 1893, 3–4).

As long as clerks and agents kept listening to pronouncements like these, actuaries had every reason in the world to keep abiding by a set of professional values that differed in significant ways from those upheld by neighboring statisticians. And the differences were clear to anyone who cared to look. Outside the Institute of Actuaries, the "taming of chance," as Ian Hacking has called it, was taking the statistical world by storm. Sociologists, eugenists, and philosophers either resigned themselves to deviant data as part of the real world, or set about trying to change the world in order to eliminate whichever deviants they thought were unsavory (Hacking 1990). With the possible exception of the economists, actuaries were by themselves when they continued to pursue what Philip Mirowski has called the "Laplacian dream" of relating irregularities in data to subjective uncertainty (Mirowski 1989, 26–30). But at least from the actuaries' perspective, this pursuit was not as quixotic as Mirowski's metaphor suggests. As they saw it, accepting the real-world implications of chance occurrences, like living with unruly insurance salesmen, was at best an annoyance and at worst a threat to professional security. The point was clear from Thomas Sprague's arguments, in a treatise on probability designed for actuaries, for rejecting the new "scientific" stance on deviance as expressed in John Venn's *Logic of Chance*. As "a matter of business," he argued, "our proper course would not be to make a large number of trials, and then be guided by the results; but rather to . . . be guided by a priori reasoning" like that embodied in Makeham's law of mortality. He revealingly concluded that "if insurance were a mere matter of chances, to be determined by the study of statistics, it would be a much simpler business than it is. There would be little scope for the exercise of judgment and skill by the Company's officials" (Sprague 1892, 99, 113). Alone among the statisticians, Victorian actuaries made a calculated decision to retain their unique philosophy of calculation.

ACKNOWLEDGEMENTS

I wish to thank Ted Porter, Andrew Warwick, Mike Power, and C. G. Lewin for comments on an earlier draft of this paper.

REFERENCES

Abbott, Andrew. 1988. *The System of Professions: An Essay on the Division of Labor*. Chicago: University of Chicago Press.
Actuaries' Club. 1848–83. Minutes of the Proceedings of the Actuaries' Club, Institute of Actuaries Library mss. 3 vols.

Adler, Marcus N. 1864. "Government Life Annuities and Life Assurances Bill."
    Assurance Magazine 12:3–32.
Alborn, Timothy L. 1989. "Negotiating Notation: Chemical Symbols and British
    Society, 1831–1835." *Annals of Science* 46:437–60.
    1991. "The Other Economists: Science and Commercial Culture in Victorian
    England." Ph.D. dissertation, Harvard University.
Anon. 1850. "Reports of Life Insurance Companies." *Assurance Magazine*
    1:87–103.
    1851. "The Institute of Actuaries." *Assurance Magazine* 2:119–36, 262–71.
    1853. "Review of E. Sang, *Essays on Life Assurance.*" *Assurance Magazine*
    3:260–64.
    1868a. "Institute of Actuaries." *Assurance Magazine* 14:333–39.
    1868b. "Review of Cornelius Walford, *Insurance Guide and Handbook.*"
    Assurance Magazine 14:409–15.
    1869a. "The Albert Life Assurance Company." *Westminster Review* 93:532–50.
    1869b. "Institute of Actuaries." *Assurance Magazine* 15:161–65.
    1869c. *Life Assurance Companies: Their Financial Condition Discussed.*
    London: E. Wilson.
    1871. *Unbiased Notes on Life Assurance.* London: Houlston and Sons.
    1872. "Institute of Actuaries." *Journal of the Institute of Actuaries* 17:145–49.
Barlow, Thomas. 1855. "Memoir of the Late Griffith Davies, Esq." *Assurance
    Magazine* 5:337–48.
Beer, Max. 1920. *A History of British Socialism.* 2 vols. London: Bell.
Berman, Morris. 1987. *Social Change and Scientific Organization: The Royal
    Institution, 1799–1844.* Ithaca, N.Y.: Cornell University Press.
Brown, Samuel. n.d. *Is the Present Competition in Life Assurance Advantageous
    to the Public?* London: W. S. D. Pateman.
    1850. "Annuities and Assurances." *Assurance Magazine* 1:20–40.
    1852a. "On the Collections of Data in Various Branches of Assurance."
    Assurance Magazine 2:200–209.
    1852b. "On the Uniform Action of the Human Will, as Exhibited by Its Mean
    Results in Social Statistics." *Assurance Magazine* 2:341–51.
    1854a. "On a Simple Plan of Classifying the Policies of a Life Assurance
    Company." *Assurance Magazine* 4:283–91.
    1854b. "On the Sufficiency of the Existing Companies for the Business of Life
    Assurance." *Assurance Magazine* 4:10–21.
Burridge, A. F. 1895. *Annals of the Actuaries' Club.* London: privately printed.
Campbell-Kelly, Martin. 1993. "Large-scale Data Processing in the Prudential,
    1850–1930." *Accounting, Business and Financial History* 3:117–39.
Carpenter, William. 1860. "Actuaries and Their Institute." *The Policyholder*
    1:264–65.
Champness, William. 1879. *An Insurance Dictionary.* London: Thomas Murby.
Crisford, G. S. 1880. Untitled excerpt from *Insurance Record* reprinted in *Journal
    of the Institute of Actuaries* 22:188–90.
Cullen, Michael. 1975. *The Statistical Movement in Early Victorian Britain: The
    Foundations of Empirical Social Research.* New York: Barnes & Noble.
Daston, Lorraine J. 1988. *Classical Probability in the Enlightenment.* Princeton,
    N.J.: Princeton University Press.

1992. "Objectivity and the Escape from Perspective." *Social Studies of Science* 22:597–618.

De Morgan, Augustus. 1838. *Essay on Probabilities, and on Their Application to Life Contingencies and Insurance Offices.* London: Longmans.

1839. *Penny Cyclopaedia,* s.v., "Mortality, law of."

1872. *A Budget of Paradoxes.* London: Longmans.

De Morgan, Sophia. 1882. *Memoir of Augustus De Morgan.* London: Longmans.

Desmond, Adrian. 1989. *The Politics of Evolution: Morphology, Medicine, and Reform in Radical London.* Chicago: University of Chicago Press.

Deuchar, J. W. 1882. "A Sketch of the History of Science of Life Contingencies." *Transactions of the Insurance and Actuarial Society of Glasgow* 1:35–71.

Downes, J. J. 1862. *An Account of the Processes Employed in Getting out the Mortality Experience of the Economic Life Assurance Society.* London: privately published.

Edmonds, Thomas. 1832. *Life Tables Founded upon the Discovery of a Numerical Law, Regulating the Existence of Every Human Being.* London: J. Duncan.

1860. "On the Discovery of the Law of Human Mortality." *Assurance Magazine* 9: 170–84.

Eyler, John. 1979. *Victorian Social Medicine: The Ideas and Influence of William Farr.* Baltimore: Johns Hopkins University Press.

Farr, William. 1860. "On the Construction of Life Tables." *Assurance Magazine* 9:121–41.

Farren, E. J. 1850. "Mental Statistics, or Edinburgh in 1850." *Assurance Magazine* 1:113–14.

Galloway, Thomas. 1841. *Treatise on the Tables of Mortality Deduced from the Experience of the Amicable Society.* London.

Gompertz, Benjamin. 1820. "Sketch of an Analysis and Notation Applicable to the Value of Life Contingencies." *Philosophical Transactions of the Royal Society* 110:214–94.

1825. "On the Nature of the Function Expressive of the Law of Human Mortality, and on a New Mode of Determining the Value of Life Contingencies." *Philosophical Transactions of the Royal Society* 115:513–85.

Guardian Life Assurance Company. 1821–73. General Court Minute Book, Guildhall Library mss. 12 vols.

Hacking, Ian. 1990. *The Taming of Chance.* Cambridge: Cambridge University Press.

Herschel, John. 1830. *A Preliminary Discourse on the Study of Natural Philosophy.* London: Longman, Rees, Orman, Brown & Green.

Hewat, Archibald. 1893. *On Training for the Insurance Profession.* Dublin: Insurance Institute of Ireland.

Hunter, Adam. 1865. *The Fruits of Amalgamation Exhibited in the Correspondence of a Palladium Policy-holder with Charles Jellicoe.* Edinburgh: Edmonton & Douglas.

Institute of Actuaries. 1848–65. Council Minute Book, Institute of Actuaries Library mss. 2 vols.

1866. *Discussions at the Institute of Actuaries, Session 1865–66.* London: Institute of Actuaries.

Jellicoe, Charles. 1853. Evidence in *Report of the Select Committee on Assurance Associations.* London: HMSO.

1854. "Rate of Mortality in the Eagle Insurance Company." *Assurance Magazine* 4:199–215.

1858. "On the Principles Which Should Govern Assurance Companies in Amalgamating." *Assurance Magazine* 7:254–58.

Jones, Jenkin. 1843. *A Series of Tables of Annuities and Assurances, Calculated from a New Rate of Mortality amongst Assured Lives.* London: Longmans.

1847. *What Is Life Assurance? Explained by Practical Illustrations of Its Principles* . . . London: Longmans.

Kindleberger, Charles. 1979. *Manias, Panics and Crashes: A History of Financial Crises.* New York: Basic Books.

King, Gregory. [1885] 1902. *Institute of Actuaries Textbook, Part II.* London: W. Sutton.

Larson, Magali S. 1977. *The Rise of Professionalism: A Sociological Analysis.* Berkeley: University of California Press.

Lazarus, William. 1862. "The Law of Human Mortality." *Assurance Magazine* 10:238–85.

Liveing, Edward. 1961. *A Century of Insurance: The Commercial Union Group of Insurance Companies 1861–1961.* London: Whiterby.

Lubbock, John William, and J. E. Drinkwater. 1830. *On Probability.* London: Charles Knight.

Macfadyen, James. 1870. *The Principles Affecting the Solvency of a Life Assurance Company.* Reprinted from *Transactions of the Glasgow Philosophical Society.* Glasgow.

Mackenzie, Donald A. 1981. *Statistics in Britain: The Social Construction of Scientific Knowledge.* Edinburgh: Edinburgh University Press.

MacLeod, Roy, and Peter Collins, eds. 1981. *The Parliament of Science: The British Association for the Advancement of Science 1831–1931.* London: Science Reviews.

Makeham, William. 1866. "On the Construction of Tables of Mortality." *Assurance Magazine* 12:325–58.

1867. "On the Law of Mortality." *Assurance Magazine* 13:325–49.

McCay, C. F. 1870. "American Tables of Mortality." *Journal of the Institute of Actuaries* 16:20–33.

Milne, Joshua. 1815. *A Treatise on the Valuation of Annuities and Assurances on Lives and Survivorships.* 2 vols. London: Longmans.

Mirowski, Philip. 1989. *More Heat Than Light: Economics as Social Physics; Physics as Nature's Economics.* Cambridge: Cambridge University Press.

Monilaws, W. M. 1891. *Life Assurance.* Birmingham: Birmingham Insurance Institute.

Morrell, Jack, and Arnold Thackray. 1981. *Gentlemen of Science: Early Years of the British Association for the Advancement of Science.* Oxford: Oxford University Press.

Nelson, Robert L., and David M. Trubek. 1992. "New Problems and Paradigms in Studies of the Legal Profession." In *Lawyers' Ideals/Lawyers' Practices: transformations in the American Legal Profession,* edited by R. L. Nelson, D. M. Trubek, and R. L. Solomon, 1–27. Ithaca, N.Y.: Cornell University Press.

Nicoll, John. 1898. "The Relation of the Actuarial Profession to the State." *Journal of the Institute of Actuaries* 34:158–251.

Orange, A. D. 1975. "The Idols of the Theatre: The British Association and Its Early Critics." *Annals of Science* 32:277–94.

Pearson, Robin. 1990. "Thrift or Dissipation? The Business of Life Assurance in the Early Nineteenth Century." *Economic History Review* 43:236–54.

Porter, H. W. 1854. "On the Education of an Actuary." *Assurance Magazine* 4:108–18.

——— 1860. "On Some Considerations Suggested by the Annual Reports of the Registrar-General." *Assurance Magazine* 9:12–41, 89–112, 149–67.

——— 1861. "Mr. Finlaison's 'Report and Observations on the Mortality of the Government Life Annuitants'." *Assurance Magazine* 9:277–88.

Porter, Theodore. 1986. *The Rise of Statistical Thinking 1820–1900.* Princeton, N.J.: Princeton University Press.

Recknell, G. H. 1948. *The Actuaries' Club 1848–1948.* London: privately published.

Simmonds, Reginald Claude. 1948. *The Institute of Actuaries 1848–1948.* Cambridge: Cambridge University Press.

Sprague, T. B. 1858. "On the Terms upon Which the Business of One Insurance Company May Be Equitably Transferred to Another." *Assurance Magazine* 7:301–10.

——— 1861a. "On Mr. Gompertz's Law of Human Mortality." *Assurance Magazine* 9:288–95.

——— 1861b. "On the Recent Imputations Made as to Mr. Gompertz's Accuracy." *Assurance Magazine* 10:32–44.

——— 1892. "On Probability and Chance, and Their Connection with the Business of Insurance." *Transactions of the Actuarial Society of Edinburgh* 3:87–113.

Strousberg, B. F. 1853. *Judgment before Trial: A Remonstrance.* London: G. E. Petter.

Supple, Barry. 1970. *The Royal Exchange Assurance: A History of British Insurance 1720–1970.* Cambridge: Cambridge University Press.

Trebilcock, Clive. 1985. *Phoenix Assurance and the Development of British Insurance.* Volume 1: *1782–1870.* Cambridge: Cambridge University Press.

Tucker, Robert. 1862. "On the Proper Method of Estimating the Liabilities of Life Assurance Companies." *Assurance Magazine* 10:312–22.

Walford, Cornelius. 1871–80. *The Insurance Cyclopaedia: Being a Dictionary of Terms Used in Connection with the Theory and Practice of Insurance.* 6 vols. London: Dent.

Woolhouse, W. S. B. 1862. "On Gompertz's Law of Mortality." *Assurance Magazine* 10:121–30.

——— 1866. "On the Construction of Tables of Mortality." *Assurance Magazine* 13:75–102.

——— 1870. "Explanation of a New Method of Adjusting Mortality Tables." *Assurance Magazine* 15:389–410.

Yeo, Richard. 1993. *Defining Science: William Whewhell, Natural Knowledge, and Public Debate in Early Victorian Britain.* Cambridge: Cambridge University Press.

Young, Thomas. 1891. "On the True Nature and Object of Insurance." *Transactions of the Birmingham Insurance Institute* 1:143–61.

——— 1896. "The Theory of Evolution Applied to the System of Life Assurance and,

Incidentally, to Insurance Generally." *Journal of the Institute of Actuaries* 32:248–59.

1897. "The Nature and History of Actuarial Work as Exemplifying the Mode of Development and the Methods of Science." *Journal of the Institute of Actuaries* 33:97–131.

5 The factory as laboratory

Peter Miller and Ted O'Leary

Introduction

The laboratory, so long neglected by science scholars, has now become the watchword. In the process, it has been made to look increasingly like a factory (Galison 1989). Science and technology studies have pointed out that the laboratory is composed of a multiplicity of instruments, ideas, inscriptions, and actors who transform the world. The laboratory is a place where "thoughts, acts and manufactures" (Hacking 1992, 30) come together. Rather than a place where researchers test theories against reality, the laboratory is a "cultural institution with a history (or rather histories)" (ibid., 33). Laboratory studies have followed scientists, scientific inscriptions, and scientific practices along the networks through which they operate (Latour 1983; Latour and Woolgar 1979). Laboratories change, and such changes are held to need analyzing in terms of a complex of questions, instruments, and forms of work organization, rather than by reference to overarching theoretical constructs (Galison 1985). The political stratagems of scientists in forming alliances and mobilizing resources are considered to demonstrate that scientific objects manufactured in laboratories are inextricably politically or symbolically construed (Knorr-Cetina 1992, 115). And the distinctions between the macro and micro, the social and the technological, that so long entranced sociologists eager to demonstrate the worth of their discipline have been argued to be unhelpful analytic categories, themselves the result of a particular "contextualist" tradition (Latour 1993; Shapin and Schaffer 1985; Mackenzie 1987; Hughes 1987).

We endorse in large part these recent developments in science and technology studies, even if we quibble about some of the details and use different words for saying similar things. But we have something to add that has largely escaped attention. We point out the remarkable extent to which the inverse of these arguments holds – viz., that *the factory resembles a laboratory*. For the factory is as much a site of invention and intervention as the laboratory populated by physicists, chemists, and the like. This is self-evident for the products made in the factory. But the factory is a site for invention and intervention in a further important sense. It is here, on the shop floor, that new realities are created out of the dreams and schemes of diverse agents and experts based in a multiplicity of locales. The rearranging of persons and things on the factory floor proposed recently by advocates of cellular manufacturing, just-in-time systems, customer-driven manufacturing, and designs for the "Factory of the Future" have made the factory into a laboratory *par excellence*. Out of such interventions have emerged new physical spaces on the shop floor, new ways of calculating, new forms of work organization, and new modes of economic citizenship. Together, these disparate devices form a complex of interrelated practices for governing economic life (Miller and Rose 1990). To adapt a phrase of Hacking's, these various initiatives that take the factory as the locus and object of intervention entitle us to analyze it as "a space for interfering under controllable and isolable conditions with matter and energy" (Hacking 1992, 36). As such, the factory is an intrinsically theoretical and experimental space, one where phenomena are created.[1]

This does not mean that there is no difference between a factory making trucks in the North American Mid-west, and the European Centre for Particle Physics in Geneva. Nor does it mean that all factories making trucks are the same. What it does mean is that science and technology studies need to take a much wider view of what counts as a laboratory (Knorr-Cetina 1992). Science and technology studies need to clear away the lingering demarcationism that characterizes the discipline and address those practices that seek to act upon and transform the world in specific and relatively bounded locales, even if this takes place outside the laboratories populated by physicists, chemists, and the like (Lenoir 1988; Miller 1994; Pickering 1992).

We focus here on one such attempt to transform the world by interfering under controllable and isolable conditions – namely, the redesign of a factory floor in a particular plant of Caterpillar Inc located in the American Mid-west.[2] Caterpillar Inc., one of the world's largest manufacturers of earth-moving machinery, construction machinery, and diesel engines, set out in the mid-1980s to effect a world-wide transformation in its manufacturing practices. This took place against a backdrop of losses of $1 billion reported between 1982 and 1985, and a perceived

---

[1] We do not strictly apply Hacking's (1992) distinction among ideas, things, and marks. However his taxonomy of the items used in the laboratory is very close to that adopted here.

[2] For a more extended discussion of these issues, upon which this paper draws, see Miller and O'Leary 1994.

structural or semipermanent reduction in demand. The concern in this paper, analyzed both at corporate headquarters and at a key manufacturing facility based at Decatur, Illinois, is with the ways in which a corporate-wide factory modernization initiative called Plant With A Future (PWAF), brought together a diverse array of ideas, expertises, and instruments for transforming the factory.

The introduction of new machines and layouts, new material flows, and new working relations in this plant could appear to be a merely "technical" matter, eminently suited to an "internalist" model of technological change. But in line with recent studies of science and technology we show that the redesign of a factory floor – a move from traditional assembly line technology to cellular and just-in-time manufacturing – is fundamentally implicated in changes that go far beyond the boundaries of the plant (Collins [1985] 1992; Galison 1987,1989; Hughes 1987; Knorr-Cetina 1992; Latour 1988; Pickering 1992; Shapin and Schaffer 1985; Wise 1988). The issues addressed here are part of a long history of attempts to transform the workplace in accordance with particular political ideals, whether in the early nineteenth century (Schaffer 1994), or in the post-World War II era (Noble 1984). The redesign of the physical space of the factory floor at a particular manufacturing plant is much more than the simple introduction of a new floor plan that partitions and links persons and machines in novel ways (Lynch 1985, 1991). The redesign of a factory floor at one of Caterpillar's key manufacturing plants in the mid-1980s is reciprocally and constitutively linked to attempts to transform the nature of economic citizenship and to remake the industrial base of a nation. The clue to understanding this remaking of a particular factory lies in untangling the complex of relays and relations formed among the physical transformation at the Decatur plant, the multiple bodies of expertise at the plant responsible for the redesign of the shop floor, and the babble of voices proclaiming the need for, and the key to, a revitalized base for North American manufacturing industry and a new form of economic citizenship. To paraphrase Ophir and Shapin (1991), such spatial arrangements are intrinsically social practices. Ideas are embedded in the most mundane parts of social reality.

But there is a considerable way to go before we can place ourselves within the new reality that is created on the shop floor. We first have to understand how it is that such a fundamental transformation of working practices and principles is made to appear *necessary*, and at the level of North American manufacturing industry as a whole. For it is from such a starting point that the search for a new reality becomes an imperative for an individual corporation and an individual manufacturing facility. We should no more presuppose this step in the invention of new factory layouts than we should assume that vast sums of money and huge numbers of hours will be spent hunting for quarks (Pickering 1984) or seeking to act upon the actions of microbes (Latour 1988). Before this can happen, the factory has to be *problematized* by a diverse and heterogeneous group of consultants, politicians, managers, experts, and commentators of varying kinds, who pronounce on the deficiencies of existing ways of making things and call for new ways to be invented. The list of such agencies is in principle limitless and infinitely varied. To paraphrase Latour (ibid., 35), we do not know in advance who the agents are who will try to remake our world.

Reality, however, does not come neatly parceled up into macro- and microlevels. "Context" – as much of the science studies literature tells us incessantly – is old hat. This applies just as much to the problematizing of the factory that was such a distinctive feature of the North American scene in the 1980s as it does to the more conventional examples in the science studies literature. So in trying to understand the problematizing of factory layouts there is a second step to be taken, one that addresses the manner in which Caterpillar made a rethinking of the factory *in their plants* seem necessary. It is therefore not only to the "outside" of the corporation, the "context," that we direct attention. Indeed, there is no "inside" or "outside" to such attempts to create new realities (Latour 1983). There are simply ways of problematizing, ways of securing acknowledgment that *this* rather than *that* is *the* problem – an often long and complex process. And there is a reciprocal and mutually constitutive relation between the different locales within which this takes place, a process of coproduction or coemergence of "problems" in which primacy goes to the relations between locales, rather than to one locale or another. To address this part of the process we have to move far beyond the analysis of "texts" conducted by others (Latour 1988). It is to the "intricacies of practice" (Pickering 1992, 6) that we have to turn our attention. Or, in Foucault's words, it is "regimes of practices" (Foucault 1991, 75) that we have to analyze, with the aim of grasping what it is that makes certain practices acceptable at particular moments. In this case it is one particular calculative practice – that of "competitor benchmarking" – that illustrates our point. For it was through this calculative practice that the image of Japanese competition was made real to those working in the North American plants of Caterpillar Inc. By this means, "competitiveness" was no longer an abstract idea, a simple invocation to work harder, to do more, to produce quicker. "Competitiveness" meant "person-to-person" competition with a Japanese worker. The "threat" from Japan to American manufacturing was to be given a face, *and* a number.

But even this was not enough. To remake the factory one has to do more than make visible the notion of competitiveness. A third step is required, one that makes possible a redesign of the physical spaces on the factory floor (Miller 1992). A diagram of the new factory floor has to be created. For if an actual factory is to be remade, one has to be able to visualize the flows of materials and products through the redesigned factory floor. Hopes and dreams of becoming competitive get you nowhere in North America in the mid-1980s if you cannot envisage a factory layout that will have imprinted on it for all to see the logic of global competitiveness and customer-driven manufacturing (Schonberger 1990). It was in systems terms that this diagram of a new reality was set out. Materials, components, subassemblies, and finished product would be made to flow across this novel diagram of the factory floor in accordance with systems principles and the requirement to conform to a computer-integrated manufacturing process. The image of the customer would be there for all to see, inscribed in the systems diagrams of a redesigned shop floor.

Yet more was required. A fourth and vital step. The concerns with the product, with competitiveness, and the dream of a "new economic citizenship" (Dertouzos et al. 1989) had still to be embedded in a new spatial and temporal ordering of production. Creating a new reality, whether on the shop floor or elsewhere, is a difficult process. Ideas, even diagrams, are not enough on their own. A factory still has to be able to produce something. To understand this step it is to yet another locale that we have to direct our attention. This time, it is the deliberations of managers, supervisors and workers at the plant in question that we address as they formulated the key concept of the "Assembly Highway". The Assembly Highway was the route, a "highway" in the shape of an inverted *T*, along which would flow all products made in the plant. Product frames would be transported along the Assembly Highway by automated guided vehicles (AGVs) and routed into assembly "spurs" adjacent to the highway. The Assembly Highway was no ordinary concept. Or rather, it was a way of both "representing" and "intervening" (Hacking 1983) at the same time. For the Assembly Highway was the new reality to be created. The Assembly Highway was a new spatial configuration of manufacture. And it was through this new spatial configuration that issues of the product, of competitiveness, and of a new economic citizenship would be embedded in the factory at Decatur, Illinois. The Assembly Highway not only gave physical form to the ambitions of the PWAF program, but made it possible to produce trucks and earth-moving vehicles according to the dictates of customer-driven manufacturing. In so doing, authority relations in the plant were transformed.

Henceforth, authority would flow directly from the customer to the work process, along the Assembly Highway, in accordance with the ideal of empowered workers responding immediately to the wants and wishes of the customer (Johnson 1992). Authority would no longer be embodied in the character of the supervisor, or in the routine calculations of a technique such as standard costing, but would inhere in the process itself. Thus could reality be reconstructed, and in conformity to the dream.

These, then, are the four steps we trace here: a problematizing of the factory at the level of North American manufacturing as a whole in the 1980s; a problematizing of the notion of competitiveness at Caterpillar Inc. through the calculative practices of competitor benchmarking; a diagraming of the ideal factory in systems terms; and the embedding of notions of the product, of competitiveness, and of a new economic citizenship in the Assembly Highway. In these four steps, discourses, diagrams, and designs come together in a new spatial ordering of production that is given actual physical form at the Decatur, Illinois plant of Caterpillar Inc. Thus was the factory floor to be remade.

Our account of this process stops at the moment when a new arrangement of persons and machines is in place on the factory floor. It is the invention of this new reality that we document. But this is no fixed point, no end of history. Nor is it a question of claiming finally to have discovered that elusive entity, "real life," or to have re-created the "thought processes" and microprocesses (Latour and Woolgar 1979) through which factory life is enacted. We leave that to those who are more confident of finally tracking down what happens in this penumbral domain. What we chart here instead is the forming of an *assemblage*, the emerging of a historically specific complex of relations around a particular issue, the establishing of horizontal linkages and relays among a multiplicity of locales and practices. Each of the components of this assemblage is itself unstable, traversed by tensions, susceptible to multiple interpretations, meanings, and utilizations. To this extent the notion "assemblage" shares with Hughes' (1987) notion of "technological systems" a concern with the heterogeneity of components that come to be linked together in such instances; but it differs in emphasizing the instability of the relations that form between such components.[3] The assemblage we chart here is nothing other than the temporarily stabilized complex of relations that formed around a particular factory in the United States in the 1980s.

[3] Hughes (1987, 53) states that "over time, technological systems manage increasingly to incorporate environment into the system, thereby eliminating sources of uncertainty." The assemblage we analyze here has no such tendency toward the elimination of uncertainty, nor does the ideal of a "closed system" capture the permeability of the factory to a diverse range of expert interventions and cultural values.

Such a complex of changing relations is ill suited to the constraints of an actor-network approach, or to the attempts by some to follow managers around so as to retrace the steps by which a stabilized end point is arrived at (Latour 1987, 1988). Indeed, there is no single group whom we might follow in this instance. Nor does the notion of "translation" fit well here. For it is unclear who might be considered to be translating whom, what is being translated into what. In any case, this would be to presuppose a movement between two given points rather than their coemergence. The forming of the assemblage we address here is instead the mutual constitution of the agents and entities that make it up, a process akin to the linking together of a plethora of "mediating machines"(Wise 1988). It is the fragile and shifting complex of *relations* that is the object of our enquiry, not a given actor who enrols and controls others. If our analysis is guided by a philosophy, it is a philosophy of the relation rather than a philosophy of objects, entities, or networks.

Rethinking the factory

We use the phrase "rethinking the factory" to refer to the multiple and diverse ways in which a transformation of North American manufacturing industry was made to appear *necessary* in the 1980s. Across this period, American industry was indicted on a number of counts: products made in America were said to be of lower quality than foreign goods; American factories were accused of inefficiency and of lacking a suitably trained work force; American managers were held to have a short-term financial orientation that was at odds with long-term goals; and the financial controls by which the factory was evaluated and managed were seen to be inadequate (Abernathy et al. 1983; Business Roundtable 1987; Congress of the United States 1987; Dertouzos et al. 1989; Holland 1989). The "American system" of mass production became the symbol of a lost economic prowess. Companies that had once been taken as emblems of America's manufacturing prowess came to achieve an inverse significance, as exemplars of the decline of entire sectors of the U.S. manufacturing economy relative to Japan (for a more detailied consideration of these issues, see Miller and O'Leary 1993).

This problematizing of a nation's products went far beyond the factory – but only to return again and again. A multiplicity of linkages was forged between the factory and other locales. Rethinking the factory was much more than a narrowly economic concern. It brought into the field of vision designers, engineers, the research community, the education system, the basis of managerial expertise, and the capital markets. For the causes were held to be deep-seated and to need tracing back to their origins. The decline of American manufacturing was seen as systemic, its consequences economic, technological, and even moral (Chubb and Moe 1990; Doyle and Kearns 1988; Hirsch 1987; Kennedy 1990). Rethinking the factory concerned many more than those who managed or owned factories. Rethinking the factory was a concern for the nation as a whole. And rethinking the factory was rapidly to become a matter of seeking to transform fundamentally regimes of manufacture and modes of governing economic life in America's factories and enterprises.

Three themes characterized this problematization of the "American system" of mass production. First, and most "self-evidently," it alighted on the *product* – its quality and integrity. From here it was only a very short step to the argument that the factory needed to be reengineered and re-created if product quality was to be enhanced and guaranteed. But the product signified more than the sum of the processes that went into making it. Products and production processes were made to evoke a set of political values. The lack of "quality" of a product was made into a test of social organization, of work practices, of government policies – indeed of collaborative endeavor itself (Clark and Fujimoto 1990; Dertouzos et al. 1989). The inferiority of American products was seen to be demonstrated and symbolized by comparing American products and production processes with those of Japan (Hayes and Abernathy 1980; Wheelwright 1981). Commentators pointed to the relative "wastes" built into the American production system. Not only did American factories need grossly more space, time, inventory, labor and record keeping than their Japanese counterparts (Kaplan 1983; Schonberger 1982, 1990), but the end result was often a lower-quality product. Poor design and deficient engineering of production systems were held to have given rise to waste, often on a massive scale. Revelations proliferated during the 1980s of materials and products that traveled hundreds of needless miles within factories because of simple flaws in factory layout. The basic message was clear, even if the precise nature of the "solution" still had to be worked out: if product quality was to be improved, then a fundamental rethinking of the factory was required.

Second, rethinking the factory was seen to be a question of *national competitiveness*. Again, this led quickly back to the factory. For a failure of national competitiveness vis-à-vis a country such as Japan was considered to be a symptom of a failure at the level of the factories from which uncompetitive products came. But the concern with competitiveness also led away from the factory, in particular to the school and the education system. The varied expressions of anxiety over American competitiveness ran far deeper than the immediate context of manufacturing management and policy (Doyle and Kearns 1988; Kennedy 1990).

According to the historian Paul Kennedy (1990, 31), there was "evidence of widespread social decay." American schoolchildren were held to be lagging behind those in other advanced societies. Throughout the 1980s, a series of reports told a similar story, pointing to the problems of American schools and linking these up with the question of national competitiveness (Business Roundtable 1987; Chubb and Moe 1990; Congress of the United States 1987; National Commission on Excellence in education 1983). All too many American students, prospective workers, were ill equipped to compete, lacking in "cultural literacy" (Hirsch 1987) and numeracy, as well as deficient in the "art of learning itself" (Kennedy 1990, 31).

The concern with national competitiveness extended to a number of other locales also. Accountants criticized themselves, and were criticized by others, for a failure to grasp the changed nature of manufacturing processes (Howell and Soucy 1988; National Association of Accountants 1986, 1988), and for the alleged resulting obsolescence of the core calculative technologies of accounting – such as discounted cash flow practices, product cost numbers, and overhead cost categories (Hayes and Abernathy 1980; Johnson 1990; Johnson and Kaplan 1987; Miller and Vollmann 1985). Overall, accounting was held to have failed in its task of representing the significance of issues of product quality and global competitiveness in the financial information it provided (Kaplan 1983). And this critique of accounting expertise extended to managerial expertise more generally, for the pervasive myopia it was held to have fostered among American managers (Dertouzos et al. 1989; President's Commission on Industrial Competitiveness 1985; Wheelwright 1981). A preoccupation on the part of managers with short-term cost reduction rather than long-term competitiveness, and with financial restructuring to bolster profits rather than technological innovation, was held to stem in large part from the financial mentality that managers learned in business schools and universities as well as from management consultants. Financial mechanisms such as leveraged buy-outs were held to allow remote entrepreneurs to exert an influence on the factory that was disastrous for the quality of American products (Galbraith 1989; Holland 1989). The productivity of particular enterprises counted for little, as a logic of portfolio analysis turned investment into speculation (Galbraith 1989; Lowenstein 1988). Similar problems arose within the enterprise itself. Managers with "grease in their blood" were replaced by managers concerned with the "tidiness of numbers" (Holland 1989). And conglomerate organization led managers further and further away from product-specific experiences that would enable them to understand and monitor the processes they controlled (Chandler 1990). Again, a transformation of North American manufacturing industry was held to be required, although in this case it was the nature of the expertise directing the manufacturing process that was problematized.

Third, rethinking the factory was seen to entail rethinking the much broader issue of the nature of *economic citizenship*. For if the factory was to be transformed, so too, it was argued, would there have to be a change in the type of persons who would work on the factory floor. Nothing less than a "new economic citizenship" (Dertouzos et al. 1989) was held to be needed, one that would entail a newly privileged role for the consumer, a more direct link between the wishes of consumers and the products made in the factory, and a new way of relating individuals to their work within the factory. Authority, so it was argued, should henceforth flow directly from the customer to the worker (Schonberger 1990). The "possibilities for personhood" (Hacking 1986) would have to be changed, a "reconfiguration" of soclal agents and the world they inhabit (cf. Knorr-Cetina 1992)[4] was required if America's competitiveness was to be restored. And, in a reworking of a familiar refrain (Donzelot 1991; Miller 1986), the ideal image of an enhancement of personal well-being was set out, one that would be made possible by a broadening of the jobs of production workers so that individuals were required to master a larger part of the whole process. No longer, or so it was argued, should employees be treated like cogs in a large and impersonal machine (Dertouzos et al. 1989). Workers, managers, and engineers should be continually and broadly trained, so that they would have an active and engaged relationship with the production process. The problematizing of the factory thus extended to the very nature of the persons to inhabit the factory floor, their capacities and attributes. Once transformed, such individuals might then not only be "empowered" (Johnson 1992) to take charge of the production process but could be made responsible for corporate and national competitiveness. Thus was the emergent assemblage opened up to multiple demands and meanings.

Within the factory, cellular manufacturing along with just-in-time principles were called upon to implant this image of the consumer. And this image of the consumer would pervade the factory itself, not just exist in the world beyond the factory gates. The ideal was to "saturate your company with the voice of the customer" (Whiteley 1991, 59). This would be achieved in part by a transformation of factory layout. There would be established "factories within a factory." Cellular manufacturing principles would mean that the output of one cell could be "sold" to its customers in the next cell along the assembly path. At the end of this

---

[4] Knorr-Cetina draws on Merleau-Ponty's terminology, and speaks of a "reconfiguration of the system of 'self-others-things'" (Knorr-Cetina 1992, 116).

"chain of customers" would be the final customer, the one who buys the product. In the words of one influential commentator, the customer should be "*in* the world-class organization, not outside of it" (Schonberger 1990, 34). By changing factory layout to a cellular organization, the "shadow of the customer" was to be cast upon each cell.

This image of a new economic citizenship was more than a disingenuous way of seeking to increase output or a crude excuse for laying off workers. Much more than "interests" was at stake (Latour 1993). This is not to say that appeals to the personal satisfaction of the worker may not be used as ploys to boost productivity. But they are also much more than that. Appeals to foster a new economic citizenship are ways of seeking to transform those entities – persons, machines, ideas – that comprise the production process. Calls for employees to give more of themselves (Dertouzos et al. 1989) are ways of seeking to invent new entities with novel relationships to a reconfigured production process. Rethinking the factory in this respect meant an attempt to create a distinctive form of individualism, one that would blend group solidarity with existing American ideals of individualism and entrepreneurship.

These three distinct and overlapping ways of problematizing the factory – a concern with product quality, a concern with national competitiveness, and a concern with forms of economic citizenship – had a common message: a transformation of North American industry in the late 1980s was a *necessity* rather than an option. And this transformation should amount to the invention of a new reality on the shop floor, rather than an adjustment or modification of existing ways of making things. Of course, this problematizing of the factory took the form of multiple and sometimes competing proposals, counterproposals, and expressions of concern. It was not a unitary or single program, but was fragmented and dispersed. Yet the heterogeneous nature of these various schemes strengthened rather than weakened the commitment to rethinking the factory. If so many agents in such diverse locales and for such widely differing reasons considered the factory to be such a problematic site in North America in the 1980s, then doubtless it needed to be reinvented. Such was the conclusion reached by plant managers and corporate executives at many North American companies, including those at Caterpillar Inc. Even though Caterpillar was renowned for the quality of its products, and its management structure focused on long-term product and market development, the company was not to escape the problematizing of American manufacture.

Bringing Japan to Decatur, Illinois

To make such a transformation possible was more than a matter of discourse. Or rather, rethinking the factory meant inventing a new idea of the factory *and* a new set of practices that would make it operable in particular corporate settings. During the 1980s this was precisely what happened at Caterpillar Inc. (Miller and O'Leary 1994, 22ff.). Questions of the product, of national competitiveness, and of economic citizenship were posed in a series of initiatives. There was a succession of attempts to rethink the factory at Caterpillar Inc., to transform employees and manufacturing processes so as to address concerns about product quality, competitiveness, and the capacities and attributes of the work force. Initially, as we show in this section, this took the form of certain calculative practices – notably competitor benchmarking – seeking to make real within the plant concerns with the competitor and the customer. As we demonstrate in the following two sections, this later took the form of a more concerted and far-reaching attempt to transform the factory. A wholly remade architecture of production would seek to embed the idea of the product and of national competitiveness in a new spatial ordering of production.

But the first step was a problematizing of corporate performance in general at Caterpillar. The year 1982 provided the perfect occasion. For it was in that year that Caterpillar, one of the world's largest manufacturers of earth-moving and related machinery, reported its first financial loss in fifty years. By 1985, losses totaling almost $1 billion had been reported. Six plants were shut. Employment was cut by 44 percent among hourly workers and 26 percent among salaried staff. Senior executives argued that demand in certain key markets had declined in a semipermanent or structural way, and that the company's cost structure would need to be adjusted to respond to this.

A contextualist understanding of these events would narrate how Caterpillar "responded" to financial difficulties – by seeking to cut costs, automate manufacturing systems, change factory layouts, and much else besides. According to this view, attempts to be more "competitive" would be direct responses to external shocks. Such a view is now discredited, at least among those sociologists of science and technology who reject the binary division of the macro- and the micro-level, the social and the technical. But in terms of our concern with charting the assemblage that formed around the factory, it is important that we not lose sight of these local conditions of emergence. It is through the relations formed between the local conditions and those that are distant that the assemblage begins to form – not as a hierarchically ordered entity but as a complex of relays and relations that link together events on the same horizontal plane. We argue that the concerns of Caterpillar Inc. need to be seen as one component in a multiplicity of problematizations of the factory. It is not a question of attributing priority or primacy to one or the other of such problematizations, but of charting their coemergence, the intrinsic links among them that make it possible for the difficulties of a particular firm to be understood as representative of a much wider phenomenon. For as Caterpillar began to rethink its manufacturing processes in relation to the losses of the early 1980s it not only invented new ideas and practices but in the process helped shape and give content to the broader rethinking of the factory that others were also instigating. Through such a complex of relations, the assemblage began to form.

During the 1980s Caterpillar devised a succession of programs and initiatives that sought to invent a new reality within the factory and the corporation. These programs included cost containment, competitor cost analysis, manufacturing resource planning, and the ambitious "Plant With A Future," or PWAF, program that took shape in late 1984. As the culmination of these initiatives, PWAF promised to be a "program of programs," a world-wide factory modernization program that would bring together and modify a diverse range of schemes that preceded it. These would be linked, in turn, with proposals to transform the layouts in all of Caterpillar's factories through a process of "simplification," "automation," and "integration" of manufacture. Functional arrangements of work associated with the mass production line were to be dismantled in all of Caterpillar's factories. In their place were to be put multiskilled cellular working arrangements that would be dedicated to specific products and, ideally, to products already sold to a named Caterpillar customer. In this way a concern with the product, with competitiveness, and with economic citizenship was to be created within the very design of the factory.

But let us begin by examining the calculative practice of competitor benchmarking. For it was this that enabled Japan – the principal character in all stories about international competitiveness in the 1980s – to be brought thousands of miles to a particular factory in Illinois. An equivalence (Callon 1986) was established by this calculative practice between the issue of competitiveness in general, Japan as the embodiment of the competitive threat to North American industry, and Komatsu as the immediate competitive challenge to Caterpillar Inc. Competitor benchmarking allowed senior executives at Caterpillar to make detailed comparisons between the cost structure of Caterpillar and that of one particular Japanese company – Komatsu Limited – "our principal and most challenging rival" (Miller and O'Leary 1994, 24). Hourly labor costs were singled out initially and argued to be some 76 percent more in the United States than in Japan. Senior accountants, economists, and others at Caterpillar sought to make these comparisons more detailed, through a formal exercise in competitor benchmarking. Japan, in the form of Komatsu, was to be brought to Decatur, Illinois – and indeed all of Caterpillar's U.S. factories – through a complex and intricate exercise in accounting. A detailed examination of Komatsu's products, factory locations, accounts, and manufacturing processes, made visible and calculable a claim that Komatsu and other key foreign competitors enjoyed at least a 22 percent cost advantage over Caterpillar. Thus was the issue of competitiveness instrumentalized, made real and calculable within Caterpillar. A single number designated for the corporation as a whole the minimum extent of the cost restructuring that would be required if Caterpillar was to remain globally competitive. And it was this number that was subsequently appealed to as demonstrating the need for a more fundamental rethinking of the factory.

The matter did not rest there. Competitiveness was not something that could be left at such an aggregated level. Competitor benchmarking was more than a summation of costs. It was an idea as well as a calculative technology. It entailed the notion that competitiveness should be understood as an accountability to the product as a whole, and that this should be felt by each of the individuals who helped make the product. Workers and managers should thus be made aware – at their desks, machines, and work stations – of the corresponding costs for their particular kinds of tasks at their leading-edge competitor, Komatsu. "We try to instill a person-to-person sense of competition," Caterpillar chairman Morgan observed as early as 1981, "for example, that there's a person at Komatsu who is doing the same job you are doing at Cat" (cited in Krisher 1981). New kinds of questions were to be posed about work tasks and to those who carried them out. These were to relate to the product and the customer, and were constantly to refer back to the key competitor – Komatsu. What does the customer, in buying a Caterpillar product, seek from this function that I perform? In what respects, and at what cost advantage, might the function be performed better at Komatsu? How am I to be involved in continually reducing the cost, along a trend line indicated by the Komatsu benchmark? This was the type of question that competitor benchmarking put to workers at Caterpillar.

As a calculative practice, competitor benchmarking is thus inseparable from the idea of competitiveness, just as the history of instrumental practices in the laboratory is inseparable from the history of theory (Gooding 1990; Gooding et al. 1989; Hacking 1992). Such practices, and the ideas they instrumentalized, are a crucial part of the assemblage that we are concerned with here. But there is an additional dimension to this attempt to invent a new reality at Caterpillar Inc, one that often goes unremarked in science and technology studies (Knorr-Cetina 1992). This is the attempt to produce a new kind of person, a new type of economic citizen, one whose activities might be governed in accordance with the idea of competitiveness rather than through the tired concept of cost. Hacking (1986) has addressed in general terms practices of "making up people"; but when discussing the "laboratory sciences" (Hacking 1992) this dimension is curiously absent. In contrast, and in line with Knorr-Cetina's (1992, 119) remark that scientists as well as objects are malleable, the making up of people is central to our concern here with the invention of a new reality on the shop floor. For rethinking the factory means not only addressing issues of product quality and competitiveness but also instrumentalizing these concerns by establishing intrinsic linkages and relays between the redesign of the factory floor and attempts to invent new forms of economic citizenship. Competitor benchmarking provided a way of making operable the abstract ideas and images concerning economic citizenship that were taking shape around the factory. It made it possible to intervene, to act upon the lives of workers and managers in the name of the integrity of the product and the competitiveness of the firm and the nation. The link between the worker on the shop floor and the global consumer and competitor was to be made direct and personal. The voice of the customer and the strategies of competitors were to be made calculable and to be traced to the multitude of tasks, actions, and decisions in the factory. And these in turn were to be linked up, via the corporation, to the attempt to enact a new basis of competitiveness for the nation.

But even this attempt to create a new mode of economic citizenship encountered limits, as advocates of the factory of the future were quick to point out. For although competitor benchmarking brought Japan to Decatur, Illinois, this was only via the calculations made of a particular competitor. Such calculations left the factory floor more or less unchanged. The idea of competitiveness might have been made calculable, but it had not been given physical form, it had not been embedded in the spatial arrangement of persons and machines on the factory floor. Or rather, whereas competitor benchmarking provided a device for making visible and calculable the issue of competition, one that was to become a key component of the assemblage that was beginning to form, it did not make a transformation of the factory floor itself the instrument by which competitiveness might be restored. This was to be the focus of a subsequent development, the attempt to diagram a new layout for the factory floor.

Diagraming the ideal factory

The assemblage we are charting here is an unstable and fragile complex of relations. Each of the locales in which it is formed is itself a multiplicity, traversed by tensions and peopled by diverse agents and expertises. To analyze such an assemblage is to chart the shifting ensemble of relations that forms among locales and to examine how the practices that emerge from them seek to transform the relations between individuals and their work within the factory in the name of the customer. Within Caterpillar, different bodies of expertise problematized the factory and sought to remake it in the image of the customer, competitiveness, and the product. Whereas competitor benchmarking was articulated by accountants and economists, a distinct way of problematizing the factory emerged from systems analysts, engineers, and others. These groups argued that practices such as competitor benchmarking could be made fully operable only if they were answerable to a diagram of the factory of the future that was provided by systems notions – one that would have embedded in it principles of cost competitiveness and customer responsiveness. To say that the systems experts had their way would be to oversimplify, although it does convey the point that it was in systems terms that notions of customer-driven, computer-integrated manufacturing were imprinted on the new diagram of the factory floor. In terms of the assemblage we are charting here, it is perhaps more accurate to say that two distinct, and not necessarily compatible practices – competitor benchmarking and systems diagrams of the factory floor – came to be aligned with each other and with the idea of customer-driven manufacturing. It was in the establishing of such relays between distinct practices and ideas that the assemblage began to emerge.

Systems analysts and others argued that the factory floor should be, transformed to enable the computer integration of manufacturing processes. Physical spaces should be remade so as to be isomorphic with the spaces of systems principles. The existing physical surroundings, machines, work contracts, and forms of association were seen to embody an obsolete functional arrangement of space. Moreover, these functional arrangements failed to impress the idea of the customer on the multitude of actions taken by the worker in the course of the day. But if workers could be located in manufacturing cells, and if these cells could be linked together by a synchronous flow principle of production, the idea of making a product for a particular customer might be embedded in the physical layout and operation of the factory floor. Such issues as the nature of a production cell, the arrangement of intracell activities, the layout of material flow paths, and the overall electronic plant-wide control of manufacturing processes became of central importance in this new diagram of the factory floor. The ideas of competitiveness, of the customer, and of a new economic citizenship were to be embedded in all those diagrams that set out in systems terms a new way of arranging persons and machines on the factory floor.

The practice of IDEF modeling (see U.S. Air Force 1981)[5] played an important role here, offering in systems terms a way of diagraming manufacturing activities at different levels of analysis (see figure 5.1). In its simplest form, an IDEF diagram consists of boxes (to represent activities and functions) connected by arrows (to represent links and relays). The hierarchical structure of IDEF modeling means that one can diagram and visualize the plant as a complete system, and can move down the hierarchy by disaggregating the plant into the activities and functions carried out in individual buildings and the ways in which these are linked together. In turn, buildings can be disaggregated into "bundles" (level "Y") – clusters of interrelated manufacturing activities, the linkages between which can be diagramed by arrows indicating the direction and sequence of flows. These in turn can be analyzed in terms of basic shop-floor operations conducted within cells (level "X"). This way of diagraming manufacturing plants as systems composed of interrelated modules made it possible to instrumentalize the ideal of a plant governed by the principle of rapid, synchronous-flow, computer-controlled manufacture.

The PWAF program, Caterpillar's world-wide factory modernization initiative, gave a central place to this new spatial ordering of production coming from systems thinking and coupled it with a temporal reordering of manufacturing processes. Global competitiveness was to be sought by integrating space and time in a cellular and modular manufacturing process. The long-standing "functional" arrangement of people and machines on the factory floor was to be dismantled. For this had, quite literally, blocked a view of products and critical subproducts. Instead, the individual's contribution to the overall process or product was to be made self-evident in a new diagram of the factory. What some had called a "new economic citizenship" (Dertouzos et al. 1989) was to be created in a distinct arrangement of physical spaces organized according to systems principles on the factory floor.

The diagram for the new factory at Decatur, Illinois, one of Caterpillar's key North American assembly plants, was required to

---

[5] Derived from the work of Ross and others at MIT (Ross and Brackett 1976), IDEF was elaborated during the 1970s and 1980s in a series of initiatives sponsored by the U.S. Air Force. The aim of those initiatives was to provide a way of modeling and governing certain aspects of a firm's transition to computer integrated manufacture.

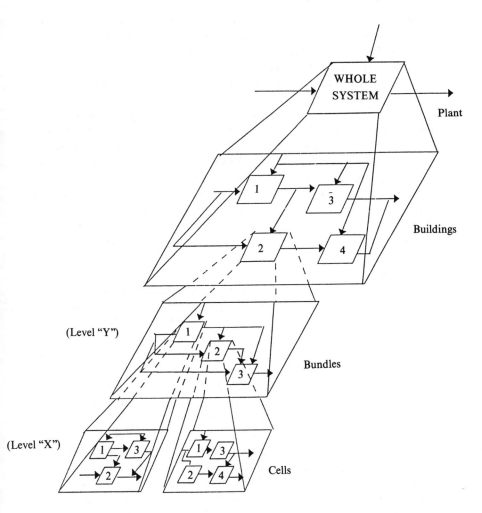

Figure 5.1. Hierarchical structure of IDEF modeling. Adapted from Ross and Brackett 1976, 40–44.

conform to a set of principles laid down by Caterpillar's head office and articulated in the PWAF program. This took the form of a number of steps that were to be followed in the modernization of any Caterpillar facility: *consolidation* (of manufacturing space); *simplification* (of product designs, manufacturing processes, and operating procedures); *automation* (of machining and materials handling processes); and finally *integration* (of engineering, logistics, and shop-floor functions into a single information system). Only facilities that could diagram their factories in terms of these basic principles would be accepted as Plants With A Future. The end point of this trajectory – computer integration – might not be realizable in the immediate future. Nonetheless, it was fundamental to the idea of cost-competitive, customer-centered production. Nothing less than a new diagram of the factory floor would make the notion of competitiveness a reality.

These concerns with the cellular reordering of manufacturing spaces, and with flows of materials and parts, were central to the Plant With A Future "vision" document circulated by Caterpillar's General Offices to the plants in February 1985. This document set out the general principles that should be built into the diagrams of the new factories. It also conveyed what was meant by the phrase "Plant With A Future." The phrase was part invitation, part injunction. For not all factories would necessarily have "a future." This was not guaranteed. It all hinged on the adequacy of the diagrams produced and the extent to which they aligned with the PWAF ideals of consolidation, simplification, automation, and integration.

The phrase "Plant With A Future" conveyed this sense of required participation. It also served to articulate an idea that was present in a similar form in the professional literature concerning advanced manufacturing systems and technologies at the time. Images and ideals of the "factory of the future" were widely prevalent, under such headings as "Factory 2000" – dreams and visions as to the nature and layout of the American production facility in the year 2000. "Plant With A Future," the phrase coined at Caterpillar's General Offices, modified these images in two significant respects: "plant" rather than "factory" signified that Caterpillar's manufacturing activities were to be understood in the widest sense; "with" a future was something to be realized by plant personnel themselves through their active participation, in contrast to the rather futuristic connotation of the phrase "factory *of* the future." Moreover, the phrase "Plant With A Future" provided an optimistic vocabulary for interpreting the plant closures and layoffs of the early 1980s, one that affirmed that "manufacturing matters" (Cohen and Zysman 1987) to Caterpillar and to the North American economy.

The new physical spaces that were diagramed in the PWAF proposals were also calculable spaces (Miller 1992). The concept of "investment bundling" made this possible. When looking at the diagram of the proposed new factory floor at Head Offices, executives were not only looking at an engineering proposal, they were also looking at a capital expenditure proposal that could be broken down into discrete physical spaces. For the PWAF program was the most ambitious investment project in Caterpillar's history. Initial forecasts were for world-wide capital spending in the region of $1 billion between 1986 and 1992. Investment bundling provided a distinctive instrument for structuring and evaluating such a massive capital spending program.

The factory floor was to be divided up into "bundles," segments, or physical areas that could be diagramed, pointed to, and when built, photographed. This "bundling" of the factory floor into areas was a densely theoretical and experimental operation, one that was conducted according to systems principles such as those of IDEF modeling discussed above (see figure 5.1). Each area, or "bundle," was to be understood according to four principles. First, it should encompass a cluster of machines and work processes with shared manufacturing processes, material handling systems, tool management systems, and computers. Second, it should be thinkable in terms of all those notions of customer-driven manufacturing – including questions of velocity of material, parts or product flow, responsiveness to customer order schedules, and quality. Third, it should be possible to identify the physical inputs of materials, parts, and components to an area or zone, as well as the outputs of subassemblies or subproducts to the next bundle. Fourth, each physical space so identified should also be a calculable space, of which one could construct a financial model. The diagram of the ideal factory was thus more than a picture of a new manufacturing regime. It was also a way of visualizing an entire new set of calculable spaces.

The path from argument to instrument and back again is long (Galison 1985, 359). In articulating the core PWAF principles, the diagram of the ideal factory gave form to all those dreams and schemes of customer-driven manufacturing. Even without building such a factory it was possible to pose questions of velocity of materials, parts, and product through a bundle; the responsiveness of processes to shifts in customer orders and demand; and the incurrence of various categories of cost. And the diagram was approved by senior Caterpillar executives in the various "concept reviews" at which proposals for the new factory were presented, assessed, revised, and reassessed. All that remained was for reality to be made to conform to the ideal, even if this entailed tailoring both so as to ensure that each might fit snugly with the other (Hacking 1992, 31).

Assembling the assembly highway

There was still further to go. Academics, consultants, and commentators of various kinds could lament the decline of the American system of manufacture and worry about the rise of Japan in the world economy. Senior corporate executives at Caterpillar and elsewhere could mandate highly general programs and diagrams of the advanced factory of the future.

But within Caterpillar's PWAF program it was to fall to managers and workers at specific plants – such as the assembly facility at Decatur, Illinois – to try to relate such diffuse and often conflicting ideas to "what it took to build machines" (Miller and O'Leary 1994, 22).

It is thus to yet another locale, and another group of disparate agents and experts, that we have to look if we are to understand the ensemble of ideas and interventions that made possible the transformation of the factory floor at a particular Illinois plant of Caterpillar Inc. For it was out of the deliberations of a small group of managers, supervisors, and workers at the Decatur plant that the notion of an Assembly Highway (see figure 5.2) was articulated as a key "enabling concept" (ibid., 33) that would seek to align the ideals of the American factory, the injunctions of the corporate PWAF program, and the task of making motor graders, wheel tractors and scrapers, and off-highway trucks. This concept made it possible both to "represent" the new reality on the shop floor as well as to "intervene" so as to make reality correspond. The Assembly Highway, it was argued, would enable the Decatur facility to be remade as a Plant With A Future. The plant space would be "consolidated" from three buildings to one – through "simplifying" flow processes, outsourcing noncore production, altering material flow paths, and investing in "automated" and "integrated" manufacturing equipment. Five traditional assembly lines, each dedicated to a particular product, were to be dismantled and replaced with a single Assembly Highway capable of accommodating the final assembly of all of Decatur's core products. The result would be a "leaner" plant with far fewer employees, managers warned. But, they added, only thus could Caterpillar constitute Plants With A Future in the United States.

As a way of seeking to make the Plant With A Future program operable, the proposal for an Assembly Highway entailed a fundamental transformation of factory space at the Decatur facility, a redefinition of work and management through cellular manufacture, and programs to stabilize production against fluctuations in market demand.

To speak of an Assembly *Highway* was to signify much of what was at stake in the novel spatial arrangement proposed for the factory floor at Decatur. Speed of manufacture, or "product velocity" as it was termed, was to be of the essence. The time needed to build a perfect, zero-defects product, from start to finish, was to be driven to its practical minimum by means of the Assembly Highway. Thereby, it was argued, the traditional focus of manufacture – the efficiency of individual functions and machine processes – would be undone. The temporal ordering of manufacture would be transformed. With this step, the cost structure of the plant, its competitiveness vis-à-vis Komatsu of Japan and other global

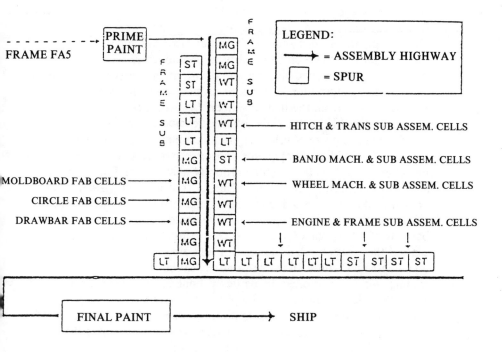

ST = small trucks, LT = large trucks, MG = motor graders, WT = wheel tractors

Figure 5.2. The Assembly Highway.
The final assembly bundle at Decatur Plant was to comprise an area of Building "B" defined by a Prime Paint booth, the Assembly Highway together with its spurs and adjacent subassembly cells, and a Final Paint booth. The "spine" of the bundle was to be formed by the Assembly Highway, along which the frames of (already sold) products were to be ferried by automated guided vehicles (AGVs). Flows of product frames along the Assembly Highway – through prime paint, in and out of the appropriate spurs for fitting of moldboards, engines, etc., and on through Final Paint – were to determine material flows and activity throughout the subassembly cells. Subassemblies were to arrive just-in-time in the appropriate spurs for fitting to the product frame. While moves along the Assembly Highway were to be fully computer-integrated, cell proprietors in each spur were to have override mechanisms to halt product moves. Investment evaluation was to embrace the synergistically linked manufacturing and logistics equipment, softwares, and hardwares needed to render the entire bundle operable and was to be assessed against the competitive cost and quality of the finished product, the altered competitive capabilities of the bundle, and Return On Investment criteria.
Source: This diagram, originally published in Miller and O'Leary 1994, is reproduced with the permission of Caterpillar Inc.

competitors, the integrity of the whole Caterpillar product, and the voice of the customer would be made real and tangible for everyone at the Decatur plant. *Product velocity*, it was argued, was the device by which the principle of "pure customer-driven" manufacture would be instantiated in the movements, actions, and decisions of everyone at the plant. Employees would no longer work to produce anonymous piles of inventory, distanced from the final customer. Instead, they would produce, as closely as possible, to the order of specific Caterpillar customers.

To maximize product velocity, the stand-alone machine for the manufacture of individual components and piece parts was to be replaced by the work cell, a U-shaped configuration of machines and people in which an entire subproduct (e.g., an engine, a transmission system, a moldboard) could be processed from start to finish. This design embodied the ideal that the output of a cell would be "sold," on a synchronous flow basis, to the "customer" in the next cell, or in a final assembly spur adjacent to the Assembly Highway. Cells and assembly spurs were to make up a dense and tightly joined network or "chain" of internal "customers," trading with one another in perfectly built subproducts (Schonberger 1990; Whiteley 1991).

But the concept of the Assembly Highway added a further crucial element to these existing dreams and schemes of the factory of the future. For the Assembly Highway linked the activities in every cell and assembly spur to the demands of an identified *external* customer. The entry of a product frame or chassis onto the Assembly Highway was thus more than the recommencement of an incessant and uniform assembly process; it meant the arrival of a product that had *already been sold*. Workers in assembly cells and spurs were to work on an individual end product. They could identify the customer from their computer screens. They could know, before the end of the day, whether 100 percent quality had been built into the product, at the first attempt, and customer satisfaction assured.

It was as though all authority was to flow directly from the customer to the work process (cf. Johnson 1992), as if authority was to be built into the architecture and spatial disposition of the Decatur plant. This dream of embedding authority relations in the physical fabric of the plant held out the hope that the "new economic citizenship" appealed to by so many commentators might be made real. A common finish paint booth installed at the end of the Assembly Highway, and through which all assembled product would have to pass, offered a way of ensuring that the gravest consequences would follow if this dream did not materialize. For if the Highway was to work at full capacity, and without bottlenecks or delays, all finished units would have to be of sufficient first-time quality to pass through the finish paint booth. "And if people don't [achieve quality assembly] every day the thing won't work," a factory superintendent remarked. "Eventually you will grind it [i.e., the entire assembly process] to a stop" (Miller and O'Leary 1994, 36).

But if the Assembly Highway was to make operable ideals of a "new economic citizenship," the newly created manufacturing spaces would have to be aligned with novel identities for plant personnel. In a plant such as that proposed for Decatur, workers should no longer be regarded as functional specialists performing stable and narrowly defined tasks. They should no longer be "assemblers," "machinists," "fabricators," or "material handlers" – terms associated with the old, functional layout of the plant. Instead they should be "proprietors" of their cells and final assembly spurs. The product rather than the function should be the primary object of attention. To ensure that this transformation would take place, labor contracts were to be revised to dismantle narrowly functional job classifications. Workers were to seek "certified supplier" status for their cells, formal corporate recognition that a cell could supply subproducts of consistently high quality. New computer systems and accounting practices were to be devised so that cells of workers could be accounted *to* rather than *for* – a transition befitting the status of "proprietor."

This was not the end of capitalism or the capitulation of bosses to demands for worker control. But it was a significant transformation of authority relations nonetheless, one that it is important to consider if we are to understand fully the creation of a new reality within the factory. For workers as "cell proprietors" were to be afforded crucial domains of discretion, albeit ones traversed by tensions and potential conflicts. They were to be delegated certain powers to pace or control the movement of products between the final assembly spurs. "Traffic lights" put in place above each assembly spur along the Highway offered cell proprietors a means of controlling the movement of products between spurs, by providing a visible signal of the on-schedule status of the product within a spur. Assemblers were entitled to continue to work on a unit even when it had run over time, in the name of product quality and integrity. Such discretion had its limits, for a disruption to the build schedule could be overruled by management. However, it reversed a key principle of the old assembly line. A space was opened up within which an alignment could be established between the ideas of product quality, economic citizenship, and cell proprietorship.

With rights go responsibilities. This applies just as much to attempts to foster a new form of economic citizenship in the factory as it does to citizenship more generally. "Cell proprietorship" was to involve an extensive set of obligations, and it was also to be linked to rewards. In the labor agreements signed between Caterpillar and the UAW (United Auto Workers) in 1986 and 1988, a further component of a "new economic citizenship" was to be set in place. Workers were to be newly accountable to the customer for the quality and global competitiveness of the Caterpillar product. As joint proprietors of their cells they were expected continually to seek ways of improving the quality of subproducts so as to outperform competition from Komatsu of Japan as well as from other competitors. To facilitate such entrepreneurship a core group of workers were to be shielded from unemployment or long-run layoff, at least within certain tolerances. Short-run cyclical swings in demand for Caterpillar products should not deter Caterpillar employees from contributing to product quality and competitiveness.

A "new economic citizenship" for employees at the Decatur plant was thus to be made operable through aligning the physical design of the Assembly Highway with a set of practices centering on "cell proprietorship," and with a stabilization of the plant work force against demand fluctuations. But contrary to Hacking's (1992) view of the laboratory, this assemblage should not be regarded as maturing in the direction of a self-reinforcing or "self-vindicating" system. Perhaps this indicates the limits of the analogy between the factory and the laboratory. Or perhaps it is more a question of saying that such a self-vindicating system is endlessly sought, even in relation to the factory, and yet endlessly eludes those who seek it. For while we share Hacking's (ibid., 30) enthusiasm for the "whole teeming world of making instruments," in the factory we see a much less stabilized or mutually adjusted relation between types of theory, types of apparatus, and types of analysis. Indeed quite the reverse. What we see in and around the factory are endless discrepancies between what is sought, the devices through which this is to be made operable, and what obtains – a perpetually failing series of programs and instruments for governing economic life. It is this *instability*, combined with a constant search for temporary stabilities, that in large part explains the process of trying to create a new reality on the factory floor in a particular North American factory in the 1980s.

By 1991, as Caterpillar engaged in contract negotiations with the UAW Union, the ideal of guaranteeing a certain level of core jobs at each Plant With A Future had already been called into question. The ensemble making up the advanced factory and giving content to the idea of a "new economic citizenship" was thus to be altered significantly. As a senior union official was to argue, the corporate emphasis had shifted from specific *Plants* With A Future to the more general issue of preserving Caterpillar's U.S. manufacturing base. And with this shift the acronym

PWAF was gradually dropped from the company's vocabulary – an indication that the assemblage we have been charting here was already undergoing further significant modification.

Conclusions

Perhaps the clearest point to emerge from the above is the importance of guarding against too narrow a view as to what counts as a laboratory. If studies of science and technology are to shed their latent epistemology, then they should address all those locales in which attempts are made to act upon and transform the world by means of diverse instruments, ideas, and calculations. The world of the factory is as much a site for creating phenomena, for "interfering under controllable and isolable conditions," as are all those seemingly more exotic locales populated by quarks, microbes, bubble chambers, electrovoltaic cells, Thyrotropin Releasing Factors and much else besides. There remains a faint whiff of scientism in the apparent reluctance of science and technology researchers to move away from some of the more cherished examples of the field. It is this that we have sought to counter in our analysis of the remaking of a factory.

But the full promise of this broadening of the sphere of science and technology studies will be realized only if the field more resolutely frees itself from its past. Affirmations that the distinction between the social and the technical is no longer viable and that the notion of interests leads nowhere have more of an eye toward the past of the discipline than toward its future. The ghost of SSK looms too large in current debates. Admittedly, much has been gained by such a rethinking of the boundaries and contents of science and technology studies. In particular, "externalist" or "contextualist" sociological concepts have been shown to be severely lacking. This has been a great benefit to the discipline of sociology more generally, even if it leaves the discipline (appropriately) bereft of a name to call itself by.

A way needs to be found to move forward, to analyze the ensemble of actors, instruments, ideas, and interventions that make up the laboratory as defined here. We have put forward the notion of an *assemblage* as a way of designating this complex of relations. Rather than following managers and others about as they came up with arguments, diagrams, systems images, and actual designs for the factory floor, we have analyzed the *assemblage* that made this possible. Rather than starting and finishing with the factory as laboratory, we have addressed the ensemble of relations and the multiplicity of locales within which the factory was problematized and in which proposals for redesigning it emerged. Only in this way, we argue, is it possible to avoid giving undue priority to either the social or the technical dimensions of change. Only in this way is it possible to give credit to the complex of relations that makes possible the invention of a new reality on the factory floor.

We have emphasized also the centrality to our example of the attempts to invent a new form of economic citizenship. Of course, the particular shape this assumed was specific to the domain in question. One would not necessarily expect to find such a project within other laboratories. But this attempt to refashion the person, to remake the individuals who populate the factory, has a wider significance. For the creation of phenomena in the laboratory may have something to do with the making up of persons in particular ways. Were it not so overused, we would invoke the word "power" to designate what is at stake here. Indeed, our preference is for the term "government" (Miller and Rose 1990; Rose and Miller 1992). But irrespective of the word used, the point remains that the attempt to instrumentalize a particular conception of the factory entailed an attempt to act upon the actions of individuals in a distinctive fashion.

Finally, a word on stability. Or rather, a call for instability. The laboratory we have studied here was not "self-vindicating" (Hacking 1992), and nor was it a stable entity. It was temporarily stabilized, but only for short periods of time and in relation to a specific set of conditions. It sought to isolate itself from the outside world. But the "outside world" kept getting in. Indeed, it was this constant "intrusion" of the "outside world" that made it possible for the factory to be remade. This suggests that we should not accord too much ontological weight to the fragile entity that is the assemblage addressed here. For this "entity" is nothing other than the complex of relations formed around and within the factory. As soon as one element in this complex of interrelated practices and locales was altered or removed, there was a possibility that the assemblage itself would be modified or transformed. As we have shown, this was the case in the final stages of our study. Whereas "customer-driven manufacturing" could mean secure jobs for a core group of U.S. workers, it could also mean something very different – exemplified in the phrase "our customers will determine where we will build our products." It is this constantly shifting nature of the assemblage charted here that is perhaps its most striking feature.

ACKNOWLEDGEMENTS

Thanks are due to two anonymous referees for comments on an earlier version of this paper. Thanks are due also to Anthony Hopwood, Andy Pickering, Mike Power, and participants at a seminar at Northwestern

University organized jointly by the Kellogg Graduate School of Management and the Department of Sociology.

REFERENCES

Abernathy, W. A., R. H. Hayes, and A. M. Kantrow. 1983. *Industrial Renaissance.* New York: Basic Books.

Business Roundtable. 1987. *American Excellence in a World Economy.* New York: The Business Roundtable.

Callon, M. 1986. "Some Elements of a Sociology of Translation: Domestication of the Scallops and the Fishermen of St. Brieuc Bay." In *Power, Action and Belief,* edited by J. Law, 196–233. London: Routledge & Kegan Paul.

Cartwright, N. 1989. *Nature's Capacities and Their Measurement.* Oxford: Clarendon Press.

Chandler, A. D. 1990. *Scale and Scope: The Dynamics of Industrial Capitalism.* Cambridge, Mass.: Belknap.

Chubb, J. E., and T. M. Moe. 1990. *Politics, Markets and America's Schools.* Washington, D.C.: Brookings Institution.

Clark, K., and T. Fujimoto. 1990. "The Power of Product Integrity." *Harvard Business Review* (November–December): 107–18.

Cohen, S. S., and J. Zysman. 1987. *Manufacturing Matters.* New York: Basic Books.

Collins, H. M. [1985] 1992. *Changing Order: Replication and Induction in Scientific Practice.* 2nd ed. Chicago: University of Chicago Press.

Congress of the United States, Committee on Commerce, Science and Transportation. 1987. *Competitive Challenge Facing U.S. Industries.* Washington, D.C.: U.S. Government Printing Office.

Dertouzos, M. L., R. K. Lester, and R. M. Solow. 1989. *Made in America: Regaining the Productive Edge.* Cambridge, Mass.: MIT Press.

Donzelot, J. 1991. "Pleasure in Work." In *The Foucault Effect: Studies in Governmentality,* edited by G. Burchell, C. Gordon, and P. Miller. Hemel Hempstead: Harvester Wheatsheaf.

Doyle, D. P., and D. T. Kearns. 1988. *Winning the Brain Race: A Bold Plan to Make Our Schools Competitive.* New York: ICS Press.

Foucault, M. 1991. "Questions of Method." In *The Foucault Effect: Studies in Governmentality,* edited by G. Burchell, C. Gordon, and P. Miller. Hemel Hempstead: Harvester Wheatsheaf.

Galbraith, J. 1989. *Balancing Acts.* New York: Basic Books.

Galison, P. 1985. "Bubble Chambers and the Experimental Workplace." In *Observation, Experiment, and Hypothesis in Modern Physical Science,* edited by P. Achinstein and O. Hannaway, 309–73. Cambridge, Mass.: MIT Press.

1987. *How Experiments End.* Chicago: University of Chicago Press.

1989. "The Trading Zone: Coordinating Action and Belief." Paper presented at the UCLA Center for Cultural History of Science and Technology Conference, "TECH-KNOW Workshops on Places of Knowledge, Their Technologies, and Economies," 2 December. University of California at Los Angeles.

Gooding, D. 1990. *Experiment and the Making of Meaning.* Dordrecht: Kluwer.

Gooding, D., T. Pinch, and S. Schaffer. 1989. *The Uses of Experiment: Studies in the Natural Sciences.* Cambridge: Cambridge University Press.

Hacking, I. 1983. *Representing and Intervening.* Cambridge: Cambridge University Press.

    1986. "Making Up People." In *Reconstructing Individualism: Autonomy, Individuality, and the Self in Western Thought,* edited by T. C. Heller, M. Sosna, and D. E. Wellbery. Stanford, Calif.: Stanford University Press.

    1992. "The Self-Vindication of the Laboratory Sciences." In Pickering 1992, 29–64.

Hayes, R. H., and W. J. Abernathy. 1980. "Managing Our Way to Economic Decline," *Harvard Business Review* (July–August): 67–77.

Hirsch, E. D. 1987. *Cultural Literacy.* New York: Vintage.

Holland, M. 1989. *When the Machine Stopped.* Boston: Harvard Business School Press.

Howell, R. A., and S. Soucy. 1988. *Factory 2000: Management Accounting's Changing Role.* Montvale, N.J.: National Association of Accountants.

Hughes, T. P. 1987. "The Evolution of Large Technological Systems." In *The Social Construction of Technological Systems: New Directions in the Sociology and History of Technology,* edited by W. E. Bijker, T. P. Hughes, and T. J. Pinch, pp. 51–82. Cambridge, Mass.: MIT Press.

Johnson, H. T. 1990. "Beyond Product Costing: A Challenge to Cost Management's Conventional Wisdom." *Journal of Cost Management* (Fall): 15–21.

    1992. *Relevance Regained: From Top-Down Control to Bottom-Up Empowerment.* New York: Free Press.

Johnson, H. T., and R. S. Kaplan. 1987. *Relevance Lost.* Boston: Harvard Business School Press.

Kaplan, R. S. 1983. "Measuring Manufacturing Performance: A New Challenge for Managerial Accounting Research." *Accounting Review,* 686–705.

Kennedy, P. 1990. "*Fin-de-Siècle* America," *New York Review of Books* (18 June):31–40.

Knorr-Cetina, K. 1992. "The Couch, the Cathedral, and the Laboratory: On the Relationship between Experiment and Laboratory in Science." In Pickering 1992, 113–68.

Krisher, B. 1981. "Komatsu on the Track of Cat." *Fortune* (20 April), 1–5.

Latour, B. 1983. "Give Me a Laboratory and I Will Raise the World." In *Science Observed: Perspectives on the Social Study of Science,* edited by K. Knorr-Cetina and M. Mulkay, 141–70. Beverly Hills: Sage.

    1987. *Science in Action.* Milton Keynes: Open University Press.

    1988. *The Pasteurization of France.* Cambridge, Mass.: Harvard University Press.

    1993. *We Have Never Been Modern.* Hemel Hempstead: Harvester Wheatsheaf.

Latour, B., and S. Woolgar. 1979. *Laboratory Life.* Beverly Hills: Sage.

Lenoir, T. 1988. "Practice, Reason, Context: The Dialogue between Theory and Experiment." *Science in Context* 2(1):3–22.

Lowenstein, L. 1988. *What's Wrong with Wall Street?* Reading, Mass.: Addison-Wesley.

Lynch, M. 1985. *Art and Artifact in Laboratory Science: A Study of Shop Work and Shop Talk in a Research Laboratory*. London: Routledge & Kegan Paul.

1991. "Laboratory Space and the Technological Complex: An Investigation of Topical Contextures." *Science in Context* 4(1):51–78.

Mackenzie, D. 1987. "Missile Accuracy: A Case Study in the Social Processes of Technological Change." In *The Social Construction of Technological Systems: New Directions in the Sociology and History of Technology*, edited by W. E. Bijker, T. P. Hughes, and T. J. Pinch, pp. 195–222. Cambridge, Mass.: MIT Press.

Miller, J. G., and T. E. Vollmann. 1985. "The Hidden Factory." *Harvard Business Review* (September–October): 142–50.

Miller, P. 1986. "Psychotherapy of Work and Unemployment." In *The Power of Psychiatry*, edited by P. Miller and N. Rose, pp. 143–76. Cambridge: Polity Press.

1992. "Accounting and Objectivity: The Invention of Calculating Selves and Calculable Spaces." In "Rethinking Objectivity II," edited by A. Megill. *Annals of Scholarship* 9(1–2):61–86.

1994. "Accounting as Social and Institutional Practice: An Introduction." In *Accounting as Social and Institutional Practice*, edited by A. G. Hopwood and P. Miller, pp. 1–39. Cambridge: Cambridge University Press.

Miller, P., and T. O'Leary. 1993. "Accounting Expertise and the Politics of the Product: Economic Citizenship and Modes of Corporate Governance." *Accounting, Organizations and Society* 18(2–3): 187–206.

1994. "Accounting, 'Economic Citizenship' and the Spatial Reordering of Manufacture." *Accounting, Organizations and Society* 19(1):15–43.

Miller, P., and N. Rose. 1990. "Governing Economic Life." *Economy and Society* 19(1) (February):1–31.

National Association of Accountants. 1986. *Cost Accounting for the 90s: The Challenge of Technological Change*. Montvale, N.J.: National Association of Accountants.

1988. *Cost Accounting for the 90s: Responding to Technological Change*. Montvale, N.J.: National Association of Accountants.

National Commission on Excellence in Education. 1983. *A Nation at Risk*. Washington, D.C.: National Commission on Excellence in Education.

Noble, D. 1984. *Forces of Production: A Social History of Industrial Automation*. New York: Alfred Knopf.

Ophir, A., and S. Shapin. 1991. "The Place of Knowledge: A Methodological Survey." *Science in Context* 4(1):3–21.

Pickering, A. 1984. *Constructing Quarks: A Sociological History of Particle Physics*. Chicago: University of Chicago Press.

ed. 1992. *Science as Practice and Culture*. Chicago: University of Chicago Press.

President's Commission on Industrial Competitiveness. 1985. *Global Competition: The New Reality*, vol. 1. Washington, D.C.: U.S. Government Printing Office.

Ross, Douglas T., and W. Brackett. 1976. "An Approach to Structured Analysis," *Computer Decisions* 8 (September):40–44.

Rose, N., and P. Miller. 1992. "Political Power beyond the State: Problematics of Government." *British Journal of Sociology* 43(2):173–205.

Schaffer, S. 1994. "Babbage's Intelligence: Calculating Engines and the Factory System." *Critical Inquiry*, 21: 203–27.

Schonberger, R. J. 1982. *Japanese Manufacturing Techniques.* New York: Free Press.

1990. *Building a Chain of Customers.* New York: Free Press.

Shapin, S., and S. Schaffer. 1985. *Leviathan and the Air-Pump: Hobbes, Boyle, and the Experimental Life.* Princeton, N.J.: Princeton University Press.

U.S. Air Force. 1981. *Integrated Computer Aided Manufacturing Architecture,* part 2, vol. 2. Wright Patterson Air Force Base, Ohio: U.S. Air Force.

Wheelwright, S. C. 1981. "Japan: Where Operations Are Really Strategic." *Harvard Business Review* (July–August):67–74.

Whiteley, R. C. 1991. *The Customer-Driven Company.* New York: Addison-Wesley.

Wise, M. N. 1988. "Mediating Machines." *Science in Context* 2(1):77–113.

6   Connecting science to the economic: accounting calculation and the visibility of research and development

Keith Robson

Introduction

The place of science and technology in modern society may seem both manifest and secure. Even those who profess to lack understanding of science and its methods can acknowledge the importance of the technical results that are present in their everyday lives. It is perhaps this taken-for-grantedness that makes "techno-science" appear as a constant and unchanging force in social life, a force that is linked to improvements in the quality of life.

While acknowledging the technical payoffs of scientific endeavor that have been achieved, certain discourses do not pronounce the status of science and technology in our societies as necessarily secure. Most prominent are those that express worries that society is insufficiently appreciative of the *value* of science, or further, that the project of modernity is threatened by the lack of attention to the scientific practices at the base of modern society (e.g., Royal Society 1985).

It is the problem of valuing and promoting science in the United Kingdom that provides the empirical focus for this paper. During the 1980s a new problematization of the value of science and technology emerged in the context of changing governmental discourses and a severe economic recession. Out of these concerns new ways of thinking about the problem of science in the U.K. economy began to address the problematical relationship between the *visibility* and *calculability* of scientific practices; accounting techniques came to be seen as one means of *connecting science* to the national economy by enhancing individual managers' *responsibility* for science and technology through economic calculation.

The structure of the paper is as follows. The next section briefly addresses the question of the varying ways in which the role of science

* The support of the ICAEW Research Board is gratefully acknowledged.

151

and technology in national contexts has been understood. It is argued that far from being practices whose values and benefits are constant, and in some senses "obvious," scientific research and technological developments have been connected, through particular discourses, to many different questions and issues. This argument is extended in the following section to focus specifically on the linkages that have been forged in the post-World War II era between national indicators of scientific endeavor and measures of national economic strength and future prosperity. To illustrate the changing relationships between scientific practices and economic calculation, the case of the development of "accounting for research and development" in the United Kingdom during the decade of the 1980s is examined. Out of a specific constellation of governmental programs and managerial discourses, the problem of promoting scientific and technological innovations in the United Kingdom was connected to the calculability of such practices and their visibility to those within and outside of the productive *enterprise*. By creating systems of individual and corporate responsibility, new forms of accounting calculation were finally cast as the means for promoting economic growth through the expansion of scientific research.

Valuing science and technology

In many of the countries of the industrialized west the degree and status of scientific research has at some time been brought into question (see Williams 1973). It seems perhaps simple to formulate such arguments in terms of the occupational interests of scientists and engineers (e.g., Finniston Report 1980), or in terms of the economic motivations of defense contractors or inventors. One might of course argue that there are those who have a clear stake in promoting an increased allocation of resources to scientific and technological practices, and therefore that such discourses merely reflect the values of the community of scientific practitioners. But this would ignore the specific contexts of such discourses and the attachment of science and technology to different social and political rationales.

While it is true that worrying about science and technology stretches back into the last century and beyond (Hobsbawm 1969; Rose and Rose 1969), the form of these worries has been shaped by a number of different problems, priorities, and rationales. The presence or absence of science and technology has been taken as a signifier of many different questions. For example, Searle (1971) explored the links between the discourse of "national efficiency," British military failures in the Boer War and the economic recession of the last quarter of the nineteenth century (ibid., chap. 2). In relation to these events a specific figuration of concerns emerged linking an apparent decline ("degeneration") in the character and mental capacities of the population with an unscientific military, educational, and productive organization at the national level. The speeches and writings of Liberal and Tory politicians, Fabian socialists, eugenicists, and journalists were constitutive of a particular pattern of discourse through which recent national failures were analyzed in terms of an attitude to science. In contrast, Wilhelmenian Germany was re-presented as an ideal of national efficiency and organization (ibid., 32). Anxieties were also expressed at the absence of scientific advice at the government level (ibid., 84–85). As Gummett (1980, 22) notes, the National Physical Laboratory, founded in 1899, was modeled on the German example.[1]

The key point here is that the character of such discourses displayed a significant break with prior discussions of science. Earlier justifications of scientific and technological endeavor emphasized their importance in terms of "high culture" (Rose and Rose 1969, 188), the legitimation of scientific quests had, previously, seemed to focus on their gentlemanly status and contribution to national "culture."

During World War II the success of key scientists such as J. B. S. Haldane, J. D. Bernal, and P. M. S. Blackett in their governmental roles provided a distinctive legitimation for scientific ventures. As Steward and Wield (1984, 196) note, for Haldane and Blackett the contribution of the scientific community to the war effort sealed the case for more national planning of science and technology. The return of the commitment to a liberal economy in the postwar era, coupled with doubts as to the radical political orientation of some of the aforementioned scientists (Gummett 1980, 29–30; Edgerton and Hughes 1989, 421), prevented the realization of this program, but a new and closer relationship between science and government was soon to emerge (see Vig 1968).

In the aftermath of World War II, and partly in connection with the program of Marshall Aid and postwar reconstruction, the formation of the Organization for European Economic Cooperation (OEEC) exemplified a new conception of science and technology as the dominant factors of successful economic production. Originally envisioned as a forum for the discussion of scientific policies and national problems of productivity, the OEEC was reconstituted in 1961 as the Organization for Economic Cooperation and Development (OECD), an association for the advancement of science and technology policies among the industrialized nations.

Whatever the success or failure of the OECD as a supposedly interna-

---

[1] This refers to the Physikalische-Technische Reichanstalt in Charlottenburg, "the State owned research and testing facilities of industrial and commercial significance" (Vig 1968, 11).

tional forum for science policy, its most lasting achievement was in the definition and promotion of *research and development* statistics. Indeed, R&D became inseparable from the rules established by the OECD for its statistical identification and collection. R&D became the measure of science and technology. As the OECD assembled cross-national statistics of R&D expenditure within member states (e.g., OECD 1965, 1968, 1975), so the constitution of R&D activity (as "pure," "applied" or "developmental") in governmental publications followed the guidelines of the OECD-sponsored "Frascati Manual"(OECD 1961). These definitions in turn influenced those of other arenas – such as, for example, accounting policy (e.g., ASC 1978), the U.K. *Annual Review of Government Funded R&D* (Cabinet Office 1986), and the costing of R&D in noncompetitive contracts with the defense department (House of Commons Defence Committee 1982).

The visibility given to science and technology by the standardization of R&D, in terms of definition and collation, facilitated the process of drawing comparisons between the commitments of individual nations to scientific research. Science and technology, principally at the national level, became a *calculable space* (Miller 1992) within which programs and policies could be focused and enacted. As Latour (1987) has emphasized, the inscribing of scientific practices translates them into "stable and combinable mobiles" capable of being aggregated, normalized, and compared. As such, the construction of R&D statistics provided a condition for the calculation of national and international norms and averages for R&D activity. For example, on the basis of the Frascati definitions, OECD and governmental reports "showed" total R&D expenditure in the United Kingdom as relatively significant when set against national gross domestic product (see table 6.1). The progress of this elementary statistic, the standard measure for national comparative purposes, was indicative of the newly perceived relationship between scientific practices and the problems of the national economy.

Given the assumption of a basic relationship that emerged between science and technology and economic growth, R&D statistics became not merely the "signifier" of scientific and technological activity but also the key indicators of future market competitiveness and long term national prosperity. Once R&D statisitics had been prepared, they could be related to other measures of economic activity to reveal new relationships and facilitate calculation. From the immediate postwar period to the late 1960s, R&D expenditure as a proportion of GDP in major industrialized countries was represented as increasing rapidly, to between 1.5 and 2.5 percent of gross domestic product. In this way R&D statistics gave a new visibility to science and technology at the level of national economies,

Table 6.1. *Trends in R&D as a percentage of GDP in selected countries*

	1963	1967	1971	1975	1979	1983	1985
Canada	1.00	1.20	1.20	1.00	1.10	1.30	1.34
France	1.60	2.29	1.90	1.80	1.80	2.05	2.20
Germany	1.40	1.70	2.10	2.10	2.40	2.45	2.50
Italy	0.60	0.70	0.90	0.90	0.80	1.00	1.20
Japan	1.30	1.30	1.60	1.70	2.10	2.50	2.80
U.K.	2.30	2.30	2.10	2.10	2.25	2.25	2.30
U.S.A.	2.90	2.90	2.60	2.30	2.35	2.65	2.90

Source: OECD (1965, 1968, 1975, 1986, 1989).

and measures of R&D in particular countries have been closely monitored for what their comparison "reveals."

R&D statistics have apparently shown that the sources of funds for R&D activities in the United Kingdom have been evenly balanced between governmental and private organizations. Another apparent national trait is that the major proportion of U.K. government-sourced R&D funds going to private business has been devoted to defense procurement (Cabinet Office 1986, chart C1, 36; cf. Williams 1973, 15–16).

The development and growth of R&D expenditure statistics provided new legitimation to a series of discourses that problematized scientific activity in the United Kingdom. The claim that national scientific expenditure is unsatisfactory is dependent on the definition of "unsatisfactory," which is itself contingent on the aims and ideals expressed through these discourses. The rationales for asserting that U.K. R&D expenditure is problematic are varied and inhabit a wide range of professional bodies, pressure groups, and state agencies.

The apparent lack of commitment to science spending has been interpreted as a symptom of an undervaluing of scientists and engineers in U.K. society. As C. P. Snow (1959) declared in his analysis of Britain's "two cultures," in the context of what he saw as the scientific revolution, science and technology were too low on the list of national priorities. A more recent statement of this view suggested that

Science and Technology play a major role in most aspects of our daily lives both at home and at work. Our industry and thus our national prosperity depend upon them. . . . Improving that understanding is not a luxury: it is a vital investment in the future well-being of our society. (Royal Society 1985)

During the 1960s the widespread belief that large numbers of British scientists were emigrating reflected emergent concerns over the status of science in the modern British economy (Gummett 1980, 41; Williams 1973, chaps. 1 and 2).[2]

Business organizations have queried national levels of R&D expenditure in terms that suggest the priorities of national education are distorted:

The question whether, if more [R&D] funds were available, there would be bright scientists to use them properly scarcely needs asking since in many fields the present shortage of funds, coupled with the expectations of greater penury to come, has dissuaded some talented youngsters from scientific careers. There must be an assurance that scientific proficiency is crucial to the United Kingdom and publicly rewarded. This must obtain right down to those teaching in junior schools to assure our future. (ICI memorandum, House of Lords 1986, part 3, p. 143)

Other accounts of the apparent U.K. R&D "crisis" have focused on problems of government. The culture and hierarchy of the British Civil Service has been said to lack interest in scientific training and expertise. The publication of the Fulton Committee Report in the late 1960s reinforced contentions that the administrative-generalist civil servant is ignorant of, and undervalues, scientific and technological activity in civil society: "Many scientists, engineers, and members of other specialist classes get neither the full responsibilities and corresponding authority, nor the opportunities they ought to have" (Fulton Committee 1968, 8).

Although there may be varying accounts of the causes of an R&D malaise (poor education; the neglectful state; unscientific culture) and conflicting evidence of its wider symptoms and effects (lack of scientific personnel – "brain drain," deterioration in terms of trade, declining market shares), statements referencing concern with the condition of R&D activity in the U.K. economy do reflect at least one common or overlapping ideal: R&D statistics are located in these discourses in such a way that they signal something more than merely a measure of scientific and technological activity. Scientific activity and R&D have been translated from a measure of techno-science into benchmarks of the health of the nation and portents for, or even determinants of (Edgerton and Hughes 1989, 420; cf. Freeman 1987), future economic prosperity: "Advances in science and technology, and the early exploitation of those advances, are essential to national success" (Cabinet Office 1987). R&D statistics, and the scientific practices to which they are presumed to refer,

---

[2] This problem of the "brain drain" was associated in particular with the program of the Labour government of 1964–70. Williams (1973, 26) argued that in the United Kingdom the brain drain concern "mounted almost to panic." The belief that the problems of the British economy were associated with the inability to translate scientific advances into new technologies (the "technology gap" – ibid., 21–34) stimulated the founding of the Ministry of Technology and a more directive science policy. At the same time, the funding given to the Research Councils was increased substantially.

assumed equivalence with competitive position, issues of national productive strength, and long-term market prospects.

The apparent need for more science, translated into problems of national competitiveness, may be familiar; but the nature and causes of the problems identified, and the strategies and solutions put forward to counter such problems, have taken different patterns in different discourses. During the 1980s conditions have contributed to an intensification of worrying about R&D. And this worrying has taken a particular form, in line with a new way of thinking about the conditions that will boost R&D activities and expenditures and thereby promote growth in the economy.

Responsibility for science and technology in the managerial society

Since 1979, Conservative governments have pursued the notion – based loosely on a particular economic analysis of the macro economy and a neoliberal political philosophy – that public expenditure had crowded out the private sector in the United Kingdom, to the detriment of the national economy – as made visible, for example, by balance of payments statistics, levels of investment, and especially inflation (Thompson 1984, 1990). Whether this analysis of the problems of the U.K. economy is true or false, expenditure cuts in the public sector were made in its name. The cutbacks in funding for research in higher education are one symptom of this program (ABRC 1987, 27; Scott 1984). Furthermore, the economic recession in the United Kingdom of the early 1980s exacerbated the decline of R&D expenditures in the private sector. Whatever the relative importance of these contingencies, the impact on R&D, as viewed through OECD and governmental statistics, appeared unambiguous. In 1986 a House of Lords Select Committee examining "civil research and development" reported that there was "now growing evidence, very considerable evidence, even on a GDP basis, as well as a per capita basis, that we are falling badly behind our competitors in R&D and in technology and especially development" (House of Lords 1986, part 2).[3]

The reduction in governmental expenditure on R&D (Cabinet Office 1986, chap. 2) was made with a very specific purpose and function. Conservative governments in the United Kingdom throughout the 1980s emphasized the need to free markets, provide the conditions for the entrepreneurial individual, and put back into the private sector those services and industries that had previously been nationalized (Thompson 1986,

---

[3] This assessment was based on the figures for 1984.

Table 6.2. Business enterprise R&D expenditure (BERD): national trends

	1985 Million $	Percentage of total	Compound real growth rates (%) 1975–85	1975–79	1979–85
U.S.A.	78,208.0	50.4	5.9	4.5	6.7
Japan	26,768.6	17.2	9.8	6.6	12.0
Germany	14,285.7	9.2	5.6	8.2	3.9
France	8,556.5	5.5	4.6	3.8	5.1
Italy	3,994.5	2.6	6.3	2.6	8.9
U.K.	9,065.9	5.8	3.3	5.0	2.1
Canada	2,729.5	1.8	9.0	7.6	10.0

Source: OECD 1989.

1990; Tomlinson 1985). The "privatization" of economic functioning was intended to apply equally to industry's provisioning for new products, technologies, and processes. The political philosophy of neoliberalism was unequivocal in apportioning the *responsibility* for funding of scientific practices. This allocation of responsibility to the "private" sector, or *enterprise*, also rested on the recognition that the most successful and innovating economies (those of Japan and [West] Germany) had had a far greater proportion of their total R&D expenditure funded by industry than had that of the United Kingdom (see table 6.2). Moreover, the relatively high rates of R&D expenditure in Germany and Japan revealed by such statistics appeared to confirm the perceived association between scientific and technological practices and national long-term strength in industrial competitiveness and production. However, the statistical information generated by such bodies as the OECD through the 1980s seemed to demonstrate that U.K. "private sector" responsibility for R&D investment was not being shouldered.

The primary thrust of governmental R&D policy was calculated to provide the circumstances within which industry would provide its own adequate level of funding for R&D activity. Some of the changes introduced by the Conservatives had been mooted before the 1979 election (Gummett 1980, 53–57); the government enacted them in a strong program of departmental committees, advisory bodies, parliamentary committees, structural reorganizations, and funding procedures (Cabinet Office 1987). A cabinet committee was formed under the chairmanship of the prime minister, Margaret Thatcher, for the assessment of science and technology policy. Each governmental department was appointed its own departmental chief scientist, and a committee of these chief scientists was created to advise the Cabinet Office. The House of Lords Select Committee on Science and Technology reported on "engineering R&D" in 1982 and "civil research and development" in 1986. The Cabinet Office's

Annual Review of Government Funded R&D was first published in 1984. And while the dominant political ideology has been neoliberal, aspects of the government's initiatives have been somewhat more *dirigiste* in an effort to spur enterprise (Edgerton and Hughes 1989, 429), particularly in the area of government-funded R&D. For example, the Advisory Body for the Research Councils (ABRC) structured the assessment procedures for funding of university research in terms of strategic, industrial, and economic importance. The LINK program has attempted to construct closer ties between university research and industrial applications. In 1987 a national Centre for Exploitation of Science and Technology (CEST) was set up, funded jointly by "the City" and industry. As Edgerton and Hughes point out (1989, 422–31), some of these policies are rather loosely coupled with the new-right, free-market philosophy.

A key feature of this program was that no significant quantities of new government funding were to go directly into R&D activity (Cabinet Office 1987); industrial managers, in accordance with the valorization of the private sector, had to be encouraged to accept their own responsibility for science and technology funding.[4] The Cabinet Office response to the 1986 House of Lords Select Committee Report argued that the "key consideration is effective management . . . Industry must take the initiative for its R&D programmes" (ibid., 1, 4).

The concept of *management* and the particular abilities and knowledges employed by management may be unclear; but again in line with certain, economic and political ideologies, in the 1980s the "manager" emerged as a key figure in the articulation of economic and national achievement (MacIntyre 1984, 26–32; Keat and Abercrombie 1990, Heelas and Morris 1992). Armed with their neutral, expert knowledges and techniques, managers had to be left to manage, as an almost sovereign "right." The Department of Trade and Industry announced in its now famous 1988 paper, *DTI – the Department for Enterprise* that the role of government was not to intervene and direct industry but to provide the conditions within which "open markets" and "enterprise" could flourish.

Yet by 1986 the foresight of management in funding and enabling R&D in their organizations began to be subject to doubt within government – in part because of the evidence of the R&D statistics. Managers

---

[4] The possibility of the government providing tax incentives was foreclosed in the Cabinet Office response to the House of Lords Select Committee, although there is some anecdotal evidence that companies supported R&D disclosure as a means of promoting such allowances. For tax allowances to be granted it would be necessary first to "reveal" R&D expenditures and then have them audited. The issue had been revived in 1986 when, in the run up to the 1987 General Election, the opposition Labour Party had declared that they would consider incentives for R&D in their next government.

had not indicated that they were fulfilling their responsibilities to this area: "The primary problem is the low level of industry's investment in R&D" (Cabinet Office 1987, 1).

Seen in these terms, direct political intervention in the functioning of private organizations offended the ideals of deregulation, free markets, and the encouragement of "entrepreneurial" initiative. There appeared to be an impasse between political concern for the relative decline in U.K. R&D activity, as revealed through government statistical returns (Cabinet Office 1984), and the rationale for creating the entrepreneurial or managerial society. One way of reconciling the two, however, was to extend the domain of economic conceptualization by promoting, within industrial organizations, new or existing modes of economic calculation for scientific practices and so encourage individual or corporate responsibility for R&D by making it visible and calculable (Hopwood 1992).

Connecting science to the economy: the role of accounting calculation

The connection forged between R&D, as the measure of science and technology, and accounting, as a form of economic calculation at the level of the organization, arose out of the attempt to reconcile science and technology with the ideals of economic growth and prosperity. Within the specific conditions of possibility that both enabled and constrained the "problem" of R&D and possible solutions, the management "tool" of accounting for R&D presented one of the interfaces between the problem of industrial management's responsibility for R&D, and science and technology.

The regulation of accounting practices in the United Kingdom was then governed by a combination of company law requirements and the accounting standards (statements of standard accounting practice – SSAPs) that were drawn up by a committee of representatives from the professional accountancy bodies, the Accounting Standards Committee (ASC). Accounting for research and development had been regulated by SSAP 13, drafted in 1977.

As an outcome of lobbying of the ASC by aerospace and defense contractors (Hope and Gray 1982), the first SSAP 13 allowed, but did not require, firms to capitalize on the balance sheet categories of "development" expenditure that met a series of stringent criteria.[5] SSAP 13 did

---

[5] The ASC had originally wanted all forms of R&D expenditure to be expensed in the profit and loss account as incurred. As this would have influenced adversely the prices paid to aerospace, electronics, and other defense-related government contractors under the regulations for the definition of capital employed governing the prices on such contracts, the ASC was the target of strong lobbying by these industries to allow some form of capitalization of R&D costs. See Hope and Gray 1982.

not require a company's annual expenditure on R&D to be revealed within company financial reports. The terms of reference of the working party responsible for revising SSAP specified consideration of R&D disclosure.[6]

By not requiring disclosure, SSAP 13 allowed firms for whom capitalization of development expenses was not an option (the majority) to pass R&D expenses through the profit and loss statement as an undisclosed element of cost of sales. In theory, and at the extreme, such firms would not necessarily need to calculate their R&D costs separately to meet the standard. Whether or not this extreme case was realized in practice, the more important issue was that under the 1977 SSAP 13, *internal* scientific and technological practices had no *external* visibility, and hence no calculability, at the level of the individual manager or organization.

Accounting calculations, and the visibility they would create, were perceived as a way of influencing managers' awareness of and responsibilities toward corporate R&D. For example, the 1986 *Report of the House of Lords Committee on Science and Technology* argued strongly for the disclosure of R&D in company accounts: "The Committee continues to believe that companies should declare their R&D expenditure in their annual reports. . . . It would bring home to *management* their shortcomings in relation to similar firms" (House of Lords 1986, part 1, para. 6.84; emphasis added).[7] The aspiration to have industrial organizations represent R&D expenditure in their annual *external* financial accounts was not directly associated with external "information," or *ex post*, effects. The House of Lords Select Committee, among others, viewed the disclosure of R&D as a mechanism for the promotion of R&D practices *within* private sector organizations in accordance with the needs of the national economy. By exposing R&D for external reporting purposes, managers would create for themselves a space for appraising their R&D activities. In accordance with the mores of the liberal economy, managers would then be free to choose their R&D strategies, by relating their current actions to industry norms and national or international averages, to calculate their firm's long-term competitive position, and to assert their role as responsible and autonomous decision makers. The calculation of R&D expenditure by management and the disclosure of R&D in company accounts were seen to supply a means of intervening in the management of research and development activities, but in a way that preserved a distance between the agencies wishing to promote R&D and the managers whose behavior they wished to guide: accounting for R&D was a mech-

---

[6] The DTI did favor R&D disclosure in its submission on the first R&D exposure draft to the ASC (Hope and Gray 1982).

[7] An earlier committee report had made the same recommendation (House of Lords 1982).

anism through which to "act at a distance" upon the issue of science and technology and its role in national economic growth (Latour 1987; Miller 1991; Miller and Rose 1990; Robson 1991,1992; Rose and Miller 1992).

Evidence of the concern with the economic visibility and calculability of science and technology is given in the oral reports submitted by the Department of Trade and Industry (DTI) and the Treasury to the House of Lords Select Committee on Science and Technology:

(MR ROITH) [DTI civil servant] The DTI is in favour of the declaration of R&D in company statements. This was a recommendation made in one of your Lordships' earlier reports.
(BARONESS WHITE) Has anything happened? Are there any movements?
(LORD GREGSON) They put a voluntary clause in the Companies Act which nobody takes any notice of.
(MR ROITH) The Committee will be aware that the Accounting Standards Committee has been considering the possibility of reporting R&D expenditure and revising their advice accordingly. It has not yet come to any conclusions. Behind the scenes the Department is encouraging the Accounting Standards Committee very strongly to introduce some proposals in this area. (House of Lords 1986, part 2, 72).

Accounting for R&D expenditure would allow the initiation of other forms of "good conduct" for management of R&D to be advanced. For example, good management of R&D also required the utilization of appropriate methods of economic calculation for R&D appraisal. Starting with the public sector, the Treasury throughout the 1980s attempted to reintroduce management to best practice in investment appraisal and policy analysis (HM Treasury 1984, 1988). Although it was felt that "the underlying principles for [science and technology] evaluation are broadly the same as those for other policy evaluation" (HM Treasury 1988, 17), this program carried over into the economic calculation of R&D with the publication in 1989 of *R&D Assessment: A Guide for Customers and Managers of Research and Development* by the Science and Technology Assessment Office of the Cabinet Office. This guide to managers outlined the main managerial techniques for monitoring and appraisal e.g., peer review, cost-benefit analysis, investment appraisal [net present value techniques], program evaluation and review technique [PERT], and rationale, objectives, appraisal, monitoring, and evaluation [ROAME]) of corporate R&D projects.

Political rationales for the disclosure of R&D were not confined, however, to the problem of management responsibility for the economic assessment of science and technology. Disclosure of R&D also presented the possibility of enhancing the long-term economic prospects of industrial firms as viewed through financial calculations of scientific and technological practices. Investors' calculations of company financial performance could be viewed as seriously incomplete if they failed to take account of the long-term nature of annual expenditures such as R&D. Paul Channon, then Secretary of State for Trade and Industry, suggested: "There is clearly with some companies a very considerable communications problem: they do not allow the City to know what their long-term aims are and what their research is for and how much they are spending and why" (ibid., 564). Here the disclosure of R&D was attached to the problem of "short termism" in the centers of investment calculation. On the one hand, undisclosed R&D expenditures would pass through the profit and loss account and thereby reduce reported earnings by an unknown amount. On the other hand, if disclosed, investment analysts could potentially allow for the reduction of earnings that is an outcome of investment in science and technology, and also reward the individual firm's potential for long-term product innovation and growth in market share. Calculations that are believed to influence share dealers behavior, such as earnings per share and price/earnings ratios, could be "corrected," with a related improvement in the market valuations placed on a company's shares.

Channon's comment laid the responsibility for the R&D problem on management, but others argued that the investment problem was centered in the "short termism" of the City's financial institutions. Managers' actions were constrained by the short-term, earnings orientation of stock market investors, portfolio managers, and analysts. The House of Lords Committee reported:

If, as many have argued, risk capital is available to British firms only on less favourable terms than those open to many of their competitors abroad, then underlining through the annual accounts the importance of R&D strength might be expected gradually to change this shortsighted view. . . . This may lead to only a gradual change in the outlook of shareholders and management; but an appreciation of the value of R&D and a more far sighted outlook must somehow be brought about. (House of Lords, 1986, part 1, para. 6.84)

Nevertheless, wherever lay the "blame" for underinvestment in R&D and to whatever the failure of the economy could be attributed, the disclosure of R&D was seen as a common solution. Those who viewed the decline of expenditure on science and technology as a management problem and those who viewed it as an investor problem could agree on the value of R&D disclosures. And the promotion of R&D disclosure enabled a form of industrial encouragement by a government concerned to avoid the ideological contradictions inherent in direct political intervention or government subsidy. The government responded to the Lords Committee on Science and Technology recommendation and accepted that "there is a need to emphasise to shareholders and managers the value of R&D. It is for companies to ensure that their bankers and major shareholders understand the advantages of investment in R&D. *The reporting of R&D expenditure in annual accounts will promote this understanding"* (Cabinet Office 1987, 6; emphasis added).

The discourses and rationales of the DTI and other state agencies therefore seemed clear. At the same time, however, there remained the requirement to enrol the support of the accounting profession, a process that was lengthy and contested. The ASC working party first met in September 1982; SSAP 13 (Revised) was issued in January 1989. The ASC working party were made aware of government views from a number of sources. Both reports of the House of Lords Select Committee on Science and Technology (House of Lords 1982, 1986) were brought to the attention of the working party through their secretariat. Views of government departments were thereby also apparently disclosed. Further, the working party met with the division of the DTI responsible for the sponsorship of the profession.[8] Government representatives from the DTI and the Head of the Governmental Accountancy Service (HOT-GAS) were also present as nonvoting observers of the ASC; and at several of the meetings where accounting for R&D was discussed, the DTI representatives spoke up in favor of disclosure. In addition, a number of ministerial statements on the public record signaled support for R&D disclosure. For example, Michael Howard, the minister for Corporate Affairs, stated that legislation would be considered to compel companies to reveal R&D expenditures (*Accountancy Age*, 24 October 1985). Other statements, however, were more in line with the argument that the government wished the ASC to deal with this disclosure issue.[9] The desire for the accounting profession to produce the necessary regulation accorded with the government's apparent non-interventionist ideology.

The chairman of the ASC argued initially that disclosure of R&D was a Companies Act problem. The DTI observers on the ASC, however, strongly supported a new standard requiring R&D disclosure. It was important that the accountancy profession be perceived as the body responsible for developing and promoting the regulation on accounting

[8] This meeting occurred subsequent to the rejection of the working party's recommendation for disclosure by the ASC (30 October 1985).

[9] A Civil Servant interviewed at the Companies Division of the DTI commented: "In common with our general sort of approach to these matters we would prefer to see the profession and the users representatives at the ASC to agree on [disclosure] and promulgate it. And we encourage that process. But if they can't agree or don't want to and don't think it should be imposed then we will have to face up to the question 'should government require it?' . . . That is a live issue at the moment."

for R&D. The Secretary of State for Trade and Industry made this clear to the House of Lords Committee:

The *voluntary disclosure* of R&D in their accounts I think is a very good idea. As I said I would prefer for it to be voluntary rather than for them to be compelled to do so by statute. No doubt there will be another Companies Bill one day. I am perfectly certain that, if there is, someone will table an amendment to that effect and, if it is carried, I am not going to cry all night, but I think it would be better if it could be done by agreement. (Paul Channon in oral evidence to House of Lords Select Committee on Science and Technology, House of Lords 1986, part 2, para. 1581; emphasis added)

The evidence of Treasury officials to the House of Lords Committee corroborates the apparent importance attached to the origination of the R&D disclosure requirement from the "knowledge experts" of the accountancy bodies:

(LORD BUTTERWORTH) Have the Treasury or the departments come up with any interesting ideas about *how industry could be persuaded to invest more in research and development?*

(MR BURGNER) [Treasury civil servant] This is a very important and, we think, difficult topic. It is one that we give quite a lot of thought to and have had discussions with the DTI.

(LORD BUTTERWORTH) I am sure you do but what are the results?

(MR BURGNER) I do not think we have, as yet, a list of results. As to the sort of thing we would like to see, we think there is a *long process of education.* The question really is what levers we can pull to speed up that process of education. The one positive idea that is under discussion at present is whether anything can and should be done to give more disclosure of R&D by companies, and I am sure you know the Accounting Standards Committee have that under discussion currently. (Ibid., 306; emphasis added)

This strategy was confirmed by other Treasury officials:

The Committee will be aware that the Accounting Standards Committee has been considering the possibility of reporting R&D expenditure and revising their advice accordingly. It has not yet come to any conclusions. Behind the scenes the Department is encouraging the Accounting Standards Committee very strongly to introduce some proposals in this area. (Oral evidence of Mr Roith, Treasury civil servant, to House of Lords Select Committee, ibid., 72)

Although it was clear that accounting expertise was being drawn upon to legitimate the disclosure of R&D, the ASC resisted the disclosure of R&D for four years; some ASC members objected to the "fashionable" demands for R&D disclosure that were put upon them. Other commentators (ASC 1988) expressed concern about the possible commercial secrecy implications or the problem of defining the relevant costs of R&D departments. But in 1987 the ASC approved a new draft standard that would demand one-line disclosure in the profit statement of companies. In January 1989 the SSAP 13 (Revised) requiring disclosure of annual R&D expenditures was published.

Conclusion

It is unlikely that the new R&D standard will produce the types of consequences that government agencies have calculated. Companies that disclose high levels of R&D expenditures could experience the "marking down" of their share valuations by financial analysts and speculators – in accordance with the effects that high levels of R&D expenditure would have on dividend returns in the short term. Further, the mere fact of expenditure on R&D says little in itself about the nature and caliber of the R&D undertaken. The U.K. accounting profession has also expressed reservations on the practicalities of apportioning organizational costs to the category of "R&D," as if such activities were wholly discrete.

Whether the desired effects are realized or not, this review portrays the central problematization of science and technology in relation to the U.K. national economy that emerged in the post-World War II era and particularly in the mid-1980s. And it is worth noting that the failure of such programs of "managing science by numbers" often become the starting point for further policies of responsibilization and calculation. Nevertheless the strategies and mechanisms for drawing science closer to the "market," recently reaffirmed by the government's White Paper *Realising our Potential* (Chancellor of the Duchy of Lancaster 1993), can be interpreted only against the backcloth of the discourses and rationales of U.K. government institutions in the 1980s. Science and technology came to be perceived as a private sector problem, and the solutions proposed aimed at the *self-regulation or responsibilization* (Foucault 1982, 1988) of managers by "revealing" and rendering calculable R&D practices at the level of the organization.

Out of the recent problematization of science and technology a multiplicity of mechanisms have emerged for connecting science to the economic. Accounting knowledges, investment techniques, and governmental statistics have gradually put in place a series of linkages for drawing together perceived problems in national scientific activity. In association with the promotion of other forms of economic calculation that would be enabled by rendering science and technology visible to internal and external agencies, accounting calculation has become a way of acting at a distance upon R&D. Chains of calculation have gradually surrounded the practices of science and technology in the attempt to make them calculable and ultimately programable. The development of "stable and combinable mobiles" representing R&D has created the space within organizations for the calculation of science and technology, and given or created a visibility to such practices within the organization. Financial institutions, productive organizations, government agencies, and other centers of calculation have, through accounting numbers, gradually become linked to the twin problems of science and the economy.

REFERENCES

Accounting Standards Committee (ASC). 1978. *Statement of Standard Accounting Practice 13: Accounting for Research and Development.* London: Accounting Standards Committee.
  1988. *Submissions to the Accounting Standards Committee on ED41: Accounting for Research and Development.* London: Accounting Standards Committee.
  1989. *Statement of Standard Accounting Practice 13 Revised: Accounting for Research and Development.* London: Accounting Standards Committee.
Advisory Board for the Research Councils (ABRC). 1987. *A Strategy for the Science Base.* London: HMSO.
Cabinet Office. 1986. *Annual Review of Government Funded R&D.* London: HMSO.
  1987. *Response of Government to House of Lords Select Committee on Science and Technology Report on Civil Research and Development.* London: HMSO.
  1989. *R&D Assessment: A Guide for Customers and Managers of Research and Development.* London: HMSO.
Chancellor of the Duchy of Lancaster. 1993. *Realising Our Potential.* Cm. 2250. London: HMSO.
Department of Trade and Industry. 1985. *Science and Technology Report 1984–85.* London: DTI.
  1988. *DTI – the Department for Enterprise.* Cm. 278. London: HMSO.
Edgerton, D., and K. Hughes. 1989. "The Poverty of Science: A Critical Analysis of Scientific and Industrial Policy under Mrs. Thatcher." *Public Administration* 419–33.
Finniston Report. 1980. *Engineering Our Future.* Department of Industry Report of the Committee of Inquiry into the Engineering Profession, Chaired by Sir Harold Montague Finniston. Cmnd. 7794. London: HMSO.
Foucault, Michel. 1979. *Discipline and Punish.* Harmondsworth: Penguin.
  1982. "The Subject and Power." In *Michel Foucault: Beyond Structuralism and Hermeneutics,* edited by Herbert Dreyfus and Paul Rabinow, pp. 208–26. Brighton: Harvester.
  1988. "The Political Technology of Individuals." In *Technologies of the Self,* edited by L. Martin, pp. 16–49. London: Tavistock.
Freeman, Christopher. 1987. *Technology Policy and Economic Performance.* London: Pinter.
Fulton Committee. 1968. *The Civil Service,* vol. 1. Cmnd. 3636. London: HMSO.
Gray, Robert. 1986. *Accounting for Research and Development.* London: ICAEW.
Gummett, Philip. 1980. *Scientists in Whitehall.* Manchester: Manchester University Press.

Heelas, P., and P. Morris. 1992. *The Values of the Enterprise Culture: The Moral Debate.* London: Routledge.

HM Treasury. 1984. *Investment Appraisal in the Public Sector: A Technical Guide for Government Departments.* London: HM Treasury.

1988. *Policy Evaluation: A Guide for Managers.* London: HMSO.

Hobsbawm, Eric. 1969. *Industry and Empire.* Harmondsworth: Penguin.

Hope, Anthony, and Robert Gray. 1982. "Power and Policy Making: Accounting for Research and Development." *Journal of Business Finance and Accounting* 83–96.

Hopwood, Anthony. 1992. "Accounting Calculation and the Shifting Sphere of the Economic." *European Accounting Review* 1 (1):125–43.

House of Lords Select Committee on Science and Technology. 1981. *Report on Science and Government* (HL [20]). London: HMSO.

1982. *Report on Engineering R&D* (HL [20]). London: HMSO.

1986. *Report on Civil Research and Development* (HL [20]). London: HMSO.

Inland Revenue and HM Treasury. 1987. *Fiscal Incentives for R&D Spending: An International Survey.* London: HMSO.

Keat, Russell, and Nicholas Abercrombie. 1990. *Enterprise Culture.* London: Routledge.

Latour, Bruno. 1987. *Science in Action.* Milton Keynes: Open University Press.

1990. "Drawing Things Together." In *Representation in Scientific Practice,* edited by Michael Lynch and Steve Woolgar, pp. 19–68. Cambridge, Mass.: MIT Press.

MacIntyre, A. 1984. *After Virtue.* Notre Dame, Ind.: University of Notre Dame Press.

Miller, Peter. 1991. "Accounting Innovation beyond the Enterprise: Problematizing Investment Decisions and Programming Economic Growth in the UK in the 1960s." *Accounting, Organizations and Society* 16:733–62.

1992. "Accounting and Objectivity: The Invention of Calculating Selves and Calculable Spaces." *Annals of Scholarship* 9:61–86.

Miller, Peter, and Nikolas Rose. 1990. "Governing Economic Life." *Economy and Society* 19 (February):1–15.

OECD. 1965. *The R&D Effort in Western Europe, North America and the Soviet Union.* Edited by C. Freeman and A. Young. Paris: OECD.

1968. *A Study of Resources Devoted to R&D in OECD Member Countries.* Paris: OECD.

1975. *Patterns of Resources Devoted to Research and Experimental Development in the OECD Area.* Paris: OECD.

1986. *OECD Science and Technology Indicators No. 2: R&D, Invention and Competitiveness.* Paris: OECD.

1989. *OECD Science and Technology Indicators No. 3: R&D, Production and Diffusion of Technology.* Paris: OECD.

Robson, Keith. 1991. "On the Arenas of Accounting Change: The Process of Translation." *Accounting, Organizations and Society* 16:547–70.

1992. "Accounting Numbers as 'Inscription': Action at a Distance and the Development of Accounting." *Accounting, Organizations and Society* 17:685–708.

Rose, Hilary, and Steven Rose. 1969. *Science and Society.* Harmondsworth: Penguin.

Rose, Nikolas, and Peter Miller. 1991. "Political Power beyond the State: Problematics of Government." *British Journal of Sociology* 43: 173–205.

Royal Society. 1985. *The Public Understanding of Science.* London: Royal Society.

Scott, P. 1984. *The Crisis of the University.* London: Croom Helm.

Searle, G. R. 1971. *The Quest for National Efficiency.* Oxford: Basil Blackwell.

Snow, C. P. 1959. *The Two Cultures and the Scientific Revolution.* Cambridge: Cambridge University Press.

Steward, F., and D. Wield. 1984. "Science, Planning and the State." In *State and Society in Contemporary Britain*, edited by G. McLellan, David Held, and Stuart Hall, pp. 176–203. Cambridge: Polity Press.

Thompson, G. 1984 "'Rolling Back' the State?" In *State and Society in Contemporary Britain*, edited by G. McLellan, David Held, and Stuart Hall, pp. 274–98. Cambridge: Polity Press.

1986. *The Conservatives' Economic Policy.* London: Croom Helm.

1990. *The Political Economy of the New Right.* London: Pinter.

Tomlinson, Jim. 1985. *British Macroeconomic Policy since 1940.* London: Croom Helm.

Vig, N. T. 1968. *Science and Technology in British Politics.* London: Allen Lane.

Williams, Roger. 1973. *European Technology.* London: Croom Helm.

7 Governing science: patents and public sector research

Brad Sherman

Introduction

Until very recently, the primary function of public sector research in the United Kingdom – that is, work carried out in universities and in state-funded research laboratories – was generally agreed to be the discovery and dissemination of knowledge and information. While continuing to function to meet these ends, there have been a number of important changes both in the way public sector research is perceived and in terms of what is expected of it. The impetus for these changes can be traced to the growing culture of public sector accountability that has developed in recent years and the general concern to "maximise the returns made when public funds are involved" (Cabinet Office 1992, 11).[1] In relation to public sector research, these changes have manifested themselves in the belief that as public resources, universities and public sector research laboratories need to justify the financial contributions that are made to them. That is, money spent on research is increasingly seen as a form of "investment" which is expected to yield a return (ibid., 3).

In a series of recent reports, press releases, and statements by experts, public sector research has been measured against these ideals and found to be wanting. At best, there is a perceived failure to capitalize on the ideas that flow from research; at worst, much of the research is said to be irrelevant or trivial. A number of reasons have been offered for this state of affairs. The fact that "the groves of academe" are separated from industry and wealth creation is said to create a number of problems (Massey et al. 1992, 22). It means, for example, that as basic research is often far removed from commercial application, it is difficult for researchers to identify or predict the potential commercial value of their

[1] I would like to thank Lionel Bently, Geoff Bowker, Steve Fuller, Alain Pottage, and Michael Power for their comments.

170

work.[2] A related problem concerns the nature and form of the knowledge that is generated within public sector laboratories. While studies suggest that industry requires highly specific knowledge to solve its problems, the results of much university research is said to be "either too general, or too fundamental and thus long-term, to be easily usable" (ibid., 73). Hand in hand with this allegation is the belief that while "genius" may exist in the university and in the public sector laboratory, researchers lack the will to reach out to the market, to commercialize their ideas.

To address these problems a number of programs for the government and management of research have recently been formulated. More specifically, seeing research as a form of investment has reinforced the growing belief that there is a need to find ways to ensure that the benefits which scientific research provides are maximized (Cabinet Office 1992, 13). This belief in turn has generated the desire to redefine and alter the nature of public sector research in the United Kingdom. As a result, we increasingly hear of the need to "enhance the value of research carried out in the public sector" (ibid., 11), to maximize the exploitation of research, to encourage innovation and enterprise, to shorten the gap between academic creation on the one hand and industrial application and commercial return on the other, to direct the balance in favor of applied as compared to basic research,[3] and to reorient research more closely to the needs of industry. Under the new program for science as set out in a recent White Paper, science not only has to provide "value for money," it also has to be realigned so as to ensure that it generates "maximum returns" and provides a means of "wealth creation" (White Paper 1993, 11).

This desire to manage research immediately runs up against a number of problems. The first concerns the question of how research centers are to be ordered, regulated, and controlled, given that they are geographically dispersed and cut across disciplines. The problems created by the fragmentation of research are heightened by the fact that there is no wish to resort to force or compulsion to achieve the desired ends. A second difficulty arises from the fact that while there is a desire to alter public sector research, to make it more meaningful in commercial and economic terms, there is also explicit recognition that "the primary purpose of [public sector] research is not financial gain" (Cabinet Office 1992, 30). Attempts to enhance the nature of research in order to make it more cost-effective run up against the problem that the "primary motivations" of

---

[2] These problems were highlighted by the failure of research laboratories in the U.K. to capitalize on research performed with government funds (e.g., hybridoma technology).

[3] The SERC set itself the goal of reducing total expenditure on basic research by 10 percent and shifting the balance between basic and applied research from 45:55 in 1991–92 to 40:60 (Dickson 1993b).

the organizations needing to be changed are "quite different" (ibid., 13). The problem is, in effect, one of how to overcome (or override) cultural differences. Perhaps more important, while there is a desire to realign both research and research practices, there is no intention to change these completely, only to redirect them to different ends. More specifically, within the programs for administering and managing public sector research, there is an aspiration to ensure that in addition to the universities continuing to provide industry with trained staff the ideals of academic freedom and "pure" research are not interfered with.[4] Underlying these concerns is a desire to preserve what is said to be the disinterested character of public sector science,[5] not least because of the possibility that it may produce unexpected results. What is needed in these circumstances is a method of government that will realign research to the objectives intended and be at the same time congruent with the ideals of academic freedom and the pursuit of basic research.

While numerous strategies, programs and techniques have been mobilized in pursuit of these objectives, this paper will focus on the increasingly important role that *patents* play in this process. It will be argued that as a specific form of technology, patents not only play a significant and growing role in facilitating the management of the scientific object, they can also be seen as a particular instance of governmentality (Foucault [1979] 1991).[6] More specifically, this paper will argue that patents have had an important impact on the culture and political economy of science. The patenting of research is changing the way researchers relate to one another; it is also altering attitudes toward research. Moreover, patents are being used as a basis from which research is measured, which in turn enables research in diverse and distinct areas to be contrasted. By providing a basis for computation and calculation that is readily translated into the language of commerce, patents facilitate the introduction of new accounting and management techniques into public sector laboratories. In this way, patents provide a

---

[4] Pure research, and the way it is meant to differ from applied research, is rarely articulated clearly. While the pure/applied research dichotomy is problematic, it plays an important role in the way the law approaches science. On the nature of "private" and "commercial" laboratories, see Latour and Woolgar 1979; Berg 1979.

[5] Although the idea of a "disinterested science" may be empirically inaccurate, it remains a central idea in the way the law perceives science. The attitude within law was summed up by Lord Camden when he said: "Glory alone is the reward of science, and those who deserve it, scorn all meaner views." Quoted in "Law of Literary Property and Patents," (1829), 446.

[6] Throughout this paper, patents are seen as a medium, a *techne*, in the process of the government of scientific practice. As such, the emphasis is placed on all aspects of patenting, from the identification of potentially patentable ideas through to their exploitation, management, and control.

mechanism by which research is, in commercial and managerial terms, made thinkable or knowable and thus offer the means by which the knowledge to govern come about. This in turn enables resources to be allocated and preexisting alliances to be altered or rearranged. In this sense patents can be seen both as a legal regime that provides limited property rights over technical information and as a sophisticated tool that can be used to regulate and manage public sector research.

The aim of this paper is to examine the role played by patents in the management of science. But this is not to suggest the existence of some mythical past in which science was free from regulation and control. While recognizing that public sector research has been and continues to be managed by a wide variety of practices and techniques, this paper concentrates on the recent introduction of new forms of regulation. It emphasizes the changes that have occurred in the way public sector research is managed, and the consequences of those changes. More specifically, the paper suggests that with the increasing use of patents as a means of governing science – a situation that *is* new – we are witnessing the growing juridification of science, the intervention of the law into an arena it hitherto largely ignored.

Patenting public sector research

For many years there was little interaction between patents and university research: the patent system had minimal impact on public sector research and public sector researchers little desire to patent their inventions. Historically patent law excluded from the scope of patent protection much of the work carried out in universities and other public sector research centers.[7] As fundamental legal doctrine teaches, "basic" or "pure" research – which is defined in law (almost tautologically) as that research which is generated within the university sector – is, along with such categories as "discoveries" and "information," explicitly excluded from the scope of patentable subject matter. Hand in hand with the idea that patents are granted only for applied research (and the pure/applied research dichotomy that this unquestionably assumes) is a particular picture of how science is organized, managed, and controlled. Based on a mixture of a legal chauvinism (which propounds that if there is no direct legal intervention, there is no regulation) and a liberal preoccupation with exchange, the law has long relied on a romantic picture of science as an unmanaged, unregulated domain.[8] While many sociologists of

---

[7] Within public sector research centers, patenting was generally seen as the antithesis of their overall aims and policies. See Noble 1977.

[8] For law – in particular, intellectual property law – public sector science has long had a special, almost sacred, status.

science and technology have rejected the ideas that public sector research operates without constraint and that it is easily distinguished from applied research, nonetheless these ideas continue to influence the way law deals with science. That is, as "real-fictions" (Hutter and Teubner 1994) these concepts significantly affect the way the law operates as a practice. While the function that these ideas serve in law is in need of examination (a task that is beyond the scope of this paper), as "legal myths" they play an important role in facilitating the regulation of research practices.

The mutual disregard of the law for public sector research and of public sector researchers for the law has over the last decade come to an end. Present attitudes in the United Kingdom toward the ownership, management, and exploitation of inventions created within the public sector are, however, in a state of flux. To understand current approaches to the patenting of research, how these attitudes are changing, and the impact these processes are having on public sector research, it is necessary to outline the changing environment within which public sector laboratories operate. The first important change is that over the last decade the United Kingdom government has pursued a policy of greater public sector accountability. This change is manifest in the fact that during the 1980s there was a marked decline in the relative level of government funding of universities. As a result, universities have been forced to look to alternative sources of income. In addition to increasing their enrollments, universities have sought to capitalize on the knowledge or, as it is now called, the information they generate. That is, in order to make up for the shortfalls in funding that have arisen, universities have begun to trade in the "products" they generate.[9]

As part of the drive toward increased public sector accountability there has also been an increase in the pressure for university research, as with most aspects of public sector life, to be rendered more "useful." One consequence of this is that in evaluating research there has been a shift away from using such criteria as the novelty or originality of the research toward an examination of its commercial relevance – or, as it was put recently, its "direct application to real problems faced by society" (Cabinet Office 1992, 33). In turn, traditional academic criteria such as the dissemination of knowledge and freedom of research have been devalued as goals. Combined with changes in the funding structure, the redefinition of the university as a public institution has led to demands for research to be placed in a position where it can best be exploited and

---

[9] As the notepaper at the London School of Economics (LSE) proudly proclaims, it was given the Queens Award for Export (of knowledge) in 1991.

traded. And one of the most obvious ways this goal can be achieved is through the use of intellectual property protection.

The second major change that has occurred in recent years relates to the way inventions created within universities are exploited. In 1981 the British Technology Group (BTG) was set up to ensure the "proper" exploitation and management of intellectual property rights generated in public sector research. To achieve this end, BTG was given the right of first refusal with regard to the products of government-funded research. The rationale behind BTG's establishment was the belief that universities lacked the expertise to protect and exploit inventions. In addition, as much research is removed from immediate commercial application, it was felt that universities were unable to identify the potential value of the intellectual property they were generating (ibid., 7).

As part of the general redefinition of the public sector that occurred over the last decade, BTG was mandatorily disbanded in 1985. With BTG deprived of its right of first refusal, universities were given the opportunity to exploit their own intellectual property rights, and many have availed themselves of this opportunity. To ensure that their charitable status would not be affected, many universities established holding companies to deal with and exploit any intellectual property rights they owned. In addition, specialist positions were created within the universities – those of the so-called industrial liaison officers, whose job it was to liaise between the university and its holding company, and to advise and educate university staff as to the nature of intellectual property rights (University Directors of Industrial Liaison 1989).[10]

The third factor that has influenced university attitudes toward patenting is an expansion in the amount of university research that is *potentially* patentable. This development can be attributed in part to changes in legal attitudes toward research. In particular, there is a growing belief in law that public sector research has recently taken on a "relevance" it hitherto lacked. Most noticeable is the perception that research, especially in such fields as biotechnology and information technology, is no longer as far removed from direct commercial application as it once was (Eisenberg 1987). What has occurred, in effect, is a shift in the boundary that distinguishes pure from applied research. A related factor is that judicial attitudes toward patents (as monopolies) have changed. In particular, courts in the United Kingdom, Europe, and America have adopted a more sympathetic approach toward the granting

---

[10] Despite the fact that many universities have altered the way they exploit patents, the Office of Science and Technology has said that only a small number of universities "appear to have satisfactory mechanisms to exploit their own [intellectual property rights]" (Cabinet Office 1992, 25).

of patents. Whereas certain products or methods of creation – such as agricultural inventions, pharmaceuticals and methods of medical treatment – were traditionally excluded from the purview of patent law, the number of areas that are said to fall outside the scope of protection has decreased markedly over the last thirty years.

While it is possible to identify changes in the environment within which decisions about patenting are made, it is not so easy to identify any clear response to these changes. The reason is that it is impossible to speak of the public sector as a unified or coherent whole. Nevertheless, it is possible to isolate two extremes within public sector research. At one end of the spectrum is the institution that has retained what could be called a more traditional approach to the patenting of research – one in which the main aim is the dissemination and production of knowledge (as compared to "information"), where "pure" research (which is defined as that which lacks any immediate practical or commercial application) and academic freedom are given pride of place over other policy goals. These policies are reflected both in the organizational structure of the university and in the way resources are allocated and decisions concerning promotion and appointment are made. In relation to the question of patenting research, the attitude of this "traditional" university is that it would not attempt to exploit the intellectual property rights it owns and certainly would not seek to have academics assign their intellectual property rights to the university. One of the best examples of this traditional approach is Cambridge University.[11] Not only does the university not seek ownership of intellectual property rights, there are also no specific provisions in employment contracts for the transfer of rights from employees to the university (*Cambridge University Reporter* 1993, 1007).

At the other end of the spectrum is the institution that takes a more

---

[11] Although Cambridge University has an explicit policy that the university should not hold patents, there is a requirement in relation to Research Council grants that individuals should approach the university's Wolfson Cambridge Industrial Unit as to the possibility of exploitation. The unit then takes over the role of ensuring that inventions are exploited. As an incentive to exploitation (and not through a belief in fairness), the university divides the royalties from the patent in the following way:

Net Income	Inventor %	Department %	University %
First £10,000	90	5	5
£10,000–£30,000	70	15	15
£30,000–£50,000	50	25	25
Over £50,000	33.3	33.3	33.3

Cambridge University Reporter 1987, 441.

proactive approach to the ownership and exploitation of research. Perhaps best typifying such institutions are Imperial College, London, and the universities of Strathclyde and Salford. For example, Imperial College seeks to retain much of the intellectual property generated within the college by its employees as well as by sponsored or collaborative research. In addition, the college now undertakes a systematic and continuous technology audit to ensure that valuable inventions are identified and then exploited, an aggressive approach to liaison with industry (that includes full costing of research overheads), and has established a holding company to provide effective technology transfer from the university (Cabinet Office 1992, 21–24).

Although it is not possible to identify any single response to the question of the ownership of research in the university sector, the vast majority of higher education institutions have moved away from the traditional approach to the patenting of research toward the idea that research is a valuable commodity that must be both protected and exploited. Researchers in the public sector in the past only occasionally patented their inventions;[12] in recent years, however, the patenting of research has become not merely accepted but seen as a necessary way of life. Similar trends are noticeable within other, non-higher education areas of public sector research.

The widespread introduction of patenting has had a number of important consequences for public sector research, one of the most important being that it has engendered certain administrative and managerial changes. To ensure that inventions are patented and properly exploited, universities are altering the methods by which research is managed. Although the nature of the changes differs among institutions, an increased dependency on patents as a source of income tends to lead to calls for better management practices. Such improvements enable public sector laboratories to protect and exploit what is increasingly seen as a major asset: the know-how and expertise embodied in their research. The methods introduced include the costing of research, the use of intellectual property audits to identify potentially patentable inventions, improved financial accountability (Cabinet Office 1992, 35), and the monitoring of progress against objectives to assess commercial potential (ibid., 17). So successful have these changes been that it was recently said that for "the

---

[12] More often than not seeking a patent was prompted by philanthropic rather than commercial motives. For example, Steenbock stated that the reason why he took out a patent on his work on irradiation was "to protect the interest of the public in the possible commercial use of these and other findings." In addition, Steenbock wanted to be able to impose ethical constraints on the potential use to be made of the product by "unscrupulous food and drug vendors" (Apple 1989, 376).

first time in UK academic institutions, the influence of management can be felt" (Baggott 1993, 19).

The growing use of patents and the technologies they facilitate and require has also led to a subtle but significant realignment in the culture and political economy of research (Mackenzie et al. 1990, 79). These changes were made clear in a recent report to arise which stated that the main benefits from the new intellectual property regime are to be found not in financial gain or in the uncovering of hidden and unexploited secrets, but rather in "second order factors such as a change in attitudes among research staff and laboratory management" (Cabinet Office 1992, 30). More specifically, patents have played an important role in promoting an "ethos of commercial exploitation" within public sector science (ibid., 9).

Many of these cultural changes can be explained by the fact that the introduction of property notions into the scientific arena destabilizes pre-existing relationships and attitudes toward the products of research. These changes not only introduce a new language into public sector laboratories,[13] they also have important consequences for the way individuals and institutions interact. The nature of these shifts is exemplified in the way researchers are coming to think of themselves and, consequently, how they relate to one another. While differences exist between institutions, it is clear that researchers increasingly see themselves, at least in certain guises, as commercial agents. For example, "academic biologists never before involved with industry have become consultants, advisors, founders, equity holders, and contractees of new biotechnological firms or new divisions of multinational corporations" (Weiner 1986, 42). One of the consequences is that researchers increasingly think of one another not only as members of an academic community but also as members of a public made up of property-owning individuals – a public whose members relate to one another as owners of commodities through the exchange of goods (Habermas 1992, 110).[14] A recent report admitted that the transition from the previous culture – which was described (somewhat romantically) as one in which data and techniques passed freely among institutions – to one in which institutions are now taking a more commercial outlook "has led to a number of disputes on ownership and revenue sharing concerning [intellectual property rights] generated at one

---

[13] A consequence of the LINK program (aimed at encouraging industry to undertake collaborative research with universities and other publicly funded bodies) was that it allowed a "common language" to be formed between academic institutions and companies (Dickson 1993a).

[14] One implication of the NIH's patent applications stemming from the human genome project is that "the human genome, the innermost essence of humanity, is just another resource for commercial exploitation" (Tom Wilkie, quoted in Kerles 1993).

institute but now a vital part of the business of another" (Cabinet Office 1992, 21).

These changes in the research culture are reflected in the fact that although the movement of molecular biology into the marketplace initially caused controversy amongst scientists, "fairly rapidly, patenting in this area became accepted as a necessary commercial safeguard" (Weiner 1986, 41). The impact of this new ethos is also apparent in the changing attitudes of such organizations as the Medical Research Council (MRC) toward the patenting of research. Claims that it was inappropriate for a research organization such as the MRC (which is publicly funded and primarily set up to pursue pure research) to patent its inventions did not stop the MRC from recently applying for patents for the partial sequences of cDNA related to the human genome they had "invented" (Cabinet Office 1992, 19). This reversal was at least partially motivated by commercial considerations. In particular, the decision to seek patent protection can be explained by the MRC's desire not to be placed in a position where it would have to pay licence fees to the U.S. National Institutes for Health (NIH) – who recently applied for patents on stretches of cDNA from the human genome (Brown 1992). Particularly interesting is the rationale given by the NIH for its decision to seek patent protection for its work relating to the human genome project – namely, that the "NIH has an obligation to ensure the public benefits from discoveries funded through tax" (Coghlan 1992). As in the United Kingdom, "benefit" was interpreted to mean return on investment.[15]

Changes in the culture of research can be seen also in the debates about the ethics of patenting. While questions about the moral and ethical nature of the patenting of research continue to appear (the latest being in relation to the ownership of the products of the human genome project and the patenting of "macrobiological organisms"), what is particularly interesting is how quickly these questions move from the realm of the moral into that of the factual. For example, it is telling that shortly after the moratorium on the commercialization of biotechnology in the United States, most of the disputes within universities tended to focus not on the nature and ethics of patenting but on the "distribution of the returns among researchers, their departments, the university and the sponsoring company" (Weiner 1986, 42). In a similar way, in recent discussions about the patenting of a genetically manipulated mouse, the

---

[15] Alan Howarth (then Britain's science minister) said that the MRC should file patents in order to protect the British position, particularly for public funded research (Charles and Coghlan 1992). Although recent reports suggest that the MRC and NIH are withdrawing their patent applications relating to the human genome, similar policies of "patent first, decide later" have been suggested for the National Health Service (National Health Service 1993, 17ff.).

main legal and scientific focus has moved from questioning the ethics of patenting to an evaluation of the risks that the invention may engender (*Onco Mouse* 1989–91; cf. Bently 1992). Add to this the fact that the letter pages of science journals now concern themselves with questions about the ownership of copyright protection for scientific papers (see "Copyright Scam" 1993), and it is difficult to suggest, as Robert Merton did, that the "scientist's claim to intellectual property is confined to that of recognition and esteem" (Merton 1973, 273).

The patenting of research also alters the alliances that exist between research centers and industry. More specifically, the fact that public sector research can be and is being patented means that we can expect to see changes in the nature of collaborative work carried out between universities and industry. In areas where there has been little contact, patenting is likely to encourage the establishment of new linkages. In areas where close links already exist between industry and science, patents open up the possibility for these relationships to be reinforced and, in certain situations, altered. While industry–public sector collaboration is usually presented as a neutral two-way exchange – "research organisations benefit from the additional revenue" while "the closer contact with the business community could also assist in the transfer of technological know-how into industry and enhance industrial innovation" (Cabinet Office 1992, 11) – it is clear that the formation of closer ties between the public sector and industry will have an impact on research and research practices. As in most situations involving the patenting of research, increased collaboration requires and facilitates managerial changes. "To attract increased income from non-Government sources, [public sector research institutes] . . . are introducing better management and financial accountability" (ibid., 35)]. More specifically, efforts have been made by the universities to introduce more sophisticated management accounting systems to enable them "to prepare more accurate estimates of the cost of research projects, including the proper assessment of overhead costs, independently audited" (National Health Service 1993, 34). Most obviously, through enhanced collaboration and increased use of the linkages provided by contracts and other legal technologies, industry will be able to exert greater control and influence over decision-making processes in the public sector (see Bornemann 1994).[16] For example, we can expect that the more "industry supports R&D, the greater will be the demand that the organization of research be structured in order to minimise risk and uncertainty" (Bell n.d, 12). While the

---

[16] Bornemann found that while there were no direct conflicts of interest among the chemical and biological research students questioned, there were delays in publication of reports.

patenting of public sector research will enable industry to exert greater influence, particularly where preexisting relationships are formalized in legal terms, this influence will not necessarily be one-way. The reason for this is that the patenting of public sector research empowers universities and provides them with greater negotiating strength, thus enabling them to wield more control over their dealings with industrial collaborators. At the same time that patent law functions to draw boundaries around information, it allows research to be treated as a form of property, or as an asset. In so doing, it enables research to become part of the commercial currency – to be mortgaged, insured, included on the balance sheet, and used as a basis on which decisions about investment can be made. Patents, then, act as a vector that enables operational links to be forged between higher education institutes and industry, and between the public and private spheres of research. When combined with the modern system of contracting, it is clear that the patent has become an important technique facilitating and reinforcing linkages between the technical, scientific, and medical domains, and the economic and commercial spheres.

Another area where we can expect to see changes in research practices resulting not only from greater collaboration but also from patenting more generally, is in the way information is recorded and divulged. Much has been written about the impact of patenting on the flow of scientific information and about the way in which it heightens the incidence, or at least the suspicion, of secrecy and fraud.[17] While many of these stories are anecdotal, occasionally they make their way into the legal arena. For example, a number of disputes have arisen from the fact that the British Home Office has attempted to use intellectual property rights to prohibit or censor the publication of research results (see e.g., *Lion Laboratories v. Evans* 1985). There is no reason why similar acts of censorship may not occur in collaborative work. Indeed one of the fears raised about collaborative work is that it may lead to the nonpublication of research results that show the industrial partner in a bad light.[18] It is also feared that in order to attract further funding or to obtain patents, researchers may falsify or exaggerate results (Broad and Wade 1982). The impact that the desire to patent may have on the way research results are described and

---

[17] See Yoxen 1985; Markle and Robin 1985; Lewin 1992; Bornemann 1994 – on the culture of secrecy among industrially funded research students; Gluck et al. 1987. This is not to suggest that research has not been influenced by secrecy in the past, only that in the past the law was not utilized in order to do so. The use of patents and secrecy is complicated by the clauses in the Patents Act that provide for Crown secrecy. For an examination of the considerable impact the military has on research, see Levidow and Robins 1989.

[18] Donald A. Hicks, then US Undersecretary for Defense, said that scientists who criticized the Strategic Defense Initiative should not receive Department of Defense funding. Quoted in Eisenberg 1988, 1376.

how this can lead to a distortion of the research agenda was made apparent in the recent dispute between the Pasteur Institute in Paris and the U.S. National Cancer Institute concerning the discovery of HIV and related diagnostic test kits.

A further restriction on the way information is disclosed arises from the requirement that for an invention to be patentable, it must be "new" (Section 1(3) *Patents Act* 1977). This means that an invention cannot be disclosed anywhere in the world prior to a patent application being lodged at a relevant patent office. In a recent study on intellectual property in public sector research laboratories, the risk of losing innovations through prior disclosure was seen as one of the most important issues that needed addressing (Cabinet Office 1992, 15). To resolve this problem, in addition to imposing contractual limits on researchers and introducing intellectual property audits that identify potentially patentable inventions, it has been suggested that managerial arrangements concerning the release of information within laboratories should also be altered. The strictures imposed on the flow of information by the novelty requirement are exacerbated by the fact that in collaborative and sponsored research the industrial sponsor may, to ensure a competitive advantage, wish to restrict the publication of research results. Some indication of the potential impact of this factor on the timing and nature of disclosure is the University Directors of Industrial Liaison's recommendation that restrictions on academic publication should rarely exceed one year and should only in exceptional cases extend beyond five years (University Directors of Industrial Liaison 1988, 3). Another indicator of the impact that patenting may have on the way research is disclosed is that in studies conducted in the United States, the areas where restrictions on information were greatest, such as genetic engineering and molecular biology – were the fields with the highest levels of industry–university collaboration.[19]

To suggest, as did the Office of Science and Technology (Cabinet Office 1992, 7–8), that patenting will have no impact on university research is to ignore the changes that have occurred in the way research is managed, recorded, and released. In addition, we can expect the *forum* where academics first read or disclose information to move from such traditional sites as journals and conferences to the patent specification.[20] Furthermore, since information embodied in a patent takes on a different

---

[19] "Biotechnology faculty with industrial support were four times as likely as their colleagues to report trade secrets resulting from their research and five times as likely to withhold research results from publication" (Weil 1988, 21).

[20] There is no reason why, after the patent has been published, this information should not be disclosed using traditional methods.

shape than when it is written up as a research paper, it is likely that the *form* this information takes will change. This is because patent claims are written for a different audience with a different aim in mind: the aim of a patent is not to present a thesis or argue a particular case but to set out and demarcate a property claim.[21]

One of the most important changes brought about by the increased patenting of public sector research is that it creates a basis from which research can be quantified and calculated. It is to this issue that we now turn.

Calibrating research

A characteristic of many programs of administration and management is that they lay claim to knowledge of the problems addressed (Rose and Miller 1992). Although they play only a minor role in the initial problematization of research, patents provide an important means by which research is made thinkable and knowable – and thus susceptible to the disciplined analysis of thought.

For many years public sector research was evaluated and measured by reputation (peer review) and by quantity and quality of publication. In recent years, however, the way research is evaluated has changed. In particular, we have witnessed the introduction of patents as a method of evaluating the output of researchers and research institutes. Instead of being judged solely in terms of its originality, novelty, or quality, research is now also judged in terms of the number of patents it generates. That is, patents are increasingly being used, both in themselves and in terms of the revenue they produce, as markers and indicators of research performance. While many other techniques have been employed to this end, what is special about patents as a means of calibration is that they are so readily accepted as a stable unit of commercial evaluation.[22]

Patents are being used to calibrate research in a wide variety of areas. In addition to patent data being used as a measure of the output of government-funded research and development (Cabinet Office 1993a; 1993b, 1003–7) and of inventive activity more generally (Cooper 1991; Schmookler 1966),[23] patents have been used as an indicator of growth in

---

[21] Frequently, the patent claim will not contain the know-how involved in or the background information to the invention.

[22] This is despite the many problems that exist in this process. The role of the accountant as expert is particularly important here.

[23] The position and relative merit of large corporations are also measured, via a league table for numbers of patents filed: "Canon was top with 1115 patents, while Toshiba, Mitsubishi and Hitachi pushed the top U.S. company, General Electric, into fifth place with 943 patents" ("Patent Power" 1992).

the hybridoma area (Mackenzie et al. 1988) and as a basis from which science parks are evaluated and compared (Massey et al. 1992, 47–48). Perhaps one of the most interesting examples of the use of patents to measure research was the recent University Funding Council (UFC) research selectivity exercise.[24] Among the factors the panel of experts considered when evaluating individual performance was the number of patents that had been generated as a result of research (UFC 1992, 39–40).[25] The figures produced, which incorporated the numbers of patents granted to individuals and departments, were converted into numerical ratings that were then used to contrast universities as well as departments within universities (UFC 1992a, 1992b). Such ratings enable research carried out in the United Kingdom to be contrasted with that undertaken in other countries and also enable it to be measured against other indicators (such as its contribution to GDP).

A number of consequences flow from the use of patents as a basis for calculating research performance. One of the most important is that insofar as patents replace publication as a means of computation and evaluation, the fulcrum of evaluation is shifted. While the calculative technologies that use the patent as a common denominator appear to operate with the neutrality and objectivity of expertise, rather than the arbitrary excess of authority, calibration is not a neutral process but one that pushes in particular directions the way in which research is judged. More specifically, the use of patents to assess research moves the center of attention away from basic research toward more applied or strategic work. The reason is that patents are granted only for inventions that are "industrially applicable." Moreover, the 1977 U.K. Patents Act specifies that certain categories of research are not patentable. In particular, patents are not granted for "discoveries" or "information," nor for "computer programs" or "algorithms." Given the favoritism inherent in the patent system, to focus on patents as a way of calibrating and evaluating research means that applied research (as defined in law) is prioritized. This helps move research away from those areas of science, such as astronomy and particle physics, that are said to be pursued primarily for "cultural" reasons (Dickson 1993a),[26] and toward areas of applied or strategic research, such as biotechnology and computer science.[27]

---

[24] This exercise was designed to measure and evaluate the research output of academic staff and individual departments in universities in the United Kingdom.

[25] Bizarrely (and suggesting American roots) the UFC exercise also extended to include "copyrights" that academics had created over the period in question.

[26] That research is pursued for "cultural" reasons exemplifies the belief in a realm of unregulated free science.

[27] The UFC exercise distinguished between basic/strategic research in relation to the physical sciences, computer science, and metallurgy and minerals (UFC 1992b, 4). Shifting the fulcrum of research enables more emphasis to be given to research that "pays."

Another important change that accompanies the patenting of research and the use of patents to quantify research is that it leads to an increase in the practices of notation, inscription, and recording.[28] These include the following: the UFC research selectivity exercise, in which individuals had to list the number of patents they had applied for (which were then computed by heads of departments); the practice of researchers having to report to industrial collaborators on their work; the drafting of the patent claim and specification; and the demands made on industrial liaison officers to list the number of patents generated within the university. These processes of transforming events and phenomena into information act as an important means of governance, because "making people write things down, and the nature of the things people are made to write down, is itself a kind of government of them, urging them to think about and note certain aspects of their activities according to certain norms" (Rose and Miller 1992, 200; Latour 1987).

The control exercised over research by the inscription process is likely to increase with continued expansion in the patenting of public sector research. Moreover, to be able to show that another researcher's patent has not been infringed, to avoid expensive, time-consuming litigation or, as patent law demands, to prove that an invention is novel and non-obvious, researchers may be asked to make detailed notes about their discoveries and work methods (always with a mind to the legality of their activities). As well as demanding that researchers follow an agreed procedure for periodically reporting their results to other participants (Cooper Report 1989, 21), collaborative agreements may specify that researchers take responsibility for identifying patentable inventions. These demands will encourage researchers to represent their laboratory activities in an ordered and logical manner – and thus reinforce what has been called the Janus-faced view of science (Latour 1987). Isolating an individual (or a group of individuals) to be named as inventor(s) reinforces the individualization of the research process and constitutes the inventor as creator of the product, rather than as author of the work (Foucault 1979).

As we saw earlier, in the process of allowing research to be presented as a bounded, stable object, patent law enables it to be translated into a unit of valuation and thus for it to become part of the commercial currency. Research thus achieves a certain level of fixity, standardization, and precision, providing a basis or denominator that reveals the "true" costs and benefits of scientific practice – a process that plays a central role in the will to knowledge and the desire to manage research and scientific

---

[28] Academic gossip and conversation are increasingly concerned with these and related issues.

practices more generally. Through standardization of research, patents make it possible for management accountants to translate research into a language that is meaningful to them. In so doing, patents help expose research to such managerial practices as auditing, costing, and budgeting. This in turn plays an important role in the transforming of public sector research laboratories into cost centers and business units – in short, into financially calculable spaces (Miller 1992).

That patents enable research to be calibrated in this particular way has a number of important consequences. One of the most important is that because patents provide a point of reference, a common currency, they make it possible for relationships to be established between individuals, organizations, and practices that would otherwise appear fragmented, autonomous, and noncomparable. In short, they render the incalculable calculable.[29] For example, they enable research in hybridoma technology in one laboratory to be evaluated against work on expert systems in another laboratory; they allow money spent on research and development in chemical engineering to be compared with that spent on developing medical diagnostic test kits.

The single figure, that is, the output of the individual or department measured in terms of patents granted and revenue received from intellectual property rights, and the development of calculable spaces not only provide a reference point from which research can be compared and contrasted, they also enable research to be governed, monitored, and reviewed. Of particular interest is the fact that the production of the single figure and the construction of calculable spaces makes it possible for the laboratory or department to be represented financially. That these numbers often tell us very little or are open to various interpretations is of little relevance. What is important is that patents facilitate a form of "action at a distance" (Latour 1987). Moreover, by appeal to the "objectivity" and expertise of the patent system, rather than by direct control of scientific research, these practices ensure that performances can be measured, standards set, and resources allocated within and among institutions.

The role played by patents and the technologies surrounding them in the management of research can be seen, for example, in Switzerland, where the number of patents granted to research centers and the amount of research needed to obtain a patent are used by the Swiss government to grade performance, allocate expenditure in the federal budget, and determine funding (Klaffke 1993). Similar criteria are being applied by research councils in the United Kingdom in the allocation of resources.

---

[29] Where they differ from other means of calibrating research is in being so readily accepted as a means of commercial currency.

For example, in distributing resources, central funding bodies in the United Kingdom were urged to place less emphasis on "traditional academic criteria" and more on the applied aspects of research – such as the possibility of it generating patents (Cabinet Office 1992, 10).

Patents are used as the basis on which resources are allocated not only among research centers but also within individual institutions. For example, at Strathclyde University, where a research review group evaluates research proposals, an important factor taken into account is the possibility that a particular research project will generate marketable technology protected by intellectual property rights (ibid., 24). Similarly, within institutions such as the MRC increasing amounts of time and money are being allocated to the task of identifying and managing intellectual property rights.

The measurement of research performance in terms of the numbers of patents generated also enables individual researchers to be treated as knowledge-objects, offering a new possibility for individuals to be assessed, managed, and supervised. Calculations can thus be made from a central point in an attempt to assess an individual's performance in relation to specified standards (Miller 1992, 65). Unsurprisingly, the standards favored are those that tie in most closely with the general programs for the management of science that have been adopted: "Rewards and incentives offered to scientific staff might take greater account of success in exploiting intellectual property" (ibid., 10). More specifically, "In staff appraisal, performance assessment and promotion reviews, research organizations might usefully place greater emphasis on patents filed and licence/royalty revenue earned rather than concentrate exclusively on numbers of papers published and standing in the academic community" (ibid., 32). Particularly noteworthy is the role that patents play not only in providing the basis for calculation, but also in setting the standards by which performances are assessed and resources allocated.

While the process of acting upon science in this absent, indirect fashion functions to constrain research in a subtle and powerful way, it does so in a manner that *appears* both to leave the autonomy of the individual intact and to provide a space in which freedom and discretion can be exercised. That is, while researchers are transformed into calculating individuals, they appear to have both the freedom and the responsibility to allocate resources as they "wish." To suggest that these practices leave (or create) a space in which individuals operate freely is to suggest not so much the absence of control as the exercise of a particular form of power. As Peter Miller has pointed out, freedom, responsibility, and discretion involve not so much the absence of government as the exercise of a particular form of it (Miller 1992, 79). This liberal mechanism of government reinforces the idea of a realm of pure science, free from constraint. More important, while it seeks to guide and encourage individuals, it at the same time renders direct control and supervision unnecessary. One reason for this is that in addition to facilitating a number of changes in the research environment, patents and the practices that surround them also operate on the researcher as *subject*. For example, patents not only serve as a mechanism enabling researchers to be acted upon, they also act as a means of ensuring that individuals come to act upon themselves.[30] As the researchers come to be enmeshed in networks of calculation, both as knowledge-objects and as active participants (as occurs with the patent royalty scheme now operating in most universities), they become both the object of highly differentiated numbers of calculation and a potential relay for them, a point of intersection of different forces. Individuals can thus be encouraged or required to evaluate their own performance and that of others through a particular set of guidelines (Cabinet Office 1992, 67). The reason for this is that the disciplinary processes that operate on researchers in this context promote and encourage a particular form of self-responsibility (Hacking 1986). In particular, these processes encourage researchers to incorporate the commercial ethos within their horizons of interpretation, to take into account certain criteria while ignoring others. The silent, non-physical control that these processes promote – reinforcing both the changes in the research culture and the use of patents to measure research output – acts as a powerful tool in the management of scientific research.

Conclusions

This paper has argued that patents play an important and growing role in the management of research, and that they facilitate the introduction of particular regimes of regulation and control. This is not to suggest, however, that research was not regulated in the past, that all research will eventually be patented, that calculation is the prime operator within the laboratory, that all laboratories or research centers are affected in equal ways, or that patents are the sole basis on which calculation proceeds. Nor is it to suggest that these programs will necessarily achieve the desired results. Indeed, there is every possibility that they may turn out

---

[30] Another situation where this can be seen is in terms of the ownership of patents generated with public sector laboratories. Given that under the Patent Act all inventions created by an employee are owned by the employer, it is likely that the status of researchers will need to be clarified. For example it was recently said that in order to ascertain ownership of intellectual property generated within the NHS it will be necessary for NHS hospitals to define exactly who the employer is – and, in so doing who is the employee (National Health Service 1993, 19ff.).

to be contradictory and counterproductive, that they may clash with other programs of government, that the programs of regulation may – as occurred with patents themselves – be put to new and unintended uses,[31] or that they may simply fail.[32]

What this paper does suggest, however, is that such regimes play an increasingly important role in the management of scientific practices. While the patenting of research in the public sector is relatively new and its ultimate impact remains uncertain, a number of factors suggest that if it does take hold, it will become a powerful technique in the management of science. One particularly important reason for this can be traced to the self-fulfilling nature of patents as a means of managing research. In other words, many of the changes engendered by patenting not only reinforce the patent process but also frequently necessitate further managerial changes. The use made of patents within the management process and the related shifts in the culture of research reaffirm both the idea of patenting of research and the use of patents as a basis from which research practices are calibrated and evaluated. Moreover, this process facilitates, even requires, greater managerial intervention. The self-fulfilling nature of patents as a management tool can be seen, for example, in the controls imposed on the release of information generated as a result of patenting. This affects the way academics relate to one another as well as the way in which information is disclosed. As research becomes more secretive, the possibility for peer review to be used as a basis from which research is assessed or evaluated diminishes. As a result, the need for reliance on other methods of review, such as that provided by patents, is increased.

The impact that patenting has on research is enhanced and reinforced by an additional range of factors. One is the increased use of training and education schemes, which are proliferating in this area. Scientists and engineers are increasingly being taught the basics of intellectual property law as a part of their university education (Cabinet Office 1992, 10). Concurrently research councils are introducing training programs or "business awareness schemes" that aim to help academic scientists understand how their discoveries can be commercialized and exploited (Dickson 1993a).[33] Reinforcing the impact of patents on science is the

---

[31] For example, the patenting of research has raised the profile of certain aspects of public sector research and in so doing seems to have increased the debate as to the public accountability of scientific practices.

[32] One of the problems identified in the assessment of the 1992 UFC research selectivity exercise was that near-market or applied research was often not put forward for evaluation because the output was confidential (UFC 1993, 8).

[33] One of the conditions under which higher-education institutes were permitted to exploit their own inventions was that they made "the guidance and arrangements [in relation to intellectual property rights] known to staff and students. The aim of the programmes of

increased use of intellectual property or technology audits (DTI, 1992a). For example, the stated aim of a pilot audit conducted at Oxford Polytechnic School of Biological and Molecular Sciences was to identify intellectual property rights (three potentially patentable ideas were noted). The audit also provided staff with new insights into their work and priorities, identified potential links with industry (such as the department's electron microscope unit and the low temperature sample preparation equipment) and highlighted the use made of laboratory resources (Bell et al. 1992). In addition to constantly reminding researchers of the importance of intellectual property rights, the audit emphasized the need for individuals to justify the use made of rooms, equipment, and laboratory time – as well as reinforcing the belief that they operate in a calculative environment. As yet only forty institutions have adopted the Department of Trade and Industry DTI "Support for Technology Audit" scheme; but given the possibility that the intellectual property audit may be made a condition both of collaborative or sponsored work and of government-funded research, its importance is likely to increase (DTI 1992b). The changes introduced as a consequence of the patenting of research are also reinforced by other factors. These include structural changes such as the development of science parks (which are intended to merge academic research with the private sector) and increased reliance on short-term contracts (which make long-term planning more difficult).[34]

While the precise degree to which patenting will have an impact on public sector research is still uncertain, it is clear that increases in patenting, and the techniques and changes that accompany it, are having an effect on the public image of science. As one commentator noted recently, "Scientists are making an uncomfortable transition from their former role as knights in shining armour to a new public image as commercial mercenaries" (Macilwain, 1993). Ironically, while patents are being used to transform scientific practices, the resulting changes are themselves having an impact on the way science is viewed in law. For example, in response to the question as to the ownership of a genetically manipulated cell, an American court declared that the "links being estab-

education and training of scientists is to provide the right climate of encouragement and to ensure that well-informed management take appropriate and immediate decisions" (Cabinet Office 1992, 29). The SERC has recently run a pilot scheme for younger academic staff, "Exploiting Research – Routes for Academic Research," with the aim of promoting the exploitation of resources and ideas. The SERC also plans to produce an introductory guide to intellectual property rights.

[34] It is also reinforced by the growing use of interdisciplinary group research, apparently better suited to resolving practical problems (see Noble 1977). These spatial changes help to achieve the aim of building intellectual property rights into the overall objectives and structures of higher education institutes (Cabinet Office 1992, 31).

lished between academics and industry to profitize biological specimens are a subject of great concern" (*Moore v. Regents of the University of California* 1988a, 509). While science has long been revered in law, with the growing commercialization of science there has been, to borrow the words of the same American court, "a commingling of the sacred and the profane" (*Moore v. Regents of the University of California* 1988b, 164). This suggests that the aura that has long surrounded science in law may, at least in certain senses, be fading. The growth of intellectual property rights in public sector research may also force the law to reexamine the romantic image it has long held of public sector research (such as the idea of a pure science that is free from constraint). Moreover, the "commingling" of the roles of the researcher – as academic and entrepreneur – undermines the faith placed by the law in the expertise of science. For example, at a hearing to discuss the safety aspects of recombinant-DNA technology, the testimony of the head of the laboratory was dismissed with the comment: "You're more than a scientist now. You are a businessman" (Weiner 1986, 43). To the extent that the commercialization of science creates conflicts of interest, be they actual or imagined, it erodes the public trust in science (Durant 1992, 13). Any further deterioration is likely to augment the demands currently being made for the public funding of science to be justified. It will reinforce the dependency of science on patenting and on the regimes that surround it, which in turn will enlarge the role played by patents in the management and transformation of public sector research.[35]

REFERENCES

Apple, Rima D. 1989. "Patenting University Research: Harry Steenbock and the Wisconsin Alumni Research Foundation." *ISIS* 80:375–94.
Baggott, Jim. 1993. "Quantum Leap for the Market Formula." *THES* 21 (May): 18–19.
Bell, Elizabeth. n.d. "Some Current Issues in Technology Transfer and Academic Industry Relations — A Review Paper." Unpublished manuscript.
Bell, Elizabeth, David R. Kingham, and Anne Powell. 1992. "Technology Audit: Methodology and Case Example." Paper presented at Technology Transfer and Implementation Conference, 6–8 July.
Benn, Stanley, and Richard Peters. 1959. *Social Principles and the Democratic State.* London: Allen & Unwin.

[35] Recognizing the role played by patents in governing science also has important consequences for the way we think of patent law and the functions it performs. More specifically, acknowledging the positive role that patents play in shaping research makes it even more difficult to argue, as so many do, that the patent system is a value-free, neutral area of the law and that political, ethical, and social questions are thus beyond its remit or concern.

Bently, Lionel. 1992. "Imitations and Immorality: The Onco Mouse Decision." *Kings College Law Journal* 3:145.

Berg, Maxine, ed. 1979. *Technology and Toil in Nineteenth Century Britain.* London: CSE Books.

Bok, Derek. 1982. *Beyond the Ivory Tower.* Cambridge, Mass.: Harvard University Press.

Bornemann, Stephen. 1994. "The Research Student and Coping with Confidentiality: A Pilot Survey." Paper presented at "The Role of IPR in the Innovation Environment: An Evaluation of Socio-Economic and Legal Issues." 23–24 March 1994.

Broad, William, and Nicholas Wade. 1982. *Betrayers of the Truth.* Oxford: Oxford University Press.

Brown, Phyllida. 1992. "Call for 'Treaty' on Human Gene Patents." *New Scientist,* 9 (May): 5.

Cabinet Office. 1992. *Intellectual Property in the Public Sector Research Base.* London: HMSO.

1993a. *Annual Review of UK Research and Development.* London: HMSO.

1993b. "Report of the General Board of the Wolfson Cambridge Industrial Unit."

Cambridge University Reporter. 1987.

Cambrosio, Alberto, and Peter Keating. 1988. "The Commercial Application of a Scientific Discovery: The Case of the Hybridoma Technique." *Research Policy* 17:155.

Charles, Dan, and Andy Coghlan. 1992. "Ministers Move to Limit Genome Patents." *New Scientist,* 14 March, p. 9.

Coghlan, Andy. 1992. "US Gene Plan Makes a Mockery of Patents." *New Scientist,* 22 February, p. 10.

Cooper, Carolyn C. 1991. "Making Inventions Patent." *Technology and Culture,* pp. 837–45.

Cooper Report. 1989. *Intellectual Property Rights in Collaborative R & D Ventures with Higher Education Institutes.* DTI paper.

"Copyright Scam." 1993. *Nature,* 8 April, p. 489.

Dickson, David. 1993a. "Britain Rediscovers Industry-Academia LINKs." *Nature,* 22 April, p. 687.

1993b. "SERC Broadens Its Role in Support of Industry." *Nature,* 1 April, p. 386.

DTI. 1992a. *Auditing Research in Higher Education Institutions: A Guide to Best Practice.* London: DTI.

1992b. *Innovation: Support for Technology Audit.* London: DTI.

Durrant, John. 1992. "Introduction." In *Biotechnology in Public: A Review of Recent Research,* edited by John Durant, 13. London: Science Museum.

Eisenberg, Rebecca S. 1987. "Proprietary Rights and the Norms of Science in Biotechnology Research." *Yale Law Journal* 97(2):177–231.

1988. "Academic Freedom and Academic Values in Sponsored Research." *Texas Law Review* 67:1363–404.

Foucault, Michel. 1979. "What Is an Author.?" In *Textual Strategies,* edited by J. Harari, 141. Ithaca, N.Y.: Cornell University Press.

[1979] 1991. "On Governmentality." In *The Foucault Effect: Studies in Governmentality*, edited by Graham Burchell, Colin Gordon, and Peter Miller. New York: Harvester/Wheatsheaf. Originally published in *Ideology and Consciousness* 6:5–22.

Gluck, M. E., D. Blumenthal, and M. A. Stoto. 1987. "University-Industry Relationships in the Life-Sciences: Implications for Students and Post-Doctoral Fellows." *Research Policy* 16:327–36.

Habermas, Jürgen. 1992. *The Structural Transformation of the Public Sphere.* Translated by T. Burger. Cambridge: Polity Press.

Hacking, Ian. 1986. "Making Up People." In *Reconstructing Individualism*, edited by T. C. Heller. Stanford, Calif.: Stanford University Press.

Hutter, Michael, and Gunther Teubner. 1994. "The Fat Plunder of Society: *Homo iuridicus* and *homo oeconomicus* as Communication-Sustaining Fictions." Unpublished paper. London School of Economics.

Kevles, Daniel J. 1993. "Flavr [sic] of the Month." *London Review of Books*, 15 August, pp. 16, 21.

Kenney M. 1986. *Biotechnology: The University-Industrial Complex.* New Haven, Conn.: Yale University Press.

Klaffke, Oliver. 1993. "Swiss Do Well on Patents but Demand Results." *Nature*, 25 March, p. 281.

Kloppenburg, Jack. 1988. *First the Seed.* Cambridge: Cambridge University Press.

Latour, Bruno. 1987. "Visualisation and Cognition: Thinking with Eyes and Hands." *Knowledge and Society: Studies in the Sociology of Culture, Past and Present* 6:1–40.

Latour, Bruno, and Steve Woolgar. 1979. *Laboratory Life: The Social Construction of Scientific Facts.* London: Sage.

"Law of Literary Property and Patents." 1829. *Westminster Review* 10:444–48.

Levidow, Les, and Kevin Robins. 1989. *Cyborg Worlds: The Military Information Society.* London: Free Association Books.

Lewin, Roger. 1992. "Pressure to Publish Leads to Increase in Fraud." *New Scientist*, 4 April, p. 7.

Lion Laboratories v. Evans. 1985. Queens Bench 526, Court of Appeal.

Macilwain, Colin. 1993. "OTA Panel Opens Inquiry into Patenting of Genes." *Nature*, 1 April, p. 386.

Mackenzie, Michael, Alberto Cambrosio, and Peter Keating. 1988. "The Commercial Application of a Scientific Discovery: The Case of the Hybridoma Technique." *Research Policy* 17:155–70.

Mackenzie, Michael, Peter Keating, and Alberto Cambrosio. 1990. "Patents and Free Scientific Information in Biotechnology: Making Monoclonal Antibodies Proprietary." *Science, Technology and Human Values* 15:65–83.

Markle, Gerald E., and Stanley S. Robin. 1985. "Biotechnology and the Social Reconstruction of Molecular Biology." *Science, Technology and Human Values* 10:70–9.

Massey, Doreen, Paul Quintas, and David Wield. 1992. *High Tech Fantasies: Science Parks in Society, Space and Time.* London: Routledge.

Merton, Robert K. 1973. "The Normative Structure of Science," In his *The Sociology of Science.* Chicago: University of Chicago Press.

Miller, Peter. 1992. "Accounting and Objectivity: The Invention of Calculating Selves and Calculable Spaces." *Annals of Scholarship* 9:61–86.

Miller, Peter, and Nikolas Rose. 1990. "Governing Economic Life." *Economy and Society* 19:1–31.

Moore v. Regents of the University of California. 1988a. 249 *Californian Reporter.* 494.

    1988b. 271 *Californian Reporter* 146.

National Health Service. 1993. *Proposal for Intellectual Property Handling and Technology Transfer in the National Health Service.* London: HMSO.

Noble, David. F. 1977. *America by Design: Science, Technology and the Rise of Corporate Capitalism.* Oxford: Oxford University Press.

Onco-mouse. 1989. Examining Division [1989]; Board of Appeal [1990] *EPOR* 501; Examining Division [1991] *EPOR* 525.

"Patent Power." 1992. *New Scientist,* 13 March, p. 12.

Rose, Nikolas. 1988. "Calculable Minds and Manageable Individuals." *History of the Human Sciences* 1:179–200.

Rose, Nikolas and Peter Miller. 1992. "Political Power beyond the State: Problematics of Government." *British Journal of Sociology* 43:173–205.

Schmookler, Jacob. 1966. *Invention and Economic Growth.* Cambridge, Mass.: Harvard University Press.

University Directors of Industrial Liaison. 1988. *The Report of University Directors of Industrial Liaison(s).* London.

    1989. *University Intellectual Property: Its Management and Commercial Exploitation.* University Directors of Industrial Liaison. London.

University Funding Council (UFC). 1992a. *Research Assessment Exercise 1992.* UFC Circular 5/92. March.

    1992b. *Research Assessment Exercise 1992: The Outcome.* UFC Circular 26/92. December.

    1993. *A Report for the Universities Funding Council on the Conduct of the 1992 Research Assessment Exercise.* June.

U.S. Congress, House Committee on Science and Technology. 1981. *Fraud in Biomedical Research: Hearings before the Subcommittee on Investigations and Oversight.* 97th Congress, 1st session.

Weil, Vivian. 1988. "Policy Incentives and Constraints on Scientific Information." *Science, Technology and Human Values* 13:17–26.

Weiner, Charles. 1986. "Universities, Professors and Patents: A Continuing Controversy." *Technology Review* (Feb./March): 33–43.

White Paper. 1993. *Realising Our Potential: A Strategy for Science, Engineering and Technology.* Cm. 2250. London: HMSO.

Wilkie, Tom. 1993. *Perilous Knowledge: The Human Genome Project and Its Implications.* London: Faber.

Yoxen, Edward J. 1985. *The Gene Business.* New York: Oxford University Press.

8   On customers and costs: a story from public sector science

John Law and Madeleine Akrich

Introduction

This is a story about a laboratory – Daresbury SERC laboratory.[1] It's a story about some of the ways in which a state scientific bureaucracy started to come to terms with the rhetoric and forces of the marketplace that became popular in government in the U.K. in the 1980s. For at the beginning of the 1980s Daresbury *bought* services and goods in the marketplace: it paid for electricity, purchased equipment, and was, to be sure, a substantial employer. So it knew about buying. But, with minor exceptions, *it did not sell anything*. And, concomitantly, it knew little about selling, or how to sell. It was not that it didn't work for outsiders. Indeed, it did so extensively. However, it did this in ways based on quite different understandings that had little to do with notions about cost or profit.

The bulk of the argument is empirical. We start by talking a little about these understandings and, more particularly, about what it meant (and still means) to be a "user" at Daresbury. Then we turn to the way in which economic liberalism and spending restrictions started to impinge on Daresbury in the middle 1980s. First we consider the significance of a category, the "customer," which did not exist in 1980 but was to become of major importance to the laboratory by 1990. Second, we explore some of the organizational problems that the laboratory encountered as it started to come to terms with the new category of customers – and then with the ways in which it sought to resolve those difficulties. As a part of this we consider the way in which the laboratory sought both to create "good customers" and at the same time to convert itself into a "good seller" (both of these terms are our own). Then we look at the way in which being a "good seller" was related to a particular set of costing practices that were closely related to the implementation of a manage-

---

[1] SERC is the acronym for the Science and Engineering Research Council, which was the major U.K. government funded body supporting research in physics, chemistry, and engineering at the time of the study.

195

ment accounting system. Finally, we consider how Daresbury's response to "market forces" influenced scientific and organizational practice.

Here our argument becomes more overtly theoretical. It is that the social technologies of governmentality performed by accountancy – but also by scientific and bureaucratic practice – are complex, discursively heterogeneous, and context-sensitive. This means, or so we suggest, that it is difficult if not impossible to mount general arguments about "science" and "the market," and that the use of such large-scale institutional oppositions impedes analysis. We conclude with a brief theoretical observation about interdiscursivity and modernity.

Users and customers

Daresbury is an SERC central facility. That is, it builds and manages experimental equipment that because of its cost, size, and complexity, is not duplicated in individual universities. At the time we carried out this study, there were two experimental centers at Daresbury: a Nuclear Structure Facility (which has since been closed) and a Synchrotron Radiation (SR) Facility (on which we focus in what follows). Physically, the SR source is a huge ring evacuated to a near vacuum. Electrons injected into this ring are accelerated by radio frequency radiation produced by a klystron – the kind of valve that powers a TV transmitter. As they move around, the electrons are deflected by powerful magnets and give off intense beams of monochromatic light or synchrotron radiation – called "beams" in the laboratory vernacular. These beams, which range from infrared through to hard X-rays, are piped down "beam lines" to the more than twenty stations where the experimental work of the laboratory is carried out.

Most of the funds for the SR facility and its penumbra of supporting equipment, laboratories, engineering services and personnel come directly from the SERC. The council supports the facility so that scientists from other institutions may come to Daresbury and gather experimental data. This is where the word "user" enters the vocabulary, for such is the term used to describe such visiting scientists. A user is likely to be an academic scientist. He or she will have written a grant application and submitted it to the SERC or perhaps to another academic research body such as the Medical Research Council (which also funds some facilities at Daresbury). The application will have been subjected to competitive peer review and, if accepted, awarded a grant that includes an allocation of a certain number of shifts of "beam time" at a specific experimental station.

For the users, working at Daresbury is a distinctive experience. This is partly because the laboratory has some of the features of a total institution. Users are away from home base, friends, and family. They live in the laboratory hostel, probably taking their meals in the canteen. And they are working round the clock, probably in a small team, at one of the experimental stations. Because when the SR machine is working (as it is most of the time if all is well) there is beam all through the night. Experimental station, hostel room, canteen – for many users for a few weeks the world is defined by this triangle.

It's important to understand the value of that beam time. As with high-energy physics (Traweek 1988), users *depend* on it. They live and die by it. It is the scarce resource, the choke point in their research. So part of the tension of a visit to Daresbury has to do with the health of the beam, and users get very fidgety if the SR source is not working. They try to be polite to "the crew" – that is, the technicians who are responsible for operating the source and producing the beam. But when things go wrong they sometimes find it difficult to keep their tempers. One of the engineers at Daresbury told us of a conversation that took place with a user (in another, quite different, facility):

USER: [Without beam] I might as well be dead.
ENGINEER: I beg your pardon.
USER: I might as well be dead. If I am not writing papers, I might as well be dead.
ENGINEER: What do you mean?
USER: To be second in science means that you might as well not do science.

Who do users see? The answer is that apart from one another they come across members of the Daresbury staff. In particular, they meet the "station master," who is the staff scientist responsible for the particular experimental station at which they are working. If they are new to the laboratory or don't have much experience in using the station, then the Daresbury staff will be teaching them how best to use it. Here is one user: "[There is a] learning curve. Brenda [from the Laboratory] did all the work the first time. She showed us [what to do]. But the second time she also set time aside. But we did it more [ourselves] though we made some mistakes."

It doesn't require a particular view of the character of scientific inquiry to see that this way of living – and perhaps in particular the conversation between the engineer and the user – indexes a set of classic themes in the sociology of science. These are academic scientists who order the world and their experience in conformity with academic procedures. And at the beginning of the 1980s they were virtually the only kind of people who came to use the SR facility.

By 1990 things were changing – indeed they had changed. Though the majority of outsiders were still users, they had been joined by a significant number of paying "customers." There were three main reasons for this. First, the facilities offered at some of the SR stations were suitable for commercially relevant work – for instance, surface science, which was important for research on catalysis. Second, Daresbury was short of money. Restrictions in SERC grant were reflected in the funds available to the laboratory. Accordingly, the management had a real incentive to find ways of selling services and so increasing income. And third, this incentive was strengthened by the impact of government policy as refracted through the SERC. The argument was that even academic and quasi-academic institutions should actively seek to market their services and engage in profitable trading with private sector customers. So Daresbury, like other public sector laboratories, was being encouraged to increase the level of such "repayment work"[2] – and was told, both as a target and as a limit, that it might secure up to 20 percent of its income in this way.

In practice the notion of repayment work is rather opaque. Thus it includes arrangements that are straightforwardly commercial in character: there was a substantial number of private sector companies who bought services or beam time from the laboratory in return for cash payment. But some work with industry doesn't fit this pattern. For instance, a group of firms (the "Industrial Consortium") had funded the construction of series of experimental stations in return for "free" beam time. And (still within the rubric of repayment work, though arguably even further removed from the commercial marketplace), the EEC was paying the laboratory to make experimental shifts available to academic EEC but non-British users. In addition, several individual overseas funding agencies had made somewhat similar arrangements with respect to specific experimental stations.

As already mentioned, such paying customers were important to the laboratory. Most obviously, they were important because they attracted income in the form of payment in cash or kind. Less directly, they made it possible for the laboratory to build up important *scientific* collaborations with certain major industrial companies that were more concerned with applicable science than immediate marketability. And again, less directly, paying customers were important because they showed that the laboratory was entrepreneurial in spirit – a not unimportant consideration in the bracing political climate provided by Thatcherism. However, along with the advantages came a series of difficulties and problems.

First, many users were edgy about the priority that attached to certain

[2] This is Treasury jargon for work done on behalf of paying customers.

kinds of repayment work. In principle 20 percent of laboratory income could come from this source, but in practice the same experimental stations were popular with both users and customers. Indeed, commercial demand would have used up most of the available shifts on such experimental stations without any risk of breaching the overall 20 percent rule. Here, then, was a moment when a logic that was commercial in character, butted up against other modes of ordering; a moment when, as it were, a form of organizational rule setting was needed to articulate the relationship between commercial customers and users. And in practice the solution was to limit commercial work at any given station to 20 percent of the shifts. However, the question of priority then emerged in a different form, for this figure needed to be added to other priority demands: the EEC had bought 10 percent of beam time across all stations, and the Netherlands Organization for Scientific Research had a right to 25 percent of the shifts on particular stations. Users were aware that more than half of the time on particular stations was not available to home users, and they sometimes complained about this: "[It is] worrying about the priority for people who pay. [After all] the UK taxpayer is [also] paying."

Users and managers were also exercised by the problems posed by the EEC contract. They knew and accepted the priority given to what was sometimes called "academically inferior" commercial work. But what about non-British *academic* work? Why should this have priority over "better" home proposals? So here again concern about priorities and how these should be exercised surfaced, a concern that once more posed itself in organizational quasi-moral language:

JOHN: [So far as the EEC is concerned] we must deliver most of the promised shifts.
DICK: So we need to guide [the committee that allocates shifts of beam time]. They should reject a proposal only if it is technically not feasible, repeats [old work, or is] poor science.

If the first problem caused by the growth of repayment work was to find a way of balancing the claims of academic users against those of commercial or quasicommercial purchasers of laboratory services, the second issue concerned costs. This was a sore point. For instance, when it was first signed, the contract with the industrial consortium mentioned earlier was seen as a triumph. However, by 1990 perceptions had altered and it was widely believed that the laboratory was losing out. One scientist told us: "They only paid a third of the costs. The problem is that we undersold by an enormous amount." So far as we could tell, no one in the laboratory was accusing the firms in the industrial consortium of having pulled a fast one. Rather, the assumption was that when it entered into the contract – and remember that it was a complex arrangement –

the laboratory had had little idea about how to calculate the cost of any of its activities. And people in the laboratory believed that the problem with the consortium was only the tip of a much larger iceberg. The perception was that the laboratory had been charging unrealistically low sums for its services – sums which meant that rather than making a profit, on many of its contracts it was really making a loss.

The third problem arising from repayment work takes us to the understandings surrounding experimental work. We've already observed that laboratory staff tended to help out inexperienced users. Indeed, there were specific arrangements for new users in the form of exploratory agreements: "At first we didn't know what we could do [with the experimental facilities of the laboratory]. So the first work was done under an exploratory agreement. [This was] very useful."

In many ways customers weren't so different from users. They might or might not have an expert knowledge of the appropriate experimental stations and protocols in the laboratory, and they might or might not have the initial expertise to determine which of the many experimental facilities was best suited to their particular needs. Thus though some were extremely skilled, knew exactly what they required, and needed no help, others might not have the know-how to set up and run an experiment, collect the data, and process those data to produce a finding. However, the *implications* of a possible absence of skill were quite different. For while teaching *users* posed no particular problem, teaching *customers* might turn out to have other and dangerous implications:

When laboratory scientists are responsible for gaining data [because they are trying to help out an inexperienced customer], is the [laboratory] responsible for getting the data, or the customer? If there were arguments after the event, they may say, "Well, you guys were responsible. It's your fault." And *we* may say, "No, *you* were responsible."

The problem, then, was that some customers tended to have a cut-and-dried notion of the agreement they had entered into with the laboratory. Not used to the uncertainties of scientific work, some assumed that the laboratory was responsible not only for the provision of experimental facilities and beam time, but also for results. But – and this was the laboratory's difficulty – this had never been the case in the past. Users might curse the laboratory, but if they went away empty-handed then that was it. They had no choice but to go through the process of applying for more beam time. But certain customers didn't see matters this way. And the fact that the laboratory guaranteed them beam time (which already distinguished them from "mere users") didn't really get to the heart of the problem.

Creating the "good customer"

Questions of priority setting, costing, and the understandings surrounding experimental work – these were the three great problems that
customers brought with them when they started to buy services from
Daresbury on a large scale. We've mentioned how the first of these problems was resolved: essentially, the solution was found in administrative
fiat. The "good customer" was rationed: it could buy up to 20 percent of
the time at any station, and that was the limit.[3]

We'll deal with the question of costing shortly, but first we'll look at
the matter of understandings. The can of worms opened up here was
nicely characterized by one laboratory manager: "The difference between
the academic and commercial users is that though the contract says
they'll be treated as academic users, the commercial users consider payment [should be made] on the basis of *results*. So they don't treat a shift
of setting-up as a part of it."

So what was to be done? The answer was that the laboratory needed
to engineer what we're going to call the "good customer." This would
take the form of a docile and disciplined purchaser that would pay a sum
of money in return for a specified service. The service would be close to
that offered to the user – though not, as we have seen, identical, because
the "good customer" was awarded unconditional beam time. On the
other hand, the customer would not make "unreasonable" demands. And
this was, as we have noted, the nub of the problem. Since some customers
had "unreasonable" expectations it was going to be necessary to teach
them to be reasonable. So how was this to be done?

The laboratory set about this in two rather different ways – though
they had in common the fact that both sought to make explicit what had
previously been implicit. First, it started to be clearer about the conditions under which it would agree contracts. Here is part of an acetate
shown by a senior manager to a meeting of the entire SR division:

A contract should only be accepted if there is certainty of delivery and at a profit.
  Correct technical evaluation is crucial (e.g., only one shift of beam time may
be needed, but it may take several shifts to set up a station). Once a commitment
has been made we have no choice but to deliver.

So contracts specified what might previously have been implicit, both
technically and financially. Leave the question of finance on one side for
the moment. How was a "correct technical evaluation" to be achieved?

---

[3] There is no direct correspondence between the formal rule that up to 20 percent of the
income of the laboratory could be generated from repayment work and the limit of 20
percent of beam time set for repayment work on each station. We are simply reporting
a managerial decision taken as a response to conflicting pressures.

The answer leads us to the second part of the laboratory strategy for engineering the "good customer." The laboratory concluded that it needed to educate prospective customers – because, it noted, there was a link between technical competence and reasonable expectations. It was those who were *least* competent who tended to make unreasonable demands. All of which meant that it could not hope to deal with "good customers" unless the latter were given certain kinds of help. "As customers get more and more discerning and demanding . . . and to make sure that paying customers get a better level of service, more and more we are telling prospective customers that the best thing to do is to buy a certain amount of personal service in order to get best value for money. And it also increases our resources."

As a part of those services, it might also be necessary to define the needs of the customer: "We needed to ask [customers] for a little bit more information, so we could judge about what was needed, even though it is commercial and confidential, so we could provide the equipment and the personal service they needed."

So in the laboratory view the "good customer" knows what it wants – or it has discussed and agreed what it wants with laboratory staff. It has bought the necessary number of shifts – even if some of those shifts don't produce data because they were needed to set up the experiment. If it isn't too experienced, then the "good customer" has probably bought the expertise and time of laboratory staff – and if it has not, and as a result has tried to do something impossible, then it doesn't blame the laboratory. But – and this is a further implication of the acetate quoted above – a "good customer" is also one that goes away from the laboratory happy. Presumably, the hope is that it will tell others, or come back again to purchase more laboratory services.

Creating the "good seller"

So far we've concentrated on the customer and on some of the processes by which the laboratory sought to convert those that were unreasonable into more tractable "good customers." Or, to draw on a different register, some of the ways in which the laboratory sought to engineer the customer as a different kind of calculating self.[4]

But it isn't possible to create good customers unless you also convert yourself into a "good seller." The two *necessarily* go together. Thus most

---

[4] See, for instance, Miller 1992, where the notion of the calculating self is linked to the creation of calculable spaces and, more generally, to issues of governmentality. See also Miller and Rose 1990. But note also Munro's (1993) comments on the consumption of control technologies, to which we return below.

of what we've described can also be seen in this light. The process of "educating" customers and trying to sell a package of services rather than simple shifts on an experimental station – this represented a change in laboratory practice. And so too, did the contentious issue of "helping out" in the case of problematic experiments. As we've seen, the laboratory learned to be cautious about this when it discovered that doing so might leave it responsible for any failure. Again, the matter of contracts has as much to do with engineering the "good seller" as with acquiring the "good customer." To quote from a part of the acetate again:

A contract should only be accepted if there is a certainty of delivery and at a profit.

Perhaps the phrase "certainty of delivery" reflects the experience with the industrial consortium; at any rate, it certainly reflects the fact that the laboratory had sometimes committed itself to work that turned out to be extremely difficult and costly. It is to the matter of profit that we now turn; for as a part of the process of turning itself into a "good seller" the laboratory also started to reorganize its costing procedures.

When it first entered the commercial game the laboratory did not think very much about the costs of its different experimental activities and had little experience of selling anything. Indeed its position on the matter of costs wasn't so different from that of Josiah Wedgwood before 1772: there was no way of discerning – perhaps we should say creating – the cost of any particular product (see Hopwood 1987). So why was this? And what were its implications? To answer this we need to go back to the question of funding. We've noted that most laboratory finance came from the SERC via one or other of its specialist committees. But this meant that if something went wrong there was a kind of division of labor between users and funders.[5] If the difficulty was small then the users tended to wring their hands and complain. But since they weren't paying and depended on the laboratory for diffuse and undefined help, it did not occur to them to send for their accountants or their lawyers and threaten to sue for breach of contract. They were, as it were, inserted into their own particular network, one that drew on university researchers and university research, but not on legal resources.[6]

In contrast with small delays and problems, if a large-scale project went wrong or absorbed too many resources, then it was the funders who started to worry. But they didn't necessarily worry about the money. This

---

[5] This is somewhat too simple, since the two categories overlapped. But for present purposes the simplification is adequate.

[6] This is an idea that has been developed in actor-network theory (see, for instance, Law 1992). Note that this approach is not about relations between people, but rather about constitutive links between entities of all kinds.

was because the presenting symptom of a major problem almost always took the form of technical difficulty or failure, followed by delay. For instance, when it was originally commissioned the SR ring suffered a series of unexpected breakdowns that led to substantial delays. Such delays were deeply worrying – they were a potential source of disaster for the scientific standing of the laboratory – and the funders took an intense interest in the resolution of the problem. Thus though senior management were concerned about financial resources, since the latter were usually inelastic, technical difficulties were typically converted into delay, or perhaps into redeployed effort and resources (which meant delay to other, lower-priority projects). To be sure, accountants from head office might ask rude questions about both deadlines *and* overspend. But overrun wasn't usually translated into either "losses" or cancellations. Indeed, the notion of a financial "loss" had little or no meaning within the laboratory.

What, then, were the consequences of all this? One was that the amount of money devoted to specific activities was usually of little direct significance. Thus though sums of money were allocated to laboratory divisions such as the Nuclear Structure Facility and the SR Facility, there wasn't much need to think about the amount spent on specific projects. And certainly there was no method for creating a cost for particular activities. So, like "loss," the notion of cost in relation to particular projects (though not to the laboratory as a whole) was more or less irrelevant. A second consequence had to do with ownership. The extent to which particular bits and pieces of the laboratory might be "owned" was rather limited. True, the laboratory, or more accurately the SERC, owned the site, buildings, equipment, staff time, and all the rest. And the divisions "owned" buildings and equipment in a somewhat looser way. But within the SR division, at the level of specific projects, the notion of legal ownership (as opposed to rights of use) didn't make much sense.

However, with the arrival of the first paying customers all this started to change. For as it started to sell its services, the laboratory found itself for the first time facing customers who expected the timely delivery of contracted goods and services for which they had paid. They did not take kindly to delay. But more important, they took the view that once they'd agreed on a price there was no reason why it should be renegotiated in favor of the laboratory. This meant that the laboratory found, again for the first time, that it needed to create an accountable cost for specific and detailed activities. And as a further aspect of this, it needed to be able to account for its spending – to demonstrate to its customers not only that it had spent their money legally, but that it had also done so on the appropriate, project-relevant, bits and pieces.

This then was the problem. To be a "good seller" the laboratory needed to know how much it cost to undertake specific activities. But it had no tradition of doing this, because in the past there had never been any need. So to become a "good seller" there was need for a large amount of backstage, organizational work. Specifically, what was required was the formation of a project-relevant accounting system: a system that would, like a set of bank balances, track, record, and report income and outgoings for each project. But how was this to be done? How should the activities of the laboratory be organized and grouped? And how should they be costed?

At this point the senior managers started to wrestle with a series of problems that has exercised managers and accountants for decades – or indeed for centuries if one chooses to delve into the archaeology of accounting (see Hopwood 1987 for an introduction). Their first step was to chop up what had previously been a seamless web of laboratory activity from the point of view of cost. This involved creating and defining specific projects, and then designating these as cost centers. To do this, project team leaders were given budgets – which included (some of) the income for work done for customers. And, as a second and related step, customers were charged for their activities and purchases. To use the terminology adopted in the social construction of accounting, this was a first step in the creation of a new kind of (financial) calculable space, and with it a novel form of calculating self (see Miller 1992). But in practice this was little more than a restatement of the problem; for there remained the question of determining charges: how "costs" and "income" should be associated with each project team. How was this to be done?

The answer was to build on existing practice. Managers and accountants were used to paying bills for equipment and services from outside contractors: indeed, the laboratory had elaborate procedures for processing, approving, and paying these. And there was an analogous set of practices for paying salaries and wages, in which the hours worked by employees were tracked and salary bills calculated. So if, as we have suggested, there were practices that grouped activities into project relevant blocks, then there were also practices for imputing costs. But – and this was the problem – *how should these be brought together*? How should activities and costs be married?

In 1990 this question was a top priority for the managers. But finding an answer – or rather, creating a set of practices that would add up to an answer – wasn't easy. For instance, the term "requisition" was laboratory jargon for equipment and services bought from outside. Some requisitions (for instance, certain kinds of equipment) came with a label already attached: they were destined for use on a single identifiable project. This meant that once projects were defined in financial terms, at least in principle it wasn't too difficult to track the bills for such items through the accounting system and charge them to the budgets allocated to the project team leaders. But this was the easy part; for there were many other bills that didn't come with project labels. For instance, telephone charges, local taxes and electricity bills, the cost of general repairs and maintenance – all these were treated as overall charges on the laboratory or its divisions and weren't linked to a particular project.

What, then, was to be done? How could project labels be attached to bills? This – the problem of overheads – is perhaps the most intractable and controversial problem in accountancy.[7] For Daresbury in some cases the answer was a technological fix – as, for instance, with the introduction of direct metering and billing of phone calls. But sometimes this wasn't possible. To take a specific instance, how could the personal computers used by laboratory management be billed to particular projects? Management absorbed resources but used them (or so the argument ran) for the benefit of the laboratory as a whole.

If many requisitions didn't have ready-made project-relevant labels, the difficulty was even more acute for the "manpower"[8] budget – an important item that amounted to nearly 50 percent of laboratory spending. Yes, the salaries were paid. Yes, they were paid to particular individuals. And yes, they were precisely calculated. But there was no way of linking them to specific projects. And neither did they come with handy, project-relevant labels. So what was to be done? How were the practices for paying employees to be linked with the effort put into particular projects?

Think of the difficulties. First, a good part of the bill for manpower was difficult to link with specific projects: Who should pay for the services of the top managers? Or the security team? Or the accountants? Or (a very large item) the services of the engineering division? Second, even those people who could be counted as working on particular projects tended to work on more than one, moving around among different jobs during the course of a week or a month. And third, assuming that these questions could in principle be resolved – that it was possible to decide who "belonged" where, and when – then there was still the problem of sorting them out in practice.

[7] As one of the referees to this paper indicated, the current preference is for "activity based costing," in which an attempt is made to locate and define cost drivers (including especially the costs of transactions), which relate variations in costs to variations in activities within cost centers. See Johnson and Kaplan 1987, chap. 10, on "New Systems for Process Control and Product Costing." Needless to say, this form of naturalized moralizing has as many opponents as supporters.

[8] In conformity with laboratory practice, we also will use this unhappily gendered term.

How, then, to track wages and salaries? How to debit them against specific projects? Here again the debates mirrored those that have taken place in the accountancy profession. One possibility was to average them across the laboratory. Or within divisions. Indeed, there was a system already in place for doing this: for charging the salaries of engineers, for instance, to the SR Division, or the Nuclear Structure Facility. But, or so ran the argument, this wasn't really sufficiently precise. Certainly, such aggregation was at a much higher level than that of the project. So about eighteen months before our fieldwork a detailed manpower booking system was created. Here's how it worked. Every month employees filled in a card saying how they'd spent their lime during that previous month. The card embodied a series of trade-offs to do with the level of detail. How many activity codes should be included? And how many time slots? In the minds of the managers the basic compromise was between precision and accuracy – a trade-off related to the effort needed to run the system itself. On the one hand, charging would be precise if there were lots of time slots and projects. On the other hand, the greater the precision the smaller the likely accuracy – and, to be sure, the more expensive it would be to run the system. We weren't around to hear these debates. However, by the time we were present the managers had designed a card with a relatively limited number of activity codes, which divided the month into half-day units. And the system was up and running.

If creating "real costs" was an important part of creating a "good seller," then the manpower booking system was another vital part of that process. But it also implied the need for reorganization. People had to be persuaded to fill in their cards. And these had then to be collected, assessed, processed, and the results reported. As we know, order generates its own forms of disorder. (The argument is outlined and explored in Cooper 1986.) Therefore it is no surprise that the manpower booking system created new forms of delinquency and resistance amongst those who did not wish, in this respect at least, to be "good employees." For instance, some failed to fill in and return their cards. Sometimes it was that they didn't understand the codes, sometimes that they did not *want* to understand the codes.

Some of this resistance appears to have been random. We were told that on the whole it was different people who didn't fill in their cards each month. And this was because, for instance, they were on leave, working off site, or had simply forgotten to do so. Sometimes, however, the absence of a card at the end of the month seems to have been more motivated. Thus the managers occasionally talked about a "hard core" of delinquents. Who were the hard core? We don't know. But we do know that many scientists had a strong commitment to their science. They saw it as a vocation. And they conceived of their work as a form of craft or profession. They didn't watch the clock (even though in theory they were entitled to time off in lieu if they worked extra hours). And in their work they evinced a passionate commitment to the process of technical or scientific puzzle solving. We also know that in a number of cases they simply resented the requirement to account for the seamless web of their day in this segmented bureaucratic and financial manner. The arguments here were thus that they didn't have time – they were working too hard – and that the divisions represented by the manpower booking form were arbitrary, indeed in large measure meaningless to what was important about their work.[9]

So what was to be done? The answer was that the Finance Office told supervisors which cards were missing. And supervisors were supposed to chase up the delinquents. Sometimes this worked; but sometimes it didn't, in which case the Finance Office had no choice: it had to fill in the cards "on behalf of" the delinquents – which in turn might lead to controversy:

NIGEL: I've discovered that if manpower booking forms are handed in later than 2.00 p.m. on the first day of the month, they allocate that manpower to any project they fancy . . .
PETER: I think that is a bit of an exaggeration!
NIGEL: Okay, well, maybe it is a bit.
PETER: I have a lot of sympathy [with them]! They wait for a period. They send round a note. And only then do they allocate a booking.
NIGEL: Well, at least at the Electricity Board they do it on the basis of last year's bill!

By the time we reached the laboratory the manpower booking system was starting to settle down in practice. And its results – the amount of manpower charged to different projects (though not yet the *financial cost* of that manpower) – was being reported to senior management. For the

---

[9] If the development of management accounting and its particular versions of the calculating self and the calculable space represents a particular discourse of governmentality, then there were certainly others operating in the laboratory; and some of the resistances may be understood as expressions or performances of these other discourses. For this argument, developed in slightly different terms, see Law 1994. Here the management of the laboratory is pictured as a self-reflexive interdiscursive space in which modes of ordering perform themselves together, sometimes in a manner that is complementary and sometimes in a way that leads to conflict and resistance. Note that there is a tendency for some of the literature on governmentality to marginalize resistance and adopt a somewhat "managerialist" tone, in which it is assumed that calculability and calculating selves can fairly easily be generated. On this see Roberts and Scapens 1990, and in particular Munro 1993, who stresses that what he calls the "production view" of accounting numbers needs to be complemented by a consumption view. We discuss this further below.

first time, at least in some measure, it had become possible for senior management to sit in meetings and "see" how much different projects were costing, and the extent to which those costs matched estimates. If we were being Foucauldian we might say, therefore, that for the first time management had constituted itself as a cost and project-relevant panopticon: that an accounting version of governmentality with its calculating spaces and calculating selves had been constituted within the laboratory.

Multivalent spaces, multivalent selves

It is widely believed that we live in an age in which links between buyers and sellers have displaced other forms of ordering in many areas of social life. Perhaps this is as much the case for science as anywhere else. Customer-contractor relations now claim to organize relations in areas of scientific work previously untouched by logics of economic calculation. In this paper we've sought to tell matter-of-fact stories about some of the economically relevant changes that came to Daresbury laboratory in the 1980s[10] by talking of the creation of "good customers" and "good sellers." As indicated, this can be linked to questions of governmentality. We've seen that the problem for Daresbury was that some customers made unreasonable demands, they tended to displace "users," or they didn't pay enough for what they were buying. But we argued that the creation of "good customers" wasn't possible without a "good seller." So our story was also about the way in which the laboratory sought to turn itself into a "good seller" by creating a novel calculable space.

Though our story is not innocent of theorizing, it may be interpreted in a number of ways. For instance, it's possible to draw on the sociology of science and insist on the specificity of the scientific gift, the scientific field, or scientific credibility.[11] Such arguments might be used to suggest that there is a necessary incompatibility or tension between "science" and "the market."[12] But there are problems with this view. In particular, it implies that "science" and "the market" perform and embody particular,

[10] Many others have offered similar matter-of-fact accounts: witness the large literature on accountability and "auditability," governmentality, and the meaning of the figures and procedures generated in accountancy and its allied trade. As examples (some of which are critical of an excessive reliance on Foucault) see, for instance, Harper 1988; Hines 1988; Hopwood 1986, 1987; Miller 1991; Miller and O'Leary 1990; Miller and Rose 1990; Munro 1993; Munro and Hatherly 1993; Power 1991, 1994; and Roberts and Scapens 1990. But there are other traditions at work. See, for instance, the fascinating description of the formation of economically calculating selves offered in Garcia 1986.

[11] On academic science conceived as a gift economy, see Hagstrom 1965. For the general theory of field and capital, see Bourdieu 1986; for its application to the case of science, see Bourdieu 1975. On credibility, see Latour and Woolgar 1979.

[12] The most obvious example in this genre, which poses the matter in terms of gift versus

specific, monolithic but distinct logics. This is a strong assumption, and not one that we take to be sustainable. Thus studies from a number of different perspectives suggest that if different logics perform themselves in social life (and there is disagreement about this), then they certainly don't map conveniently onto the divisions between such great institutions, but rather infuse through them and operate alongside one another within particular locations.[13]

A second theoretical possibility is Foucauldian and would say that we are witnessing the development of an apparatus for surveillance and discipline, with its separations, normalizations, and panoptical foci (see, in particular, Foucault 1979). As we've indicated, there is a strong tradition of such work in the social analysis of accounting (see, for instance, Miller 1992; Miller and O'Leary 1990; Miller and Rose 1990). We wouldn't seek to resist such a view. Indeed, we touched on it above, and its concern with calculating selves and calculable spaces is central to our understanding of the formation of the "good customer," and the "good seller." Our story, as we have noted, is not theoretically innocent.

However, there's a third possibility, which seeks to make more of contingency. This can be treated empirically, by considering how far-reaching the effects of "the market" have been for Daresbury and for the practice of its science. But it also has theoretical implications to do with the complexity of locality, with interdiscursivity, and with what Rolland Munro calls the "consumption" of the figures generated in accountancy. And it is this third, complex, possibility to which we now turn by touching first on the empirical before using this to consider the character of interdiscursivity.

Note first that *even in principle* commercial and quasi-commercial repayment work accounts for only 20 percent of laboratory income, and

market is Titmuss 1973. The argument is that market transactions, which tend toward the simple and the specific, tend to erode the more diffuse and complex understandings to be found in economies of gift giving. In the case of Bourdieu's field theory, the story would be about the tensions that exist between different methods of reconverting capital. In this version users would be located in the field of distinction such that their first preoccupation would be with the accumulation of symbolic capital (which might subsequently be reconverted into economic capital). In contrast, customers would be more concerned with the direct accumulation of economic capital. Latour and Woolgar do not elaborate a specific theory of economic capital. Nonetheless, credibility is a movement or a flow, or a set of relations; it is not reducible to (though it sometimes takes the form of) money.

[13] This is a possible implication of work from symbolic interactionism (Becker 1970a; Star and Griesemer 1989), discourse analysis (Foucault 1979; Miller and Rose 1990, Miller 1992; Power 1994), and actor-network theory (Latour 1988; Law 1994). In their concern with what Foucault describes as the "micro-physics" of power, all of these operate at a different level of aggregation, locating strategies and orderings that permeate through the divisions erected by the macro-social.

that in practice it is lower than this. But what have been the practical effects? How far have managers and others been turned into economically calculating selves? Here we note that there has indeed been substantial reorganization of parts of laboratory practice in conformity with a logic of financial calculation. This is particularly visible if one approaches the laboratory, as we did, via its management meetings. These are the changes that we've outlined above: the creation of cost centers, methods of accountancy for supporting (indeed constituting) those cost centers, budgeting, and the manpower booking system – all represent substantial changes in management, and therefore in organizational practice.

But when we start looking at the textures of laboratory practices we start to uncover complexities. Here is one of the senior managers: "All the pressure on [the project team leader] is to press the work and maximize his manpower. The sign of success is to get the job done, *not* value for money."

Seemingly, cost or profit are (or were[14]) not usually uppermost in the mind of project team leaders. But why? The quotation suggests that they calculate, but they calculate in ways that don't have much to do with costs. They think, for instance, that success depends on getting the job done – which means that professional or organizational concerns have displaced economic considerations in the way in which they reason.

It's possible to make this point in an almost architectural fashion. For the project team leader may be a budget holder, and she may, indeed, be worrying about her budget when she sits in her office looking at the monthly financial printout. But with the 100 yards walk to the experimental floor, her context starts to change and scientific or technical questions start to form in her mind. How well is the experiment working? How good is the beam today? Have the users sorted out the problem of keeping the crystal cool? Has the alignment of the mirror in the new beam line been sorted out? Have the ducts for the air conditioning been delivered? Questions of this sort tend to crowd out thoughts of budgets as she passes through the corridor that joins the office block to the SR ring.

Our argument, then, is that the project team leaders are indeed constituted as calculating selves, but that they are located in several spaces of calculation. Or, perhaps better, that they are constituted in a *multivalent calculative space*. If this is right then concern with financial calculation rubs up in contingent ways against other kinds of reasoning. And (or so we want to suggest) it does so in ways that are context-sensitive. We want

---

[14] Note that this reports conditions at the end of 1990. Further innovations were in preparation that were intended to change the circumstances we report in this paragraph. See below.

to illustrate this sensitivity by briefly exploring four examples. We have already considered the first. It is the quotation above. The point is straightforward but it merits notice. If the cost of manpower, unlike that of requisitions, is not charged to the budget of a project, then this acts to decouple manpower distribution from a concern with cost. Instead manpower is distributed through a series of diverse and quite different organizational, bureaucratic, and informal transactions that may have nothing to do with cost or economic efficiency. It is true that these transactions might reflect management views of priorities, but they are also likely to reflect quite other concerns – which is the point of the quotation above.[15]

Our second example also points to the sensitivity of calculation to context: "Did you hear about Bill? He went to the stores, signed for a box of screws, and as he started to walk away they called him back and took them away because the project had overspent on requisitions!"

This story was recounted as an example of lunacy. It was intended to show the way in which financial reasoning was cut off from, and indeed impeded, what was taken to be the real business of the laboratory. But it also shows that there are contexts – here to do with requisitions – where the creation of costs is having real effects on the nature of calculation. In addition, it illustrates the sensitivity of these effects to the presence or absence of other forms of calculation. Thus it appears that the stores clerk had been told not to allow overspend. But, unlike the scientists, he had no particular commitment to the conduct of experimental work. In these circumstances the logic of accountancy was stiffened by a bureaucratic mode of reasoning, so he simply (as they say) followed orders. "Administration" and "economics" – two calculative spaces – here worked to complement each other, with no basis for resistance in some other calculative mode.

Our third case takes us to Munro's point about the *consumption* of figures. Thus one of the strategies for resistance is that of deliberate overspend. The logic is straightforward: once money is actually spent, there's a good chance it won't be clawed back because there is likely to be underspend elsewhere.[16] This is an old strategy, not one created by the formation of cost centers. It is just that the transparency of the accounting system sometimes makes it easier to play this game. The figures become resources for resisting the economic reasoning they are supposed to entrench.

[15] As we finished our period of fieldwork the laboratory was preparing to change this. The next step was to arrange that manpower budgets should be costed and charged to projects.

[16] This game was played at every level in the laboratory. Indeed, Treasury rules limiting the amount of money that might be carried forward from one year to the next provided an added incentive for the players.

Our fourth example takes us to a management meeting:

ANDREW: I'm trying to nip the problems in the bud, if there are any problems. Let's just review the situation. . . . If we look at the last report . . . this is okay. Jimmy Smith says that the superconductor itself is okay. So the problem is with the experimental instruments. The manpower used was low, [but] it was said that it would pick up. We aimed to use nineteen in-house man years, but we [actually] used seven in-house man years. . . . So there is a big gap developing. I think that this means we've got a problem. Is this right?

Andrew is our pseudonym for the managing director. But, though he's sitting in the panopticon, what he is talking about has little to do with financial control or cutting costs. Rather it has to do with the classic Daresbury concern of making sure that a big project doesn't fall behind schedule. So the way in which he's talking is not so different from that of the project team leader described above: he wants to get a job done. Except (here is the difference) he also knows that he'll have to make difficult decisions. "I am much relieved," he goes on to say. "You are addressing priorities!" This is the language of choice. Or discretion. But it is a matter of scientific or organizational rather than financial discretion ("The Second Wiggler is top priority. . . . Nothing is as important as the Second Wiggler"). So what we're witnessing in this case is the conduct of a bureaucratic and scientific calculation by quasi-economic means.[17]

Our conclusion, then, is that the introduction of a space of economic calculability produces complex, contingent, and often unanticipated effects. And that this is because it combines with other spaces of calculability in ways that are local and relatively unpredictable. Similarities and differences, coexistence, conflict, cooperation, subversion: the relations between such spaces are constructed in quite specific ways.[18] However, one more general consequence is that the calculating selves within the organization are multivalent. And, perhaps more strikingly, they are also relatively unstable. Thus we often watched managers who had been poring over budget figures and complaining about overspenders on a Friday turn into different people, as it were, by going on to put in a 12-hour day down in the experimental area on a Sunday. Sunday was a day devoted to science, to calculations on data, to setting up crystals in X-ray beams, to cursing and trying to work round the vagaries of the SR

---

[17] This suggestion brings together the (otherwise very different) analyses of power developed by Foucault (1982) and Barnes (1988). The argument is that discretion is constituted first as a location within each individual calculable space and second as an aspect of the *multivalence* of those spaces. See also Law 1991a.

[18] This point has been developed at length by Annemarie Mol. See Mol 1991, and Law 1994.

ring. For senior managers it was often the only day on which they could do science. But this is just an example of a more general point: to imagine that agents are consistent between contexts is a strong assumption – and not one that our data bear out. Or, to put it a little differently, to imagine that spaces of calculability perform themselves uniformly through organizations to generate consistent contexts seems to be an equally strong assumption.[19] All of which means that there can be no simple answer to the question about how the development of management accounting has influenced scientific work. And, though this is doubtless frustrating, we wouldn't even care to make a generalization about Daresbury, let alone other scientific laboratories. The question seems to pose itself at quite the wrong level of aggregation.

We want to conclude by touching on what we take to be a double dialectic. One half of this dialectic has to do with the multivalence of calculable space that we have just described. The other concerns the relationship between face-to-face interaction and action at a distance. Hopwood writes of Josiah Wedgwood after he introduced his first accountancy reforms:

No longer did he have to rely solely on walking around the pottery on the lookout for "unhandiness," scolding those individuals who did not follow his instructions . . . Such personal observation and supervision could start to be complemented by the exercising of control at a distance, both in time and space. Wedgwood now had available to him the basis of a more anonymous and continuous means of surveillance. (Hopwood 1987, 218)

The idea that accountancy is a form of action at a distance related to the construction of calculable spaces is one that has been well developed in the literature (see, for instance, Miller 1992, 65). But versions of the argument as applied to other social technologies can be retrieved from half a dozen other literatures.[20] The contention is always the same: that with the development of these technologies there is less need to move, to walk, to touch; and that, as a consequence, other senses are subordinated to the ocular. The eye starts to displace the body. And visibility from a central place becomes the dominant metaphor for ordering.

This is fine, but only if it is imagined dialectically. For (and this is a further statement of Munro's point) with action at a distance, bodies do

[19] In this respect our analysis leads us in the opposite direction to that of Becker 1970a, which assumes that consistency is the result of accumulating side bets or investments in different but interrelated courses of action. It's also in tension with the argument mounted by Elias 1978 about the civilizing process and the consistency of calculation.

[20] It is central to the Foucauldian analysis of governmentality (Foucault 1979), to the actor-network analysis of ordering (Latour 1990), to historical writing on the development of printing (Eisenstein 1979), literacy (Ong 1982), and linear perspective (Alpers 1989), to neo-Marxist understandings of the imperialist control of space and time (Harvey 1989), and to anthropological interpretations of the importance of writing (Goody 1977).

not go away. Interactions still take place. The proximal (that is, action by contact) still performs – indeed it *helps* to perform – the apparent stabilities of the distal.[21] So what is the nature of the interaction of these two dialectics? How does the proximal/distal dialectic relate to the dialectics of multivalent calculation? We have two tentative but interrelated thoughts. The first is that the consumption and uses of figures (and other modalities generated from action at a distance) may be imagined as a bodily effect of multivalent calculation. Or, to put it a little differently, it is that the creativity, the unpredictability, and the specificity of action and interaction may be imagined to reside in the heterogeneity of the spaces of calculation that constitute the ordering self. Our second thought is that the governmentality of modernity may be understood as a combination of more or less loosely related calculable spaces.[22] Indeed, it may be that this is what constitutes what is most distinctive about modernity. In which case it becomes important to ask, as we have briefly here, how such calculable spaces relate together. Do they, for instance, amount to an episteme, a relatively coherent set of knowledges? Are they expressions of a grand narrative? Doubtless there are reasons for pressing these possibilities, but we are skeptical. For the thrust of our argument has been that the relations between the various social technologies of calculation are contingent rather than representing the expression of a deeper consistency. In which case accountancy is merely another addition to the more or less ramshackle technologies of modern governmentality, the latest wheeze of modernism as it performs diversities and fragmentations while dreaming of an impossible order. But all is not lost, for (this is the place where the two dialectics come together) such diversities and fragmentations tend to increase, albeit ambivalently, the creative and hetereogeneous specificity of the face-to-face.

ACKNOWLEDGEMENTS

[21] For discussion of the distinction between proximal and distal, see Cooper and Law 1995. Note, however, that the arguments about bodies have been rehearsed in many fields. In the present context it is perhaps useful to note that much of the thrust of T. S. Kuhn's understanding of the nature of science lay precisely in an attempt to resist the notion that science is a set of disembodied ideas that correspond to or look down on reality; and with this, to recall the notion that these ideas arise from the application of a general set of relatively stable scientific methods. Against this, he insisted on the craft nature of science and sought to rehabilitate the body of the scientist, emphasizing that much scientific knowledge is tacit, contextual, and embodied (see Kuhn 1970).

[22] There are many possible citations here. For an important general line of argument on representation, see Cooper 1992, 1993; note that Cooper presses the importance of material heterogeneity, which for purposes of simplicity we have ignored here. On the loose coupling of ordering forms see Latour's "Irreductions" – which is found with Latour 1988 – and Law 1994.

We are grateful to all those who work in Daresbury SERC Laboratory for their support and encouragement before, during, and after the period of fieldwork undertaken by John Law. We would also like to thank the Economic and Social Research Council and the Science Policy Support Group for their generous financial support within the Changing Culture of Science research initiative. Without this, the extended period of fieldwork that led to this paper would not have been possible. We are most grateful to Mike Power and an anonymous referee who made many helpful suggestions about an earlier draft of this paper. Finally, we would like to thank our colleagues, and in particular Michel Callon, Bob Cooper, Bruno Latour, Annemarie Mol, Rolland Munro, and Leigh Star for their continuing intellectual support, dialogue, and encouragement.

REFERENCES

Ahonen, P., ed. 1993. *Tracing the Semiotic Boundaries of Politics.* Berlin: Mouton de Gruyter.

Alpers, S. 1989. *The Art of Describing: Dutch Art in the Seventeenth Century.* Harmondsworth: Penguin.

Bacharach, S., P. Gagliardi and B. Mundell, eds. 1995. *Research in the Sociology of Organizations*, vol. 13. Greenwich, Conn.: JAI Press.

Barnes, B. 1988. *The Nature of Power.* Cambridge: Polity.

Becker, H. S. 1970a. "Notes on the Concept of Commitment." In Becker 1970b, 261–73.

——— 1970b. *Sociological Work: Method and Substance.* Chicago: Aldine.

Bourdieu, P. 1975. "The Specificity of the Scientific Field and the Social Conditions of the Progress of Reason." *Social Science Information* 14 (6):19–47.

——— 1986. *Distinction: A Social Critique of the Judgement of Taste.* London: Routledge.

Bromwich, M., and A. G. Hopwood, eds. 1986. *Research and Current Issues in Management Accounting.* London: Pitman.

Cooper, R. 1986. "Organization/Disorganization." *Social Science Information* 25 (2):299–335.

——— 1992. "Formal Organization as Representation: Remote Control, Displacement and Abbreviation." In Reed and Hughes 1992, 254–72.

——— 1993. "Technologies of Representation." In Ahonen 1993, 279–312.

Cooper, D., and T. Hopper, eds. 1990. *Critical Accounts.* London: Macmillan.

Cooper, R., and J. Law. 1995. "Organization: Distal and Proximal Views." In Bacharach, Gagliardi and Mundell 1995, 237–274.

Dreyfus, H. L., and P. Rabinow (with an afterword by Michel Foucault). 1982. *Michel Foucault: Beyond Structuralism and Hermeneutics.* Brighton: Harvester.

Eisenstein, E. L. 1979. *The Printing Press as an Agent of Change: Communications and Cultural Transformations in Early-Modern Europe.* Cambridge: Cambridge University Press.

Elias, N. 1978. *The History of Manners.* Oxford: Blackwell.

Foucault, M. 1979. *Discipline and Punish: The Birth of the Prison.* Harmondsworth: Penguin.

——— 1982. "The Subject and Power." In Dreyfus and Rabinow 1982, 208–26.

Garcia, M.-F. 1986. "La Construction sociale d'un marché parfait: la marché au cadran de Fontaines en Sologne." *Actes de la Recherche en Sciences Sociales* 65:2–13.

Goody, J. 1977. *The Domestication of the Savage Mind.* Cambridge: Cambridge University Press.

Hagstrom, W. O. 1965. *The Scientific Communication.* New York: Basic Books.

Harper, R. R. 1988. "Not Any Old Numbers: An Examination of Practical Reasoning in an Accountancy Environment." *Journal of Interdisciplinary Economics* 2:297–306.

Harvey, D. 1989. *The Condition of Postmodernity: An Inquiry into the Origins of Cultural Change.* Oxford: Blackwell.

Hermsen, J. J., and A. van Lenning, eds. 1991. *Sharing the Difference: Feminist Debates in Holland.* London: Routledge.

Hines, R. D. 1988. "Financial Accounting: In Communicating Reality, We Construct Reality." *Accounting, Organizations and Society* 13:251–61.

Hopwood, A. G. 1986. "Management Accounting and Organizational Action: an Introduction." In Bromwich and Hopwood 1986, 9–30.

——— 1987. "The Archaeology of Accounting Systems." *Accounting, Organizations and Society* 12:207–234.

Johnson, H. T., and R. S. Kaplan. 1987. *Relevance Lost: The Rise and Fall of Management Accounting.* Boston: Harvard Business School Press.

Kuhn, T. S. 1970. *The Structure of Scientific Revolutions.* Chicago: Chicago University Press.

Latour, B. 1988. *The Pasteurization of France.* Cambridge, Mass.: Harvard University Press.

——— 1990. "Drawing Things Together." In Lynch and Woolgar 1990, 19–68.

Latour, B., and S. Woolgar. 1986. *Laboratory Life: The Construction of Scientific Facts.* Princeton, N.J.: Princeton University Press.

Law, J. 1991a. "Power, Discretion and Strategy." In Law 1991b, 165–91.

——— ed. 1991b. *A Sociology of Monsters: Essays on Power, Technology and Domination.* Sociological Review Monograph 38. London: Routledge.

——— 1992. "Notes on the Theory of the Actor-Network: Ordering, Strategy and Heterogeneity." *Systems Practice* 5:379–93.

——— 1994. *Organizing Modernity.* Oxford: Blackwell.

Lynch, M., and S. Woolgar, eds. 1990. *Representation in Scientific Practice.* Cambridge, Mass.: MIT Press.

Miller, P. 1991. "Accounting Innovation beyond the Enterprise: Problematizing Investment Decisions and Programming Economic Growth in the U.K. in the 1960s." *Accounting, Organizations and Society* 16:733–62.

——— 1992. "Accounting and Objectivity: The Invention of Calculating Selves and Calculable Spaces." *Annals of Scholarship* 9:61–86.

Miller, P., and T. O'Leary. 1990. "Making Accountancy Practical." *Accounting, Organizations and Society* 15:479–98.

Miller, P., and N. Rose. 1990. "Governing Economic Life." *Economy and Society* 19:1–31.

Mol, A. 1991. "Wombs, Pigmentation and Pyramids: Should Anti-Racists and Feminists Try to Confine 'Biology' to Its Proper Place?" In Hermsen and van Lenning 1991, 149–63.

Mol, A., and J. Law. 1994. "Regions, Networks and Fluids: Anaemia and Social Topology." *Social Studies of Science* 24:641–71.

Munro, R. J. B. 1993. "Just When You Thought It Was Safe to Enter the Water: Accountability, Language Games and Multiple Control Technologies." *Accounting, Management and Information Technologies* 3:249–71.

Munro, R. J. B., and D. J. Hatherly. 1993. "Accountability and the New Commercial Agenda." *Critical Perspectives on Accounting* 4:369–95.

Ong, W. 1982. *Orality and Literacy: The Technologizing of the World.* London: Routledge.

Power, M. 1991. "Auditing and Environmental Expertise: Between Protest and Professionalisation." *Accounting, Auditing and Accountability Journal* 3:30–42.

1994. *The Audit Explosion.* London: Demos.

Reed M., and M. Hughes, eds. 1992. *Rethinking Organization.* London: Sage.

Roberts, J., and R. Scapens. 1990. "Accounting as Discipline." In Cooper and Hopper 1990, 107–25.

Star, S. L., and J. Griesemer. 1989. "Institutional Ecology, 'Translations' and Boundary Objects: Amateurs and Professionals in Berkeley's Museum of Vertebrate Zoology, 1907–39." *Social Studies of Science* 19:387–420.

Titmuss, R. M. 1973. *The Gift Relationship: From Human Blood to Social Policy.* Harmondsworth: Penguin.

Traweek, S. 1988. *Beamtimes and Lifetimes: The World of High Energy Physics.* Cambridge, Mass.: Harvard University Press.

9 A visible hand in the marketplace of ideas: precision measurement as arbitrage

Philip Mirowski

Initiates into the social studies of science in the 1990s could easily be forgiven if they tended to equate the "social" with the "economic." Marxist analyses of science date back to the "Hessen thesis," if not earlier. Representatives of various earlier sociologies of science have more or less self-consciously used the metaphor of a "marketplace of ideas" as their starting point; while representatives of a more postmodernist bent, from Latour and Woolgar to Pierre Bourdieu, have reveled in the language of the market and the accumulation of credit in their debunking exercises. Perhaps more ominously, there are now signs that more conventional analytic philosophers of science such as Radnitzky (Radnitzky and Bernholz 1987), Goldman (1992), and Kitcher (1993) are appropriating mathematical models from neoclassical economics in order to reach some accommodation with what they regard as outlandish constructivist accounts of science. All of this newfound enthusiasm for economics amongst those who thought only a few short years ago that it should be safely quarantined on the far side of the demarcation divide is a phenomenon that deserves close scrutiny by philosophers and historians alike; but it is one to which justice cannot be done here.[1] Instead, I shall begin from the observation that if economic analogies in science studies are to have any bite, to count as something more than coffee-room chatter, it would be wiser not to start with *rough qualitative* analogies in the manner of the above, but rather with *quantitative* ones, which at least have the added advantage that mathematical models expressing their insights would derive a modicum of support from the quantitative character of the subject matter.

The crucial issue, as with all such exercises, is to identify a plausible starting point in science for economic comparisons. This paper suggests that we pursue the analogy to the very heart of the image of scientific enterprise – namely, to the precision measurement of physical constants. Curiously enough, all of the above authors have neglected the one literature where economic reasoning abounds: that of the treatment of error

[1] One author who has begun to sort out the issues is Hands (1994a and 1994b).

in inductive inference. It so happens that all modern accounts of the stabilization of quantitative error possess an economic account of rationality at their very core; the purpose of this paper is to propose an alternative account, based on rival economic concepts. The reason such an account appears here, rather than in a journal of metrology or of statistics or analytic philosophy, is that this theory of scientific practice is explicitly intended to resonate with modern social studies of science, especially the recent work of Latour, Shapin and Schaffer, Gooday, and Porter. As such, it encompasses (a) an explicit mathematical model of the stabilization of constants in a quantitative science, (b) a framework for the writing of a history of practice with regard to quantitative measurement error, (c) resources for the comparative sociology of scientific disciplines, and (d) a platform for the critique of "accounting" or "economics" as a discrete theory of social life. Individual components of this program have been elaborated upon elsewhere.[2] The purpose of this paper is to provide an introduction, synthesis, and overview of (a) to (c).

The assignment of number as a process of give and take

It is striking just how quickly the paradigmatic exemplars of rationality in our culture, the physicists and the economists, ascend to ethereal realms of mysticism whenever they take it upon themselves to discuss the role of mathematics within their disciplines. Appeals are ubiquitous to an "unreasonable effectiveness of mathematics," to a partially obscured Book of Nature written in mathematical dialect, to an inborn utilitarian calculus, to a magic language more transparent than any vernacular and to a conflation of number and the phenomenon that somehow manages to escape crass numerology. Number and/or mathematics in these narratives are endowed with transcendental epistemic significance, which is subsequently used to explain empirical progress in the successful sciences. The problem with this mode of argumentation is that it grasps at legitimation from the wrong end of the stick, from the side of abstract formalism rather than from the side of *error* accounts.

From Pierre Duhem and C. S. Peirce onward, some philosophers have realized that the key to understanding the assignment of number is to focus on the problems of accommodation to error in a world where there is no prospect of its complete extirpation. In the early twentieth

---

[2] The mathematical model of arbitrage is discussed at greater length in Mirowski (1991 and 1994). A more elaborate version of the history of physical constants is presented in Mirowski (1993). That paper can also be read as a companion to Mirowski (1992), which discusses the cultural legitimations of the physical constants. The problems of statistical inference are covered in Mirowski (1990 and 1995). The critique of economics dates from Mirowski (1989).

century, this concern was tamed by conflating it with the theory of probability and reducing it to an instrumental concern of the discipline of statistics. The two dominant accounts of the treatment of error in our century, the theory of Neyman-Pearson hypothesis testing and the Bayesian theory of subjectivist probability assignment, constitute the scaffolding upon which all modern empirical activity in all the quantitative sciences is draped. It is therefore no accident that many contemporary accounts of the rationality of science take one or the other of these stories as their point of departure.[3] What has been neglected in the interim, however, is the fact that each of these two grand metanarratives, in turn, is itself based on a core notion of economic rationality: a metaphor for the trade-offs and compromises encountered in quotidian practice.

The version of Neyman-Pearson found in the plethora of undergraduate statistics texts is a garbled and distorted version of the original doctrine (Gigerenzer and Murray 1987); and there is substantial evidence that the two protagonists themselves did not agree on its content (Mayo 1985; 1992); but for our purposes it will suffice to recall the major components of the doctrine. It presumes the ability to specify two rival quantitative hypotheses before the fact of data collection; the ability to assign probability distributions to a unique variable under both rival hypotheses; and the ability to define regions of acceptance or rejection of the null hypothesis as a function of the power of the test statistic. Neyman in particular motivated the last step by explicit reference to the costs and benefits of acceptance or rejection of the null; and this economic reasoning has been ensconced in the tradition by reference to loss functions, optimal estimators, and the like. The pervasive dissatisfaction with the Neyman-Pearson organon among philosophers and statistical theorists (Howson and Urbach 1989; Gigerenzer and Murray 1987) derives from observations that this economistic calculation as an a priori categorical imperative does not seem to capture the actual behavior of scientific researchers, even when they themselves sincerely believe they are adherents of the Neyman-Pearson doctrine.

The Bayesian doctrine, while clearly in the ascendant in terms of attracting adherents, also has its version of economic rationality and its own peculiar drawbacks. While it allows that probability assignments might be individually idiosyncratic and even inconsistent at times, this doctrine depends on some version of the "Dutch Book" argument to

[3] The modern champion of the Neyman-Pearson school is Mayo (1985). The latest enthusiasts for a Bayesian theory of science are Howson and Urbach (1989) and Franklin (1986, 1990). A very important historical work, one which demonstrates that the two rivals have not been kept as pristinely separate as conventional wisdom supposes, is Gigerenzer and Murray (1987). A more recent work revealing some of the dark sides of the Bayesian ascendancy is Earman (1992).

assert that personal probabilities ultimately obey the Kolmogorov axioms (de Finetti 1974). Here the inconsistent actor is to be "punished" by some external agent who makes a sequence of bets with the first party that pay off with probability one, thus transforming personal inconsistency into a hemorrhaging "money pump." The role of the virtual economy here is clear: its job is to police the otherwise unexplained diversity of opinion. The drawback is that in science, as opposed to the racetrack, it is not clear how the Dutch Book is supposed to work and who is to play the role of the venal bookie. When combined with other complaints about the a priori need to restrict individual prior probabilities and the freedom of actors to update their conditionalized priors as they like, it would seem that economic arguments are not sufficient to clinch the determinacy of error in the way imagined by avid Bayesians (Earman 1992; Kahneman, Slovic, and Tversky 1982).

A further reason to be skeptical of both of these accounts, at least within the social studies of science community, is their wilful methodologically individualist character. The Neyman-Pearson doctrine imagines a frequentist theory of probability underwriting a mechanical decision process fully implementable by any isolated self-contained individual inquirer. The Bayesian model is often retailed as being founded on a utilitarian or "rational choice" conception of individual action. This orientation, which seeks to ground rationality in the epistemic capacities and inclinations of isolated individuals, that has encouraged recourse to economic metaphors: some sort of "invisible hand" must then reconcile these marooned Robinson Crusoes of science, and the discipline most willing to supply such notions has been economics.

Because scholars in more recent manifestations of science studies may be more disinclined than most to endorse such invisible hand explanations, it would seem that the time is ripe to rethink the treatment of quantitative measurement in the history and sociology of science. We shall therefore begin our sketch by drawing on a relatively recent literature in economics that conceptualizes the social constitution of value as the outcome of a process of arbitrage within the institutional constraints of a monetary system and a set of external definitions of the identity of commodities. This literature treats the market as an evolving network, thus resonating with certain versions of the philosophy of science (Hesse, Latour) as well as certain connectivist themes in complexity theory (Farmer 1991). For obvious reasons, the mathematical component of the economic theory cannot be developed in detail here; citations are provided for the curious.[4] Rather, I shall provide a brief description of

---

[4] The basic mathematical model is surveyed in Ellerman 1984. Further elaboration and description in the economic context can be found in Mirowski 1991 and 1994.

the analogy between commodity exchange and the assignment of quantitative error in the vernacular using diagrams, and follow with the relevant central theorem before moving on in subsequent sections to sketch the uses to which it may be put in science studies.

The governing trope of my account in both the economic and measurement cases is one of the process of creation of numerical invariance through arbitrage. In the marketplace, the prices of most commodities can be stated in terms of prices of other commodities; in physics, most constants can be defined by other constants. The key variable in the market situation is *profit*; in scientific measurement it is *error*. In markets, exchange is deemed arbitrage-free when any sequence of trades between commodities, however circuitous, always ends up with identical numerical relative prices of the initial and final commodities. One can think of this as the transitivity of value relations: knowing the going rates of corn for gold, gold for oil, oil for beef, and beef for silver means the going rate of corn for silver can be directly inferred without actually consulting the marketplace. In parallel, a set of physical constants is *consistent* (arbitrage-free) when any sequence of measurements, however circuitous, always gives the same numerical value for the resultant implied physical constant. One can think of this as the transitivity of measurement relations through successive theories. The root phenomenological problem both in markets and in physical science is that the numbers are never really arbitrage-free (actual prices are never mutually consistent; actual measurements never completely transitive), and therefore the algebraic systems that they embody do not strictly possess invariants. The absence of invariance in both instances is initially comprehended as *error*: Did we make a mistake at any node of the calculation? Was the valuation in a particular market in some ill-specified way "wrong"? Are the theories in fact in conflict? Was the experimental setup somehow at fault? Within a certain indeterminate range of quantitative discrepancy, actors are willing simply to ignore the problem of consistency: in arbitrage, it is within the band of "transaction costs"; in precision measurement, it is outside of the band of "significant figures." But there is more to it than that, since a major part of the problem is to foster interpersonal agreement as to where the band lies.

It is noteworthy that the arbitrageur always claims to halt the dark threat of infinite regress at the "fundamentals" – the underlying real determinants of value – while an experimentalist claims to halt the threat of infinite regress at nature. One of the triumphs of the science-studies literature, and particularly of the work of Harry Collins (1985), has been to undermine this account and show in actual circumstances how the "experimenter's regress" is short-circuited in practice. The parallel devel-

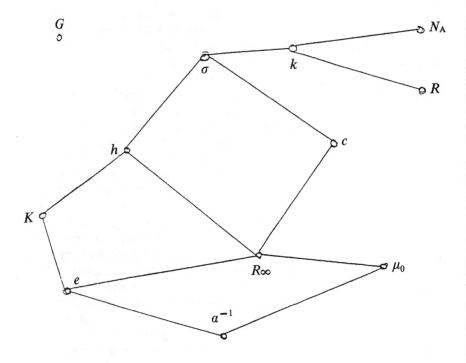

G = gravitational constant; σ = Stefan Boltzmann constant; k = Boltzmann constant; N_A = Avogadro constant; R = gas constant; h = Planck constant; c = speed of light; K = Josephson constant; e = electron charge; R_∞ = Rydberg constant; μ_0 = permeability of vacuum; a^{-1} = fine structure constant.

Figure 9.1. A simplified graph of some physical constants.

opment in economics has been to show that "the fundamentals" are effectively by-passed in the course of closing a deal (Bernstein 1992). The advantage of the economics literature is that it shows how this closure can be achieved in a quantitative manner, whereas Collins has so far confined his commentary to the qualitative phenomenon. Important in extending this formal analogy to physics is the convention that all physical constants be treated as though they were ratio combinations of other, derived, physical constants. A fact rarely commented on is that many of our present constants do exhibit this character: for instance, the Josephson frequency-voltage quotient is $2e/h$, the fine structure constant is $\mu_0 ce^2/2h$, the electron specific charge is e/m_e, the Boltzmann constant is R/N_A, and so forth. I shall make use of this algebraic curiosity in figure 9.1, above.

There is, however, one extremely critical way that the market analogy *does not* fully carry over into the process of physical measurement. In the marketplace there is an entire class of transactors who are on the lookout for price inconsistencies, because the unit magnitude of those divergences are realized in the form of money profit. This is often stated as a truism: No $50 bills will be found lying on the sidewalk. In physics, the unit magnitude of divergences are denominated in errors; and in that sphere we shall not presume that anyone is motivated to accumulate error units for their own sake. Therefore, while one could imagine a "laissez-faire" situation in which transactors police price consistency in a market out of nothing more than venal self-interest, it is highly unlikely that such a situation would ever arise in physical measurement. Far from crippling the effectiveness of the analogy between market and measurement, this divergence is responsible for our first empirical finding: that historically, arbitrage emerged much later in the process of physical measurement than in the evolution of the marketplace, and that its emergence required the imposition of an "artificial" actor whose whole purpose was to develop a set of error accounts. This persona was the invention of a real historical figure, the physicist Raymond Birge.

The theory of arbitrage that undergirds this account is based on the work of Ellerman (1984) on the formalization of "market graphs." A *directed graph* $\zeta = \{\zeta^0, \zeta_1, t, h\}$, is a set of ζ^0 nodes numbered $1,...,N$, a set of ζ_1 arcs or darts numbered $1,...,L$, and head and tail functions which indicate that arc k is directed from tail node $t(j)$ to head node $h(j)$. A "path" from node $j = 1$ to $j = n$ is an unbroken sequence of arcs connected at their heads or tails that extends from node j^1 to j^n node. A graph is called "connected" if a path exists between any two arbitrary nodes. When we endow graphs with economic significance, we associate each generic commodity with a single node and associate each arc with a permitted exchange. In order to discuss prices, each arc is assigned a nonzero rational number r_k, here called a "rate." One unit of the commodity at the tail node can be exchanged for r_k units of the commodity at the head node.

In the arbitrage theory of physical constants, we instead assign nodes to physical entities that are supposed to exhibit some fixed quantitative attribute: it could be the electron charge, or the Planck quantum of action, or the Avogadro number. A truncated graph of a selective subset of physical constants is illustrated in figure 9.1. The arcs here represent theories that connect the entities in fixed quantitative relationships: for example, the BCS theory of superconductivity links the electron charge and Planck quantum through the Josephson effect, while the permeability of the vacuum and the speed of light are linked through spectroscopy and the Rydberg constant. The role of the graph both in economics and in measurement theory is to stress that no value can ratify itself (no self-loops) and that a specific node can be reached only along a subset of all possible paths. Market graphs must be connected for successful arbitrage to take place; measurement graphs must be connected for successful error arbitrage to take place. The gravitational constant is portrayed as an isolated node in figure 9.1 because it is the least well connected of the physical constants; as a consequence, the gravitational constant has the least successful history of error stabilization of all the fundamental physical constants (Petley 1985, 11).

Why can an individual measurement not ratify itself? Quite simply, because no single laboratory can simultaneously fix the values of all the constants used in measuring other constants. The danger of self-ratifying constants is called by Petley (ibid., 8–9) the "Zanzibar effect." Reportedly, in that exotic clime a watchmaker set his clocks by the report of a noonday cannon fired by a fusilier who consults a watch that he borrows daily from the watchmaker . . . Another way to think about this is to see it as a concrete elaboration of Latour's (1987) analytical insight that inscriptions must pass through other labs and enroll other workers in order to become black-boxed. Here, at the most basic level, the analogue of money becomes the fundamental yet arbitrary standard of length, time, mass, and charge. Metrology thus stands to the physical sciences as central banking stands to market economies.

It is the purpose of this theory to illustrate how the introduction of money/standards, in conjunction with other social structures, renders the system of "rates" an algebraic group or, in this case, the multiplicative group of nonzero rationals. It is indispensable to this portrait that the existence of the money/standards is a necessary prerequisite for movement along a path to be reversible: here, if a path traverses an arc in the opposite direction, the rate is treated as the reciprocal r_k^{-1}. Reversibility is induced because many actual trades cannot be reversed (the BMW lost substantial blue book value the minute it was driven off the lot), and many physical measurements cannot be unproblematically inverted (remember, we cannot ourselves generate all the quantitative values needed). Let us define a composite path as the product of the relevant rates over each segment of the path, namely $r[a] = \Pi_a r_k$. Under these circumstances, we will be able to assign a number ($\mathbf{p}$ for price, $\mathbf{c}$ for constant) to each node as a function of the rates associated with the graph. The triple $\{\zeta, r, \mathbf{p}\}$ is called a market graph in economics; I propose that in physics we call the triple $\{\zeta, r, \mathbf{c}\}$ a "measurement graph."

The main conditions for the practical existence of such a graph are that (1) there are no self-loops at any node (no self-measure stabilizes itself); (2) the graph ζ must be connected (theories must use each other's variables); and (3) any circuit, of either exchange or measurement, beginning and ending at the same node results in a composite rate $r[a] = 1$ (this is the desideratum of consistency). Under these conditions, Ellerman proves the following theorem:

Cournot-Kirchoff Arbitrage Theorem. Let $\{\zeta, r, \mathbf{p}\}$ be a market graph with $r[a]$: $\zeta_1 \rightarrow T$, taking values in any group T. Then the following conditions are equivalent:

1. There is a price system P derived from the rate system r.
2. The exchange rate system r is path-independent.
3. The exchange rate system is arbitrage-free.
    The theorem may be restated for measurement graphs $\{\zeta, r, \mathbf{c}\}$ as:
1. There is a system of physical constants C derived from the theoretical rate system r.
2. Quantitative measurements in the theoretical rate system r are path-independent.
3. Measurements in the theoretical rate system r are error-free.

The advantage of the arbitrage approach to the phenomena of both markets and the measurement of physical constants is that it provides a structural framework within which one can argue that both phenomena are made, not discovered. Even with the vast social technologies of money, banks, and accounting, prices do not "naturally" conform to the Cournot-Kirchoff theorem: prices are rife with inconsistencies and therefore informational anomalies. One way this is made manifest is through the existence of arbitrage opportunities; and the way a "consistent" system of prices is approximated is through the activities of the arbitrageurs. Likewise, even with the vast laboratory resources of SI units, the National Institute of Standards and Technology, and the metrologists, the measured physical constants do not "naturally" conform to the Cournot-Kirchoff theorem; at any moment in time the constants are rife with inconsistencies and therefore informational anomalies. One way this is made manifest is through inconsistencies uncovered by meta-analysis; and I shall argue in the next section that the Raymond Birges of the world are their arbitrageurs. Thus the history of error would have to trace the joint evolution of the self-seeking arbitrageur and the institutions that render new versions of arbitrage conceivable and achievable. The narrative in section 2 was constructed with just such an outline in mind.

A natural history of quantitative error

Until very recently, the history of the fundamental physical constants was in a state of deplorable neglect. Depending on the source, one might have got the impression that some of our more hallowed constants were quickly identified and measured in the seventeenth century, close upon the spread of structured experimentation; or perhaps that they were quite securely nailed down by the spread of precision instrumentation and an Enlightenment "quantifying spirit" in the eighteenth century; or surely, that they were codified as an uncontentious compendium of reliable numbers in the industrialized standardization of the nineteenth century. Hence it must come as a bit of a shock to read the assessment of Raymond Birge, a major protagonist in the natural history of the physical constants, in a retrospective on the state of play in the 1920s:

A distinguished scientist would obtain a value of some such constant, which he believed more accurate than any previously found. He would make such a claim in a published paper, and thereafter, for some longer or shorter period, his value would be generally accepted and used throughout the scientific world. . . . In that case there was only one exhaustive investigation. Another situation tended to develop when research workers residing in two or more countries were involved. If, for instance, a distinguished German scientist obtained one value, and a distinguished French scientist another value of the same constant, one usually found the German value used subsequently in German papers and texts, and the French value in French papers and texts . . . Another unfortunate aspect of the situation, as I found it, was that the generally adopted value of each constant was chosen quite independently of the value of other, often related constants, so that no *consistent* set of values of the general constants existed . . . There have even been instances of two *different* values of an auxiliary constant (the velocity of light) used in the *same* equation. (Birge 1957, 40–41; emphasis in the original)

This certainly does not resonate with many of our commonplace notions of the special character and status of physics, ranging from the bracing regimen of quantification, to the relentlessly impersonal ethos of scientific knowledge, to the quest for clarity and consistency in the painstaking reproduction of the physical phenomenon. There is a simple explanation for this yawning gap between image and actuality. Everyone who has sought to write a history of the physical sciences has done so in the terms used by their subjects: precision, accuracy, replicability.[5] Yet this language is curiously ahistorical, in that each generation tends to

---

[5] This is true even of more "postmodern" historians, such as many of those gathered at a recent Princeton symposium on the history of precision in quantitative science (see Wise 1995). It is entertaining to observe how much more "radical" are modern physicists than the postmodern historians in this regard: "Modern physics is based on some intrinsic acts of faith, many of which are embodied in the fundamental constants" (Petley 1985, 2).

claim some such virtue as an attainable goal and then, essentially by fiat, claims to have attained their version of it.

But how to write a more sophisticated history of error? Are there not so many potential ways things can go wrong in all empirical endeavor that any attempt to present them in an organized or systematized manner can only come to grief? Not if one consults any standard textbook or practitioner's account of the modern status of the physical constants (Petley 1985, 10). There we learn that all uncertainty about the legitimacy of the values of the constants may be divided into two categories: (1) random error and (2) systematic error, which corresponds to the modern distinction made between "precision" – the closeness with which measurements agree with one another – and "accuracy" – the closeness of measurements to their "true" value. The distinction, as one might expect, has something to do with the canons of statistics versus discrepancies between theory and evidence. Ideally, in the former category there exists an irremediable element of variance that cannot be completely banished, though it can be neutralized by statistical techniques like ordinary least squares; the latter category is conversely something that could be eliminated by dint of the diligence of the experimentalist and/or the theorist, again ideally in the limit. When systematic error has been vanquished, the conventional index of success is the finding that all that remains is a Gaussian distribution of reported results, justified by reputedly uncontentious limit theorems, which in turn yields to readily understood estimation techniques.

Giora Hon (1989, 476ff.) finds this all quite useless for the historian of error, if not positively misleading for the practitioner. He insists that "the dichotomy between systematic and random errors does not focus on the source of the error; rather, it examines the nature of the error by applying a mathematical criterion." In the sense that the distinction tells us nothing interesting about the potential sources of error, or indeed about the practices used for either eradication of or accommodation to error, he is certainly correct. There is also the further consideration that methods for justifying and ascertaining the Gaussian status of random error are preponderantly groundless by the standards of *fin-de-siècle* probability theory.[6] Yet contrary to Hon, there is a grain of truth in the distinction, which may provide the beginnings of an analysis of a history of error. The distinction between random and systematic error, taught in every introductory laboratory practicum, is a fair description of the way in which the actors practically constitute the meaning of error and then allocate it to various "causes" as a prelude to rendering it harmless. The

---

[6] For a discussion of more general central limit theorems and stable distributions, see Zolatarev (1986) and Mirowski (1990).

analogy, which is explicitly acknowledged in such standard terminology as "error budgets," is with the allocation of profits to various sequences of transactions. In this way of thinking, precision is to arbitrage as accuracy is to the actual pattern of realized exchanges.

Let us begin our brief retrospective history with any practitioner's survey of suitably ancient fundamental physical constants – such as that found in, say, Petley (1985). On page 228 we find a table of the major laboratory measurements of the gravitational constant. Prior to the 1870s they are few and far between, dating back to 1798. Petley reports standard deviations back to the beginning, starting with Cavendish in 1798 and Reich in 1837. Or take the determinations of the velocity of light on pages 56–57. Values there date back to Römer in 1676, but again they are few and far between before the 1870s, with no standard deviations reported prior to that watershed. Without wishing to impugn Petley's tables (for, after all, his first interest is in metrology, not history), the few occasions when standard deviations are reported prior to the 1870s are of dubious status. For instance, recourse to his cited texts reveals that whereas extreme values of relevant variables are reported, individual observations are not; all we are tendered is a "best" or "mean" value. Therefore no legitimate statistical "error" is reported, nor can one be extracted from these early experimental reports. A similar problem arises with Romer's determination of the speed of light, once the historical context is taken into account (van Helden, 1983). Indeed, it would be extremely difficult to form any independent opinion concerning the nature or extent of quantitative errors in any of these texts, for while we are tendered the seeming minutiae of endless verbal descriptions of the apparatus, the delicate "corrections" and attentions required, and protestations of the diligent patience of the experimenter, it would be effectively impossible to compare the outcomes to roughly contemporary experiments, much less to modern determinations of the "same" constant.[7] So the distinction between precision and accuracy cannot be carried back

---

[7] Take, for instance, Petley's citation of Reich, which turns out to be a verbal report by the president of the Royal Astronomical Society of London on Reich's German experiments (*Philosophical Magazine* 1838, 283–84). On the determination of the gravitational constant, supposedly a repetition of and improvement on Cavendish's experiment, the commentator remarks: "The arm itself appears to have been nearly of the same length as that used by Cavendish, but we are not informed of its weight, nor of the weight of the small balls." Even the gathered company recognized this might be a source of variance, if not error. While on this topic, it might be noted that the widespread impression that early paradigm determinations of the physical constants might be "restaged" for modern audiences is more a theatrical than an epistemic prospect, given the spotty character of early experimental reports, combined with vast differences in the very character of the materials used between then and now. This point is nicely made for nineteenth-century practices in physics by Stansfield (1990).

into the earlier history of the physical constants – at least not, say, prior to 1870 or so.

If there is one thing which sets apart the eighteenth-century notion of error from the complex of practices that came afterwards, it is that error was almost always associated exclusively with the virtues (or lack thereof) of the individual experimenter. As one contemporary put it: "Everything Sir Isaac Newton handled became Demonstration" (quoted in Gooding et al. 1989, 99). The central icon of the process of measurement inherited from the Enlightenment is that of the experimenter as engaged in an unmediated asocial encounter with nature, even though this flies in the face of all the social technologies involved with the institution of an "experimental form of life" (Shapin and Schaffer 1985). "The historical rhetoric of solitude typically signified a series of normatively patterned disengagements from specific institutions or sectors of society . . . solitude was often an intensely public pose, intended to express an evaluation of the society from which the isolate represented himself to be disengaged" (Shapin 1991, 195). When the savant returned from his private communion with nature, his own virtue and reputation were thought to be the primary guarantors of truth or error. This act of communion, like the faith that often underwrote it, possessed a private, ineffable, mystical dimension that would not bear too close scrutiny, especially given the tensions between science and religion. Thus physical inquiry was a "calling" to which many responded but for whom few were chosen by nature to bestow her secrets. "Great exactitude and a spirit of order – these are the principal requirements of the physicist who devotes himself to these sorts of observations" (Cotte quoted in Frängsmyr et al. 1990, 166). Error itself was regarded as too amorphous and polymorphous to display any structural order in its multifarious manifestations. What is central to this ethos of exactitude is that it is a matter of vigilance and sensibility – rarely a communal phenomenon and not inherent in the observations themselves.

This extreme personification of error explains many of the curious aspects of eighteenth-century experimental reports and protocol statements that so perturb more modern observers, often expressed in such comments as "Precision and reliability, in fact, did not trouble early eighteenth-century natural philosophers" (T. Feldman quoted in ibid., 148); "In eighteenth-century quantitative science no need was felt for a theory of errors as a vehicle for the discussion of discrepancies between data and the proposed laws describing them" (Tiling 1973, 56); or "The physicists and chemists of the eighteenth century, unlike the astronomers and mathematicians, did not find it imperative to make use of very great accuracy in their measurements" (Daumas 1963, 430). For instance, there was a tendency to report not more than one or perhaps two trials of experiments, even while openly admitting that they were extracted from a much larger sequence of trials. As Newton once wrote of his optical investigations: "The historicall narration of these experiments would make a discourse too tedious & confused & therefore I shall lay down the *Doctrine* first and then, for its examination, give you an instance or two of the *Experiments*, as a specimen of the rest" (quoted in Gooding et al. 1989, 68).

The doctrine of *experimentum crucis* was intended to convey efficiently the distilled insight of the savant in illustrating the discovery, which itself would be validated by witnesses of impeccable credentials. The extirpation of error was something best done alone and in private, although, of course, disputes in public could not be altogether avoided.

The major watershed in our prospective history of error was the deconstruction of the convention that the lone individual was morally and intellectually responsible for its extirpation. The new history of "objectivity" has made us aware of the extreme confusion and lack of specificity in our own uses of the term; it also has stressed the profound changes in the early nineteenth century of the various referents of the status of the objective (Daston 1992). The rise of the aperspectival connotation of objectivity in the early nineteenth century was intimately bound up with changes in the social structures of science, as well as with the reconstitution of the category of quantitative error. The expansion of scientific communities tended to undermine earlier presumptions of personal acquaintance and contact with the then small number of competent researchers in any single subject area. As the experimenter came increasingly to depend critically on the results of strangers for quantitative inputs and inspirations, the ideal of the interchangeable observer and the "view from nowhere" came to dominate the earlier moral economy of the laboratory. In place of simply conveying what was known about a measurement, it became incumbent on experimental reports to try somehow to convey what was *not* known (Olesko 1991, 139). But of equal importance, the network of theoretical terms began to attain a critical state of connectedness, whereby "identical" numbers might be reached by several different methods. All of this had far-reaching implications for the conceptualization of error.

Three manifestations of this depersonalization of measurement led jointly, over the course of the nineteenth century, to the systematization of quantitative error: the spread of ordinary least squares as a research technique for the reduction of data; the promulgation of the notion of a "personal equation" of error; and the drive toward metrological standards. With respect to a history of error, it should become apparent that the concerted construction and maintenance of invariant standards and the circulation of representatives among laboratories certainly helped to break down the earlier reliance on an unmediated personal confrontation with nature, as well as to bring home the significance of personal frailty in the reproduction of such basic entities as the units of mass, time, and length. Babbage's proposal for a compendium of the "constants of Nature" in 1856 was merely the beginning of the realization that the contemporaneous codification of standards in trade among nations might also be prudent, if not inescapable, among laboratories.

Hence by 1870 the problem of transpersonal error in precision laboratory measurement was no longer avoidable; it is only at this point in history that the distinction between systematic and random error was regularly made explicit, and the derivative distinction between precision and accuracy thus became uncontentious. This was instantiated in that era in many activities and aspects of physical science. First, as noted in our perusal of Petley (1985), above, after circa 1870 we actually start to get multiple readings of precision measurements commonly reported in individual published papers, so that the authors (or for that matter we historians) can calculate standard errors of estimated physical constants of a specific vintage. Graphical presentation of experimental results becomes a standard rhetorical trope, attesting to an ethic of candidness with regard to error. This same period witnessed the rise of the physics teaching laboratory in the British and American pedagogical contexts (Gooday 1990; Olesko 1988); and much of what was taught within the practicum was the correct protocol to separate out systematic from random error to the extent then thought possible.

The next landmark in this prospective history of error is the work of the hero of modern metrology (but not of any recent histories of physics), Raymond Thayer Birge (Helmholz 1990; Petley 1985, 153; Cohen et al. 1957, 105). His major achievement was single-handedly to create the role of the meta-analyst in atomic physics and therefore to make more explicit what had until his efforts been merely latent: the ineluctable social character of error and thus precision. While primarily remembered for his discovery of the isotope carbon 13, Birge's main contributions to physics were his talent for reevaluation of the experimental reports of others, his appreciation of the (almost Peircian) implications of statistical practices, and his bold willingness to challenge some of his most famous contemporaries in experimental physics. His critical review of the physical constants (Birge 1929) was the first to examine the relationship of the entire constellation of numbers (as then understood) to the errors reported by their individual assayers. His reconsideration of the relevance of least squares in the estimation of structural relations between constants and across experimenters (Birge 1932) led to the graphical analysis of error bars and what are now called Birge ratios and Birge-Bond diagrams (Petley 1985, 296, 304). The former compared standard errors between experimenters' reports with errors reported within individual experiments, while the lattter developed a statistical technique of fitting the "best" configuration of individual constants, given some imposed constraints. Birge ratios will occupy pride of place in the next section.

While these might appear dry technical considerations, in practice they served to bring to light the deeper problems of the definition of errors of measurement. As Cohen et al. (1957, 104) admitted, it is not generally the concern of the individual experimentalist "to enquire how *consistent* the overdetermined set is . . . Aside from the exercise of vigilance in the experiments themselves, this test of consistency is in fact the only safeguard we possess against systematic errors." The distinction between systematic and random error had been initially intended to demarcate those discrepancies that were the responsibility of the analyst from those residua to be tamed by statistics; but once statistical constructions of error became ensconced, they tended to usurp the causal character of the "systematic" residual. As Birge himself noted: "We never know the *true* errors of individual measurements. We know only their deviations from some calculated average value. Hence we can only state an estimate of probable error . . . and a corresponding estimate of the odds to be attached to the stated measure of uncertainty" (Birge 1957, 61). But in such a regime the physical constants became the product of averages of averages of averages – the Russian doll as an act of measurement, with personal responsibility for the extirpation of error grown ever more diffuse and difficult to isolate with each subsequent revelation.

But although my original object was thus merely to bring about consistency in the field, I have, as a result of such detailed recalculation, occasionally come across serious errors in the published reduction of the data . . . Naturally I am both surprised and shocked at such discoveries, and I am often placed in a most embarrassing position. But the only point I am making now is that it seems necessary, in all serious work of a critical nature, to take nothing for granted. In fact, the great complaint of everyone who attempts to do such work is that the average investigator – to be sure, under pressure from the editor – fails to include sufficient detailed observational material in his published paper to make even possible a valid recalculation of his results. (Birge 1945, 64)

In this regime it made more sense for someone not embroiled in any specific experimental protocol or laboratory to oversee the work of averaging in order to provide an external review of possible systematic errors, cast a critical gaze upon the publishing practices of the relevant outlets, and also survey all potential interconnections. This, of course, just rephrases the point made in the previous section about the absence of any story of laissez-faire based on individual self-interest. As Birge observed, "It is really difficult for one who has not worked in the field to visualize the maze of interconnections that exists between the general physical constants" (ibid., 63). What was missing was the person who would sketch out the measurement graph, inspect it for connectedness, and gauge the discrepancies along its multiple paths. Hence Birge's innovation of the persona of the meta-analyst – or better, the "scientific arbitrageur" – and the relatively open acknowledgement of the social character of the final numbers inscribed in the reference tables.

Birge's genius was to realize that far from being a glorified anthologist, the job of the meta-analyst was to supervise actively the attribution of error throughout the interconnected network of constants (as in figure 9.1), doggedly imposing consistency in the teeth of error. In his 1929 survey, he suggested that the metrologist begin with those constants least dependent on all the others and most "solid" in his estimation, selecting a path through the subsequent constants that was predicated on fairly accepted conversion factors and auxiliary constants, compounding the least statistical error along the way. This might end up being a thankless task, given the need to deflate egos not accustomed to having their laboratories turned upside-down by outsiders. In this regard Birge was brazen, reserving especially sharp criticism for Robert Millikan's oil-drop experiment, among others.[8] But even this procedure did not result in a unique set of final values, prompting Birge in the 1930s to research further techniques for the minimization of overall statistical error, as well as the development of expository techniques such as plotting error bars and calculating Birge ratios to render error more explicit. Yet the more attention was lavished on error, the more apparent it became that the systematic/random distinction was persistently compromised. In one of the major fruits of meta-analysis, the exposure of the estimation of random error to the light of day opened up the possibility that there might be yet further systematic patterns to such attributions.

The story of Millikan's determinations of the charge of the electron (e) provides one illustration of the conundrum. Birge, working *only* from published data, made a number of criticisms of the reported value of e, which he claimed was "accepted without question by everyone, [with] no one else even attempt[ing] similar work of comparable precision" (Birge 1957, 43). Initially noting an inconsistency between values of e derived

[8] See, for instance, the discussion in Birge 1957 (pp. 43–47). In light of the crusade by Allan Franklin (1986, chap. 5; 1990, 132) to rehabilitate the reputation of Millikan after the problems identified by Holton (1978), this singling out of the Nobel Prize winner is especially interesting.

from X-ray crystal diffraction and Millikan's oil drops, he tended to attribute the discrepancy to use of an incorrect auxiliary constant for the viscosity of air. Further digging revealed that Millikan had also used discrepant units of voltage, and that he had derived a slope estimate from a freehand plot and not least squares, thus revealing that his "error" estimate was relatively subjective and not dependent on statistical calculation. Recourse to Millikan's laboratory notebooks, an option not open to Birge, has revealed even more patterns in the treatment of error. As described by Holton (1978), Millikan's earliest published work on water droplets assigned subjective ratings of validity to braces of observations. By the time of the oil drop experiments, Millikan had learned the hard lesson of impersonal statistical rhetoric in his writing; but it did not appreciably alter his private behavior in the laboratory. There he regularly dismissed events that would have implied nonintegral units of charge, not including them in his final error estimates. Holton regards this as an illustration of the theory-dependence of observation, since if free quarks were thought to exist, then one would be on the lookout for fractional charges. While quarks could not have been imagined before the fact, the existence of fractional charges was advocated by the Austrian contemporary Felix Ehrenhaft, who, although even going so far as to reprocess Millikan's published data, did not have his own findings taken into account by Birge and others. From our own vantage point, this highlights not so much older Kuhnian notions of incommensurability as much as the pervasive adulteration of reports of "random" error by unspecified systematic components. All Birge's meticulous care and concern over air viscosity and international voltage units could still have been for naught, swamped by the systematic effect of unreported selection on the part of the original investigators.

The ultimate implication of the modern explicit rendering of error practices is to realize that the uniform approach of the physical constants to some invariant asymptote is itself a myth. Without suggesting that Birge ever doubted the palpable reality of the physical constants, he certainly developed a shrewd appreciation for anomalies in the patterns of error attributions toward the end of his life (Birge 1957, 51): "The tendency of a series of experimental results, at a certain epoch, to group themselves around a certain value raises a very interesting psychological question." That question, rephrased in modern terms, is: To what extent does the experimenter fight the systematics until he or she gets the "right" answer? This is now known as the problem of "intellectual phase locking" or (following Allan Franklin) the "bandwagon effect." Prior to the advent of meta-analysis, with its calculation of Birge ratios, and the whole panoply of error analysis, this problem could never even have been isolated in the act of quantitative measurement of physical constants, so in that sense it is characteristic of the late twentieth century. But from an alternative perspective, it is the same old problem of the sociology of knowledge – namely, how findings come to be stabilized in a community of inquirers.

The bandwagon effect is common knowledge among practicing metrologists (Youden 1972; Langenberg and Taylor 1971; Petley 1985; Rosenfeld 1975, 581; Franklin 1990, 135); and it should be made better known among historians and philosophers of science. Briefly, it is the tendency of individual estimates of physical constants plotted chronologically to bunch together in certain eras, then to jump outside of previous error bound estimates, only to cluster within the new range for another indeterminate length of time. This behavior violates almost every assumption buttressing the use of statistics in the assessment of measurement error; however, it is entirely consistent with the practical blurring of the systematic/random distinction described above. Practicing ₋etrologists have commented on this:

One has to remember that some errors are random for one person and systematic for another. . . . It is not possible for one person to perform every single experiment to prepare his own determination of something. One has to take other people's results. So if one uses those results and they are the same all the time, they are systematic to this particular investigation. (Vigouroux, quoted in Langenberg and Taylor 1971, 524)

Yet combining this observation with the knowledge that everyone's results are jointly and severally dependent on everyone else's in a simultaneous manner, we can imagine the situation where very small changes somewhere in the web can shift the entire structure discretely and discontinuously. And far from being a hypothetical possibility, metrologists are also aware that this has actually occurred in the past and, more important, do not find it daunting or distressing.

No cry of anguish was heard from the general scientific community when it was discovered in 1967, as a result of the Josephson effect measurement of $2e/h$, that many of the previously accepted values of the constants would have to be changed between 20 and 100 ppm (four to five times their assigned [standard] errors). (Taylor, quoted in ibid., 496)

In summary, this historical sketch of the estimation of the physical constants has been one of the construction of more and more elaborate institutions and social structures for the production and allocation of quantitative error. Meta-analysis is itself a thriving industry. For example, the Particle Data Group at Berkeley – the final arbiter of numerical characteristics of subatomic particles – throws out roughly 40 percent of all experimental reports before reporting a preferred estimate of a measured constant (Rosenfeld 1975, 578). Many laboratories engaged in precision work now internalize this process by producing their own "error budgets," allocating error bars to individual components of any multitiered experiment (Mackenzie 1991, 267; Cartwright 1989, 68).[9] Just as economists have long wondered why large firms often internalize various functions that might potentially have been performed by "the market," a looming problem in science studies will be to plumb the reasons why some laboratories in the age of Big Science now manage to perform some of their meta-analysis in-house.

It is no accident that the bureaucratization of error audits spreads in tandem with the bureaucratization of scientific inquiry. For instance, the Defense Department is at present the largest employer of metrologists in the United States; the ohm now follows the barrel of the gun (O'Connell 1993). Political worries about the appearance of accountability and fraud in the era of Big Science have threatened to superimpose yet another layer of oversight on the existing error attribution process, only this time at the level of congressional subcommittee investigations or judicial intervention. *Science* magazine and the Sunday tabloids now endeavor to take sides in public accusations of shoddy laboratory protocols. Sociologists and risk analysts have even been getting into the act of late, subjecting the "subjective" probability estimates of measurement error to the traditions of decision science (Henrion and Fischoff 1986). There is no end in sight to the ongoing evolution of a novel social process of intervention in the interests of the stabilization of error.

Quantitative indexes of the social construction of error

One of the advantages of a mathematical description of the economics of error arbitrage is that it not only suggests a diachronic account of the history of error but also provides a synchronic set of indexes of the status of error arbitrage both within and between sciences. The quantitative measure of greatest simplicity in this tradition is the one already pioneered by the meta-analysts – namely, the Birge ratio. The purpose of the Birge ratio is to provide a quick diagnostic comparison of the consistency of a field's own assessment of its success in taming error with the assessment of the outsider examining its published reports – in other

---

[9] I must here enter a demurrer concerning the way in which error budgets are regarded by Nancy Cartwright. Whereas she views them as evidence of the "totally controlled experiment" (Cartwright 1989, section 2.4.2) in pursuit of novel findings, I see them instead as ultimate evidence of an absence of tight prior knowledge and control, which is staunched by means of a relatively arbitrary assessment of what magnitudes of error will be countenanced. It is an approach of the engineer or the grants administrator, rather than being her exemplar of the Millian inquirer after tendencies and capacities.

words, the relative magnitude of internal and external consistency of measurements (Petley 1985, 304). Suppose in some empirical endeavor of interest each experiment reports an estimated value X_i of some relevant constant and an estimated standard error σ_i. Let us collate a number N of individual published experiments in the particular science claiming to estimate the same constant, construct the mean of their estimates $\overline{X}$, and use it to define a value of the external error consistency as:

$$\sigma_E = \left[\sum_{i=1}^{N}(X_i - \overline{X})^2 / \sigma_i^2 \right] \left[(N-1)\sum_{i=1}^{N}(1 / \sigma_i^2) \right]^{-1}$$

If one then defines as σ^* the sum of the reciprocals of the individually estimated standard errors, then the Birge ratio is defined by $B = \sigma_E/\sigma^*$. When $B = 1$, the assessment of error bars within experiments could readily account for the distribution of errors in the network of constants of estimates of X between experiments, or in our economic language, error is being successfully arbitraged between constants. However, if B is very much greater than unity, then one or more experiments have severely underestimated the uncertainty surrounding the value of X, or else the presumption of joint independence between experimental determinations may be violated. In either case the meta-analyst uses the diagnostic to search out sources of interexperimenter inconsistency. In our economic terminology, there are profits to be made by eliminating some experiments or else by reestimating the magnitude of some of the network of constants or, most drastically, by reconfiguring the entire theoretical network.[10]

Metrologists use Birge ratios in their quotidian endeavors; it is my contention that they should also be a part of the tool-kit of the sociologist of science. To show how they might be used in science studies, I shall reproduce a few collections of Birge ratios reported in greater detail elsewhere and then draw out a few social implications of their relative magnitudes. The fields chosen for comparison are modern physics, modern

[10] It is necessary to stress that the Birge ratio cannot indicate where the problem lies; nor is a low Birge ratio prima facie evidence for experimental success, since collusion could equally well produce a $B = 1$. There are also many proposed refinements of the Birge ratio in the metrology literature, discussed in Petley (1985, 305–6). It is also prudent to point out that we have only just begun to sketch the social theory of the various options open to the individual scientist when confronted with a large-scale arbitrage opportunity as described above. Mathematically, "error" can indifferently be reduced by throwing out some experiments, reallocating error among existing experiments, or changing the theory and reconfiguring the graph. In real life, the options are not so indifferently available to every scientist. Birge himself is not remembered in standard histories of physics because he did not engage in the high-status occupation of theorists to banish error, nor did he generate more estimates of the relevant constants. To put it bluntly, metrology is not a royal road to a Nobel Prize. This clearly will bias the distribution of reactions to error. (I owe this point to Michael Power.)

Table 9.1. *Birge ratios for physical constants*

Constant	Dates	B	N^a
Speed of light	1875–1958	1.42	27
Gravitational	1798–1983	1.38	14
Magnetic moment proton	1949–67	1.44	7
Fine structure[b]		2.95	24
Fine structure[c]		1.26	14
Muon lifetime	1957–80	3.28	10
Charged pion mass	1957–80	2.23	10
Lambda mass	1957–80	4.34	10
Lambda lifetime	1957–80	2.72	27
Sigma lifetime	1957–80	1.62	16
Omega mass	1957–80	0.86	11

Sources: Upper panel, Henrion and Fischoff (1986, 794); lower panel, Hedges (1987, 447).
[a] Number of studies estimating value of constant.
[b] "High accuracy" measurements of inverse fine structure constants. No dates given.
[c] "Low accuracy" measurements of inverse fine structure.

experimental psychology and modern neoclassical economics.

In table 9.1 we have two samples of Birge ratios, one for the fundamental physical constants over longer periods of time and one for some more recent subatomic constants over much shorter time frames. The first aspect of the table which jumps out at the novice is the fact that most Birge ratios in physics exceed unity. This would seem a counterintuitive result, except for the considerations already broached in the two preceding sections. To recap, inconsistencies always exist in any densely connected network of quantitative constants, and no individual experimenter can effectively personally allocate the error across the net. Moreover, quantitative error itself has changed in epistemic significance over longer stretches of time, due in no small part to historical changes in institutions identified in the previous section, so no single interpretation could be legitimately attached to reported errors over time. And then, more recently, there is the bandwagon effect, which would tend to violate the independence of experimenter reports presumed by the Birge ratio. In economic terms, arbitrage opportunities are always present in precision measurement; it is only a question of their greater or lesser magnitude. Thus Birge ratios should be considered a comparative device, indicating rough orders of magnitude of quantitative disagreement.

Our second brace of Birge ratios (table 9.2), compiled by a psychologist, reports results for a set of quantities deemed as legitimate constants by the relevant experimental community. Again we observe that the pre-

Table 9.2. Birge ratios for psychological measurements

Subject	B	N
Sex/spatial perception	1.64	62
Sex/spatial visualization	1.27	81
Sex/verbal ability	4.09	11
Sex/field articulation	1.75	14
Open ed./reading	5.87	19
Open ed./math achievement	2.73	17
Open ed./school attitude	2.16	11
Open ed./self-concept	1.39	18

Source: Hedges (987, 449).

ponderance of Birge ratios exceeds unity. While a few ratios are above four, by and large one might claim that the magnitude of "agreement" in psychology was roughly comparable to that in physics, which was indeed the interpretation of the compiler of the statistics (Hedges 1987). Before psychologists embark on a round of hearty self-congratulations, however, it is imperative to recall that many things can account for low Birge ratios, and that one should not confuse low ratios with unqualified empirical success. Nevertheless, this finding is significant for science studies, since it does call into question an often implicit ranking of the empirical hierarchy of the sciences.

Table 9.3 reports Birge ratios from some of my own work on the empirical practices of post-1945 neoclassical economists. (The underlying data and sources are documented in an appendix that is available on request.) It should be stressed at the outset that these "constants" are not the product of controlled experimentation, but rather the output of econometric statistical packages. The relationship of econometrics to controlled experimentation has been a contentious issue throughout its brief history; but the belief of many economists is that their statistical devices serve as an adequate substitute for controlled experimentation.[11] Here let us take those beliefs as a given, simply so as to be able to report on their own practices with regard to the attribution and arbitrage of error. We observe that Birge ratios in economics are orders of magnitude above those generally found in physics and psychology, if we accept the values reported in tables 9.1 and 9.2. It seems that there may exist a myriad of unexploited opportunities for error arbitrage within the community of neoclassical empirical economists.

This seeming divergence of the amount of agreement among physicists,

[11] For claims along these lines, see Morgan (1990) and Cartwright (1989). The problems with these assertions are discussed in Mirowski (1990 and 1995).

Table 9.3. *Birge ratios, economics*

Model	N	Years	Birge
US Money Demand Elasticity	9	1971–88	49.66
UK Money Demand Elasticity	7	1971–91	73.34
Purchasing Power Parity, 1920s FF/$	6	1973–88	3.14
US Import Income Elasticity	14	1974–90	29.87
US Import Price Elasticity	10	1974–90	5.49
US Export Income Elasticity	13	1963–90	24.90
US Export Price Elasticity	9	1963–90	4.89
Employment-Output Elasticity,			
US Manufacturing	6	1967–74	22.70
Male Labor Supply	5	1971–76	1.26
Welfare Spell Length and Race	5	1986–92	2.23

Source: Appendix available on request.

psychologists, and economists, respectively, has many causes, most of which can be traced to their divergent histories. Clearly justice cannot be done to that inquiry here; the theory of error arbitrage is intended as a prelude to a research program in science studies, not its culmination. However, there is one very salient reason for this pattern that is germane to the thesis of this paper. As I have argued, it is very unlikely that a laissez-faire pattern of arbitrage would successfully serve to stabilize the empirical measurement of quantitative constants, because of the fact that no one is personally motivated to accumulate the results of arbitrage – namely, the error units themselves. This is the most striking way that a conventional market differs from the process of error arbitrage. The primary reason that both physics and psychology display distinctly lower Birge ratios than does economics is that *they have institutionally acknowledged that fact:* at some juncture in the twentieth century, both have managed to institute structures of meta-analysis both to foster and to enforce the reconciliation of error attributions on the part of individual experimentalists. Physicists have their particle data groups, and psychologists have a special journal and the subdiscipline of meta-analysis. The empirical economists have nothing comparable.

Here is where the history and sociology of science reenter the meta-narrative with a vengeance. Why do economists not acknowledge the problem of which the astronomical Birge ratios are a symptom? The short answer is that neoclassical economics is a peculiar social theory that has its own special problems of reflexivity. The standard Walrasian general equilibrium tradition is a theory that claims to describe how a market works to reconcile individual desires and activities as if by an invisible hand, without the intervention of any conscious external agency. Many, though not all, neoclassical economists thus imbibe a deep skepticism toward the claims of government to be capable of allocating resources according to any standards of efficiency or welfare. Indeed, some psychological researchers have claimed that one result of socialization in the economics profession is a pronounced antipathy toward social cooperation (Frank, Gilovich, and Regan 1993). Economists, not surprisingly, have also been one of the most serious advocates of applying their own theory reflexively to themselves, regarding their discipline as a "free market of ideas" (Hands 1994). Thus any movement to set up an agency devoted to meta-analysis has been blocked by a vocal coalition as the encroachment of Big Brother on their academic freedom, in a manner very different from attitudes in physics and psychology.

I shall close this survey on what may seem a note of irony. In this paper I claim that a model of arbitrage taken from one version of economics could help us better understand the process of the stabilization of quantitative measurement in all the sciences. Yet, upon deployment and elaboration of this model, it was discovered that economics itself was an egregious outlier in terms of the lack of agreement in its attempts at precision measurement and stabilization of its quantitative empirical practices. Is there not here also some sort of reflexive problem? Not if we insist that the theory of arbitrage (which, by the way, is not an integral part of the neoclassical school) is a generic theory of the imposition of an algebraic structure on a heterogeneous network. The reason that economic metaphors seem so helpful in its understanding is probably due to the historical fact that they evolved first in the economic sphere and only later in other realms of quantitative activity. The fact that the theory can be turned into an auto-critique of economics, rather than another triumph of an imperial imperative of the most imperious of the social sciences, should stand as one of the strongest arguments in its favor.

REFERENCES

Bernstein, Peter. 1992. *Capital Ideas.* New York: Free Press.
Birge, Raymond. 1929. "Probable Values of the General Physical Constants." *Physical Review Supplement* 1:1–73.
   1932. "Probable Values of *e, h, e/m* and *a*." *Physical Review* 40:228–261.
   1939. "The Propagation of Error." *American Physics Teacher* 7:351–57.
   1945. "The 1944 Values of Certain Atomic Constants." *American Journal of Physics* 13:63–73.
   1957. "A Survey of the Systematic Evaluation of the Universal Physical Constants." *Nuovo Cimento*, supp. 6, 39–67.

Bourdieu, Pierre. 1975. "The Specificity of the Scientific Field." *Social Science Information* 14:19–47.

Cartwright, Nancy. 1989. *Nature's Capacities and Their Measurement.* Oxford: Oxford University Press.

Cohen, E. R., K. Crowe, and J. Dumond. 1957. *The Fundamental Constants of Physics.* New York: Interscience.

Cohen, E. R., and B. Taylor. 1987. "The 1986 adjustment of the Fundamental Physical Constants." *Reviews of Modern Physics* 59:1121–48.

Collins, Harry. 1985. *Changing Order.* London: Sage.

Daston, Lorraine. 1992. "Objectivity and the Escape from Perspective." *Social Studies of Science* 22:597–618.

Daumas, Maurice. 1963. "Precision of Measurement and Physical and Chemical Research in the Eighteenth Century." In *Scientific Change,* edited by A. C. Crombie. London: Heinemann.

de Finetti, Bruno. 1974. *Theory of Probability.* New York: Wiley.

Duhem, Pierre. 1977. *The Aim and Structure of Physical Theory.* New York: Atheneum.

Earman, John. 1992. *Bayes or Bust.* Cambridge, Mass.: MIT Press.

Ellerman, David. 1984. "Arbitrage Theory: a Mathematical Introduction." *SIAM Review* 26:241–61.

Farmer, J. D. 1991. "A Rosetta Stone for Connectionism." In *Emergent Computation,* edited by S. Forrest. Cambridge, Mass.: MIT Press.

Frängsmyr, T., J. L. Heilbron, and Robin Rider, eds. 1990. *The Quantifying Spirit in the Eighteenth Century.* Berkeley: University of California Press.

Frank, R., T. Gilovich, and D. Regan. 1993. "Does Studying Economics Inhibit Cooperation?" *Journal of Economic Perspectives* 7:159–71.

Franklin, Allen. 1986. *The Neglect of Experiment.* Cambridge: Cambridge University Press.

——— 1990. *Experiment Right or Wrong.* New York: Cambridge University Press.

Gigerenzer, Gerd, and David Murray. 1987. *Cognition as Intuitive Statistics.* Hillsdale, N.J.: Erlbaum.

Goldman, Alvin. 1992. *Liaisons.* Cambridge, Mass.: MIT Press.

Gooday, Graeme. 1990. "Precision Measurement and the Genesis of Physics Teaching Laboratories." *British Journal for the History of Science* 23:25–51.

——— 1992 "The Morals of Measurement: Precision and Constancy in Late Victorian Physics." Paper presented at the December 1992 meeting of HES, Washington, D.C.

Gooding, David. 1990. *Experiment and the Making of Meaning.* Boston: Kluwer.

Gooding, D., T. Pinch, and S. Schaffer, eds. 1989. *The Uses of Experiment.* Cambridge: Cambridge University Press.

Hands, Wade. 1994a. "The Sociology of Scientific Knowledge and Economics." In *New Perspectives in the Methodology of Economics,* edited by Roger Backhouse, 75–106. London: Routledge.

——— 1994b. "Blurred Boundaries: Recent Changes in the Relationship Between Economics and the Philosophy of Natural Science." *Studies in the History and Philosophy of Science.*

Hedges, Larry. 1987. "How Hard Is Hard Science, How Soft Is Soft Science?" *American Psychologist* 42:443–55.

Helmholz, Carl. 1990. "Raymond Thayer Birge." In *Biographical Memoirs of the National Academy of Sciences* 59:73–84.

Henrion, Max, and Baruch Fischoff. 1986. "Assessing Uncertainty in Physical Constants." *American Journal of Physics* 54:791–97.

Holton, Gerald. 1978. *The Scientific Imagination.* New York: Cambridge University Press.

Hon, Giora. 1989. "Towards a Typology of Experimental Errors." *Studies in the History and Philosophy of Science* 20:469–504.

Howson, Colin, and Peter Urbach. 1989. *Scientific Reasoning.* La Salle: Open Court.

Kahneman, D., P. Slovic, and A. Tversky, eds. 1982. *Judgments under Uncertainty.* New York: Cambridge University Press.

Kitcher, Philip. 1993. *The Advancement of Science.* New York: Oxford University Press.

Kuhn, Thomas. 1977. *The Essential Tension.* Chicago: University of Chicago Press.

Kyburg, Henry. 1992. "Measuring Errors of Measurement." In *Philosophical and Foundational Issues in Measurement Theory*, edited by C. Savage and P. Ehrlich. Hillsdale, N.J.: Erlbaum.

Langenberg, D., and B. Taylor. 1971. *Precision Measurement and the Fundamental Constants.* Washington: USGPO.

Latour, Bruno. 1987. *Science in Action.* Cambridge, Mass.: Harvard University Press.

1993. *We Have Never Been Modern.* Cambridge, Mass.: Harvard University Press.

Latour, Bruno, and Steve Woolgar. 1986. *Laboratory Life.* Princeton, N.J.: Princeton University Press.

Mackenzie, Donald. 1991. *Inventing Accuracy.* Cambridge, Mass.: MIT Press.

Mayo, Deborah. 1985. "Behavioralistic, Evidentialist, and Learning Models of Statistical Testing." *Philosophy of Science* 52:493–516.

1992. "Did Pearson Reject the Neyman-Pearson Philosophy of Statistics?" *Synthese* 90:233–62.

Mendoza, Eric. 1990. "Delaroche and Berard and Experimental Error." *British Journal for the History of Science* 23:285–91.

Mirowski, Philip. 1989. *More Heat Than Light.* New York: Cambridge University Press.

1990. "From Mandelbrot to Chaos in Economic Theory." *Southern Economic Journal* 57:289–307.

1991. "Postmodernism and the Social Theory of Value." *Journal of Post Keynesian Economics* 13:565–82.

1992. "Looking for Those Natural Numbers." *Science in Context* 5:165–88.

1993. "Unholy History of Error." Notre Dame Working Paper.

1994. "Arbitrage, Symmetries and the Social Theory of Value." In *New Directions in Analytical Political Economy*, edited by Amitava Dutt. Cheltenham: Edward Elgar.

1995. "Three Ways of Thinking about Testing in Econometrics." *Journal of Econometrics.* 67: 25–46.

Mirowski, Philip, and Steven Sklivas. 1991. "Why Econometricians Don't

Replicate (Although They Do Reproduce)." *Review of Political Economy* 3:146–63.

Morgan, Mary. 1990. *A History of Econometrics.* Cambridge: Cambridge University Press.

O'Connell, Joseph. 1993. "Metrology: The Creation of Universality by the Circulation of Particulars." *Social Studies of Science* 23:129–74.

Olesko, Katheryn. 1988. "Michelson and the Reform of Physics Instruction." In *The Michelson Era in American Physics,* edited by S. Goldberg and R. Stuewer. New York: American Institute of Physics.

——— 1991. *Physics as a Calling.* Ithaca, N.Y.: Cornell University Press.

Petley, Brian. 1985. *The Fundamental Physical Constants and the Frontiers of Measurement.* Bristol: Adam Hilger.

Pickering, Edward. 1873. *Elements of Physical Manipulation.* Boston: Houghton Mifflin.

Porter, Theodore. 1986. *The Rise of Statistical Thinking.* Princeton, N.J.: Princeton University Press.

——— 1992. "Objectivity as Standardization." *Annals of Scholarship* 9:19–59.

Radnitzksy, G., and P. Bernholz, eds. 1987. *Economic Imperialism.* New York: Paragon.

Rosenfeld, Arthur. 1975. "The Particle Data Group." In *Annual Review of Nuclear Science* 25:555–98.

Serres, Michel. 1982. *The Parasite.* Baltimore: Johns Hopkins University Press.

Shapin, Steven. 1991. "The Mind in Its Own Place." *Science in Context* 4:191–218.

Shapin, S., and S. Schaffer. 1985. *Leviathan and the Air Pump.* Princeton, N.J.: Princeton University Press.

Smith, C., and N. Wise. 1989. *Energy and Empire.* New York: Cambridge University Press.

Stansfield, Ronald. 1990. "Could We Repeat It?" In *Physicists Look Back,* edited by John Rocke. Bristol: Adam Hilger.

Stigler, Stephen. 1986. *A History of Statistics.* Cambridge, Mass.: Harvard University Press.

Swijtink, Zeno. 1987. "The Objectification of Observation." In *The Probabilistic Revolution,* vol. 1, edited by L. Kruger et al. Cambridge, Mass.: MIT Press.

Taylor, B., and W. Phillips, eds. 1984. *Precision Measurement and Fundamental Constants II.* Washington, D.C.: National Bureau of Standards, Special Publication no. 617.

Tilling, Laura. 1973. "the Interpretation of Observational Errors in the Eighteenth and Early Nineteenth Centuries." Ph.D. diss., University of London.

van Helden, Albert. 1983. "Roemer"s Speed of Light." *Journal of the History of Astronomy* 14:137–41.

Wise, M. N., ed. 1995. *The Values of Precision.* Princeton, N.J.: Princeton University Press.

Youden, W. 1972. "Enduring Values." *Technometrics* 14:1–11.

Zolatarev, V. 1986. *One-Dimensional Stable Distributions.* AMS Translations No. 65. Providence, R.I.: American Mathematical Society.

10 Toward a philosophy of science accounting: a critical rendering of instrumental rationality

Steve Fuller

The project of "social epistemology" draws on the resources of history and the social sciences to address the normative problems classically posed by epistemologists and philosophers of science (Fuller 1988). A core tenet of this project is that once these normative problems have been sufficiently historicized and sociologized, they will resemble the problems associated with evaluation and policymaking in other social arenas (Fuller 1988, 263–94; 1993a, 143–207; 1993b, 227–318). This essay will drive home the point by translating certain classical debates over the nature of scientific rationality into issues of science accounting. First I distinguish the social epistemologist's position on science accounting as a "constructive" and "reflexive" one, to use two terms that help position me in recent social theoretic discussions. Next I argue that attempts – especially by the Frankfurt School – to make an absolute distinction between "critical" and "instrumental" forms of rationality capture only the constructive but not the reflexive side of science accounting, whereby instrumental rationality can be rendered critical. Four "accountability conditions" are then provided, under which instrumental rationality may be rendered critical. This defines adequacy conditions for the social epistemologist's sense of science accounting From there I move to consider competing critico-instrumental accounts of science offered by Ernst Mach and Max Planck at the dawn of Big Science, a turning point that proves instructive in trying to account for science in today's world.

The kind of science accounting appropriate to social epistemology

We may distinguish two general kinds of science accounting, *deconstructive* and *constructive*. The first is familiar from empirical studies of "science in action" influenced by ethnomethodology. Following Harold Garfinkel (1977, 17), one speaks of social life being "accountable" in the sense that there are ready-made verbal formulations that members of a society routinely use to normalize their activities. The ethnomethodologist is typically struck by how similar formulations are used to account for a wide range of events, many of which deviate significantly from what one would normally expect to fall under such accounts. Thus Knorr-Cetina (1981) found that laboratory scientists could mobilize a positivistic repertoire for writing up their results into publishable form, no matter how chaotic their work at the lab bench had turned out to be. An important social function of accounts, in this view, is to reinforce the idea that the world is governed by a certain "mundane reason" (Pollner 1987). Perhaps the most salient sign of this mundaneness is that audiences largely trust the accounts they are given. In a fashionable phrase, the accounts enclose the accounted-for events in a "black box." The ethnomethodologist's job, then, is to open the black box by describing the disparate events that culminated in the provision of a particular account. Once this disparateness is made evident, it becomes clear that an account does not possess some special power to "represent" reality but is itself just another part of that reality. If anything, accounts, by virtue of their perceived trustworthiness, may be especially able to *conceal* other parts of reality (Lynch and Woolgar 1990).

What makes the first sense of science accounting "deconstructive" is its preoccupation with showing what is *not* accounted for. But it is also usually *unreflective*. Ethnomethodologists situate accounts in the social worlds that produce them without situating themselves in those worlds. This gives ethnomethodology its much-vaunted "indifferent" attitude toward the phenomena it studies, which is meant to simulate much of the experience associated with being "objective." However, not all ethnomethodologists have been happy with the coupling of deconstruction and unreflexivity. In the case of science studies, this dissatisfaction has erupted into the field's principal epistemological debate. Mulkay, Woolgar, and Ashmore – in somewhat different ways – have all advocated that science accountants must account for themselves as they account for the scientists whose accounts are under investigation (Woolgar 1988). Thus, insofar as science accountants subvert the trustworthiness of the accounts of the scientists they study, they also subvert the trustworthiness of their own accounts, as they too claim to be engaged in a scientific inquiry. In practice, reflexive deconstructive science accounting throws into doubt the determinateness of such distinctions as true/false and fact/fiction.

Without denying the value of this first sense of science accounting, it is, at best, propaedeutic to the social epistemologist's sense, which, in turn, may be characterized as *constructive* and *reflexive*. A "constructive" approach to accounting holds that the significance of actions and events do not speak for themselves but require the kind of articulation and definition that only discourse can offer. Of course, a variety of standards may be introduced to evaluate the actions and events. However, the crucial point is that without the construction of such accounts, the significance of the actions and events would remain indeterminate. In part, I am appealing to the intuition that informs public-spirited calls for "greater accountability" in politics or, for that matter, science. However, to appreciate the difference between a "reflexive" and "unreflexive" version of constructive science accounting, let us briefly consider a mildly fanciful case of unreflexive science accounting.

Suppose that state science policymakers decided that Larry Laudan's (1981) criterion of "pursuitworthiness" in science was the standard by which research programs would be evaluated. The policymakers might then hire a science accounting firm to compare research programs according to whether they are solving the most empirical problems while causing the fewest conceptual problems in the process. I would call the activity of this firm "constructive but unreflexive" science accounting. The firm does not participate in the creation of the accounting norms – or offer reasons for why a research program *should* adhere to the Laudan standard – but simply applies the norms in the relevant cases, as the policymakers wish. In fact, if the accountants were unemployed philosophers, they would probably harbor doubts about Laudan's scheme but feel that it was not their job to register complaints.

In contrast, the social epistemologist sides with the "reflexivists" in science studies, that science accountants must situate themselves in the accounts they give. However, such reflexivity need not be self-deconstructive; it may be "constructive" if the science accountant assumes responsibility for the norms to which the scientists are held accountable – as if he or she helped legislate the norms into existence, not merely made judgments in accordance with them. As noted above, ethnomethodologists have simply been content to reveal the divergence of accounts from the accounted-for events. No judgment is passed on the normative significance of this divergence: Does it mean a breakdown in social order, a sign of social change, or what? If anything, the refusal of ethnomethodologists to remark on the topic has led more critically minded social theorists to infer that they tacitly endorse the status quo: specifically, that we would do better to alter our attitudes toward accountability than to alter the relationship between accounts and what they account for (cf. Gouldner 1970, Gellner 1979). A similar criticism has been lodged against ethnomethodological studies of scientific practice, with Latour (1987) coming under attack for what seems to be his enthusiastic depiction of scientists operating in a Machiavellian universe (Lynch and Fuhrman 1991).

Ethnomethodological indifference to making science more (or differently?) accountable reflects the origins of empirical science studies as a backlash against philosophical attempts to hold science accountable to norms that are alien to the day-to-day practices of scientists (Lynch 1993). Indeed, the case that science studies makes for having "refuted" positivist and Popperian norms of scientific rationality is not unlike the case made a generation earlier by Michael Polanyi for literally keeping the government accounts out of the laboratory (Fuller 1992b). In both cases, such expessions as "form of life," "culture," and especially "practice" play a prominent role. They are meant to convey that what scientists routinely do in their laboratory settings does not require the sort of constructive science accounting favored by philosophers of science and, now, social epistemologists. That scientific practice is governed by its own tacit norms is evidenced by the fact that scientists have their own ways of going about business, creating and resolving disputes, and so forth. They have managed to do all this – and produce the results they have – without the interference of external scrutinizers. It is suggested (though never argued) that any interference with these practices is bound to make matters worse.

Although it is increasingly fashionable to speak of the work done in a modern scientific laboratory as consisting of "practices" (e.g., Pickering 1992), a citizen of the Athenian polis would find little in this usage that cohered with his understanding of *praxis*. Indeed, I would venture to say that our Greek progenitor would see the social epistemologist, not the laboratory scientist, as engaged in a true *praxis*. In what follows, I rely on Maurice Godelier's survey of recent historical and anthropological work on ancient Greece (Godelier 1986, 130–37).

For the Athenian, a *praxis* was an activity that was done "for its own sake" in a special sense of the highlighted expression. The activity had to have a natural trajectory and ending that would be recognized by the person engaged in the *praxis*. In addition, a *praxis* could define the trajectory and ending of other activities that did not have such self-defining qualities built into them. For example, before the introduction of slavery, agriculture was the paradigm case of a *praxis*. The cultivation and harvest of food were not interminable affairs but ones pursued only as long as was needed to sustain a household. The emphasis was placed not on transforming nature but on participating in an activity pursued by many at once. Such *praxis* was the primary means by which a sense of civility was instilled, as each household tilled the soil in ways that enabled others to sustain themselves. However, after slaves started doing the agriculture, *praxis* was limited to free speech, that is, speaking one's mind (and *only* one's mind). Here we find the roots of the "constructive" sense of accounting.

Two related notions need to be introduced here: *techne* and *poiesis*. The former designates any of a variety of client-oriented trades that require specialized (usually esoteric) training, while the latter refers to the characteristic products of such a trade. The client engages in *praxis* by directing the tradesman to make something to the client's specifications. The tradesman's job is to realize the client's idea in the medium of his trade. The client may oversee the tradesman's work, just to make sure all is going to plan. If the final product is judged good, then the *client*, not the tradesman, will receive credit for its successful execution. (The tradesman will receive payment for his labor, of course.) While such a merit system may seem odd by modern standards, consider the case of today's teachers who typically receive credit for the excellent performance of their students on exams. In both the ancient and the modern case, merit lies more in the design of realizable standards of performance than in the sheer ability to realize those standards in performance. If *techne* enables a tradesman to infuse matter with form, *praxis* enables the client to infuse the tradesman with direction. The social epistemologist proposes that science accounting places the public in the role of the client/teacher and the scientist in that of tradesman/student.

Various complications can be added to this story. For example, what if some enterprising people try to turn speech itself into a *techne*? Would undergoing the relevant training enhance or diminish the status of speech as *praxis*? Such were the worries that animated Plato's and Aristotle's philosophical response to the Sophists. Nevertheless, our Athenian forebears would be in agreement that crucial features of today's "scientific practice" disqualify it from counting as *praxis*. First, consider the claims made for the open-ended, indeed interminable, nature of scientific inquiry, as well as the stress placed on the essentially unintended ("serendipitous") character of major scientific achievements. But perhaps even more telling is the image of a mounting body of scientific literature that seemingly diminishes in its ability to capture its objects of inquiry. More and more is written about less and less.

In short, the sorts of reasons that have often been given for why the Greeks would never have countenanced the unbounded market mentality of capitalism can be used to show why they would refuse to dignify modern science with the title of *praxis*. Someone endlessly driven to make money may be quite skilled, in the sense of possessing a *techne*; but the lack of purposeful closure to his activities would mark it as pathological.

At this point one objection to this characterization of *praxis* is worth facing. Alasdair MacIntyre (1984, 187ff.) includes in his list of *praxes* scientific inquiry as well as musical performance. However, the difference between the two kinds of cases is important. A musical performance is properly regarded as a *praxis* because each moment of a competent performance recognizably contributes to an overall goal, the execution of a piece of music, during which both the performer and the audience experience pleasure. One's musicianship crucially depends on one's ability to execute a piece of music successfully. There is no such clear connection in scientific practice. Given the long hours of unproductive labor often involved in laboratory science, scientists are taught *not* to tie their efforts too closely to the likelihood of success. Rather, they are taught to see themselves as *potential* players in a story that will eventuate in a complete world picture (cf. Kuhn 1970, 38). In the case to be considered below, Max Planck was quite explicit about the *vicarious* character of the pleasure that most scientists would receive from their activities. And if, as we shall see Planck maintain, a mark of mature science is that increasing effort is needed to achieve comparable results, it would seem that we have on our hands less a *praxis* and more an *addiction* – with hallucinatory elements thrown in to capture the virtual status of any given scientist in his or her paradigm's narrative of progress!

In what follows, the difference between the unreflexive and reflexive approaches to constructive science accounting will appear as, respectively, "uncritical" and "critical" forms of instrumental rationality. The social epistemologist's own position as science accountant will then be formally presented in terms of four accountability conditions for critico-instrumental rationality.

Instrumental rationality: critical and uncritical

Following the early Frankfurt School (esp. Horkheimer [1932] 1972), it has been common throughout most of this century for social theorists to draw a sharp distinction between types of rationality that might be called, respectively, "instrumental" and "critical." The former seeks the most efficient means to a given end, whereas the latter calls the end itself into question, thereby subverting any straightforward sense of efficiency. I would maintain, however, that such a distinction mixes logical types. In particular, instrumental rationality is a specific form of thought (means-ends reasoning, or Max Weber's *Zweckrationalitaet*) that may be either "critical" or "uncritical," depending on when, where, and by whom it is deployed. In contrast, "critical rationality" does not refer to a specific form of thought but rather to the oppositional relationship in which one form of thought stands to another, presumably dominant, form of thought.

More than logical niceties are at stake here. The Frankfurt School distinction fails to acknowledge the historically variable role of instrumental rationality in Western culture. True, in the aftermath of World War I it was easy to see instrumental rationality as an especially uncritical form of thought. This was the first war in which natural scientists were mobilized in great numbers to design technologies of mass destruction, weapons whose sense of efficiency was predicated on their ends not being called into question. Indeed, the prestige of physics and chemistry had never been higher and never more closely implicated in the plans of the state and industry. The ease with which serious scientists could be swept up into the jingoism of the time remains striking even today. They simply took for granted – until Germany's humiliating defeat in 1918 – that instrumental rationality was an unmitigated good (Forman 1971).

However, if we turn back the clock another 150 years, instrumental rationality appears in a quite different light. During the Enlightenment it was tied to the emerging bourgeoisie, with whom the state and the Church had yet to come fully to terms. By decrying the "inefficiency" of religious and aristocratic practices when taken on their own terms, and revealing the often embarrassing "latent functions" performed by those practices, the Enlightenment thinkers helped break down taboos that had made such traditional habits of mind and action appear above criticism. Instrumental rationality was crucial to this task by its insistence on treating practices *not* as *sui generis* but as among an array of alternatives that might be compared along a variety of dimensions: Are the advertised benefits really delivered by current practices? Even if so, could some other practice provide the same benefits at a lower cost? It was in this spirit that Voltaire and Rousseau periodically presented "anthropological" evidence for the superiority of certain "savage" practices to comparable "civilized" ones.

Moreover, instrumental rationality has not completely lost its critical edge in our own century; though increasingly such appeals have been read in an ironic light – sometimes not even as a serious argument but as a piece of satire. Consider, for example, Thorstein Veblen's (1934) thesis that the "conspicuous consumption" and "conspicuous leisure" of rich capitalists undermine the ethic of industriousness that enabled them to accumulate their wealth in the first place. While the rich may complain that they deserve to enjoy the fruits of their labor, Veblen would want to hold them to the logic of capital, which regards excessive time off from work as wasteful – not just for workers, but for anyone encompassed by the system. Thus the best producers will be the most efficient consumers – which in Veblen's mind suggested the need for a professional class of "engineers," whose ascetic devotion to production would supersede an increasingly idle class of "businessmen."

Still closer to home is the case of Paul Feyerabend (1975), whose "anything goes" philosophy of science reflects a rather pure – perhaps literal-minded – application of instrumental rationality with critical intent. It is worth recalling here the enlightenment-like link that Feyerabend's mentor, Karl Popper, repeatedly made between criticism and means-ends reasoning (much to the bafflement of his Frankfurt School opponents). For purposes of this discussion, Feyerabend may be read to argue as follows: If truth is the overriding goal of inquiry that everyone says it is, then different means should be compared with respect to their efficiency in meeting the goal. In that case, it may well turn out that some of our most cherished means of inquiry do not work as well as we thought. To then continue pursuing those means – say, for "good philosophical reasons" – would constitute a form of irrationality, call it "methodolatry," and the philosophical reasons would be rendered a form of superstition. Feyerabend's famous case in point is Galileo, who is portrayed as having willfully violated the methodological canons of his day yet was later shown to have gotten closer to the truth than any of his proto-positivistic persecutors.

In the right hands, then, instrumental rationality remains a powerful critical tool. But whose hands are these? The general answer is that the critic needs to have clearly articulated *ends* that serve as an explicit standard in terms of which alternative means may be compared for their efficiency. Although this condition sounds like the *sine qua non* of accountability, it is in fact rarely met, which may help explain the general feeling that instrumental rationality is "uncritical."

To see what I mean here, consider a critical strategy common to Popper and his followers (including Lakatos and Feyerabend), one that has not endeared them to professional historians of science. It is the "rational reconstructionist" approach to the historiography of science. In simplest terms, it involves presuming that later science is better science, with ours being the best for now. The question is then posed: Why did the history of science not take the shortest possible path to this end point? The Popperian proceeds to construct the shortest possible path (a counterfactual historical trajectory), with the actual history appearing as fraught with deflections from this path. As became especially clear in Popper's (1981) response to Thomas Kuhn's work, the upshot of this strategy is to show just how *inefficient* science normally is, especially when measured against its own self-image as an activity that asymptotically approximates the truth by removing the various institutional and psychological barriers to free inquiry. In fact, the only truly efficient episodes in the history of science turn out to be the "revolutionary" ones, such as those involving Copernicus, Galileo, Newton, and Einstein – as these made great strides toward our current epistemic state.

Interestingly, when historians want to question the propriety of the Popperian approach, the first thing they do is deny the premise that the history of science has discernible overarching ends. The premise may be denied in at least two ways, depending on whether one attacks the "overarching" or the "discernible" character of ends in history. In the first case, common in sociological histories, the scientists are permitted locally defined ends, or "interests"; but these do not add up to anything purposeful on the global level. In the second case, common in more philosophical histories, the overarching end of truth may be retained, but only as a noumenal entity, one that remains mysterious from the standpoint of our latest science. In both cases the historian does not possess the standard by which the history is held accountable. In the former case the history is accountable to the various scientists under study (not just the winners), whereas in the latter it is accountable to God – or whoever else may be waiting for us at the end of inquiry.

Talk of God may seem flippant in this context, but it is meant to be deadly serious. After all, instrumental rationality did not arise spontaneously out of the scientific and capitalist revolutions of the seventeenth century. From the earliest days of Christianity there have been speculations about how each creature and event functioned in the divine plan. Indeed, starting with Augustine of Hippo, events that appeared to do much harm and little good were taken to be signs that the ends of creation were ultimately beyond human comprehension. The more intellectually ambitious natural theologians then constructed *theodicy* – the study of how apparent liabilities such as monstrous births, natural disasters, human atrocities, and the like may be seen as contributing to an overall picture of ours being "the best of all possible worlds," the only kind of world that an omnipotent and omnibenevolent God could create. By the late seventeenth century, as much of this theorizing began to lose its theological baggage, philosophers like Leibnitz spoke of *the economy of nature*, governed by *the principle of sufficient reason*. This principle enjoined the inquirer to seek the end that would be served by a given event, if we presume that the event is part of the most efficient means to that end. In other words, one was to rationalize the event as a "means" rather than to question it as an "end" (cf. Elster 1983).

God may have been disappearing from philosophical view at this point, but in his place was emerging the uncritical attitude toward instrumental rationality so decried by the Frankfurt School. The Leibnitzian inquirer, satirized as Dr. Pangloss in Voltaire's *Candide*, was to take for granted that there is a point to everything that happens and that any alternative action would have been worse. Examples of such "naturalized" instrumental rationality can be found in much "functionalist" and "evolutionary" thinking in the nineteenth and twentieth centuries. In these cases, it is presumed that there is something charmed about the existence of stable social or biological systems, even when these systems maintain their "equilibrium" at the cost of the oppression, waste, and death to some of their parts. Whoever ends may be served by this process, they are most certainly *not* those who must bear the burden of these "costs." But, then, whose ends are served? "Spirit" and "Life" acquire rhetorical force here, as they seem eligible to subsist through a succession of expendable and replaceable material parts (Richards 1987). More mechanistic thinkers, ranging from Herbert Spencer to Herbert Simon, have put the point less metaphysically, claiming that evolution is the story of how organisms come up with increasingly more sophisticated means to achieve the same old ends (Simon 1981). But here, too, "ends" remains radically underdefined, typically glossed by an empirically self-fulfilling term such as "survival."

However, it would be a mistake to assume that this uncritical appeal to instrumental rationality is limited to *apologists* for the status quo. The flipside of believing that the world displays a preestablished *harmony* is believing that it displays a preestablished *hegemony*. This latter view presents ours as the worst of all possible worlds, one where everything that happens – even the most seemingly generous and innocent of acts – contributes to the overall oppression of the human condition. For example, ideologies of individualism, which would seem to encourage workers to take responsibility for their lives, end up preventing the workers from seeing the systemic character of their oppression because they are persuaded to blame themselves when they fail. Such a perspective corresponds to extreme forms of structural Marxism that require an inexplicable "rupture" in the mechanisms of domination for radical social change to occur. While these Marxists would hardly want to be confused with apologists for the status quo, nevertheless they share certain assumptions that render them "uncritical." In particular, they refuse any role as participants in the construction of the ends to which social actions are held accountable. Consequently, the role of social accountant is detached from that of political agent. Of course, such detachment can give the account an air of objectivity, a point not lost on Michel Foucault – or his detractors, especially Jean Baudrillard (1977). Under these circumstances, criticism is reduced to a form of "fascination."

On the basis of this brief historical survey of what has made instrumental rationality "critical" and "uncritical," I would define pure *critico-instrumental rationality* in terms of four *accountability conditions*. These conditions pertain to qualities of the ends in terms of which some form of social action is held accountable. They also capture the sense in which the project of social epistemology is one of constructive and reflexive science accounting:

(1) *Discernibility*: The ends are known to the social accountant, mainly because the accountant chooses them or participates in their construction. The ends are not mysterious or accessible only to some undefined entity.

(2) *Transcendence*: The ends are more than the sum of the immediate ends of the individuals whose actions are being held accountable.

(3) *Responsibility*: The ends are not idiosyncratic to the social accountant but are ends to which the accountable individuals would reasonably consent.

(4) *Revisability*: The ends may change, even quite radically, as the knowledge or identity of the social accountant changes.

Few of the instances of critico-instrumental rationality canvassed in our survey are pure cases. Feyerabend perhaps comes closest. In contrast, Popperians may adhere to conditions (1), (2), and (3) in their accounts of science, but probably not (4). In fact, part of the rhetorical force of their rational reconstructions is the suggestion that *future* rational reconstructions will include all the episodes that have so far been identified as contributions to scientific progress: Copernicus, Galileo, Newton, Maxwell, and Einstein will remain – supplemented by the revolutionary breakthroughs of tomorrow. However, (4) is needed to ensure that the social accountant fully participates in setting the standards of accountability and is not reduced to a rationalizer of whatever history has delivered up to the point at which the account is taken. In other words, an absence of (4) can weaken (1) and (2).

This point may be illustrated by one species of naturalized theodicy that is well represented in contemporary philosophical accountings for science. It is the so-called invisible hand account provided by, *inter alia*, Hull (1988) and Kitcher (1993). The basic strategy here is to account for scientific progress in terms of the spontaneous self-interested transactions of scientists, which over time have been conventionalized as "peer review." Implicit in this view is a relatively abundant and unregulated material environment for science. Peer review works not only because scientists have an interest in criticizing one another, but also because the scientific community is sufficiently endowed to enable scientists to receive exactly the resources that their peers deem their research to merit.

A natural question to ask at this point – one relevant to condition (4) being met – is whether science has yet reached an optimal level of non-regulation: Would a still less visible hand produce still better science? Hull and Kitcher are suspiciously silent here, suggesting that their appeals to the invisible hand are less to a well-grounded accounting procedure and more to a rationalization of contemporary views about the history of science. In contrast, a principled libertarian like Feyerabend (1979) wanted to push invisibility to the limit. He anticipated that the next step in the deregulation of scientific inquiry would be the decentralization of the science-funding apparatus, preferably by curtailing the state's ability to concentrate wealth through taxation. Only a policy environment that is insulated from democratic processes, Feyerabend reasoned, would tolerate a research program whose survival depended on monopolizing the material resources available for inquiry. For example, no one ever put the scientific "megaprojects" of our time – including the Superconducting Supercollider and the Human Genome Project – to a formal vote of the populace – or of the "republic of science," for that matter.

Thus even if science succeeds insofar as it approximates the invisible hand, additional steps toward increasing invisibility may cause science accountants to revise their estimation of what good science has been and can be. For example, a critical science accountant following Feyerabend's lead may believe that the charter of the Royal Society of Great Britain marked the beginning of a spontaneously self-organizing system of inquirers. However, the intellectual descendants of the Royal Society's founders may have become victims of the advantages that the natural sciences have accumulated over the last 350 years. Specifically, as the sciences have participated in the material reproduction of society, scientists have lost not only the flexibility to change their own research trajectories on the basis of peer criticism but also a sense of tolerance for many competing trajectories. Too much else is at stake for scientists to judge knowledge claims on their merits alone; hence the spirit of gamesmanship, and even play, associated with the idea of science as a free market has been lost (cf. Munevar 1981). Hence Feyerabend's policy advice: Today's scientists should not inherit the cumulative advantage of their precursors, even if that means divesting support for research projects currently touted by the elite members of the scientific community. We shall see an argument of this sort advanced by Ernst Mach in the next section (cf. Feyerabend 1979, 195–205).

As the above example suggests, (4) is in clear tension with (3), since prima facie it is difficult to imagine that the same individuals would consent to be held accountable to what might seem to them radically different standards. However, one practice that seems to overcome this difficulty reasonably well is embodied in the history of the U.S. Supreme Court. Here the "intentions" of the framers of the Constitution have been regularly projected into contemporary situations and reinterpreted accordingly. Judicial decisions are often rendered in the following form:

"If the framers were alive today, they would adjust their views, in light of evidence and reasoning that was unavailable to them in 1787." Thus the framers are portrayed as counterfactually revising their intentions to conform to the legal standards of the time in which the case is being decided. Similarly, we might imagine the founders of the Royal Society – even Sir Isaac Newton – counterfactually agreeing with the Feyerabendian accountant that maintaining an atmosphere of free inquiry overrides the success of a project such as the Supercollider, whose monopoly over U.S. physics funding would nevertheless have contributed to cosmological research in which Newton would have had a direct personal interest.

Now what if we have a situation in which two rather different critico-instrumental accounts of science are competing for public acceptance *at the same time*? This is certainly possible in periods in which the seat of power in society is not consolidated. Suppose, on the one hand, that we have a physicist who spends the bulk of his career as an elite functionary for the scientific establishment. He identifies "the ends of science" with the interests of professional scientists, yet he continually needs to demonstrate the relevance of arcane and expensive research to a public who still think of Galileo and Newton as their paradigm cases of scientists. Then suppose, on the other hand, we have a physicist who spends a good part of his career as a parliamentary champion of democratic education. In his view "the ends of science" are nothing more than a repertoire of techniques for ameliorating the human condition, one of whose burdens may turn out to be the scientific community itself. The two exemplary science accountants in question are Max Planck and Ernst Mach, respectively.

A tale of two critico-instrumental rationalists: Mach and Planck

Nowadays it is common to interpret the Mach–Planck exchanges as a debate in the philosophy of science. Much of the substance of their arguments was informed by the changing fortunes of atomism as a research program in physics, and the overall positions staked out by Mach and Planck resemble those of "instrumentalists" and "realists," respectively, as they appear today in the philosophy of science (cf. Leplin 1984). However, their exchanges arose at a specific conjuncture in the history of science accounting, one where the demands of research and education had to be met simultaneously. The scientific community was entering a period of unprecedented research growth and specialization just as the imperial powers of Europe were expanding and modernizing citizen education so that the populace could be more easily mobilized for economic and military purposes (Albisetti 1983).

The imagination of educational reformers was captured by the strategy that Count von Moltke had used to lead the Germans to a stunning victory in the Franco-Prussian War of 1870–71. Von Moltke had realized that the same material infrastructure could be mobilized for either industry or defense, depending on whether the nation was at peace or war. The success of this strategy seemed to refute the opposition between commerce and war that had been a staple of classical political economy arguments for free trade (Inkster 1991, 133). Indeed, the free trade arguments were increasingly treated as a British ideological maneuver to halt the rise of Germany. The Franco-Prussian War showed that factories could be readily converted to manufacture arms, and railroads to ship supplies. The key to national preparedness in the future, then, would be a citizenry trained in skills that would enable them to adapt quickly to either mode. Although science was arguably still more instrumental in the explanation and legitimation of new technologies than in their actual creation, the German chemical industry had already established a precedent for science-based technological innovation (ibid., 138). The practical question concerning the development of this "spiritual infrastructure" was how and where natural science courses should be introduced into the curriculum. Mach and Planck both realized that in the balance hung the social reproduction of scientific knowledge itself.

Generally speaking, educational reform moved on two orthogonal fronts: on the one hand, educational opportunities were expanded for the populace; on the other hand, educational credentials were introduced to differentiate and stratify occupations (Mueller et al. 1987). Today, movement on both fronts is taken as a defining feature of modernizing societies. Indeed, in the writings of systems theorists "growth through specialization" sometimes enjoys an axiomatic status, bolstered by a strong organismic analogy and little empirical argument. However, the relationship between the expansion and specialization of education was much more controversial at the end of the last century.

When relatively few people received formal schooling, education served as a vehicle for social mobility, enabling the lower classes to improve their social standing and the upper classes to move easily between careers. Not surprisingly, democratic theorists called for universal formal education as a means of completely equalizing employment opportunities. Yet many educational reformers feared that, left unchecked, the mobility of the newly educated masses would lead to social disorder. They wanted to reinvent within the "liberalized" educational system the sorts of discriminations that had traditionally restricted access to education. In practice, this meant predicating employment on credentials, the acquisition of which required the student to undergo a course of study whose content would be controlled by the relevant academic specialists.

In Germany, much of the public debate over these matters centered on the implications of introducing the natural sciences into the secondary schools, the *Gymnasien*, the curricula of which had remained uniformly humanistic throughout the nineteenth century (Blackmore 1973, 135–37). Most parties agreed that some form of (natural) science education should be made available in at least some of these schools – but in what form, and to what end? Answers to these questions turned on what was taken to be the distinctive epistemic contribution of the natural sciences, and its relevance to the "modern" German citizen who might not pursue scientific research as a career but whose continued support would be needed for science to continue at its current pace.

Against this backdrop, Mach and Planck engaged in a sustained and highly personalized debate about "the ends of science" that attracted considerable public attention from 1908 to 1913 (for the texts of the major rounds, see Blackmore 1992, 127–50). Broadly speaking, Mach's instrumentalism drove him to see mass empowerment and scientific credentialism as incompatible goals for education, whereas Planck's realism led him to endorse credentialism as a necessary complement to a rapidly expanding educational system. Mach's vision of "spreading science" throughout the school system could not have been more different from Planck's. As we shall see, where Mach envisioned a more *mobile* citizenry, Planck saw one that was more *mobilizable*. In Mach's accounting scheme science *saved labor*, whereas in Planck's it *added value*.

The cases of Mach and Planck are especially illuminating because they lived their respective ideologies. Mach championed the cause of adult education in the Austrian parliament and authored a series of middle school and college science textbooks for nonscience majors (Blackmore 1973, 235). Through these texts many of the leading scientific thinkers of this century – including Einstein, Heisenberg, Carnap, Popper, and Wittgenstein – were introduced to Machian instrumentalism (ibid., 141). Planck, on the other hand, administered many of the institutions responsible for shaping the professional identity and public voice of the German natural science community both before and after World War I. These included the German Physics Society, Berlin University, and the corporate-sponsored national research institutes known as the Kaiser-Wilhelm-Gesellschaften, as well as several international scientific unions (Heilbron 1986, 47–86).

Mach, as is well known, located the value of science in its ability to economize on thought: Phenomena that once could be handled only with great mental and physical effort – because they were thought to be disparate in nature – could now be epitomized in a single mathematical equation or set of formulas. In most general terms, science is an abstract labor-saving device that facilitates the satisfaction of human needs, thereby freeing up time for people to pursue other things. Mach did not hold the practice of academic science to be itself an especially interesting or ennobling pursuit. He went so far as to ridicule the practicing scientist's taste for the odd and the exceptional that was often pedagogically dignified under the rubric of "curiosity" (Blackmore 1973, 133). Not surprisingly, Mach concluded that secondary schools could do justice to science without requiring an inordinate amount of specialized science education. Indeed, beyond the point of showing science's historical tendency toward economizing on effort, science education might even become self-defeating. The last thing Mach wanted was to replace the time students wasted on mastering humanistic arcana with their mastering scientific arcana (ibid., 134). In fact, he wanted to reduce the amount of time students spent in school generally (ibid., 136).

Notice that Mach's economy of *thought* is diametrically opposed to the economy of *nature* that figured so prominently in our account of uncritical instrumental rationality. If the economy of nature adapts human expectations to the complexity of nature (by rationalization), the economy of thought works in reverse as the means by which humanity focuses its finite energies strategically to reduce that complexity (ibid., 174). Mach held that human survival was the end in terms of which the economic value of various intellectual projects, including the natural sciences, should be judged. He was unique among late nineteenth-century physicists in regarding evolutionary biology – and not some ultimate branch of physics – as the background constraint on all inquiry. Moreover, Mach's joint commitment to psychologism and liberalism distinguished him from some of his fellow evolutionists; for he believed that "human survival" was determined not by natural forces beyond human recognition or control but by the collective interests of humanity at the times when accounts are taken. (For Mach, survival was not "brute" at all but closer to the modern concept of welfare.) Even if our biological natures and environmental conditions determine the times in which accounts are taken and decisions made, Mach held that they do not dictate the content of those accounts and decisions (Blackmore 1992, 137–38).

Planck focused his public battle with Mach on whether "economy of thought" should be included among the ends of science. To appreciate what bothered Planck about Mach's thesis, consider a passing observation that the economist Nicholas Georgescu-Roegen (1971, 27, n. 14) made about it. When Mach cites examples of economized thought from the past, he treats, say, the multiplication tables and Snell's law on a par. Both save human labor by providing for the efficient storage, transmission, and retrieval of large amounts of information. As a result, people do not need to work so hard to repeat the past and duplicate each other and can move on instead to more personally satisfying and socially enriching projects. Georgescu-Roegen then notes that this tendency in human history probably has more to do with the introduction of writing as a prosthesis for memory than with the actual development of scientific thought. In fact, the sciences are only one among many social practices whose development has been fostered by the spread of writing and its technological descendants, printing and computerization.

Looking back at scientific debates in the early twentieth century, it is easy to get the impression that such words as "economy," "simplicity," and "unity" are used interchangeably and mean the same things to all parties. On closer inspection, however, this is not the case at all. For example, Planck repeatedly asserted science's mission to arrive at the unified theory of physical reality but refused to interpret this goal as "economic" in Mach's sense. For Mach, science is one means – perhaps heretofore the most prominent one – of helping people save labor as they go about the business of living. For Planck, science is an end to be pursued in its own right, independently of its ability to ameliorate the human condition; Planck would treat any convergence between the ends of humanity and the ends of science as a lucky coincidence (Blackmore 1992, 142–43).

Given his construal of "the ends of science," Mach held that the natural sciences' historical role in the economy of thought should not be presumed to extend indefinitely into the future. Contemporary society was not obliged to complete some ongoing scientific project that began (as Planck maintained) with Newton's *Principia Mathematica*. In other words, the past track record of natural science must be treated as a "sunk cost" when determining the direction that tomorrow's science policy should take. As suggested above, Mach was specifically concerned with the prospect that increasingly specialized scientific research would exhibit diminishing returns on investment. The chief indicators here included the accumulation and persistence of anomalous phenomena, as well as the appeal to arcane mathematics and unobservable entities. To pursue research under these conditions would clearly require more expensive and customized laboratory equipment. Until then heavy capital investment in scientific research had been mainly limited to state-corporate sponsorship of chemistry, where the practical dividends were very apparent. But is the extension of this policy to all the natural sciences warranted, especially if public benefits are not likely to be forthcoming?

Planck recognized this problem as well, but his gaze was firmly fixed on the future of the physics community. However much Mach's views on science education might lead students to respect the accomplishments of science, they were not designed to encourage students to enter science or even to adopt a scientific mind-set – at least one that bore the stamp of the physics community. Planck's own strategy was to enroll the entire citizenry in the mission of mature science via science education. In today's terms, Planck wanted students to acquire something of the "paradigm" of contemporary physics.

Planck held that science imparted an increasingly coherent world picture (*Weltbild*), whose strictures could deepen the understanding and formalize the practice of virtually any field. For example, engineers became better engineers by mastering some of the problem-set of physics. Planck's focus, then, was on teaching students how scientists construct and solve well-formed problems, thereby enabling them to acquire what we would now call "exemplars" and "disciplinary matrixes" that can be used for shaping their own practices. This was more than a matter of applying theory-neutral equations as one pleased. It required that students be sufficiently committed to some overarching model of physical reality – such as atomism – to think through its implications for some experimentally testable cases (Heilbron 1986, 42, 55). Presumably students would then be persuaded that they could not fully grasp the formulas and techniques without internalizing some of the scientist's professional orientation. If such a strategy did not actually entice students to enter scientific careers, the students' efforts at mastering some of the theory would at least enable them to sympathize with the labors of future cutting-edge scientists even when they were not producing anything of immediate practical benefit.

With this much of Planck's rationale revealed, a standard realist objection to instrumentalism becomes vivid: Without a theoretical framework to suggest objects beyond phenomena that have already been economically saved, what motivation would there be for continuing to do science? In practical terms: If you do not convey some of the research orientation of professional scientists in general science education, how do you expect to recruit the next generation of scientists and to sustain public support for cutting-edge scientific research? For Mach, science was a fit subject for general education as long as students could easily assimilate it into their normal lives; Planck, in contrast, wanted students to become acquainted with the more demanding qualities of science that contributed to its distinctive place in modern culture. Moreover, contrary to the labor-saving image of science that Mach promoted, Planck believed that as physics approached unification, each additional increment of knowledge would require increased effort without necessarily issuing in any direct practical benefits. A public accustomed to seeing science as an economizing tool could well become discouraged by such prospects.

Planck argued that the epistemic distinctiveness of physics lay in its ability to reach closure on an ever-wider body of observations by an ever-larger number of observers, all encompassed under a single unifying theory. This theory might not make sense to someone without the proper training; but then the validity of such a theory would be checked not by such anthropocentric means but by its ability to deliver the same results to any inquirer anywhere, even on Mars (Blackmore 1992, 128–29). Any critique that failed to respect this fundamental aspiration did not deserve the title of "science". Planck's appeal to the "independent" and "invariant" character of ultimate reality was certainly a familiar one; yet his argument implicitly conceded to Mach that universal convergence on this reality presupposed the elimination of individuality from the creative process by the enforcement of a uniform research orientation (ibid., 130–31). We see here a vivid admission of the paradoxical interdependence of scientific realism and the theory-ladenness of observation.

The unified theory that Planck desired was "simple" in that it explained the most diverse phenomena by the fewest common principles. He cited Boltzmann's statistical unification of thermodynamics and mechanics as evidence that this sense of unity was immanent in physics (Blackmore 1973, 213–20). Such a theory, however, would not be "simple" in Mach's economical sense because it would require that people reinterpret their experience of reality in terms of the esoteric language of physical theory. What would ordinarily appear as qualitatively different experiences – such as heat and magnetism – would now be discussed as the product of the statistical motions of unobservable entities – namely, atoms.

Planck portrayed scientific unity in terms of the exhaustive explanation of one type of phenomena in terms of a "deeper" type to which only cutting-edge physicists had epistemic access. Mach's own vision of unity corresponded to his sense of simplicity, the prototype of which was Fechner's laws of psychophysics. Here the mathematical formulas were said to correlate sets of experiences – physical stimuli and sensory responses – that were regarded as ontological equals (ibid., 29–30). If Planck's principle of unity was reduction, Mach's was translation.

From a pedagogical standpoint, Planck's view implied that ordinary people would either have to learn how to rearticulate their experiences in terms of the new physics or simply have to let the physicists speak on their behalf. Mach found neither option appetizing: the former added to the labor that students would need to expend in schools, while the latter subtracted from the power that people would have to do what they wanted. Here it is important to appreciate the role that Mach saw between scientific research and scientific education, as that has been subject to considerable misunderstanding by such self-professed Machians as the logical positivist Rudolf Carnap.

Mach's pedagogy primarily aimed to rid students of fixed ideas that prevented them from making intelligent judgments about their experiences. These fixed ideas included not only the esoteric categories of contemporary physics but also the implicit ontology of common sense, which Mach believed owed more to medieval scholasticism than to phenomenological authenticity. Thus unlike the American pragmatists, whose phenomenalism easily lapsed into commonsensical modes of experience, Mach maintained that teachers needed to make students conscious of the metaphysical baggage imported even in such expressions as "Heat causes objects to feel hot." In this respect Mach advocated a kind of language therapy in the classroom (Blackmore 1973, 137–38). However, unlike Carnap of the *Aufbau*, Mach did not believe that this therapy had to be followed by an axiomatic reconstruction of the world in terms of a formal language of sensory elements. Indeed, Mach made it very clear that Euclid's *more geometrico*, the model for Carnap's project, was at bottom responsible for making both scientists and lay people less receptive to their own experience, as they are forced to reason through the implications of artificially chosen first principles (ibid., 303–4).

Mach objected that the Euclidean method turned what is essentially a tool for facilitating thought into a model for thought itself. The formal presentation of Newton's laws and their consequences under particular boundary conditions may enable people to locate problematic propositions more precisely without saying a thing about the cognitive contexts in which such searches can and should be made. A more generalized version of this critique appears in Mach's aversion to mechanistic explanations: To promote the use of labor-saving machines is quite different from claiming that reality is mechanical or that we think like machines (ibid., 192–93). In fact from Mach's standpoint, to the extent that we can populate the world with machines, we can allow the nonmechanical aspects of ourselves to flourish.

Among Carnap's colleagues in the Vienna Circle, Otto Neurath's thinking about scientific research and education was more in line with Mach's. Neurath followed Mach's lead in supporting adult education, extending this to the idea of "social museums," which workers could visit to learn about their socioeconomic conditions and political opportunities (Dvorak 1991). Neurath was preoccupied with developing a theory-neutral language of experience that would allow the workers direct understanding of their situation. However, Neurath's frequent allusions to mass advertising should make us wary of overintellectualizing "understanding." Neurath's interest was more in enabling collective action than in creating a common mind-set. Much as Mach suspected the theoretical neologisms of physicists, Neurath wanted to avoid relying on the introduction of a new *verbal* language, as that would bias understanding in favor of those with prior exposure to the lexicon from which the words were chosen (so that even logical syntax would be biased toward the algebraically adept). In other words, a universal language must be universally *accessible*, especially if the information conveyed in that language was likely to upset preconceptions and focus action.

In this spirit Neurath invented a language of visual icons called ISO-TYPE, which was used at the Vienna social museum. The ISOTYPE was influenced by three pictorial conventions: (a) artistic renditions of historical battles in which the size of the rival forces represents their relative strength; (b) Egyptian art, which marked social rank by clothing and body image; (c) children's art, which tends to abstract only important data and ignore the rest (Sassower 1985, 115–19). The last influence was especially significant as an effort to capture a distinction Mach drew between "presentational" and "representational" forms of experience. The ultimate lesson that Mach tried to teach was how to draw this distinction in practice so as to separate one's actual experience from whatever inferences may be unconsciously attached to it. The leading academic psychologist in Neurath's Vienna, Karl Buehler, had argued that children's art constituted a "pre-representational" form of experience focused entirely on whatever grabs the child's attention. Buehler's project, then, was to see how the child comes to learn to draw in the ways that adults find "representational." For Neurath, Buehler's work exemplified how scientific research could inform pedagogy without simply replacing one totalizing world view with that of another. (See Bartley 1974 on Buehler's influence on two other philosopher-pedagogues: Popper and Wittgenstein.)

But Mach's objections to Planck's pedagogical strategy were not limited to the cost-effectiveness of nurturing diseconomic forms of inquiry and forcing students to learn artificial modes of thought. Mach's reservations extended to the ideological content of natural scientific knowledge itself, given its combination of high societal prestige and intense theoretical contestation. Mach's worries here marked a new chapter in the history of academic freedom. When debates over the place of science in the secondary schools first erupted after the Franco-Prussian War – and the principal antagonists were Ernst Haeckel and Rudolf Virchow – the issue was whether socialist supporters of evolutionary theory might jeopardize the gains that the natural sciences had recently made as university subjects (Baker 1961). Now, it would seem, the tables had turned. The question had become whether natural scientific research could continue to flourish *without* the ideologies associated with these fields dominating the secondary school classrooms. Certainly, Planck thought not. However, the price of such dominance, as Mach saw it, was the prospect of two equally unsavory scenarios.

On the one hand, science educators might try to pass off as fact theories whose ultimate validity had yet to be decided by the scientific community – a practice that would then subtly put pressure on scientists to support theories that already had a popular following. This worry would be realized in the Weimar Republic, as quantum physicists adapted to the irrationalist sentiments already present in general education by plumping for an indeterminist interpretation of microphysical reality (Forman 1971). In essence, Mach was merely extending the German university doctrine of "value-free" pedagogy from the humanities to the natural sciences. This doctrine is often associated with Max Weber's call for professors to exercise ideological self-restraint in the classroom. The contemporary descendant of this sensibility may be found in Feyerabend's (1979, 73ff.) insistence that creationism be taught alongside evolutionary theory so as not to rob students of the right to believe what they want, especially when the truth (concerning the origins of life in this case) is far from clear.

On the other hand, students who are introduced to scientific theories in general education and later enter public life may try to give extra rhetorical weight to their political pronouncements by drawing metaphorically on scientific concepts. Mach had in mind the tendency of jingoistic German politicians to use Newton's laws – suitably refracted through the philosophical lens of German idealism – to justify the inevitability of international conflict. Thus colliding inertial masses easily metamorphosed into egos with opposing wills (Blackmore 1973, 234–35). Mach's view was simply that if a theory such as atomism is true, then its truth will be borne out in the formulas and techniques to which it gives rise – which in turn will render the atomic theory itself redundant for classroom instruction. Until these results are forthcoming, the theory has the status of a heuristic device for research, but one without purchase outside that area.

So far it seems as though Mach had a completely negative attitude toward the advancement of science. Is his a truly critico-instrumentalist approach, or just sheer skepticism, as Planck liked to portray Mach? To answer this question, we must recall the end to which Mach was holding the history of science accountable – namely, relief from the burdens of survival. From that standpoint, organized inquiry can be a help or a hindrance. It can be a hindrance if the perpetuation of a particular community of inquirers takes precedence over the survival of entire species. It was in this light that Mach portrayed Galileo's Jesuit inquisitors as a hindrance. Galileo's studies of the heavens pointed toward the amelioration of the human condition, even as it meant the destabilization of the Roman Catholic church.

This picture conformed to the "science versus religion" motif that was popular in histories of the day. However, in his celebrated *Science of Mechanics* ([1883] 1960), Mach went further and applied this motif to the contemporary scene in physics, arguing that the sort of theoretical orthodoxy demanded by Planck artificially restricted thought's economizing tendencies. Mach offered as evidence the fact that fundamental objections to Newtonian mechanics that were only now beginning to be taken seriously had originally been made soon after *Principia Mathematica* was first published. The insistence on a common paradigm in physics had suppressed the teaching of these historical objections, yet they refused to go away – and indeed Einstein credited Mach with keeping them alive long enough to suggest the need for what became relativity theory.

But Mach did more than give voice to scientific dissidents in his historical writings. He also promoted (often in his own students) the revitalization of defunct research programs that attempted to develop scientific principles based on regularities in the experience of ordinary people. This sometimes involved experimentally examining "unschooled" Czech and Austrian craftsmen whose folk knowledge was based on highly developed perceptual capacities (Blackmore 1973, 59, 89, 206–7, 222). In one sense these projects in, say, phenomenological optics, acoustics, and chemistry can be understood as attempts to resurrect early nineteenth-century *Naturphilosophie* – a German competitor to Newtonian mechanics associated with the poet Goethe that was superseded once the rest of the physical sciences started to match the mathematical and experimental sophistication of classical mechanics. However, from a broader perspective, these Mach-inspired projects aimed at constructing "folk sciences" as alternative sources of epistemic authority that would enable the enlarged student body of the modern school system to recover some of the cognitive ground that was rapidly, albeit implicitly, being ceded to the emerging class of scientific experts.

This interest in "empowering the masses" was integrally tied to Mach's economic approach to education, which called for students to learn the most by applying the least effort – in this case by making maximum use of what they already know before entering the classroom. In our own time, pedagogical reforms aimed at recovering "indigenous knowledge" fit the Machian mold. Even in his own day, Mach joined chemist Wilhelm Ostwald in providing moral and financial support to Buddhists in Ceylon who were resisting the overhaul of native educational practices that accompanied British imperial rule. Here Mach willingly indulged Ostwald's "energeticist" metaphysical maxim "Always conserve energy!" as grounds for the Ceylonese not having to replace their traditional epistemic practices (Blackmore 1992, 185).

In retrospect, a crucial factor in Mach's long-term loss to Planck was the former's strict, perhaps even anachronistic, adherence to Wilhelm von Humboldt's original 1810 plan to revive Socratic dialectic in the German university system by casting students as active inquirers in their own right, not passive recipients of knowledge. The research and education functions of the university were thus never sharply distinguished in Mach's mind. All students were, as the social psychologist Jean Lave has put it, "legitimate peripheral participants" in the knowledge production process (Lave and Wenger 1991). According to Mach, the tractability of science to common modes of experience should constrain the development of science nearly as much as science should revise and discipline common modes of experience. As noted earlier, Mach conceptualized psychophysical laws more as principles of translation between equally valid modes of experience than as principles of reduction.

No such reciprocal arrangements figured in Planck's thought. Planck sharply distinguished between the research and educational functions of the university. In practice, the state and the scientific community struck a deal. The state invested heavily in cutting-edge research as "bets" on the curriculum that would be needed to qualify the next generation of citizens for jobs that would ensure the smooth operation of the social system (cf. Stinchcombe 1990, 312–13). In return, the scientific community offered its services in designing new principles of social stratification – ones based not on "status" or "class" but on "general intelligence" and "problem-solving ability." These qualities supposedly pertained to all kinds of jobs, but ultimately they were modeled on one's facility with the kind of "work problems" found in classical mechanics textbooks. Indicative of this new insertion of science into the mechanisms of social reproduction and control was the attitude of Gestalt psychologist Wolfgang Koehler toward the widespread use of intelligence tests in schools.

Koehler had originally studied physics with Planck in Berlin. He later credited Planck – especially in a speech made during his exchanges with Mach – with having discovered that the mind strives toward the kind of closure that would come to characterize Gestalt experimental findings (Koehler 1971, 112–13). Planck had described the solution to a problem in physics as a part needed to complete a preexistent whole, or "field." Thus the Gestaltists generalized across individuals and sensory modalities a process that physicists more abstractly and selfconsciously enacted whenever they constructed equations with a unique set of solutions. That physicists should have beaten the psychologists to this insight was explained by the electromagnetic "isomorphism" of psychological and physical fields (ibid., 237–51). All of this was a far cry from the simple capacity for precise observation and critical judgment that Mach wished to carry over from physics to general education.

The influence of this physics-centered view of thinking and intelligence was felt throughout Gestalt psychology. In their textbooks Gestaltists were at pains to deny the Machian/popular view that physics was an inappropriate model for studying normal psychological processes because of its preoccupation with unobservable entities in artificial settings (Koffka 1935, 57). The earliest Gestalt experiments on problem solving, which inspired the "cognitive revolution" of Newell and Simon (1972), were based on accounts of the electrical discoveries made by Benjamin Franklin and Michael Faraday (Humphrey 1951, 142–43). These experiments, conducted by Otto Selz, highlighted the ability of subjects to transform their environments – essentially turning them into thought laboratories – and thereby remove the obstacles in the way of their problem-solving tasks. Moreover, while the subjects typically could not recount their thought patterns as a train of images, they nevertheless felt an unconscious "determining tendency" that kept them motivated until a solution was reached.

The report of such experiences suggested that even ordinary people normally partook of some of the committed and slightly mysterious character of physical inquiry as Planck portrayed it. Perhaps Mach had overstated the case for the exotic nature of physics. Nevertheless, younger adherents to Mach's critical approach to science, such as Karl Popper, remained concerned. Part of Popper's dissertation was devoted to showing that these early cognitive psychology experiments did not clearly distinguish between thought that was simply driven to fit the facts into preexisting patterns – as is often connoted in the idea of a "mental-set" – and a genuine scientific breakthrough that addressed the facts in ways which substantially reconfigured preexisting patterns. We see here a psychological basis for Popper's famous falsifiability criterion (Berkson and Wettersten 1984). Given this lineage, it is hardly surprising that Kuhn (1977, 309–19) found his studies of paradigm acquisition in the physical sciences moving him toward more general considerations of how children learn concepts. The relevant developmental psychology experiments, which built on the early Gestalt work, presuppose that children are inchoate physicists before they are anything else.

On the specific topic of intelligence tests, Koehler (1971, 187–88) revealed his Planckian sensibilities most clearly. He sharply separated the administrative role of the tests from their proper scientific merit. In fact, Koehler held that the primary function of the tests was to reduce uncertainty in how teachers classified students when tracking them through the educational system. Such bureaucratic efficiency was worth whatever interpretive confusions the tests' coarse-grained measures might breed in the public – as in encouraging the idea that "intelligence" is a univocal substance that people have in varying amounts. Psychological researchers would not be so fooled, since (so Koehler believed) intelligence tests are clearly artifacts of the cultures that construct them and not the royal road to cognitive capacity. The ease with which Koehler could harbor vastly different attitudes to the educational and research value of such tests is reminiscent of Plato's tolerance for "noble lies" that serve to stabilize the social order. While Planck and Mach would disagree on the import of this resemblance, both would agree that only practices that appear to have the warrant of the natural sciences are in a position to manufacture such myths in the twentieth century.

Conclusion: some lessons for the social epistemologist's science accounting

Although both Mach and Planck would probably have been lumped together as uncritical "positivists" by critical theorists of the Frankfurt School, nevertheless both were offering rather bold visions of the future of science at a time – the first decade of the twentieth century – when the future seemed up for grabs. The natural sciences had been fully incorporated into the university system only in the previous generation, and academics were ambivalent at best about the industrial model of research and the credentialist model of education associated with those fields – though most acknowledged emerging tendencies in those directions.

In terms of their significance, the exchanges between Mach and Planck resemble those between Thomas Hobbes and Robert Boyle, as presented in *Leviathan and the Air-Pump* (Shapin and Schaffer 1985). "Hobbes versus Boyle" represents a turning point in the history of science in which social and epistemological problems are solved simultaneously. Coming into the debate, each fork in the road toward which the two contestants pointed seemed as viable as the other. In the mid-seventeenth century, serious questions had been raised about the possibility of gaining knowledge exclusively through verbal reasoning (Hobbes' path), yet the experimental mode of knowledge production had not proven itself in a wide range of settings (Boyle's path). Which way to go? Likewise, "Mach versus Planck" represents a turning point – one of more contemporary relevance perhaps, given the increasing calls today to downsize Big Science and relate scientific research more directly to the educational needs of ordinary citizens. Is a return to Mach possible – or even desirable?

To address this question, let us return to our four accountability conditions, which we will take in reverse order – starting with "Revisability" of ends and then moving on to "Responsibility," "Transcendence," and finally "Discernibility." Revisability is the easiest place to start because a critico-instrumentalist argument always presupposes a historical disjuncture, a fork in the road, that requires the revision of ends. Mach and Planck differ interestingly here on account of their different temporal orientations, which are reflected in contrasting attitudes toward history. Both are clearly situated in "the present." But is the present continuous or discontinuous with what might be called "the past" and "the future"?

Analytic philosophers of language have long discussed the logic of the words people use to identify themselves in time and space. Among these words are such "token-reflexive" indexical expressions as "here," "now," "there," "then." A common thread in this literature is that the scope of an indexical expression may vary quite substantially, depending on the context of utterance. For example, "Now" may mean "right this second" or "the twentieth century" or "the modern era," according to context. Thus in certain contexts, "the past" and "the present" or "the present" and "the future" may significantly overlap.

Mach treats the past as continuous with the present. This enables him to interpret the failure of contemporary physicists to answer 200-year-old objections to Newtonian mechanics as the suppression of voices in an ongoing conversation. Mach is also thereby able to appeal to the lost "opportunity costs" (to mass empowerment) involved in silencing more phenomenologically based approaches to science. By making the past continuous with the present, Mach is able to make it seem as though those opportunity costs would still be recoverable if enough scientists followed the example of his students and saw how experimental approaches might be used to develop the insights of *Naturphilosophie* and craft knowledge. At the same time, Mach's past-oriented present is discontinuous with the future. This explains the ease with which he can regard the successful history of Newtonian mechanics as a sunk cost that should not bias our judgment as to the kind of science that requires support in tomorrow's world. Straight induction is no ready guide here.

In contrast, Planck draws a sharp boundary between the scope of "then" and "now" and aligns the present with the future. For him, objections raised two centuries ago are irrelevant to contemporary concerns. The past is dead and best left to historians, who, in turn, should stay away from the education of practicing scientists. Interestingly, Kuhn (1970, 167) sides with Planck against Mach on this one. But whereas Kuhn's interest is in protecting historians of science from the interests of contemporary scientists, Planck's was the other way around. The result is the same, however, in that neither Kuhn nor Planck enables history to intervene critically in contemporary science accounting. Moreover, Planck's future-oriented present enables him to challenge the recoverability of lost opportunity costs in the history of science. Even if Mach were correct that Goethe's science was given shabby treatment one hundred years earlier, it is now too late to repair the damage. The Newtonian paradigm has displayed further strengths, and scientific culture has remade society in its image. Past opportunities are not permanent possibilities for action.

Turning now to the other conditions of accountability, we see that simultaneously meeting the Responsibility and Transcendence conditions may be difficult if the interests of the accountant and those of the accountable individuals are sufficiently at odds with each other. Given his interest in seeing the physics community radically alter its current course, Mach has problems with Responsibility. Planck on the other hand naturally runs afoul of Transcendence because he does not clearly distinguish the goal of physics from the interests of contemporary physicists. Mach's solution is to portray physicists first as human beings and then as scientists. Thus the labors they perform as scientists to alleviate ignorance and suffering are repaid by the labor they save as human beings. Planck's solution is trickier, but luckily he received help from his student Moritz Schlick, who was eventually appointed to Mach's chair in the history of inductive sciences at Vienna and in that capacity organized the Vienna Circle.

To appreciate Planck's solution, let us start by observing that the clarity of the very distinction between "realist" and "instrumentalist" philosophies of science reveals a presumption in favor of Planck's view, certainly in our own day but maybe even at the time of the Mach–Planck exchanges. When those unschooled in the philosophical arts have a hard time seeing the difference between realism and instrumentalism, it is often because they take for granted that science's increasing ability to predict and control phenomena implies that it has a more comprehensive understanding of nature: Does not instrumentalism simply presuppose realism (and maybe even vice versa)? Indeed, prior to the Mach–Planck exchanges this conflation was quite common even among sophisticated philosophers and scientists. Only once a scientific research program had been allowed to develop in a sufficiently autonomous fashion for a sufficiently long time did it become clear that the one need not imply the other. At that point, about one hundred years ago, people began to discern that the search for truth and the search for utility might involve trade-offs.

Planck's view – and the autonomy of the scientific realist position it legitimated – was aided by the publication of Schlick's *The General Theory of Knowledge* in 1925. Explicitly harking back to the Mach–Planck exchanges of the previous decade, Schlick (1974, 94–101) once again sought the source of "the value of knowledge." At first glance, Schlick seemed to give a Machian answer that addressed the question within an evolutionary naturalist framework. However, on closer inspection it became clear that he neutralized Mach's arguments against Planck's perspective.

Schlick grants that knowledge was originally sought to maximize pleasure while minimizing pain. However, after a point people realized that the pursuit of knowledge itself brought pleasure and thus started to pursue it as an end in itself. Indeed, knowledge turned out to be such an exquisite pursuit that other needs in life became subordinated to it. This is the mark of civilization. Such an explanatory narrative had been previously used by Wilhelm Wundt to show that teleological and deontological ethics were earlier and later phases in the moral development of humanity. Schlick then purported to show an evolution in the conception of economy, with Mach representing the earlier phase of "minimal effort" and Planck the later phase of "minimal principles," the pursuit of which may actually involve much (pleasurable) effort. The crucial ambiguity in Schlick's account, which carries over into contemporary philosophy of science and science policy, is whether he is talking about the development of the individual inquirer or that of a community of inquirers. The ambiguity matters when interpreting the idea that other life needs come to be subordinated to scientific ones. Is Schlick talking about the self-sacrificing scientist or the society that increasingly adapts its other functions to the needs of scientific institutions? The elision of these two interpretations clearly worked to promote Planck's vision of science in society.

Finally, we turn to the Discernibility of ends. And here we see the Achilles' heel of Mach's position. It rarely suffices to be held accountable to an end in the abstract – some general goal whose concrete realization remains elusive – especially if the accountant wants to be in a position to criticize specific things people do. Thus ends need to be tied to institutions. But then the desirability of the ends can turn out to rest on the feasibility of the institutions. For his part, Mach identified the ends of science with the classical humanistic mission of the university. He imagined that the absorption of the natural sciences into the universities (and the *Gymnasien*) would serve to divest these institutions of their residual elitism. Moreover, Mach held to a resolutely *praxis*-oriented view of scientific activity, one in which the ends of science were regularly co-realized by professor and student in the classroom. This Humboldtian image – modeled on Plato's academy – was quite opposed to Planck's vision of a community of scientific researchers whose work remains quite separate from what they do in the classroom. *Praxis* here, if any such notion remains in Planck's vision, lies in the role that science plays in reproducing the social order. Plato's philosopher-king is the classical bench mark in this case.

It is beyond the scope of this essay to explain exactly how Planck's vision came to triumph, but the signs of its success are relatively easy to mark. In the first place, the unity of research and teaching of the classical humanist university underwent a subtle metamorphosis, one that can already be detected in the reactions to Max Weber's famous "Science as a Vocation" address of 1918 (Weber 1958). Few academics any longer talk about students intellectually maturing as they participate in the professor's scholarly interests. Rather, the professor himself is the one who now undergoes self-transformation through the process of scholarly discipline. Weber's particular way of characterizing this process – which involves subsuming one's ego to an endless and largely vicariously realized quest – was roundly criticized for its obvious reliance on the image of natural scientific inquiry fostered by Planck and the physics community. Thus humanists familiar with the classical pedigree of *praxis*, such as Ernst Robert Curtius, found Weber's vision a monstrous perversion of the ends of inquiry (Lassman and Velody 1989). However, in its place Curtius could invoke only the scholar's solitary participation in the thought of past minds and the intuitive sense of private closure that it brings. Yet this, too, was certainly a far cry from the dialectical participation of professor and students in the Humboldtian classroom. It had become clear to all that academics were no longer in the business of bringing their students to intellectual maturity, let alone to personal empowerment (Ringer 1979, 19).

The social historian Fritz Ringer has examined the long-term effects of basing access to secondary and tertiary education on entry and exit examinations – the so-called merit-based system that has prevailed in Europe since the end of the Franco-Prussian War. Ringer (ibid., 27–29) observes that while the merit system has reduced the differences in social advantage among average members of the old class and status groups, it has also tended to increase the differences *within* those groups, as each of the old groups has roughly a normal distribution of people in the various categories of academic merit. In other words, criteria of academic merit have gradually collapsed traditional ways of categorizing people and have become *the* basis of social stratification. And rather than being a vehicle of democratization, the examination basis of academic merit has made possible degrees of discrimination – percentile rankings – unprecedented in their precision. It may even be that whatever original appeal mass education had as a mechanism for increasing social mobility has been offset by a decline in *alternative* paths to upward mobility. Thus when academic credentials are required even for low-level management positions, opportunities for working one's way up from the stockroom disappear.

As the employment opportunities of academically qualified people have increased over the last century, they have also displayed a distinct pattern, which Daniel Bell (1973) originally took to mean "the coming of post-industrial society." The pattern is one of *intermediation* – that is, the increasing need for academically qualified people to survey, digest, and translate the work of other academically qualified people for a third group of academically qualified people. In some recent popular works (e.g., Reich 1991), this labor process has been described as "symbolic analysis" and "knowledge brokerage." For science policy analysts, intermediation is the institutional correlate of cognitive complexity (Pavitt 1991); for critical political theorists, it marks the corporatist sublimation of democratic impulses (Held 1987, 143–220). For still others, especially the German systems theorist Niklas Luhmann (1983), these are two ways of talking about the same positive development – namely, an increase in social integration brought about by the continual redistribution of uncertainty across the various "intermediators." However, in contrast to these diagnoses, I would argue that intermediation is symptomatic of the growing disparity between the *content* and *function* of scientific knowledge, a tolerance for which we can already see in Planck and especially in his students Koehler and Schlick.

If the ends of science are not merely distinct but increasingly divergent from other societal ends, then greater efforts need to be made to render the two compatible. The problem is made especially acute if the ultimate *Weltbild* seems to recede into the indefinite future and scientists are left with sheer "productivity" as their metric of progress. Later research is made possible by the rapid obsolescence of earlier research. Indeed, according to standard science indicators, the "harder" sciences are also the more "brittle," as measured by the rate at which research is superseded (cf. De Mey 1982, 111–31). However, the plethora of fads and jargons associated with such volatility is in striking contrast to the stabilizing function that science continues to serve as the premier mechanism of social reproduction. To make the two ends meet, intermediators emerge who rationalize bits of the difference to each other; but none can make it all the way around from content to function, showing, say, how the continued administration of aptitude tests squares with our best theories of how human cognition develops. Given such a disparity, one might wonder whether both science and society have lost their ends.

REFERENCES

Albisetti, James. 1983. *Secondary School Reform in Imperial Germany*. Princeton, N.J.: Princeton University Press.
Baker, John. 1961. "The Controversy on Freedom in Science in the Nineteenth Century." In *The Logic of Personal Knowledge*, edited by J. Baker, 89–96. London: Routledge & Kegan Paul.
Bartley, W. W. 1974. "Theory of Language and Philosophy of Science as Instruments of Educational Reform." In *Boston Studies in the Philosophy of Science*, vol. 14, edited by R. Cohen and M. Wartofsky, 307–37. Dordrecht: Reidel.
Baudrillard, Jean. 1977. *Oublier Foucault*. Paris: Editions Galilée.
Bell, Daniel. 1973. *The Coming of Post-Industrial Society*. New York: Basic Books.
Berkson, William, and John Wettersten. 1984. *Learning from Error: Karl Popper's Psychology of Learning*. La Salle, Ill.: Open Court.
Blackmore, John. 1973. *Ernst Mach*. Berkeley: University of California.
    ed. 1992. *Ernst Mach – A Deeper Look*. Dordrecht: Kluwer.
De Mey, Marc. 1982. *The Cognitive Paradigm*. Dordrecht: Reidel.
Dvorak, Johann. 1991. "Otto Neurath and Adult Education: Unity of Science, Materialism, and Comprehensive Enlightenment." In *Rediscovering the Forgotten Vienna Circle*, edited by T. Uebel, 265–74. Dordrecht: Kluwer.
Elster, Jon. 1983. *Sour Grapes*. Cambridge: Cambridge University Press.
Feyerabend, Paul. 1975. *Against Method*. London: Verso.
    1979. *Science in a Free Society*. London: Verso.
Forman, Paul. 1971. "Weimar Culture, Causality, and Quantum Theory: 1918–1927." *Historical Studies in the Physical Sciences* 3:1–115.
Fuller, Steve. 1988. *Social Epistemology*. Bloomington: Indiana University Press.
    1992a. "Being There with Thomas Kuhn: A Parable for Postmodern Times." *History and Theory* 31:241–75.
    1992b. "Social Epistemology and the Research Agenda of Science Studies." In Pickering 1992, 390–428.
    1993a. *Philosophy, Rhetoric, and the End of Knowledge: The Coming of Science and Technology Studies*. Madison: University of Wisconsin Press.
    1993b. *Philosophy of Science and Its Discontents*. 2nd ed. New York: Guilford Press.
Garfinkel, Harold. 1977. "The Origin of the Term 'Ethnomethodology'." In *Ethnomethodology*, edited by R. Turner, 15–18. Harmondsworth: Penguin.
Gellner, Ernest. 1979. *Spectacles and Predicaments: Essays in Social Theory*. Cambridge: Cambridge University Press.

Georgescu-Roegen, Nicholas. 1971. *The Entropy Law and the Economic Process.* Cambridge, Mass.: Harvard University Press.

Godelier, Maurice. 1986. *The Mental and the Material.* London: New Left Books.

Gouldner, Alvin. 1970. *The Coming Crisis in Western Sociology.* New York: Basic Books.

Hacking, Ian, ed. 1981. *Scientific Revolutions.* Oxford: Oxford University Press.

Heilbron, John. 1986. *The Dilemmas of an Upright Man: Max Planck as Spokesman for German Science.* Berkeley: University of California Press.

Held, David. 1987. *Models of Democracy.* London: Polity Press.

Horkheimer, Max. [1932] 1972. *Critical Theory: Selected Essays.* New York: Seabury Press.

Hull, David. 1988. *Science as a Process.* Chicago: University of Chicago Press.

Humphrey, George. 1951. *Thinking: An Introduction to Its Experimental Psychology.* London: Methuen.

Inkster, Ian. 1991. *Science and Technology in History: An Approach to Industrial Development.* London: Macmillan.

Kitcher, Philip. 1993. *The Advancement of Science.* Oxford: Oxford University Press.

Knorr-Cetina, Karin. 1981. *The Manufacture of Knowledge.* Oxford: Pergamon.

Koehler, Wolfgang. 1971. *Selected Papers.* Edited by Mary Henle. New York: Liveright.

Koffka, Kurt. 1935. *Principles of Gestalt Psychology.* New York: Harcourt, Brace & World.

Kuhn, Thomas. 1970. *The Structure of Scientific Revolutions.* 2nd ed. Chicago: University of Chicago Press.

——— 1977. *The Essential Tension.* Chicago: University of Chicago Press.

Lassman, Peter, and Irving Velody, eds. 1989. *Max Weber's "Science as a Vocation."* London: Unwin Hyman.

Latour, Bruno. 1987. *Science in Action.* Milton Keynes: Open University Press.

Laudan, Larry. 1981. "A Problem-Solving Approach to Scientific Progress." In Hacking 1981, 144–55.

Lave, Jean, and Edward Wenger. 1991. *Situated Learning.* Cambridge: Cambridge University Press.

Leplin, Jarret, ed. 1984. *Scientific Realism.* Berkeley: University of California Press.

Luhmann, Niklas. 1983. *The Differentiation of Society.* New York: Columbia University Press.

Lynch, Michael. 1993. *Scientific Practice and Ordinary Action.* Cambridge: Cambridge University Press.

Lynch, Michael, and Steve Woolgar, eds. 1990. *Representation in Scientific Practice.* Cambridge, Mass.: MIT Press.

Lynch, William, and Ellsworth Fuhrman. 1991. "Recovering and Expanding the Normative: Marx and the New Sociology of Scientific Knowledge." *Science, Technology, and Human Values* 16:233–48.

Mach, Ernst. [1883] 1960. *The Science of Mechanics.* 6th ed. La Salle, Ill.: Open Court.

MacIntyre, Alasdair. 1984. *After Virtue.* 2nd ed. Notre Dame, Ind.: University of Notre Dame Press.

Mueller, Detlef, Fritz Ringer, and Brian Simon, eds. 1987. *The Rise of the Modern Educational System: Structural Change and Social Reproduction, 1870–1920.* Cambridge: Cambridge University Press.

Munevar, Gonzalo. 1981. *Radical Knowledge.* Indianapolis: Hackett.

Newell, Allan, and Herbert Simon. 1972. *Human Problem Solving.* Englewood Cliffs, N.J.: Prentice Hall.

Pavitt, Keith. 1991. "What Makes Basic Research Economically Useful?" *Research Policy* 20:109–19.

Pickering, Andrew, ed. 1992. *Science as Culture and Practice.* Chicago: University of Chicago Press.

Pollner, Melvin. 1987. *Mundane Reason.* Cambridge: Cambridge University Press.

Popper, Karl. 1981. "The Rationality of Scientific Revolutions." In Hacking 1981, 80–106.

Reich, Robert. 1991. *The Work of Nations.* New York: Knopf.

Richards, Robert. 1987. *Darwin and the Emergence of Evolutionary Theories of Mind and Behavior.* Chicago: University of Chicago Press.

Ringer, Fritz. 1979. *Education and Society in Modern Europe.* Bloomington: Indiana University Press.

Sassower, Raphael. 1985. *Philosophy of Economics: A Critique of Demarcation.* Lanham, Maryland: University Press of America.

Schlick, Moritz. 1974. *The General Theory of Knowledge.* Berlin: Springer Verlag.

Shapin, Steven, and Simon Schaffer. 1985. *Leviathan and the Air-Pump.* Cambridge: Cambridge University Press.

Simon, Herbert. 1981. *The Sciences of the Artificial.* 2nd ed. Cambridge: MIT Press.

Stinchcombe, Arthur. 1990. *Information and Organizations.* Berkeley: University of California Press.

Veblen, Thorstein. 1934. *The Theory of the Leisure Class.* New York: Modern American Library.

Weber, Max. 1958. "Science as a Vocation." In *From Max Weber,* edited by H. Gerth and C. W. Mills, 129–58. Oxford: Oxford University Press.

Woolgar, Steve, ed. 1988. *Knowledge and Reflexivity.* London: Sage.

Index

Cambridge Studies in Management